HUDSON TAYLOR

&

CHINA'S OPEN CENTURY

Book Two: Over the Treaty Wall

**Overseas Missionary
Fellowship
1058 Avenue Road
Toronto, Ontario M5N 2C6**

HUDSON TAYLOR

&

CHINA'S OPEN CENTURY

BOOK TWO
Over the Treaty Wall

A J Broomhall

HODDER AND STOUGHTON
and
THE OVERSEAS MISSIONARY FELLOWSHIP

Chinese calligraphy by Michael Wang. Cover design by Melvyn Gill
based on the insignia of a Qing (Ch'ing) dynasty viceroy or provincial
governor (courtesy of the Victoria and Albert Museum, Crown
copyright).

Subsequent volumes in this series will be in large format paperback. The publishers
intend to reissue the first volume in this format, subject to demand.

British Library Cataloguing in Publication Data

Broomhall, Dr A J
    Hudson Taylor & China's open century.
    Book Two: Over The Treaty Wall
    1. Missions – China – History – 19th Century
    I. Title

ISBN 0 340 27561 8

*First published 1982. Second impression 1986. Copyright © 1982 by the Overseas
Missionary Fellowship. All rights reserved. No part of this publication may be
reproduced or transmitted in any form or by any means, electronic or mechanical,
including photocopying, recording, or any information storage and retrieval system,
without permission in writing from the publisher. Printed in Great Britain for
Hodder and Stoughton Limited, Mill Road, Dunton Green, Sevenoaks, Kent by
Richard Clay (The Chaucer Press) Ltd, Bungay, Suffolk. Photoset by Rowland
Phototypesetting Ltd, Bury St Edmunds, Suffolk.*

Foreword to the Series

China appears to be re-opening its doors to the Western world. The future of Christianity in that vast country is known only to God. It is, however, important that we in the West should be alert to the present situation, and be enabled to see it in the perspective of the long history of missionary enterprise there. It is one of the merits of these six remarkable volumes that they provide us with just such a perspective.

These books are much more than just the story of the life and work of Hudson Taylor told in great detail. If they were that alone, they would be a worthwhile enterprise, for, as the *Preface* reminds us, he has been called by no less a Church historian than Professor K S Latourette 'one of the greatest missionaries of all time'. He was a man of total devotion to Christ and to the missionary cause, a man of ecumenical spirit, a man of originality in initiating new attitudes to mission, a doctor, a translator, an evangelist, an heroic figure of the Church.

The historian – whether his interests be primarily military, missionary, or social – will find much to interest him here. The heinous opium traffic which led to two wars with China is described. The relationship of 'the man in the field' to the society which sent him is set before us in all its complexity and (often) painfulness. And the story of Biblical translation and dissemination will be full of interest to those experts who work under the banner of the United Bible Societies and to that great fellowship of men and women who support them across the length and breadth of the world.

Dr Broomhall is to be congratulated on writing a major work which, while being of interest *primarily* to students of mission, deserves a far wider readership. We owe our thanks to Messrs Hodder and Stoughton for their boldness in printing so large a series of volumes in days when all publishers have financial problems. I believe that author and publisher will be rewarded, for we have here a fascinating galaxy of men and women who faced the challenge of the evangelisation of China with daring and devotion, and none more so than the central figure of that galaxy, Hudson Taylor himself. The secret of his perseverance, of his achievement, and of his significance in missionary history is to be found in some words which he wrote to his favourite sister, Amelia:

'If I had a thousand pounds, China should have it. If I had a thousand lives, China should have them. No! not *China*, but *Christ*. Can we do too much for Him?'

Sissinghurst, Kent   Donald Coggan

PREFACE

In the first book of this series the groundwork was laid, the essential foundation of a true understanding of Christian missions in China, and therefore of the life and work of James Hudson Taylor. In this second book he comes into his own, and it is time to be increasingly selective in attempting to show him in the perspective of history. For the purposes of this record we must now keep to what bears most directly on his own life and activities, as the personal archives become fuller. The youth is plainly seen as father of the man. His developing personality takes on individual characteristics which make him in some ways unique. With hindsight the pioneer and founder of missions can very early be recognised. His fitness for greater responsibilities was proved in the testing he surmounted.

So the period of Hudson Taylor's apprenticeship, before he went to China and while he found his feet there, holds the key to what followed. The man in the making is the man who in the hands of God made history. His initiative as a beginner matured into leadership along unprecedented paths. But at every step his indebtedness to others is important and apparent, as the first book, *Barbarians at the Gates*, set out to show. *Over the Treaty Wall* continues the story without a break, assuming familiarity with the characters and events described. The whole series is in fact one book, divided for the convenience of handling.

To pick up the threads again is impracticable, but the résumé in Appendix 1 will serve as a reminder. The general preface to Book One, and the chronological tables and personalia supply other links.

As before, five strands are interwoven:

Chinese and Western secular history:
Catholic and Protestant missions to China;
Western trade and diplomacy in China as they affected missions;
Individuals involved in the unfolding drama; and
Hudson Taylor's personal story, to show the sources of his innovations.

Again, these books are primarily a compilation of facts and statements unearthed from the records, allowing the historical sequence of events to shape the structure. The narrative would be improved if material of only minor interest to some readers were to be left out, but a basic aim in writing is to expose to the light of day what has been buried for a century. A truer picture of the man should result. *Over the Treaty Wall* takes up the narrative in 1850 and sees Hudson Taylor through seven turbulent years to the eve of his independence from any organisation or visible means of support. *If I had a Thousand Lives* then follows, to the turning point of June 1865.

AJB
1981

KEY TO ABBREVIATIONS

American Board =	American Board of Commissioners for Foreign Missions (ABCFM)
Bible Society	= British & Foreign Bible Society (B&FBS)
BMS	= Baptist Missionary Society
CES	= Chinese Evangelization Society
CIM	= China Inland Mission
CMS	= Church Missionary Society
LMS	= London Missionary Society
P & O	= Peninsular & Oriental Steam Navigation Company
RCS	= Royal College of Surgeons
RTS	= Religious Tract Society
SPCK	= Society for Promoting Christian Knowledge
SPG	= Society for the Propagation of the Gospel
The Society	= Chinese Evangelization Society (CES)

ACKNOWLEDGMENTS

The Hudson Taylor (OMF) archives have formed the main source of material for this second book. Other sources acknowledged in the first volume have again provided much of value (for details *see* Notes): special thanks are due to the Church Missionary Society for quotations and information from Eugene Stock's *History* of the CMS; to Collins Publishers for permission to quote freely from Richard Collier's biography of General William Booth, *The General Next to God*; to Harvard University Press for material from Prof J K Fairbank's *Trade and Diplomacy on the China Coast*; to Harper & Row, Publishers Inc, and the First New Haven National Bank, Trustees of the late Prof K S Latourette's estate, for the use of material from his books (as detailed); to Drs F R Coad and H H Rowdon for quotations and help from *A History of the Brethren Movement* and *The Origins of the Brethren*, respectively; also to the St Andrew Press, Edinburgh, for a quotation from *The Seed of the Church in China* by M Boone; to Dr George Woodcock for more racy quotations from *The British in the Far East* (Weidenfeld & Nicolson); and to Messrs Allen & Unwin and Arthur Waley for the poem about Charles Gutzlaff (Appendix 8). To the Librarian and Public Relations Officer of the London Hospital and the Librarian of the Royal College of Surgeons I am grateful for help in describing conditions in 1852–53.

The distinctive advice of each of my very helpful critics has put me deeper into their debt: Peter Harvey, Jane Lenon, Leslie Lyall, Pauline McIldowie, Howard Peskett and, especially, Bishop Stephen Neill; while Mollie Robertson's immaculate typing has made months of work a constant pleasure, crowned by more of Val Connolly's line drawings and maps. The responsibility for the end result is mine, but full credit must go to all these good friends, and to my tolerant publishers.

AJB

BOOK TWO: OVER THE TREATY WALL

CONTENTS

MAPS

ILLUSTRATIONS

PART 1

THE ALL – OR – NOTHING APPRENTICE

1850–54

PROLOGUE

CHINA OPEN?
1850

China in ferment

When the Dao Guang emperor died on February 25, 1850, momentous upheavals began to shake China. A change of emperor meant a change of officials, with all the potential for trouble that such a ferment contained. But the nineteen-year-old Xian Feng (Hsien Feng), who succeeded to the Dragon Throne, exhibited signs of instability which presaged no good for the nation. Already a widower, he had acquired the reputation of a layabout, dissolute and spineless. With responsibility thrust upon him he turned to an idolatrous, superstitious form of Buddhism. And when the persecution of Christians was resumed, the report was circulated that he had issued secret orders annulling the edicts of toleration decreed only five or six years previously. He labelled Christians the enemies of the public good. The most charitable assessment of the change of attitude in the government was that the new mandarins were ignorant of Dao Guang's concessions or after his death ignored them. But explanations mattered little, the antagonism was intensified.

Xian Feng was unfortunate in having inherited two major problems: the assertive presence of foreigners on Chinese soil, enlarging the foothold they had gained by the first opium war and subsequent treaties; and the rebellion of the sect in the hinterland of Canton known from its quasi-Christian tenets as the Worshippers of Shangdi. Linked with anti-Manchu secret societies they began to resist the imperial government and showed all the signs of developing into a serious menace. The seeds of the devastating Taiping rebellion had indeed been sown, a movement which was almost to topple the dynasty.

While the Court at Peking (Beijing)[1] vacillated in the face of both threats, the Church suffered the repercussions. In the Canton area sullen malevolence made open preaching impossible, and Dr Peter

Parker's hospital was able to keep going only with difficulty. The heroic Chinese missionary Liang A-fa[2] and his fellow-Christians had to tread very warily. In Fujian province the missionary pioneers met with furious opposition. Bishop George Smith of the Church Missionary Society (CMS), who arrived at Hong Kong in March 1851 with six new colleagues, set them to work in Fuzhou (Foochow), Ningbo and Shanghai, but a riot followed attempts to occupy premises near a meeting place of the Fuzhou literati and for ten or eleven years it was all 'slog and danger' without a sign of results.

The Court had good reason to be anxious about the foreigners' intentions, for bellicosity in Queen Victoria's government was never more strident than at this period. For twenty years, since 1830, Lord Palmerston and the Duke of Wellington had alternated at the Foreign Office, Palmerston with Lord Melbourne as Prime Minister and Wellington with Peel. But in 1846 Palmerston became Lord John Russell's Foreign Minister and an overbearing spirit came over him. Loud and self-confident, he lectured foreign governments, became reckless in his decisions, and not content with impertinence and disobedience went so far as to disregard the Queen's constitutional rights until she dismissed him. After an interval he was back again, and in February 1855 he himself became Prime Minister. Twenty-six years after the annexation of Western Burma in 1826, Britain returned in April 1852 to capture Rangoon and occupy Lower Burma. China still looked upon Burma as part of her commonwealth and sphere of influence. The acquisitive Westerners, who had so alarmed her by occupying the Philippines, much of the Indonesian archipelago and great areas of India before forcing concessions from the powerless Dao Guang emperor by the opium war of 1840–42 and the Treaty of Nanking, had begun to subjugate China's immediate neighbours. How far would they go?

Caught on the wrong foot

Britain herself was in turmoil of a different kind. An ecclesiastical furore had arisen over new initiatives from Rome to reconvert England to Catholicism. Widespread indignation was aroused by the creation of an archbishopric of Westminster and bishoprics throughout the country with titles appearing to claim equality of status with those of the established Church of which the Queen herself was the head. Little more than twenty years had passed since the repeal of the Test Act and Catholic emancipation, yet the new archbishop spoke of 'Catholic England' being 'restored'. The effect upon foreign missions was immediate, as strong feelings diverted interest and financial support. Eugene Stock, General Secretary and historian of the CMS wrote,[3] 'An outburst of indignation arose instantly from the whole country . . . From the Tweed to the Lizard rang the cry of "No Popery." Great meetings were held everywhere to protest against the "insolent and insidious" aggression of the Papacy, as the Premier phrased it.'

But that was not all. Trouble had arisen within the Anglican Church itself. When the Privy Council ruled in the Gorham Judgment that the views held by GC Gorham, an evangelical clergyman,[4] were 'not contrary or repugnant' to the teaching of the established Church, many Tractarians, including the future Cardinal Manning, left the Church of England. The CMS suffered more than most. The Society exhorted its members 'still (to) keep in view the great missionary effort to which the present crisis calls and invites us.'

Failing support for missions was not the only effect of these developments. The cleavage between the Roman and Protestant Churches meant that in China each continued to go its own way. The antagonism to Robert Morrison and his colleagues at Macao had from the beginning made communication, let alone cooperation between the two Churches, improbable, but a wide divergence of beliefs and practices perpetuated the rivalry, and these new trends made more rigid their isolation from each other. If it had not persisted far into the twentieth century, the matter might be happily passed over, but throughout the 'open century' each Church in China was to regard the other as too deviant to allow of friendship. Polarisation in Europe extended to East Asia and inevitably affected the development of missions and the personal experiences of Hudson Taylor.

With the signing of the treaties of 1842–44, Catholic and Protestant missionaries had moved rapidly to take advantage of the new diplomatic climate and the opening of the five ports of Canton, Amoy,[5] Fuzhou, Ningbo and Shanghai to foreign trade. In 1850 the *Annals of the Propagation of the Faith* contained a letter from the Administrator Apostolic of the Catholic diocese of Nanking saying, 'It is scarcely five or six years since the diocese of Nanking contained no more than three or four European missioners, and seven or eight native priests, most of them old and infirm. I can now already reckon twenty-eight European missioners, four native priests, five students of theology . . . and four lay brothers. . . . My college contains thirty pupils.' Of new missionaries disembarking at Shanghai he went on, 'The apostles land (in crowding numbers) who are destined for . . . almost three-fourths of China.'[6] Only residence and trade in the five treaty ports had been authorised, and penetration of the interior remained illegal and hazardous under Xian Feng's renewed persecution. The trouble was that while the Catholic Church was responding with a will to the new opportunities, Protestant Churches in Europe were obsessed with political distractions.

The total number of Protestant missionaries to the Chinese in East Asia was fifty, not including wives. In India there were in 1851 some ninety-one thousand Protestant Christian adherents of whom fifteen thousand were communicant members of the Church.[7] And because of a people's movement among the Karens, church members in Burma numbered ten thousand and adherents about thirty thousand. But the grand total of Chinese Protestant Christians was only about two hundred, and most of them were in Malaysia.[8] Forty-five years after Morrison began at Canton success seemed as remote as ever. A few years later, it is true, there were seventy-five male missionaries to the Chinese, and sixty women, with Americans outnumbering the British by two to one, but in Britain interest in the stony field of China was at a low ebb, compounded by the notorious failure of Charles Gutzlaff's Chinese Union.

At this dismal stage in events the Chinese Evangelization Society which Gutzlaff had initiated began circulating its magazine *The Gleaner in the Missionary Field* to rally the disheartened and to challenge the Church with the claims of neglected China. Examining the question, 'To what extent is China open to the preachers of the Gospel?' it said, 'If the zeal of the Roman Catholic missionaries leads them to brave the dangers and hardships connected with residence in the interior, is it too much to expect of self-denying (Protestant Christians) that they should do the same . . .?'

CHAPTER ONE

THE GREAT OBSESSION
1850–52

'China in all my thoughts'   *1850*

Eighteen-year-old Hudson Taylor read his copy of *The Gleaner* and was impressed. According to the veteran Walter H Medhurst in the second issue, between 1843 and 1850 the number of missionaries in Shanghai free to take the gospel to neighbouring towns and villages, had increased by only five, from two to seven, representing six different missions. At first it had been necessary for these pioneers to return to Shanghai within twenty-four hours but now they could be absent in the interior for a month – disregarding treaty restrictions.

> When missions at the five ports are fully supplied [said Medhurst provocatively] and there are men to spare for these trips and experiments, it will be time to try whether a mission cannot be fixed among the people in the interior.

The prospect spurred young Hudson Taylor to action. On August 7, 1850, he wrote to George Pearse of the Chinese Society,

> though the aspect of the Institution (the Chinese Union) is at present in many respects discouraging, we may hope for better days. (With supervision, Chinese Christians would still achieve a good deal.) We cannot be too much in earnest in the prosecution of this great work. The missionaries should be men of apostolic zeal, patience, endurance, willing to be all things to all men. May the Lord raise up suitable instruments, and fit me for this work.

It had to come out. Each sentence led him nearer, and the stockbroker reading and thinking, 'Who is this young man?' would not have been surprised to see the personal commitment. 'On Dr Gutzlaff's return will the Institution be remodled (*sic*) or can further frauds be prevented in any way?', Hudson Taylor's letter went on, followed by a request for books or cards about the work and for authorisation to 'gather a few pounds if possible'.

At some point during 1850 Hudson Taylor heard that a Congregational minister in Barnsley possessed a copy of Medhurst's tome on *China: Its State and Prospects*, and asked if he might borrow it, explaining that God had called him to spend his life as a missionary in China. 'And how do you propose to go there?' the minister asked. Hudson Taylor admitted he did not know. He would probably have to go 'without purse or scrip', relying on the One who was sending him to supply his needs. The minister was down to earth. 'Kindly placing his hand upon my shoulder, he replied, "Ah, my boy, as you grow older you will get wiser than that. Such an idea would do very well in the days when Christ Himself was on earth, but not now."' 'I have grown older since then, but not wiser,' Hudson Taylor said in his *Retrospect*.[1]

He immersed himself in Medhurst's book and emerged with the conviction that medical work was the key to acceptance by the Chinese. So his father's medical books came down from the shelves and he began dissecting any animal he could lay hands on. He was no longer only an assistant. As he told Mr Pearse, he was prescribing and dispensing for patients. Eighteen months later his father proposed leaving him in charge of the business. Meanwhile he devoted all his available time to preparation for going to China.

He paid a visit to Barton-on-Humber during his sister Amelia's summer holiday and wrote revealingly to her on his return at the beginning of September. Marianne Vaughan, with whom he was in love, was probably there, for he enquired after her. He was living in a euphoric glow of spiritual liberation since his self-consecration to God's service.[2]

> Dear Amelia, remember me in all your prayers . . . I am determined to devote myself body, soul and spirit to (God's) work. I feel a stronger desire than ever to go to China. China is ever in my thoughts. Think of three hundred and sixty million souls without hope or God in the world . . . For every man, woman and child in Barnsley, four thousand are dying in China. [It was a miscalculation but the figures matter little.] Poor China is neglected – no (one) scarcely cares about it . . . Nearly one-third of the inhabitants of the whole world is almost left to its own ignorance; '. . . shall we to men benighted the lamp of life deny?' – enlist all you can to pray for the Chinese . . .

He had sensed the truth. China was neglected and too few cared. For a letter written at the pharmacy counter, bucking 'like a rocking-horse with the mortar going rap, rap, rap', as his father or

John Hodson, his cousin, prepared medicines, it came from a full heart.

The friendship between brother and sister was deep and uninhibited. They wrote as freely as the conventions of letter-writing would allow. For her birthday, for example,

> You will be fifteen . . . O my dear sister, keep very close to Jesus . . .
> Devote yourself to His service, body, soul and spirit . . . Pray for the
> cause of God and expect an answer. *Pray for China* . . .

Ten days later, after telling her that he was still having trouble with his eyes from reading in all his spare time, in spite of wearing spectacles, he gave her his off-duty time-table: Up at 6 am; on Monday – Latin; Tuesday – theology; Wednesday – Chinese; Thursday – pharmacology; Friday – 'the science of disorders' and physiology; Saturday – Chinese. And in the context of a long, mature exhortation on not giving way to temptation, 'Determine to live by faith, simple faith . . . I go into the warehouse or stable or anywhere, for private prayer, and some most blessed seasons I had . . .' And then in November,

> We are studying anatomy . . . when I feel tired of it, I think of China
> and the thought braces me up and I persevere. China is the subject of
> all my thoughts and prayers, at night many times when the others are
> sound asleep. [But not only China. The problem was how to get there.]
> I have not the slighest idea *how* I shall go, but this I know, I *shall* go . . .
> I know God has called me to the work, and He will provide the means
> . . . Who is to send me? Wesleyans have no station (in China) . . . The
> Church have one but I am no Churchman and will not sacrifice
> principle for anything . . . The Chinese Association is very low in
> funds, and so *God* and *God alone* is my hope, and I *need* no other.

Fuel for the flame   1850–51

Month by month *The Gleaner* kept Hudson Taylor and his parents informed of the progress of the Chinese Associations. Admitting anxieties about Gutzlaff's Chinese Union as the facts became better known, the editors urged their readers not to underrate the principles, or the value of measures being taken to print and distribute the Scriptures and to call and train European missionaries to supervise the work in China. While the prospects in China were in doubt they made much of missions in other parts of the world, but in December the whole issue was given to China and the leading editorial was addressed 'To the Friends of China'. The Chinese

Union in Hong Kong might be failing, it declared, but the cause
could not fail.

> The claims of China upon the disciples of Christ are great and
> overwhelming . . . The whole country is far more open and accessible
> than can be taken advantage of by the whole host of God's people. The
> encouragements to go forward are so many, that it would be a reproach
> to allow temporary hindrances to stop the current of our sympathies on
> its behalf.

The attempts made by one and another might fail but the *object* in
view could not, for it was God's own cause. Christian supporters
must not lose heart from the single error of 'a hasty thrusting forth of
untried men'. Charles Gutzlaff's policy had not received a fair trial.
They should realise that all through Europe men and women were
uniting to do what needed to be done and some were offering to go.

> [The foreign missionary] should identify himself with the people and
> their interests, mix familiarly with them, if practicable, adopt their
> dress, and enter into the interior, not to take the place of haughty
> superiority but, as far as possible, become a Chinese that he may win
> the Chinese.

A significant letter was quoted from the LMS *Chronicle*.[3] A
missionary named Gilfillan had penetrated to a city fifty miles inland
from Amoy and considered it preferable as a mission centre.

> But as things are [he advised] perhaps prudence forbids an attempt to
> establish a Mission there [while the Treaty provided only for the five
> ports]. Yet it may become a grave question for the consideration of
> wise men at home, whether all our missions in China should seek to
> nestle under the wing of British law. Whatever the variety of opinion
> on this point . . . a missionary can work for days together in an inland
> city without let or hindrance. The wall of Chinese exclusiveness is
> surely breached and crumbling . . .

– prophetic and provocative ideas not lost on his readers.
    A letter from Wilhelm Lobscheid in Hong Kong reported on the
freedom with which he and Ferdinand Genähr were working on the
mainland in eastern Guangdong and stressed the necessity of
medical work, as a commendation of themselves and the gospel. He
endorsed Gutzlaff's plea for women missionaries 'for female education', saying, 'the Chinese are an intelligent and a very interesting
people, who can be educated easier than the children of Europeans.' All this was meat and drink to Hudson Taylor. His whole

outlook and personal approach to work after he reached Shanghai showed how deeply he absorbed these articles.

Christmas came and went, and the first *Gleaner* of 1851 maintained the tone. Distracted still by Church politics and the debacle of the Chinese Union, friends of the association and its magazine dwindled badly, for all the exhortations. 'The expansive power of this Gospel,' the January *Gleaner* said, 'will bind (a believer) in heart to those who have likewise felt its power.' Quoting what the LMS called a 'fundamental principle' of the Society's foundation, *The Gleaner* applauded the 'catholic spirit' which rose above sectarian differences in order to be united in presenting the gospel to the world, leaving the Church which sprang from such efforts, 'to assume for themselves such form of Church government as to them shall appear most agreeable to the Word of God.' Hudson Taylor approved, and this expansive ecumenism in the biblical sense, learnt in part from the LMS, characterised him for the rest of his life.

Another article in *The Gleaner*, reproduced from the contemporary periodical *The Christian Spectator*, asked, 'How shall we give the gospel to the dying myriads . . .?' and answered, 'The PRESS is fast becoming the ruler of the world.'[4] This new force must be mobilised for spreading the gospel. Colportage was an embodiment of 'two of the mightiest agencies for good that the world has ever known – the living voice and the printed page.' As William Milne had said, 'Tracts can easily put on a Chinese coat and may walk without fear throughout the land; they may penetrate silently even into the chamber of the emperor.'

Then came two reports on itinerant evangelism by Karl Vogel, the Kassel missionary in Guangdong, and a Chinese, in the form of daily journals. As lessons in how to go about this pioneering and how to report it, they were all an aspiring missionary like Hudson Taylor could desire. But in a postscript came a warning, '(to) show the importance of availing ourselves of the openings for the Gospel in China, as we little know how long they may be continued. In one of the Provinces an edict against Christianity has been issued by the Prefects. It pronounces Christianity to be illegal, incredible and absurd.'

Restless to get going   1851

Spending Christmas with Amelia and Marianne again was disturbing for the lovelorn Hudson. As long after their return to

Barton as February 1851 he was still disconsolate. He had apparently spoken his mind during the holidays. His calf-love was becoming deeper than infatuation. But after a bleak February he managed to resolve a major problem that was contributing to his tensions. For years he had been directly under his father's eye and found it a strain. On March 16 he plunged into effusive outpourings of love for Amelia and the Lord. 'I love you, from the bottom of my heart I love you . . . My heart longs for sweet communion with you' – and then: 'I have determined to leave home and I want you to pray God to guide me into a good situation where I may . . . get fitted for China . . . Give my best love to my dear Marianne . . .'

Their holiday together had been good fun. The moors of what is now the Peak District national park were only a few miles from them and they had gone riding in the country together. Long conversations about China can be assumed. *The Gleaner* had published two letters about women being needed there and a Ladies' Association had been formed to help women with a desire to go to China. Amelia was interested.

On March 27, after referring to notes from Marianne, Hudson wrote,

> I have been out on the pony this afternoon. Father wanted me to go and exercise it . . . I went the route Miss Vaughan, you and I went the first time. She rode on Prince. The water was higher than his body owing to the late heavy rain . . . and the current was so strong it almost took us away. Then I went into a field and took several leaps and while leaping over a small stream I lost my hat . . . About China . . . If you were ever to go you would have much to put up with, but that is not the question. The question is *are* you called? The call may be given directly as in Paul's case, or a strong impression that it is your duty to go, or you may be moved, like Christ, to go about doing good . . . If you see any of these is the way, walk in it. Pray, Pray, Pray, Pray . . .

Hudson Taylor was looking for employment with access to the anatomy and surgery books he could not afford and with a prospect of learning practical surgery. He wrote to Mr Pearse that he had been collecting contributions from friends and family for the Chinese Union, 'to forward the evangelisation of the Chinese by Native Agency' and consulted him about how to send them. A postal order would cost sixpence but to remit through Glynn's or any other bank would save three or four pence. This faithful attention to detail came from his parents and stayed with him through life. It impressed Pearse, inspired confidence among his future supporters and was cited by Latourette as one of Hudson Taylor's strong qualities.[5]

It was not until June that *The Gleaner* was declared to be the organ of the Chinese Society (no longer the Association) so it was not surprising if Hudson Taylor was uninformed. Only once had the Association and its committee been named. If Mr Pearse would send reports of the Society and how the funds were applied, Taylor continued,

> I have no doubt when more is known . . . I shall be able to collect more . . . I have devoted myself to (the Lord's) service (in China) in obedience, I believe, to His call and for this purpose I am studying medicine and surgery, that I may have more opportunity of usefulness and perhaps be able to support myself when there. However, I leave this in His hands, believing if I seek first the Kingdom of God and His righteousness all these things will be added.

Then he asked for suggestions. How could he promote the cause and fit himself for the work?

Pearse jumped to conclusions. He asked for a statement from Hudson Taylor about himself, his spiritual experience, religious views, education and health, as if he were already a candidate for service with the Society, not only replying to his immediate proposition. If he would come and study medicine in London the Chinese Society might or would help with grants. (The letter has not been preserved, but subsequent correspondence revealed its content.)

On April 25 Hudson Taylor wrote, thanking Mr Pearse for the suggestion of a book on China. He did not name it but very likely it was Wells Williams' *The Middle Kingdom*, a two-volume tome published four years previously, in 1847, but the last word on things Chinese. He would 'endeavour to procure it'. '(I) am grateful to your Committee for the kindness in promising access to an Hospital, and to the Lectures (but) I have no means of supporting myself in London' and as employment there would not leave time to attend the hospital, it would not be possible to accept the offer.

He then gave at length the story of his spiritual awakening and conversion, his 'Covenant' with God and his efforts to learn about China and to equip himself with medical knowledge.

> My age will be nineteen on the 21st of May, 1851. Of course I am unmarried. As to the general state of my health, I have never had any serious illness, but cannot be called robust. I have never been better than at present . . .

Then more about his education, his occupation as assistant to his father, and his resignation from the Methodists, together with his parents and hundreds of others 'not being able to reconcile the late proceedings with the doctrines and precepts of the Holy Scriptures'.

Apart from nine months in the bank Hudson Taylor had been helping his father since 1845. He was ready for a change. He accepted an invitation from the Hull surgeon Robert Hardey, his aunt Hannah's brother-in-law, to become his assistant. So for the present nothing came of the Chinese Society's conditional offer of help with hospital fees.

The last few weeks in Barnsley were busy ones. Hudson Taylor preached his first sermon in a cottage about a mile out of town and preached again two days later at Royston in May – the village where his great-grandfather had been converted on his wedding morning. Special evangelistic meetings were being held in the Barnsley area and he was involved as a counsellor and sometimes as a speaker. For the first time the joy of leading others to the point of reconciliation with God through faith in Jesus became his own. His letters to Amelia were full of it.

> At night we crammed about 500 in the room and at least as many went away without being able to get in . . . Afterwards we had a glorious prayer meeting and twelve adults and five children came to the penitent form and were saved. There were five or six others I know of who were under deep conviction but they would not come up. Oh! it was a glorious time.

It was not a flash in the pan. Hudson Taylor had entered upon a new phase in his development. It blossomed at Hull, but this was the beginning. His attention was drawn to the biblical principle of tithing his income, as he was soon to start earning. So he studied what the Bible had to say on the subject and decided before he went away from home, and was placed in circumstances which might bias his conclusions, to set apart 'for the Lord's service' not less than one-tenth of whatever money or possessions he might acquire. It was more easily said than done, but he made it his life-long practice.

To be a practising Christian was now his whole aim. He could not forget the just criticism of that bank cashier, that so many Christians said one thing and did another. His own Christianity must be genuine, at any price. He was praying for Amelia 'seven times a day', he told her. A friend of his own age, the surgeon to be, Thomas Neatby, was struck 'as were all who knew him' with his spiritual depth during these last weeks in Barnsley.

Hull and Mr Hardey   *1851–52*

The Hull period of Hudson Taylor's life was one of the most important. He was there from May 1851 until September 1852, a mere sixteen months, but during that time he matured rapidly and a series of personal experiments developed much of the Christian personality for which he later became known. The convictions he reached and the principles he adopted for his own life at Hull, and subsequently in London, became not only the principles of the mission he inaugurated and led, but with little change are the principles of that mission a hundred and thirty years later. To observe the process in Hudson Taylor's youth is to observe the sapling stages of the centenarian mission of today. Without these experiences – his faith and obedience to what he believed to be the will of God – no such future might have been possible. Experimental faith, groping after God's guidance, and faltering obedience they undoubtedly were, but the common denominator of submission of his own preferences to the leading of the Holy Spirit is apparent in both.

In 1851 Kingston-upon-Hull, as it had been called since the thirteenth century, was predominantly a fishing town straddling the River Hull where it joined the Humber. At that time it was little more than the Whitefriars island, the depressed district of dockland and the Paragon where many Irish famine labourers were crowded into slums and lodging houses, and the quiet residential area around Charlotte Street and Kingston Square. A few minutes' walk from there led into open country.

The Hull, Barnsley and West Riding Junction Railway deposited Hudson Taylor at Cannon Street station, then set in the fields, but where the tentacles of early industrial expansion were probing out from the town. He made his way to Kingston Square as he had often done before, and presented himself at the home of Richard and Hannah Hardey (*see* Appendix 2). It looked on to an oval garden in the centre of the square and beyond that to the medical school on the other side. Aunt Hannah, the portrait painter, had her studio on the top floor. On Monday, May 21, his nineteenth birthday, he reported for work.

Mr Robert Hardey's home and surgery were on Charlotte Street, the Harley Street of Hull, where most of the profession had their consulting rooms. Besides his private practice, Mr Hardey was a surgeon at the Royal Infirmary near the Paragon, a lecturer in

obstetrics and gynaecology at the medical school and surgeon to
several factories. As his assistant Hudson Taylor at once found
himself plunged into treating frequent minor and major accidents.
Hardey was a pleasant person, tall and manly, with a cheerful sense
of humour that his patients loved – the right antidote for his wife,
the starched, severe and unfriendly hostess who showed Hudson to
the bedroom assigned to him. There was a consulting room in the
house for prestigious[6] patients, but Hudson's work-place was the
surgery at the far end of the garden, opening on to a side street.

It was nearly eleven, after his first day at work, that he was at last
able to write to Amelia. 'I scralled (*sic*) a note to Mother at dinner
time', so hastily, he said, that he questioned whether she could read
it.

> From what I have seen of my new situation I think I shall like it
> exceedingly. Of course I felt very strange and awkward at first but I
> have begun to feel more at home now and know better where to find
> things. [He could see that he would need to do some tidying up and
> cleaning, he said.] I almost think I shall be able to slip over to Barton at
> night by a little arrangement and being willing to stay a little longer
> when they are busy etc. . . . You cannot think how happy I feel in my
> Saviour's love.

Their mother was a wise woman. In her first note to Amelia after
Hudson Taylor left home she warned her not to visit him too often
or make a convenience of her aunt's house. And she confided in
Amelia that the wrench of his rather abrupt departure from home
gave her a taste of the pain of parting soon, perhaps for ever.

So Hudson Taylor settled down to work, dispensing medicines,
keeping the accounts, dressing wounds, accompanying Mr Hardey
to midwifery cases, and attending lectures at the medical school.
Robert Hardey guided his reading of medical books and taught him
in the course of their work. This was the way that medical students
of the day began their training. Quickly they struck up a friendship.
Hardey was a Methodist class leader and a true Christian. So they
had their foremost interests in common. They began to pray
together in the surgery. We can visualise them standing or kneeling
there, the older man in a double-breasted frock-coat and the
younger in the cutaway morning coat of the age, each with a
stand-up collar and bow tie, Hudson's more fashionably fuller than
the doctor's, as shown in Aunt Hannah's portraits of him. The
propriety of dress mattered. But both were busy and Hudson had
many hours alone, making up the medicines Hardey prescribed,

and instructing the patients on how to use them. When Amelia visited Hull she too had to dress appropriately. The high neck-line was in vogue and a throat ribbon with dangling ends. Skirts were full over a whalebone crinoline. Despite her mother's advice, she found her relatives welcoming and saw a good deal of Hudson at the weekends.

The lodging-house area was notorious for vice, violence and crime and the police seldom dared to visit it with fewer than half a dozen men together. It was the Irish priest who was called in to thrash his tipsy parishioners when they were too riotous. Possibly because he was soon known as Mr Hardey's assistant, Hudson Taylor quickly found he could go into this area with a companion or even alone, not only to see patients and to hand out tracts but to preach to small groups of people in the tenements. Garden Street, Middle Street and West Street became familiar in his correspond-ence, synonyms for vice and suffering. Hull had been the home of William Wilberforce, emancipator of slaves. Monuments to him stood in the town hall and town centre. As a founder of the Church Missionary Society and Bible Society he was of interest to Hudson Taylor though he had died in Hudson's infancy. But so close to Wilberforce House, the pride of Hull, degradation went unheeded. Rich and poor lived side by side and social conscience was slow to awaken.

If Hudson wrote home during June and July, no letters have been kept. During this time he made the acquaintance of an independent congregation of 'Brethren' under the ministry of Andrew Jukes and began to attend their meetings. The great strides he made in spiritual development at Hull were directly due to the Bible teaching he received from them, and to their companionship in his evangelistic work in dockland. They were in touch with George Müller of Bristol and Hudson Taylor often heard letters from that man of God read out in the meetings. At the time Müller was caring for three hundred orphans and planning to receive a thousand, without any visible means of support. All he needed, premises, clothing and daily food was coming in answer to his prayers. And in addition he was contributing to the support of forty-five mission-aries overseas. To Hudson Taylor, already believing before he left home that if God called a man or woman to any work he would faithfully provide for him, this was practical confirmation. It set him thinking about how to apply the principles to his own circumstances.[7]

In August he wrote thanking his mother for music scores she had copied for him. His fingers were tired, he said, from practising on Aunt Hannah's piano. On Sunday he had not finished dispensing until after six and did not get to the chapel with Amelia until after eight, but later he and a friend had been out to the lodging houses and had forty or fifty people crowding to hear the gospel from them. A week later he wrote again, telling his mother in detail about George Müller. An anonymous donor had sent Müller £3,000 when he was being tested by receiving nothing for some time. Then Hudson opened his heart to her.

> I think it is very difficult to set our affections on things above, exclusively. I try to be a 'living epistle' of the Lord's, but when I look at myself, I many a time wonder He does not utterly cast me off. I try to subdue my will (but) I seem to have an impression that I shall lose my dear Miss V. and God only knows what struggles I have to say 'nevertheless, not my will but *thine* be done'.

Marianne was undoubtedly fond of him but kept asking, 'Must you go to China?'

Again there is a gap of two months in the letters. He admitted that one had been lying unfinished in his pad. He was 'fretting and stewing and puzzling' as he later put it, over Marianne. He could see clearly that unless she was also called by God, he would have to say goodbye to her. And he was unwilling. He had not yet read about Henry Martyn's renunciation of love and marriage for the same reason, on the eve of sailing for India, and like him could not contemplate it without a battle.[8] Yet he knew what the outcome must be. China and the Lord unquestionably came first. If Marianne was not for China she was not for him. But he could not bear the thought. He suffered five months of misery before he emerged the victor.

Lobscheid in London   *1851–52*

The adventurous Wilhelm Lobscheid was on his way from Hong Kong to England. As one of Charles Gutzlaff's young German colleagues he already had a name for boldness as a pioneer. Hudson Taylor read of it in the July number of *The Gleaner*. He had often admired Lobscheid's exploits on the mainland, as described in his journals.[9]

The Gleaner had become expressly the organ of the Chinese Society and in June published its report and aims, 'The Promulgation of the Gospel in China and the Adjacent Countries by Means of Native Evangelists', setting out its principles of operation. 'Missionary efforts of the Church at large in all parts of the world' would still be reported, the edition announced, but China was now to take precedence.

So closely did Hudson Taylor follow the same aims and principles as the Society in his own missionary life, that the connection is significant and the Society's gradual development into an organisation sending its own missionaries deserves to be noted.

At this stage its first aim was to enlist prayer, for missionaries to be sent and sustained overseas; secondly, to make the progress of the work known and to assist those who went; and finally to be a channel for the receipt and application of funds entrusted to the Society. Moreover,

> The promotors . . . have no desire to interfere with any existing Societies, or trench upon their means . . . They earnestly desire the co-operation of all who love the Saviour, and who cordially combine *on purely unsectarian grounds* (to make Him known).

A separate fund would be used for printing and circulating Scripture. The object was to further Christ's cause and honour in China, by prayer, information and forwarding of funds without reference to any denominational views, and without interfering 'with the internal organisation or arrangements of those on the spot who are engaged in the work'. It was still a service agency, not a missionary society.

'China Open! How Far Can This Be Said?' was the title of the second article in June. For half a century Christians had been praying 'Let China be opened, let the walls of exclusion be thrown down . . . And God . . . has answered that appeal . . . by fire and blood', through the 1840–42 war and Treaty of Nanking. Now,

> in return for the evils which have been rendered to the people by the poisonous opium drug, it seems to be demanded of us to give them the antidote to their misery – the glorious gospel.

Apart from the seventy-five missionaries and sixty women already[10] in the ports and Hong Kong, three members of the Rhenish Mission had succeeded in working on the mainland for two years and Rudolf Lechler of the Basel Society at another place.

> To one who possesses the knowledge of surgery and medicine, there appears an unlimited opening of usefulness even on the mainland . . .

China is far more open to the labours, even of foreign missionaries, than they are prepared to take advantage of.

With an explanation of the failure of the Chinese Union and resignation of Charles Gutzlaff, *The Gleaner* urged all the greater need for reliable missionaries and Chinese Christians to be supported. Another headline read 'Discouragement in Missionary Efforts No Ground for Abandoning Them'. Failure in several other parts of the world, and the Societies involved, were named. There was nothing to be ashamed of. The tides of battle would not always flow in our favour. The lesson to be drawn was, 'We have advanced by our reverses.'

In July and August 1851 *The Gleaner* returned to the theme. If God could so honour one poor congregation of six hundred Herrnhut Moravian exiles as to send them to Greenland, Labrador, America, the West Indies, Africa and Asia, sustain them –

> amidst incredible hardships and self-denial from generation to generation and multiply them to a membership of ten thousand at home, fifty thousand abroad and three hundred missionaries, should we not also give ourselves to prayer for missionaries to be sent from among ourselves to China? (Because) the little body of Moravian Brethren was saved from extinction by the living energy which wrought amongst them, leading them to care for the perishing world and the honour of their God, (ought not we to show) the same single-minded devotedness . . . in the present day?

A passing reference to the rebellion in Guangxi (Kwangsi) probably attracted little notice. It was tucked in among other things. In September Lobscheid's arrival was announced and an appeal made for men to go to China. Every type of evangelist was encouraged to volunteer, 'especially if he possesses a knowledge of medicine'. 'Hermetically sealed Japan' was in the news too. 'That despotic, proud and haughty ruler was making life most harassing' for Dr Bettelheim of the Loochoo Naval Mission of Okinawa.

Wilhelm Lobscheid did not reach the United Kingdom until August 18, 1852, but on the 16th Hudson Taylor was writing to his mother for advice.

> Do you think I should be justified in going to London and expending . . . money at a time when I need it to attend lectures? If it was only for *my own* pleasure, I could soon decide . . . but sometimes I think Lobscheid might give me some information worth going for.

Prince Albert's Great Exhibition in a scintillating palace of glass, the Crystal Palace, was about to open in Hyde Park. The concept was startlingly original. And cheap excursion trains were enticing visitors to London by the hundred from every corner of the country. Amelia's sixteenth birthday was on September 20 and she was leaving school. Their parents rose to the occasion, Mr Hardey gave Hudson Taylor a week off, Uncle Benjamin Hudson booked rooms for them in Mrs Ruffell's place in Soho, where he had an apartment for use when he was in London, and on the 17th they boarded the train.

The Crystal Palace was a fairyland, exquisite with the sun reflected from the glass and lighting up the ferns and tropical plants and exhibits, Amelia reported. But Hudson was a poor companion. His mind was elsewhere, set on meeting Mr Pearse and Lobscheid. So after touring the exhibition and celebrating with a juicy pineapple in a restaurant, a birthday treat for Amelia, they found their way to the Bank of England, and were met by Mr George Pearse. He could not spare them long during Stock Exchange hours so he arranged for them to spend Sunday at his home in the village of Hackney, in the country a few miles north of the City. They went

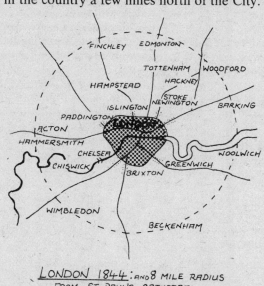

LONDON 1844: and 8 MILE RADIUS FROM ST. PAUL'S CATHEDRAL

LONDON AND VILLAGES IN HUDSON TAYLOR'S YOUTH

out by horse-bus and he took them to meet other members of the Chinese Society at Tottenham. Unrealised by any of them, this was the start of a momentous acquaintance which would outlast the century.

Everything in London was new to Hudson and Amelia and all they met were strangers, but at Tottenham it was as if they were welcomed by relatives. The friendliness and warmth of the circle in which they found themselves at once put them at ease. Most of those present were not yet middle-aged. Robert and John Eliot Howard, manufacturing chemists, and their young families, W T Berger, a manufacturer of starch, Miss Stacey and her Quaker ladies, all became lifelong friends. After reading in *The Gleaner* about the impersonal 'Ladies' Association' of the Chinese Society, formed to help women to go as missionaries to China, it was pleasant to find that the secretary and treasurer, Mrs John Eliot Howard and Mrs Robert Howard were just mothers of young children and very approachable. Forty years later, when John Eliot Howard died, Hudson Taylor felt his loss so deeply that for several days he seemed stunned by it.[11]

At the Sunday service in the Brook Street chapel, built by the Howards three years before, they were introduced to Mr Lobscheid, not as famous as Charles Gutzlaff but well known to the Chinese Society for his unprecedented success as a medical missionary. Here was a man who hobnobbed with mandarins, the class notorious for strangling or deporting foreigners in hip-high cages.[12] Lobscheid looked Hudson Taylor up and down and spoke without consideration for his feelings. Hudson was short and fair with blue-grey eyes. 'They call me a red-bristled barbarian devil' he said 'and you see how dark I am. *You* would never do for China.' 'But God has called me', Hudson answered, 'and He knows the colour of my hair and eyes.' Within a few months he was planning to travel with Lobscheid on his return to China.

Life at Drainside   *1851–52*

The week ended and on September 24 they were back at Hull. Hudson Taylor's room at the Robert Hardeys' was needed and he moved over to Aunt Hannah's. She had no children of her own and was fond of him. But he was faced with a new problem. In lieu of board and lodging, Mr Hardey added to his salary the exact amount he was to pay his aunt. How could he tithe that? If it was a matter of tax he would have no option but to pay up. So why not tithe this sum also? He thought it over for a month and started looking for somewhere else to live.

A few minutes' walk out of town and 'quite in the country' a terrace of cottages was being built along the banks of a stream called the Cottingham Drain. In Lincolnshire and the Hull area low-lying ground was converted from marsh to arable and pasture land by drainage channels, and the larger ones carrying the water away were called 'drains'. Kingfishers and herons fished in them, and water-fowl nested in the reeds. Cottagers sank their milk churns to the rim to cool the milk. It was quiet and peaceful. The road out to the railway station crossed Cottingham Drain and another called Drain-side branched off to the west following the south bank to where a rutted farm track came out of the poorer part of town and crossed into the fields by a wooden bridge.

A ship's captain owned one of the cottages facing on to the Drain between the bridges, and his wife, a Christian, let a ground-floor room to Hudson Taylor. It was only a few minutes' walk from Kingston Square and Charlotte Street, and in daytime he could use the farm track across the fields to the hospital and dockland. It was unsafe after dark. There were deep water-filled ruts and pits from which it took several men to extricate a trapped cart; and footpads liked its loneliness, to relieve late travellers of their cash. Hudson Taylor's mother made him promise to go through the lamp-lit streets even though it gave him fifteen minutes' more walking, after his evening visits to the slums. Even so, much of the way was in darkness if there was no moon.

No 30 Drainside was cosy and he was his own master, free to eat what he liked and to save how he liked. There was a fireplace for a flicker of 'a fire on cold winter evenings', if he chose to afford it, and Captain Finch's family kept him from feeling lonely. He went through their living room to his own room. From his window he could look across the Drain to the open country. He was there from November 1851 to September 1852, a period in which he ceased to be a boy and became a man with strong convictions and convincing experience of spiritual realities.

He decided to live frugally and to be a missionary in Hull in preparation for the life ahead of him in China. On October 21 before he moved to Drainside he had written to his mother, expecting a visit from her. It was five months since they had parted, 'yet it is not really long compared with a life-time'. Both were thinking more and more of the day when he would go overseas and, if things worked out as they did for many, stay on without returning to Europe. His mother wrote to Amelia at school,

> If I am to be bereaved and thus give my Isaac back to God, I pray not only for Divine support, but that he may be a 'workman that needeth not to be ashamed'.

Now Hudson was able to say 'I feel very happy in the Lord.' His heartache over Marianne was still gnawing at his composure, and a sense of guilt perhaps prompted the remark,

> I wonder He has not left me to my own way [referring to his wilfulness]. But His love is unbounded, therefore I will praise Him. . . . I did not get at liberty [from the surgery] till nearly 8 o'clock last Sunday night, so I went into the town and down to the Pier to distribute some tracts. There had just been a Packet landing an immense number of people . . . I have often wished for courage to stand up there and preach the unsearchable riches of grace, but never was able before. I began to give away some sheet tracts on the love of God, and soon had a crowd gathered around me. I . . . then took out my Bible, and began to read part of . . . John's Gospel . . . But there was soon such a row I had to stop; some were shouting, others laughing, some crying hush, and some throwing nut-shells at me. I told them it was no use me reading unless they were still, so in a little while quiet was restored and I spoke from 'God so loved the world' for about 10 minutes, when a policeman came up and stopped me, saying . . . they wanted no lecturing there. Of course I had to go; a few however followed me, and I gave them a few tracts. On the night previous there was a fight in the same place and no one interfered then.

Living alone Hudson gave more time to visiting the poor. Years later he recalled:

> Brought into contact in this way with many who were in distress, I soon saw the principle of still further economising, and found it not difficult to give away much more than the proportion of my income I had at first intended . . . Butter, milk and other such luxuries I soon ceased to use; and I found that living mainly on oatmeal and rice, with occasional variations, a very small sum was sufficient for my needs . . . I had more than two-thirds of my income available for other purposes; and my experience was that the less I spent on myself and the more I gave away, the fuller of happiness and blessing did my soul become.

But that happiness was only possible after a crisis through which he came successfully.

His surviving letters do not say exactly what the 'painful circum-stances' were, but in their biography his son and daughter-in-law have reconstructed the situation as being due to Marianne Vaughan. 'Seeing that nothing could dissuade her friend from his missionary purpose, the young music teacher made it plain at last that she was not prepared to go to China. Her father would not hear of it, nor did she feel herself fitted for such a life.' Only a year later, however, the situation was back to where it had been. Hudson Taylor found himself on Sunday, December 14, two years since he fell in love with her,

> as wretched as heart could wish. I seemed as if I had no power in prayer nor relish for it, and instead of throwing my care on *Him* I kept it all myself until I could get on no longer. Well, on Sunday I felt no desire to go to Meeting and was tempted very much. Satan seemed to come in like a flood, till I was forced to cry mentally 'Save Lord, or I perish' . . . but thank God 'the way of duty is the way of safety', and I went . . . One hymn quite cut me to the heart . . . In the afternoon as I was sitting alone in the Surgery, I began to reflect on the love of God to me . . . and how small my trials were compared with what some had and have to endure . . . The thoughts of His love melted my icy, frost-bound soul, and I did sincerely pray for pardon . . . Then, though He did not deprive me of feeling my trials, He enabled me to sing, 'Yet, *nothwithstanding*, I will rejoice in the Lord, I will joy in the God of my salvation'. . . Now I am happy in my Saviour's love, and can *thank* Him for *all*, even the most painful circumstances I have passed through, and I can 'trust *Him* for all that's to come'. [That was how he wrote to Amelia. To his mother he simply said,] Trusting in God does not deprive one of feeling . . . but it . . . enables us to see Christ in the storm – the refiner watching the fire – and be thankful . . . Good-night, I wish you were here.

From then on he was less introspective, more objective and involved in his work, and more positive about China. Alone for Christmas he was wistful, thinking of the family at home 'very likely enjoying yourselves famously', so he went for a walk, 'bought some treacle parkin' at fourpence a pound,' ('it was very poor compared with yours') and 'as the young Finches were wishing me a "merry Christmas" I divided it among them and helped to make them "merry".' As he could not be at home, he went on, 'I indulged myself with a treat', a shortbread biscuit and a glass of raspberry vinegar and water, 'and enjoyed it very much'.

A bow at full stretch   *January–February 1852*

At Andrew Jukes' chapel which Hudson attended Sunday by Sunday, he was among mature Christians steeped in the Scriptures and under an expositor with an exceptional gift for teaching. Jukes, Amelia recalled in later years, was a 'man with a message, a prophet or seer of rare spiritual illumination'. He thought deeply and he made others think, by striking and stimulating questions. After school at Harrow and two years with a commission in the army of the East India Company he was ordained deacon in the Church of England. But his views on 'believers' baptism' alienated him from his superiors and he was refused full ordination. Rejection did not remove his vocation to expound Scripture and, more at home in the environment of the early Brethren, he seceded and joined their first assembly in Hull. But by the time Hudson Taylor arrived he had left them and built a hall where until the early sixties he led and taught his own Brethren-type congregation. According to his daughter this was Jukes' happiest and most effective period. George Müller and Robert Chapman of Barnstaple stayed with him from time to time, and among his friends were William Berger, John Eliot Howard and others who were also to become Hudson Taylor's closest friends years later.

Hudson Taylor's letters reflected the illumination he was receiving. The New Year came and went and in his rented room he wrote copiously to Amelia, at home now for six months, and to his mother. Torrents of biblical language poured from his pen. He thought, wrote and probably dreamed in the words of the Bible. He was living and working in the golden glow of a new awareness of his wealth and privileges 'in Christ' both here and for all eternity. Jukes was building on a solid Wesleyan foundation and Hudson Taylor was thrilled. He had been baptised as an infant but now he accepted baptism again as a believer. Jukes' teaching in fact unsettled him on this subject. One day when Amelia was visiting Hudson from Barton, he himself baptised her in a stream. She always regretted it, acknowledging that they were immature and over-zealous.

Another who was in touch with Hudson Taylor at this time was Thomas Neatby, his friend in Barnsley. For years they had been in and out of each other's homes and had weathered the Reform Movement secession together. Like Hudson Taylor before him Neatby was going through 'spiritual conflict and depression', but

Hudson had emerged in time to help him. Years later when Neatby was a well-known surgeon and Bible expositor he wrote,

> . . . it was the truth of Romans 6 that ultimately set me at perfect liberty . . . I had one week of more intense conflict than any other. At the close of that week I received a letter from Hull . . . Its contents . . . will never be erased from my memory . . . I felt as if forsaken by God, but God . . . had been causing his servant in Hull to think of me too. I cannot tell you the relief that this of itself was.

The fact was that during the whole of that week Hudson Taylor had been very concerned for his friend, prayed often for him, and wrote to tell him so.

> The letter went on to dwell upon the pure grace of God as unfolded in . . . Ephesians 2 . . . it was a living, hearty, sympathetic application of what God is and had done to my own need at the time.

On another occasion Hudson Taylor wrote to Neatby, Amelia and his mother a series of overflowing letters of his expectation of 'the Second Coming of the Lord'. An article in *The Gleaner* and teaching from Andrew Jukes common to the Brethren movement throughout the country, brought him to see that Christians live from day to day and meet around the Lord's Table in the constant anticipation of his return, 'until He come'. 'These letters', Neatby wrote, 'were a spiritual feast to me. . . . My grasp of the Word of God was greatly strengthened and my way of studing it revolution-ized.'

Thomas Neatby was also hoping to go to China, another link in their friendship. He aspired to writing poetry and sent a copy of some verse to Hudson Taylor, who commented in reply, 'I think you will excel in prose.' Neatby attributed his lifelong association with the Brethren to Hudson Taylor's influence at this period of their lives.

Hudson's mother, however, was alarmed by what seemed to her new notions from Scripture, so he expounded them at length and exhorted her to open her heart to them for her own enrichment. 'I wish, dear mother, you saw clearly the truth of the second coming of our Lord . . . One, if genuinely believed in, which would alter the indolent and apathetic state of the Church.'

The practical effect on Hudson Taylor himself was to make him go through his possessions and weed out any that he would not want to have to answer for if Christ was suddenly to appear, or that other people could put to better use.[13] Thereafter, throughout his life he would from time to time go through his house 'from basement to attic' eliminating the unnecessary and sharing what he could spare with others. His intention was always to be ready 'with oil in our vessels and our lamps trimmed'.

All through the nine months he remained in Hull these letters continued, too full for us to do more than pick and choose amongst them. The influence of *The Gleaner* is frequently detectable, with its articles on the value of medical work in China, more accounts by Lobscheid of his experiences, and reports from other parts of the world.[14] The cruel old anti-Christian King of Siam had died and the new King Mongkut was enforcing religious toleration and inviting missionaries to return. There were one hundred thousand Chinese in Siam, themselves a mission field. But in Indo-China a Catholic priest had been executed and his head thrown in the river.

'I see there is a good work going on in India,' Hudson wrote to Amelia, but his one-track mind went on, 'I hope you will not neglect collecting something for the Chinese Society . . . Oh! I do wish I was ready and long to be engaged in the work. May God bless and fit me and open my way . . .' And on the same day, January 23, 1852, to his mother, 'I am sorry you make yourself so anxious about me. I think it is because I have begun to wear a larger coat, that everybody says "how poorly and thin you look."' He had had a cold for a week, but 'I can eat like a horse, sleep like a top and have spirits like a lark. I do not know that I have any anxieties save to be more holy and useful.' He was taking the long way through lighted streets from the poor quarter of the town to his lodgings, 'tho' ever so tired, because you wish it . . . As to my health, I think sometimes I have almost too much, for I have such a flow of spirits I often have to restrain myself . . .' from talking too much and cracking too many jokes.

In the unlit stretches of his walk he could enjoy the aurora borealis, its 'subdued splendour almost unearthly, its six or eight streams of light with intervals between them', like veiled windows of heaven revealing the inexpressible glory. He thought of the love of God and of parting from his loved ones. As he walked he wept and sang.

> Oh! mother, I cannot tell you . . . I cannot describe how I long to be a missionary – to preach the Gospel to poor sinners – to spend and be spent for Him who died for me. I feel as if for *this* I could give up all, everything, every idol, however dear.

But he felt so unworthy and unfit for it.

> Tell Father . . . if he will only go to China, I will work like a slave, and
> live cheap, and send him 25 or 30 pounds a year myself till he gets
> established; or if he prefer it . . . come and manage the business for 5
> or 6 years for him . . . Tell him there are plenty of Christians in
> Barnsley, but who cares for poor China?

Three days later, his mother's birthday, he was writing again, the
coming separation always very much in their minds,

> . . . though we may be at opposite ends of the world . . . He will be as
> near as ever. Glory be to God. I shall be as near Home as you, and you
> will be as near Home as I shall be. Should your remains be buried in
> Barnsley . . . and mine repose in peace in China, we both I believe and
> trust shall meet where the wicked cease from troubling . . . for ever
> with the Lord.

The next letter, on February 6, was typical. On the Sunday he had
been taken by the Hardeys to the doctor's parents' home and was on
his best behaviour.

> After the (evening) sermon there was a prayer meeting and the chapel
> bottom was full. I got into a corner and determined to be quiet, but you
> know whether I could, when I tell you there was a revival. I was soon
> looking out for penitents, and when I found there was no getting to the
> form, I stopped and pointed out the way of salvation to an old woman,
> a backslider, 60–70 years of age, and she got into liberty. Then I got
> into the singing-pew to the penitents and two others found peace while
> I was talking to them. Praise the Lord. I think I never seemed to have
> such clear views of the plan of salvation or such ease in expressing
> them. When I left at ten o'clock six persons had found peace. . . I was
> very happy indeed.

At Drainside he was reading Henry Martyn's life – so appropriate to his own situation – analysing human blood, dissecting a cat,
studying anatomy, posting the doctor's accounts, keeping the
surgery journal, and doing a great deal of reading over his solitary
meals. Everything had a bearing on his great obsession, to fit
himself for the life to which he was called. To Amelia he said, 'I
almost wish I had a hundred bodies; they should all be devoted to
my Saviour in the missionary cause . . .'

Amelia could not match Hudson's euphoric other-worldliness and
was taken to task for writing him pages of 'newspaper' news, when
he wanted news 'of those I love'.

The next day he had to come down to earth himself to answer his
mother's questions. She was worrying about his health. Was he

going to be fit to go abroad or would he only throw his life away? 'The missionary work is the most noble mortals can engage in,' he told her, dropping into the stilted English her generation used. 'You would be far more unsettled if I were to give it up and . . . fall into sin; would you not?' He was never 'so well and hearty . . . I take as much good, plain, substantial food as I need, but waste nothing in luxuries.' Brown-bread biscuits and herring for breakfast, prune and apple pie for lunch, and sometimes roast potatoes and tongue 'as inexpensive as any other meat', biscuit and apples in the evening. For variety, peas instead of potatoes, 'and now and then some fry or a fish, cheese, rhubarb, lettuce, pickled cabbage, so at little expense I enjoy many comforts. To these add a comfortable home, where every want is anticipated, and "the peace of God which passes understanding" and if I were not happy and contented, I should *deserve* to be miserable . . . it certainly does seem folly to spend time writing such stuff, and would no doubt be thought so by any but a mother . . .'

The Gleaner for January and February 1852 renewed its emphasis on medical missionary work. Several writers from China, not least Lobscheid, were stressing the value of it in a land full of suffering, and for winning a welcome from the Chinese. Lobscheid himself was attending lectures and hospital practice in London to increase his effectiveness. Resolutions by the Edinburgh Medical Missionary Society set out the necessary qualifications, and an editorial under the title 'China's Claims on Medical Christian Men' pressed home the appeal. 'China is, of all others, the field needing the medical missionary.' The magazine seemed focused on Hudson Taylor.

The case of a young west-country farmer probably set him thinking. A local preacher without much education, George Piercy, was convinced that God was calling him, and saved up enough to take him to China and keep him going for two years. He booked his passage on a ship with Chinese in the crew so as to study the language during the voyage, and reached Hong Kong. Dr James Legge, large-hearted as always, made him welcome, and by visiting the barracks and hospital he soon found some Christian soldiers, established a 'Wesleyan society', opened a chapel and proved himself adequate as a missionary. If Piercy could do it in days when academic degrees and ordination were considered necessary, Hudson Taylor knew he could also.

CHAPTER TWO

A MATTER OF WHEN
1852–53

To go or not to go?   *March 1852*

After the March *Gleaner* in which George Piercy's story was told, Hudson Taylor's letters became full of talk about going soon. He referred to the Moravians, to saving towards his passage money, to working his way out, even before the mast. When Captain Finch was at home, Hudson picked his brains on how to go about it.

Amelia told him again she wanted to go to China too, but was God calling her? She was not sure. Starting a long reply at eleven pm on March 1, Hudson felt that all he wanted to say was 'Pray for me, pray for me . . . if ever you did pray for me, *pray now*, and get Father and Mother and John and all my Christian friends to pray for me, that I may be led aright by the Spirit of Truth.' It was his frequent theme, to pray before acting, and to pray until light was thrown on what he should do.

As for her thoughts about China, 'I do not doubt that you will be most useful there eventually.' He did not know how to advise her to prepare, but 'store your mind with knowledge and by no means forget French'. She had been taking French lessons with a M de Mirimonde, after his runaway marriage to a cousin of theirs. Captain Finch said he had never been to a country or port where French was not known by someone. But 'above all things, seek a closer walk with God . . . God bless you, my dear Amelia – *dearer to me than all* my other friends and relations put together . . . I feel I have not long to stop in this country now . . . I am forewarned that I may be prepared.'

To delay for two years and save enough to pay for his fare would land him in China no richer than if he worked his passage out. And if in that time he could lead even one Chinese to the Lord, what would the hardships of a four-month voyage be by comparison?

He wrote to his mother the next day in the same strain but with more evidence of growing maturity.

I can sing,

> I all on earth forsake,
> Its wisdom, fame and power;
> And Thee my only portion make,
> My Shield and Tower.

But, he asked himself,

> It is no use talking and thinking of what you *could* do. What *will* you do? . . . I have felt for several weeks that I have not long to stay in England . . . Praise the Lord He will not leave me in doubt or darkness respecting His will, and till He shall shew it to me *indubitably*, I will, by *His* grace, wait patiently. I feel at perfect peace . . . I don't wish to force circumstances.

He told her about his experiences in the lodging house area and the joy of preaching the gospel. It made him long to do the same in China.

> I have done my best to be a Surgeon, but I thank God, He has thwarted all my plans; if perhaps I had succeeded, I should not have given all the glory to God.

He thought of giving notice to Mr Hardey in May and leaving in August.

> I have counted the cost, but you are my parents; are you willing, should the Lord convince me that it is my duty, to let me go? . . . *my own dear Mother.*

Ten days later Hudson was on the same theme. What his mother had replied can be surmised from his comment, 'Though I do not think your objections are unfounded, I do not think they are very important ones.' His health would bear changes of climate better in youth than later on, 'a sapling can be bent better than an oak'. The heat would depend on where in China he was. 'China contains all the climates of Europe.' He would go as assistant to a ship's surgeon, 'which from all I hear I shall probably succeed in. *But if not* if I was sure it was the will of God for me to go, that would not hinder me one *minute*. I would go as a *common sailor* . . . I have talked about it to many men . . . Captain Finch has been commander in the Indian Seas; he says, never go as a common sailor; you could never bear it . . . The company of sailors was low and debasing.' But in a page or two Hudson showed that he had thought it all through. It was possible to go as a deck-hand, without duties in the rigging. As for clothing, he had already saved fifteen or twenty pounds, enough for all he would need. None of these were the chief concern, however. What mattered was, 'What is the will of God? . . . He will direct me *how* and *when* to move. *He* is Light, and those who walk in Him shall not go stumbling about in the dark.'

By prayer alone?   *March 1852*

On March 22 Hudson Taylor told his mother his mind was made up. The Hull brethren had advised as she did, that he should postpone his going to China. He would stay on in Hull and pray for the Lord's guidance. He had prayed that God would bring them all to one mind on the subject and was very pleased when it happened.

> If it is His will for me to go sooner, He can thrust me out or open my way unmistakably.

And he added some soulful paragraphs about Sunday being the happiest day he ever spent. There were many by the same description. 'I feel that peace . . . that flows like a river, deeply, stilly, and calmly along, not an exciting joy that wearies the system, but that perfect peace that comes from dependence on the Rock of Ages . . . I cannot tell you how much I love you.'

Running through his letters are the latest bulletins on his visits to the poor quarter of town, sometimes with a friend but often alone. Finding a crowd unable to cope with a chimney on fire Hudson Taylor pressed in, advised blocking the lower end, saw the fire extinguished and had an appreciative audience for his preaching.

Understandably, nothing was said about one experience which he recalled in his *Retrospect* years later. He was giving away up to sixty per cent of his earnings and living frugally but adequately, in his opinion, on the rest. The effect on himself was 'unspeakable joy all day long'.

> It was to me a very grave matter, however, to contemplate going out to China, far away from all human aid, there to depend upon the living God alone for protection, supplies, and help of every kind. I felt that one's spiritual muscles required strengthening for such an undertaking. There was no doubt that if faith did not fail God would not fail; but, then, what if one's faith should prove insufficient? I had not at that time learned that even 'if we believe not, he abideth faithful, he cannot deny himself'; and it was a very serious question to my own mind, not whether *He* was faithful, but whether I had strong enough faith to warrant my embarking on the enterprise set before me. I thought to myself, . . . my only claim will be on God. How important, therefore, to learn before leaving England to move man, through God, by prayer alone![1]

Only seeing that this theory worked in practical situations would satisfy him. Mr Hardey expected Hudson Taylor to remind him when his salary was due, so here was an opportunity to put his belief to the test. He would say nothing but instead ask God to do the reminding. Sure enough, it worked. But the time came when 'My kind friend', no mere employer, said nothing and days passed while Hudson's cash steadily ran out. One Saturday night he had only a half-crown piece left, just two shillings and six pence. He went on praying, accepting the situation as a test of his faith and determination, but by the next day he would be penniless.

'That Sunday was a very happy one. As usual my heart was brimming over with blessing . . .' He spent the afternoon and evening as always in lodging houses and slums, so filled with happiness 'that all that could be looked for was an enlargement of one's capacity for joy'.

When he packed up at ten o'clock a poor Irishman told him his wife was dying and asked him to go and pray for her. Why didn't he send for the priest? He had, but could not afford the fee of one shilling and six pence which the priest demanded. The family were starving. Immediately Hudson Taylor thought of his solitary half-crown and no food for Sunday. He chided the man for letting things reach such a state. He himself was in a quandary. If he had had loose change he would have given some of it to buy food for the sick woman and children. 'I little dreamed that the real truth . . . was that I could trust God plus one and six pence, but was not yet prepared to trust Him only, without any money at all in my pocket.' Worse still, the man led him to some premises in which he had been roughly handled, his tracts destroyed and a warning given not to try coming there again. On another occasion the children had been set on him and had baited him unpleasantly.

In the tenement room four or five obviously starving children and their mother with a newly-born baby stared at him hollow-eyed. He tried to say comforting things to them but inside he was thinking 'You hypocrite!' He tried to pray with them but his conscience said 'Dare you mock God? . . . with that half-crown in your pocket?' He struggled through his prayer. The words came into his mind 'Give to him that asketh of thee' and, looking back in later years, he knew that this was the moment of moments in his spiritual Odyssey. God was teaching him a lesson and he was at the dividing of the ways. He dug into his pocket and handed over the coin. Now he could tell them light-heartedly that it was his own last but that he could trust

God to provide whatever he needed, and he went home singing.

> Not only was the poor woman's life saved, but I realised that my life
> was saved too! It might have been a wreck – would have been a wreck
> probably, as a Christian life – had not . . . God's Spirit been obeyed.

The morning post brought him a surprise, 'the landlady came in
holding a letter or packet in her wet hand and covered by her apron.'
It contained a pair of gloves but no letter. And out of the gloves
tumbled a gold half-sovereign. 'Four hundred per cent for twelve
hours' investment!' he chortled. So far so good, but the rest of the
week went by, the money ran out again and still Mr Hardey did not
think of Hudson's salary. Mrs Finch's rent was due on Saturday.
Now the problem was, should he admit defeat, abandon his experiment and ask for the money? He went on praying.

On Saturday evening his employer was lying back in his armchair
and chatting pleasantly with Hudson when he said, 'Isn't your salary
due again?' Hudson gulped and agreed. But Mr Hardey went on, 'I
wish I'd thought of it sooner . . . Only this afternoon I sent all the
money I had to the bank, otherwise I would pay you at once!'

About ten pm Hudson packed up and put on his overcoat to go
home. As he was going to put out the gaslight he heard Mr Hardey's
footsteps on the garden path. He was chuckling, highly amused
about something. At this late hour one of his wealthiest patients had
come in to pay his bill. Hardey handed the cash to Hudson Taylor
and Hudson went home praising the Lord 'that after all I might go to
China'. 'To me the incident was not a trivial one.' It fully satisfied
him that the principle was right, even small faith placed in a faithful
God would always be honoured, and God was prepared to 'move'
men' in answer to his children's prayers. Even on the other side of
the world his needs would be supplied. This was better than
dependence on human resources.

Fifth commandment   *April–July 1852*

For the first time in a year Hudson went home for a week, at
Easter, and so was away from Hull when Mr George Pearse visited
his friends there. Andrew Jukes' congregation had sent good donations to the Chinese Society. But before long Pearse and Hudson
Taylor were to meet again in London.

On his return from Barnsley Hudson wrote cheerfully about

sowing a little vegetable patch and dissecting a cat and a weasel. Life settled down again to the usual routine. While at home he had declined to sign the pledge not to drink alcohol, and felt the need to set his mother's mind at rest about it. 'I am not a teetotaller,' he wrote, 'I *am* and *intend* to *remain* a total abstainer from all intoxicating drinks with the usual exceptions (medicinal and sacramental).' Firstly, he went on, *her* aversion to it and to tobacco and snuff was sufficient reason for him to abstain from all three by choice. Secondly, he had 'a great personal objection to it' as well as smoking, an '*injurious, growing and extravagant habit*'. Therefore, if he were to go against these natural inhibitions, '*voluntarily* and *wilfully* with my eyes open', he could not expect to be kept from temptation to indulge to excess. Finally, to use them at all would not be avoiding 'the appearance of evil' as Scripture required. '*These* reasons are *far more powerful* than *any* pledge can be.'

He discussed many subjects of a general nature with his parents, political elections, the Militia Bill, the use of force in suppressing mobs – the Scriptures he was convinced taught non-violence, taking 'joyfully the spoiling of your goods'. 'To a Christian who sees his Heavenly Calling *loss* is *impossible by outward means.* And again, are the mob *in that state* fit to be sent into another world?'

His unconventional views troubled his parents. They were afraid he was becoming unbalanced. They did not recognise these echoes of their Wesleyan pioneer forebears who had willingly suffered violence for Christ's sake.

But his mother was anxious about other things too. She had given him to the Lord and nothing would make her take him back, but the sword had entered into her soul and every twist brought a stab of pain as she feared losing her first-born and only surviving son. 'Tell Mother I will remember her caution as to dissecting,' Hudson told Amelia. Fulminating septicaemia from a cut or scratch while handling a corpse was the danger his mother feared. Smallpox and scarlet fever epidemics were raging so he was very busy doing vaccinations, and she imagined him starving and overworking himself. How well she knew him. 'Tell Mother I will neither pinch brain, stomach nor bed. So she need not be alarmed at all,' he went on. On his birthday he assured her that he was getting plenty of eggs and not suffering from privation. 'Everyone says how well I am looking.' One of his Aunt Hannah's portraits painted at about this time, when he was just twenty, leaves room for doubt.[2]

June came and went and Amelia left home to keep house for their uncle Joseph Hudson, vicar of Dodworth, whose wife had died leaving a two-year-old child motherless. Hudson's correspondence with Amelia was all the more welcome. Even if he did pontificate, it was all in a friendly spirit. 'Employ all your spare time, as I try to do, in acquiring or communicating more knowledge of Scripture and of the mind of God . . .' he advised. And he took to writing to Louisa, now twelve. He was concerned about her, that so like him in his early teens she showed no spiritual life.

Then a serious misunderstanding with his father blew up. Hudson had offered to run the pharmacy and support his father while he went to preach the gospel in China. William Burns had managed to preach after about six months out there, so surely a scholar and preacher like James Taylor would do the same. His father however was restless, wanting to go and visit relatives in Australia. Through Amelia he asked Hudson to take over the Barnsley pharmacy while he was away. This was a very different matter. Hudson was caught on the wrong foot. He had just written to George Pearse asking for Lobscheid's address. He was wondering if he could travel to China with him. His relations with his father were never the smoothest at any time. He replied pointing out all it would involve of changed plans and frustrated hopes.

The first hint of trouble came from his mother. He must not mention Australia in his letters but he ought to write apologising for pleading the sacrifices he himself would have to make, without any sign of gratitude for all his father's sacrifices for him. On June 24 Hudson Taylor wrote to Amelia. He was rebuking himself for being an undutiful son. The fifth commandment was to honour your father and mother and he had not done so. Nor could he bring himself to write appropriately now, for his father's wish ran counter to Hudson's understanding of God's will for himself.

He made detailed enquiries about immigration costs and formalities – a model of business efficiency and precision – for 'Grimshaw's son' who also wanted to go to Australia, and sent them to Amelia. A few days later he wrote that Miss V had moved to London, and continued, 'I have thought lately, if Father does not go abroad; if I could return with Brother Lobscheid . . . he could teach me a good deal of the language in the four months of the voyage.' And so much more than the language. Lobscheid's intimate knowledge of life on mainland China would be invaluable.

The Gleaner was tantalising, month after month full of details. In April an analysis of the population of China and each dependency was printed. China's four hundred million were compared with Britain's thirty-one million. China's 'colonies' of Manchuria, Mongolia, Tibet and Ili (Chinese Turkestan) made another twenty-five million. Nominally tributary Indo-China and Korea added twenty-two million more, and countries where Chinese were to be found from Burma to Celebes, another thirty-one million. Hudson Taylor's thinking about China was in terms of how many were living and dying without Christ. In two letters his calculations were wrong but their significance was the same. Reading on he found page after page of field news from China. A quotation about Ili from Abbé Huc's *Travels in Tartary, Thibet and China* caught his attention. For many years Catholic Christians had been exiled to this remotest of remote corners of the empire. Huc advocated sending missionaries to care for them.

And then came the May *Gleaner* with its suprise announcement of the formation of the Chinese Society into *The Chinese Evangelization Society* with expanded aims. No longer content with aiding missionary work in China, it intended to send missionaries, and Lobscheid was to be its first 'agent'. A mere twenty-three missionaries from Europe to China was a disgrace. America had sent twice as many already. 'We trust it may please God to raise up another European medical missionary . . .'

The June and July issues were no less provocative. Long extracts from Lobscheid's journals told of the freedom he had had to preach the gospel, at first in Charles Gutzlaff's company and then alone. Page upon page developed the theme that '*China is ripe for the gospel*, but if it is to be reaped we must go amongst the people', not settle in the treaty ports. Rudolf Lechler of the Basel Mission and others had been quietly living on the mainland, but as a repercussion from the rebellion of the 'Worshippers of Shangdi' edicts were issued denouncing him and he had to withdraw.

All this was meat and drink to Hudson Taylor. He took himself in hand and wrote to his father. Half measures were impossible, he had to put himself fully into the hands of God.

> My dear Father,
> I cannot come, so I write in the language of the prodigal son to say, 'Father, I have sinned against heaven and in thy sight, I am no more worthy to be called thy son'. My conscience has repeatedly troubled me about the answer I sent to your enquiry . . . I can no longer rest without writing to you and confessing my sin . . . Though I mentioned there the sacrifices I should make in coming home, I said nothing about

those you have made for me, the sleepless hours – the anxious thoughts – the expenses . . . the education you have given me and the business you have taught me . . . You have toiled for twenty years for my benefit. Father, I have been an undutiful son, an ungrateful son – I have always been a rebellious son to you . . . if you wish me to come home for two years, I will readily do so. Then afterwards, if the Lord will, I hope to be able to engage in His work in China . . .

The painful part over, Hudson wrote about the current election. A placard with the words, 'The Tories are dead, the old Whigs are dying, the people are coming into power' with its rumble of the tumbrils struck him as proof that the end times were near and the Coming of the Lord could not be far off! But it was one thing to write, another to have a reply. Had his father felt ill-treated by his going to Hull instead of continuing as his assistant in Barnsley? So Hudson added,

I know I do not deserve a letter and you have only written to me once . . . since I came to Hull, but if you will write I will be much obliged. Also, if you have *decided* either on going abroad or on staying at home, will you be kind enough to let me know . . . I have just cut a man's finger off . . . entirely by myself.

It was his first amputation.

A fortnight later he wrote again. He still had not heard from his father. Apologies for his 'scroll', changed to 'scrawl', but Mr Hardey was away and Hudson claimed to be 'almost run off my feet'. Then, if his father really had determined on going abroad, why be cooped up in any sort of old tub of a ship? Why not sign on as surgeon's assistant on a first class ship? 'Either way, do let me know what you have decided.'

Last week in Hull   *August–September 1852*

Things began to move faster after that. Mr Pearse wrote saying that Lobscheid was preparing to get married and to sail for China. If Hudson Taylor would come to London to consult with them the Society would pay his travelling expenses and the Pearses would put him up. Hudson wrote to Louisa.

I expect I shall be going to London soon, and if so, and I pass through Barnsley Station, (at Cudworth), I shall be glad to meet you there for a few minutes; perhaps I may stop a day on my return.

He told her that he found it strange to be going far away to the heathen and leaving his own sister whom he loved still unconverted.

This time James Taylor replied promptly to his son's enquiry, agreeing to let John Hodson stand in for Hudson at Mr Hardey's during his absence in London, from August 4. Apparently he also relinquished the idea of his own long voyage, for Hudson returned from London with the decision already made 'to leave Hull to attend the medical course at the London Hospital'.

At mealtimes Hudson was reading part of the *Narrative* of George Müller's life, in which he had recounted instance after instance of the dramatic supply of his needs, to clothe and feed his orphans. It inspired him to put his own faith into practice from day to day. In November 1840 Müller had recorded that one shilling was put into the offertory box at the Bethesda Chapel in Bristol 'with the words "Jehovah Jireh – the Lord will provide"'. So 'refreshing to my soul' did he find this message that when a valuable diamond ring was given for his orphans, he used it to engrave 'JEHOVAH JIREH' on his window-pane before selling it; and 'when in deep poverty', he wrote, 'the words often cheered my heart.'[3]

Such literal application of Scripture to daily life appealed to Hudson Taylor, and in particular Müller's attitude to debt as a denial of God's faithfulness in keeping his promises. So Hudson wrote,

> My faith has been strengthened and I do think I have been taught through it one lesson, to owe no man anything. I intend by the grace of God . . . to borrow no more of anyone under any circumstances whatever. May God help me.

Never again did he allow himself to go into debt. By strong strides he was learning new lessons and one by one making them his own by deliberately accepting and putting them into practice.

While in London he had taken steps to look for an assistantship with a doctor not too far from the London Hospital. Without it he would have no means of livelihood. But with it he could be prevented from attending enough lectures and hospital practice. Here was a new problem to face. He knew George Müller was living and running his orphanage in Bristol without human assurance of support but in dependence on God for provision for all his needs. But even in Christian circles the idea was still *avant garde* and to Hudson Taylor's parents with their insistence that God could be trusted to keep his promises, this new notion of Hudson's was as questionable as his views on the Second Coming and mob control.

> With regard to London, [he continued to his mother] when I returned to Hull after prayer I considered why I desired to take the step contemplated, and I believe my reason is that I may be enabled to serve the Lord better . . . Then why do I not take it? Simply because I have doubts about the means. If my earthly Father had offered, in case I required it, to lend me five or six pounds, without the least hesitation I should have given notice; how much more then shall I leave trusting in the Living God, who in His Word says, take *no* thought, saying What shall we eat? or what shall we drink, or where withal shall we be clothed? . . . for your *Heavenly Father knoweth* that ye have need of all these things; and 'Trust in the Lord and do good, so shalt thou dwell in the land, and verily thou shalt be fed (*see* Psalm 37.3–6). So I thought it seemed like doubting the Lord to depend on circumstances, and consequently gave notice on Saturday, August 21st and shall go to London whether I meet with the situation or not, trusting in the Lord.

Robert Hardey was sorry to lose him and offered him a formal apprenticeship, at that time one of the steps towards registration as a doctor. He could graduate in Hull instead of London. But London was a step nearer the Chinese Evangelization Society and China. At Hull he had weaned himself from home. Now he needed full independence from family props and scrutiny.

By this time Hudson Taylor had moved on from useful experimentation to the measured application of his convictions. The Word of God was no longer only a devotional manual to worship and pray by. It was a practical handbook to live by and act upon. Bible and timetable belonged together.[4] His letter to his mother went on,

> I have heard today of a situation and shall write about it, tho' I do not think it will suit me on account of the distance (from the medical college). As to getting any salary, as you mention that is *altogether* out of the question, and if I get a situation allowing me 6 or 8 hours a day for lectures etc., that is *all* I can expect . . . My mind is quite as much at peace as it would, nay more than if I had £100 in my pocket to go with. May *He* ever keep me thus, simply depending on *Him* for every blessing, spiritual or temporal, for Jesus sake.

James Taylor released John Hodson to follow Hudson at Mr Hardey's, and Thomas Neatby took John's place as Mr Taylor's assistant. Both were also to be Mrs Finch's lodgers after Hudson left. When John moved on as a medical student to hospital, Thomas went to Hardey, then to St Bartholomew's Hospital to qualify as a surgeon. Hudson Taylor led the way a lap ahead of them in practical as well as spiritual progress.

On September 4 he wrote to John, telling him that the unsettledness he spoke of would leave him for ever if he read his Bible more, treasured it more, believed it more and prayed for the Spirit of Truth to guide him by it. John valued his letters and carried some of them in his pocket-book to read from time to time.

> You ask what I shall do if no situation turns out for me. If the Lord will, I shall go to London, endeavour to trust in the Lord and do good (see Psalm 37) and in all my ways acknowledge Him and seek to do His will, for He knows best what His children need . . . I have not yet heard of a situation, nor am I anxious to do so, if it be the Lord's will for me to wait. I received a note from Uncle Benjamin [in Soho] yesterday, offering me board and lodging as his guest until I find a desirable situation in London. I shall probably (D.V.) go there, though I have by no means decided how far it is proper to receive aid from the unconverted . . .

Benjamin Hudson, brother of both Hudson's and John's mothers, was not a believer. To Amelia Hudson wrote on the same day,

> No situation has yet turned up, that will suit me, as to distance; but I do not feel at all concerned about that as He is the same today, yesterday, and for ever . . . I know He only tries me to increase my faith, and that it is love and not anger that causes it. He is glorified, I am content.

A week later and only ten days from ending his job, he told Amelia,

> How kind of the Lord to keep my mind in perfect peace, and full of joy divine and happiness now, when in outwardly the most difficult circumstances. Had I left the question, Shall I go, or stay? to be answered by circumstances, how unsettled I should have been! And how unsettled John would have been. But as the Lord enabled me to take the step unhesitatingly, because it was for His glory, and leave all things in His hands, my mind has been just as peaceful as it would otherwise have been unsettled. In all probability had I been very anxious about it, I should not have been able to sleep properly, and what with that and my business which fully occupies my time I should have been thoroughly knocked up. Praise the Lord for His goodness, He has provided all that is necessary so far. Now I have a home to go to – money to pay the fee of the Ophthalmic Hospital – the practice of the London Hospital, which costs £90, and some Christian Friends in London . . . And when He sees fit, if He sees fit, He will find me a suitable and appropriate situation, and if not, will provide for and

occupy me as seemeth *Him* best. I leave it all to *Him* . . . Last autumn I was fretting and stewing and reckoning and puzzling myself how to manage this and that, like a person who cannot swim, in water, or a fish out of it, but it all came to nothing. *Now*, when the *Lord* opens the way, when everything seems adverse, He first removes one difficulty and then another obstacle, plainly saying, '*Be still* and know that I *am* God!' . . . Always *cast all* your care on *Him* for *He* careth for you . . .

When a few more days had passed and still no prospect of a job had appeared, Hudson wrote again to his mother. The Duke of Wellington, idol of the nation, died on September 14 but he had no thought for him. His thoughts were too deep. He copied out a hymn about confidence in Jesus, to strengthen her. For the first time he quoted his father's favourite words of Scripture, as if he had assimilated them as his own capital asset, 'If we believe not yet he abideth faithful; He cannot deny Himself.' James Taylor would add, 'He would not be God if He could'. A satisfying concept of effortless confidence, never betrayed, was becoming his working philosophy.[5] And he was little more than twenty.

Hudson Taylor's convictions were firm but his experience of their viability was so far minimal. It mattered to him that he should see more of God's faithfulness in action. And at this stage, with no prospect of a job, the potential for another experiment fell into his lap.

When he understood from George Pearse that the Chinese Evangelization Society had 'kindly offered to bear my expenses while in London',[6] Hudson Taylor was also considering a similar offer from his father. He could have accepted either as the Lord's provision in answer to his prayers, but he knew that 'owing to recent losses, it would mean a considerable sacrifice' for his father at that particular time. He wrote to both that he would 'take a few days to pray about the matter before deciding', and mentioned to each the offer made by the other. Then, while he was praying for guidance,

It became clear to my mind that I could without difficulty decline both offers. The secretaries of the society would not know that I had cast myself wholly upon God for supplies, and my father would conclude that I had accepted the other offer. I therefore wrote declining both propositions . . . I was simply in the hands of God . . . He, who knew my heart, if He wished to encourage me to go to China, would bless my effort to depend upon Him alone at home.

When he reached London it was not to be the plain sailing that he might have hoped for. He soon learned that rejecting one form of the Lord's provision in order to receive another is neither more spiritual nor right than accepting the first. But this time God honoured the young zealot's zeal and gave him a demonstration of how his promises come true. Meanwhile he worked for Robert Hardey to the last minute.

He was booked to sail from Hull on Tuesday, September 21, but John Hodson, always happy-go-lucky, arrived too late to be shown the ropes. Then 'almost a hurricane' blew up and there was nothing to be done but to sail by a later ship. Amelia came to see him off and spent her seventeenth birthday and the last few days at Mrs Finch's cottage. They only had the evenings and meal-times together, he was so busy, but it meant a great deal to them. Apart from a few holidays in the company of others, it was to be the last opportunity to enjoy their close childhood friendship. His days were spent in the practice. 'On Thursday morning I brought into the world as fine a little girl as ever you saw,' he told his mother in a pencilled note from the old paddle steamer *London*. At last he got away at four pm on Friday, the 24th, leaving his Amelia in her bonnet and crinoline on the pier among the friends who came to see him off.

Soho, Tottenham and the CES   September 1852

Instead of the twenty-hour journey of the newest steamer, Hudson Taylor's old coaster crawled slowly up the Thames estuary sounding its foghorn and dropped anchor at eight-thirty on Saturday evening, unable to go further. He had woken at daybreak, and was on deck for two hours before six am enjoying the morning star, a mill-pond sea and the excitement of embarking upon a new life. Travelling cheaply meant providing his own food. He took brown bread and pickled herrings, but by his chosen standards that was no hardship. It was late on Sunday morning, September 26, before the fog lifted and noon before they tied up in London Pool. The Thames was busy with sail and steam, a crowded thoroughfare in those days. Hudson Taylor left his baggage on board to be collected later and walked through the City and Holborn to his uncle Benjamin Hudson's 'apartment' in Mrs Ruffell's establishment at 24 Church Street, Soho, close to Shaftesbury Avenue.

Benjamin Hudson was good company, clever, amusing and a born raconteur. His portrait painting took him away frequently but he was there to welcome Hudson Taylor and see him settled into the apartment adjoining his own, determined to introduce him to the surgeons in his wide circle of friends, with the hope of their giving him an apprenticeship. He was impatient with Hudson's talk of praying for the Lord to guide him, and would have swept him off to meet them at once, but Hudson had first to meet the secretaries of the Chinese Evangelization Society (CES). George Pearse, the Foreign Secretary, and his colleague Charles Bird, responsible for 'Home' affairs, might have other ideas. They had.

For a start George Pearse was too busy to see him. He invited him 'to spend some Sunday with him' as if Hudson Taylor was already well established at hospital. That meant the loss of at least a week, but the medical schools were opening on the following Monday. When Hudson Taylor managed to get his interview, however, he found to his surprise that the offer of the CES to pay his hospital fees was not an unconditional grant and moreover was only tentative. The Committee would have to meet and decide about it. On October 2 he could only tell his parents, 'Really you know almost as much of my future plans as I do, for I have nothing certain yet, except "I will never leave thee"'. Even after another week he had to say, 'I am *altogether* in the Lord's hands and He will direct me.'

He started to study on his own and after mid-October to pay his own rent, more per week that it had been monthly in Hull. Soho was a far cry from Yorkshire. 'London is a trying place – so much noise and bustle and distraction of every kind. You can have no idea of the difference it makes to be among a light, thoughtless and worldly-minded company.'

In a room round the corner in Dean Street, but in and out of 'Ruffell's', was John Hodson's brother Thomas, a student at the School of Design at Marlborough House, intending to become an interior decorator, Mr Ruffell's profession. When Hudson Taylor knew where he stood and decided not to take an assistantship for the present, he accepted Thomas's invitation to share his room at the top of the house in Dean Street. It threw them together even more, and while Hudson had to pray and read his Bible under observation, Tom was intrigued by talking with him about his ideas on 'faith' and the future.

At first Hudson Taylor attended an assembly of 'Brethren' at Kennington, 'in the Surrey part of London', where three to four hundred met in the morning 'besides a good congregation' at two other meetings in the day. He wrote, 'It was so nice to be in a quiet private family', when one member took him home for meals; when they made toast by the living room fire 'it reminded me so strongly

of old times I could have cried with pleasure'. But the Kennington
Brethren were of an exclusive persuasion. At first their critical
influence on him was strong and Hudson reflected it in his letters.
'Oh! dear Mother, I do wish you were out of that Babylon of
Confusion, Sectarianism,' he wrote. 'The moment a man is called
Reverend he takes on a higher standing in the eyes of the world and
worldly Christians than his poor local brother who may be far more
holy.'

For a few weeks he was tarred with the brush that made him decry
'cults, heresies and denominations' all in the same breath. But it was
not long before he was of a different mind. He soon found the
independent, open congregations, and looking back on that brief
encounter with exclusivism he wrote, 'I saw enough of their spirit to
keep me from ever joining them.'

At Tottenham where he enjoyed the fellowship of like-minded
men and women of several denominational backgrounds it was
different. His brief acquaintance in 1851 with the Howards and Miss
Stacey, and with the Pearses and William Berger at Hackney, now
began to grow into the lifelong friendships so inseparable from his
future actions, and in their open-hearted attitudes the ecumenical
spirit of the Hudson Taylor of later years and of the mission he
founded can be recognised. Among such people he received a
welcome and was encouraged in his non-sectarian views. Some of
them were members of the council and committee of the Chinese
Evangelization Society, together with Anglican ministers, Quakers
and members of the Free Churches.[7]

While waiting for Charles Bird, the secretary, to hand him the
fees and an introduction to the Ophthalmic and London Hospitals,
he reported on Monday, October 11, to his mother 'a very serious
delay'.

> While unbelief sees the difficulties Faith sees God between itself and
> them . . . The Chinese Committee met on Thursday and considered
> my application for Hospital Practice, and on Friday I received a note
> from Mr Bird desiring me to procure certain testimonials.

The nature of them worried him. He was not applying for charity.

> I intend to see Mr Pearse today if possible . . . The required testi-
> monials I do not altogether understand – and if all of them are
> necessary I shall thank the committee for their kindness and
> trouble them no further . . . I thank God I feel quite as willing to
> lose as to gain their assistance.

As he saw it he had already been offered a grant. Why then these puzzling formalities? The next day he wrote again,

I got up early this morning and went over to Hackney and saw Mr Pearse and soon set all right. Mr Pearse however wishes me to write to you and Mr Robert Hardey and get you to write to Mr Bird. You can just state your opinion as to whether you think me converted or not, if you think me seriously intending to go to China, and anything you may know in me which would make me either *suitable* or *unsuitable* for missionary work. I do not wish you to write as my *mother*, but as you would if your candid opinion was asked, in so momentous a matter, on any other person.

Another fortnight went by and at last the committee reached a conclusion. But not until the Saturday night did Hudson Taylor hear from Bird that he could start at the London Hospital in Whitechapel on Monday. Then a new distress arose. Well-meaning though James Taylor was, he still seemed unable to understand his son. He sent him a message that if he ran out of resources in London he could always come home and count on a livelihood. His son's new philosophies were beyond him. If Hudson's reply had been passed on to him, James Taylor would have been surprised, 'Thank Father for his kind offer of a home, but tell him, those who trust in the Lord *always* "have something to depend on".' Reconciliation had not yet bridged the gap between them.

So at long last, a month after reaching London, things began 'assuming a more settled appearance' and Hudson Taylor started work at 'The London'. 'Give me neither poverty nor riches' was the biblical ideal and by his own spartan standards he was being adequately housed, clothed and fed. His fees were paid and he had his savings to live on for the time being. What happened when they ran out would be interesting to see. He would try to win a scholarship, and God would supply, not plenty but all he needed. Meanwhile careful economy must stretch what he had in hand as far as it would go.

Whether or not the scholarship he hoped for was in connection with the Preliminary Examination of the Royal College of Surgeons is not stated. At this or some stage soon, Hudson Taylor had to demonstrate his general education by translating from Caesar's *De Bello Gallico, St John's Gospel* in Greek, Voltaire's French and Schiller's German, as well as by examination in English grammar and composition, geography, history, mathematics, mechanics, chemistry, zoology and botany.

From Soho to Whitechapel was a long four miles, through
Holborn, past St Paul's Cathedral, along Cheapside, through
Aldgate and for the last mile along Whitechapel Road. It was
possible to go by bus, horse-drawn of course, costing as much each
week as the rent of his room, or by cab if he were really well-off.
Hudson Taylor could afford neither. He would have to walk, as very
many did in those days. But on the Thursday he had sprained his
ankle. 'I determined to walk the pain off, and succeeded admirably
in walking it *on*, and have been lame ever since,' he told his mother.
But walk he had to. Every day he walked the eight or nine miles,
there and back. If he knew that he was doing as Robert Morrison
did, with his long walks from Bishopsgate to Greenwich, he does
not mention it in the surviving letters. On the way home he bought a
large loaf of brown bread, and asked the baker to divide it for him,
half for the evening meal and half for breakfast. That, with 'a few
apples for lunch' was his staple diet. It became his custom to set off
for Whitechapel in the morning without breakfast and to eat his
ration when he stopped for a rest somewhere along the way.[8]

London in 1852 was a hurly-burly of horse-drawn carriages,
pedestrians, mounted men and hand-carts rattling over the cobble-
stones. They jostled uncomfortably, dependent on shouted warn-
ings in the near absence of rules of the road. There was no Holborn
viaduct. As he climbed the hill from Farringdon Road Hudson
Taylor passed drovers leaving Smithfield Meat Market after delivering their herds of bullocks. If he had been attending St Bartholomew's Hospital he would have needed to go no further, but 'The
London' it had to be. Once through the City he came into another
world.

London was still 'the great wen', the abscess, of Cobbett's time.
Its unsewered streets, littered with accumulated filth, reeked from
another cause. Existing streams, so foul that covering them over
was simply to smother the stench, were the only sewers until long
after 1859 when sewerage construction began. Most houses had
cesspools beneath them. In Richard Collier's vivid 'Book Society
Choice' about William Booth, *The General next to God*,[9] he de-
scribes the East End in 1865 with its 'stifling alleys east of Aldgate
Pump'. It was the same or worse in 1852.

Match-sellers and orange-women blocked his path . . . hulking labourers, women clad only in soiled petticoats. Children with wolfish faces

foraged at his feet . . . [Drunkenness at all hours of day and night added danger to the degradation . . .] silent savage men with ashen faces . . . lunged and struck and toppled heavily and watching women, faces animal with passion, screamed 'strike! strike!' The streets were their eating place – breakfast doled out by the hot-baked potato man, supper from the hot-eel seller . . . Yankee foremast men from the windjammers with tarry trousers and case-knives strung from their girdles . . . bearded Jewish old-clothes vendors . . . street-girls in poppy-red Garibaldi blouses. The noise was shattering, a babel of sound. In the dark alleys near the docks, the sick, the dying, often the dead, lay side by side on the bare floors of fireless rooms covered with tattered scraps of blanket . . . Their homes smelt of red herrings, stale bedding and last week's rain . . .

This was the East End in which the London Hospital had been built, a mission field waiting twelve more years for its William Booth and Thomas Barnardo; a morass of poverty for which Karl Marx was working at that very time in a very different way in the British Museum library.

At last Hudson Taylor's daily traipse would end, and as he walked up the ramp and under the arch into the hospital he entered a new world.[10] The London Hospital had been there since 1759 after the long cold winter in which thirty thousand died. In 1840 the appalling death rate of mothers in childbirth was one in every hundred. That was one in every twenty women with five children, but many had ten. Epidemics periodically swept through the country. Cholera raged in London in 1848 when sixteen thousand died, and in 1853 and 1854. Medical knowledge was still woefully inadequate and hospital care was still primitive. Bed bugs were rife.

Until 1840 crude hussies attended the sick. 'Every vice was rampant among the women and their aid to the dying was to remove pillows and bedclothes and so hasten the end.' The rare exceptions of some commended for kindness and ability were recorded in the annals. But in 1840 under the influence of the philanthropist Elizabeth Fry a society of the 'Protestant Sisters of Charity' had been proposed. It petitioned the hospital to take 'two or three respectable women for training'. When Hudson Taylor arrived, both types were there, attending about three hundred patients. A resident apothecary was in charge, dignified after 1854 with the title of Resident Medical Officer. Each ward was issued with seven candles per week. Additional ones were permitted only if ordered by the surgeon in an emergency.

Anaesthetics other than inebriation by alcohol were not in use. As a student at University College Hospital Joseph Lister had amputed a leg under neat ether in 1846, and the following year, appalled by the barbarity of cruelty common in the practice of midwifery, James Simpson, Professor of Obstetrics in Edinburgh, experimented with chloroform on himself and some friends. But prejudice was too strong and before 1860 little advance was made. In Hudson Taylor's time patients for operation were held down by attendants or strapped to the table if too strong. A great bell 'loud and harsh enough to make all Whitechapel shudder' was sounded when more manpower was needed. The surgeon donned a frock coat stiff with blood and pus from previous operations. One of the older surgeons said he 'liked a good honest scream' as an indication of the patient's vitality and endurance. But often the operation could not be performed because of the effect of the pain inflicted. From his year with Mr Harvey in Hull, Hudson Taylor was inured to most of this and took it for granted. The conditions are not mentioned in his letters.

The medical college was only then going up and, three weeks late, Hudson Taylor joined the students in a wing of the hospital. T B Curling, Jonathan Hutchinson and Andrew Clark, famous men, were on the staff. It was to Curling, Honorary Secretary or Dean of the medical school and a considerate man that Hudson Taylor reported. Only the previous year he had called the attention of the hospital committee to the fact that the duties of the students as dressers, doing almost all the repulsive routine work in those days of 'good and laudable pus' was 'very onerous'. 'The smell of gangrene and decay in the wards was, in Simpson's own notes, described as "even worse for a medical student to become accustomed to than the scene during the operation itself."'

Curling appears to have taken a liking to this slight, sensitive new student, for the lengths he later went to in helping him sound extraordinary to us.

If exchanging home and the Christian gentility of Hull for Soho and Benjamin Hudson's world was difficult, sudden immersion in the company of the fifty or sixty blasphemous medical students was pure suffering, Hudson Taylor admitted in after-years. The crudity of their duties seemed to make brutes of the men, coarseness was their best defence against going under, if they had no spiritual alternative. He made some friends, however, by helping them with their dissecting and out-patient dressings. 'I don't mean to lose or waste many opportunities,' was his policy, but in fact he was soon so busy that the Ophthalmic Hospital had to wait. If he suffered emotionally his letters did not betray it. They were objective and carried an air of excitement over the progress he was making.

In early November a letter from home enquired how he was using his spare time. The tone of his reply betrays the gasp he must have given.

> I begin in the morning (by having) to be at the Hospital at 8 am, before which time I have a short walk . . . I get my breakfast on my way to rest me a little. [Then his timetable] 8–9 ward rounds with M.Ds. 9–10 lecture on surgical anatomy. 10–10.30 dissecting room or library, 10.30–11.30 chemistry or dissecting demonstrations, 11.30–1 pm dissecting room, museum, library or dressings and operations in out-patients. Then lunch. 1–3 operations and rounds with surgeons, 3–4 lectures on surgery or physiological anatomy and once a week an exam, 4–5 'medicinal lecture'. On Saturdays 7–8 am a lecture on dental physiology and surgery. (Then walk home and) *if possible* read up on some subject, transcribe notes, answer letters and then employ 'spare time' as may happen, with eating and sleeping . . . Sometimes I have been so tired I was forced to ride part of the way home . . . all but about half a mile for three pence or a mile and a half for one penny . . . [With two or three weeks' vacation at Christmas] I actually thought of popping down if there were any cheap trains, and I could save by getting any *grub* out of you, but that is done away with . . .

Some student vocabulary was rubbing off on him already. Dissecting was expensive, 'Nine shillings a member – so I have to watch others.' But to Amelia he wrote a week later that he could not do without some dissecting. 'I have twice as much to do, as I can possibly get through . . . Tell Mother not to be alarmed about me, but when I am quite worn out I get into a "Bus" . . .' Predictably he wished Amelia could be in London, but was resigned to the impossibility.

> There are now about 300 in-patients besides out-patients. I am sorry I have no opportunity of giving them any spiritual instruction as I am only with them when the Surgeons and Physicians together with 50–60 students are present and so we have to pass quickly to get through them all. We are not allowed to give them anything . . . but they are provided with Gospel Tracts and Bibles etc. by the Chaplain. I can assure you, it does need watchfulness, for if one was once to give way, among such a set, it would be all over with them. Pray for me . . .

At last, two months after the Duke of Wellington's death, preparations for the pageantry of his state funeral were complete. Passing St Paul's Cathedral day after day, Hudson Taylor was appalled. It was 'like a workshop, public service given up'. Excursion tickets from Hull to London and back were only five shillings, but no one came from home and he himself deliberately missed the celebrations.

> The crowding during the lying-in-state and funeral have been terrific, several persons have actually been crushed to death . . . Uncle had a seat . . . to see the funeral procession. Thos. [Hodson] saw it from Marlborough House . . . I had the offer of a seat, but declined, thinking it was the world worshipping its Idol and classed in the lust of the flesh, the lust of the eye and the pride of life.

He was working hard for his scholarship when he received a request from Mrs Finch. Captain Finch was commanding a London ship and had asked Hudson Taylor to collect and remit part of his salary month by month to Mrs Finch in Hull.[11] Her request was for him to send the next amount as early as possible. Rather than take time to collect it he sent his own money, intending to refund himself as soon as the examination was over and he could get to the shipping office. The medical school closed for a day on account of the Duke's funeral, however, so Hudson Taylor called at the office. To his dismay he was told that Finch had abandoned his ship and gone to the gold diggings, but Hudson Taylor reminded himself that he was 'depending on the Lord for everything, and His means were not limited'. So this was only a matter of looking to him sooner than otherwise for his necessities.

With the onset of winter the mud and slush in the streets were making the walking more difficult.

> Thank Father for the loan of Turner's *Chemistry* and for the boots [he wrote home]. They are a little too large but . . . will be very welcome this dirty winter weather . . . I have had some most miserable walks lately. Don't be afraid of me cutting myself in Dissecting. Numbers of students have cut themselves, but they always suck the cut and apply caustic to it, and it gets well directly. I was going to have a leg in a subject we have just got in, but as I have a little cold, Mr Ward recommended me to delay a little . . . so you need not be frightened now at any rate.

The cadavers were not embalmed.

Each time he wrote home he complained that his mother and

Amelia did not write often enough. They teased him about his 'insatiability'; they were writing as frequently as usual. But he was hungry for the daily Christian fellowship he was used to, and confessed that he felt starved. Previously he had written, 'Your letters are like angels' visits, few and far between'. But now 'I have been thinking I don't half value my privilege of hearing so often from you – soon probably it may not be so.' That was the underlying thought, the long separation had begun.

He was thinking over what he read in *The Gleaner*. So much of it was applicable directly to him. The Chinese Evangelization Society was coming into the limelight. Meetings in the Savoy Chapel, Glasgow, Cheltenham, Leamington, place after place, were well attended, and donations were flowing in. The sailing of Mr and Mrs Lobscheid as CES missionaries had given the needed stimulus.

The editorial in the November *Gleaner* was on *The Advantages of Medical Missions to China*, a good article mobilising opinion from the CMS and other sources and quoting Liang A-fa.[12] And there was more on mission hospitals. A notice giving news of George Piercy[13] announced the decision of the Wesleyan Missionary Society to support him and to send two young men to join him. Things were moving. With December came the reminder that tea came from China, so 'With every cup of tea pray for China'! But this month's magazine carried other exciting news. With an article on Japan, still inaccessible, came the information that seven American warships under Commodore Matthew Perry[14] had sailed for Japan to demand the release of some American citizens held prisoner. And a letter from Issacher J Roberts[15] claimed that Hong Xiu-quan (Hung Hsiu-ch'üan), the leader of the Worshippers of Shangdi, far from being dead as previously reported, was struggling for religious liberty in China, and had been taught Christianity by one of the founding members of the Chinese Christian Union. Moreover, Mrs Gutzlaff was still in Hong Kong carrying on her husband's work.

On his visits to Hackney and Tottenham Hudson Taylor was able to discuss these things with George Pearse and the others and learn more. But where did he personally fit in? On December 1, 1852, he wrote home, as from 24 Church Street, Soho,

> As I am still Dissecting of course I have no time to spare. It does not injure my health, on the contrary everyone says how well I look, some even I am getting fat. This I believe however requires rather a brilliant imagination to perceive. The walks do not fatigue me as they used to do, but the profane conversation of many students heartily does sicken

> me and I need all your prayers . . . My expenses, of course, they are
> very great, but as you say the future is in the Lord's hands, and where
> else could you wish it?
>   I have had many thoughts lately, as to what part of China I shall go
> to, and it seems to be impressed on my mind I shall eventually go to Ili
> on the Thibetan border of China. There I am afraid it will be impos-
> sible to correspond with one another . . . It must however be some
> years before I can go . . .

Although far from Hull he was thinking still of John Hodson,
assistant to Mr Hardey. The pastoral gift that was to be one of
Hudson Taylor's strong points as a leader of men is seen in his letter
of December 6 to John whom he knew so well. He urged him to
'Cleave closely to the Rock of Ages' and 'be *diligent* that you may be
found *without spot* and blameless.' But he was an evangelist too. In
mid-November Thomas Hodson turned to Christ; 'soundly converted' was how Hudson Taylor put it a month later. But by then he
was more than fortunate to be able to write at all.

'You are a dead man!'   *December 1852*

On December 14 Hudson Taylor was sewing sheets of notepaper
together to make a notebook when he pricked his right hand. It was
nothing, and in a moment he had forgotten about it.

> The next day at hospital I continued dissecting as before. The body was
> that of a person who had died of fever, and was more than usually
> disagreeable and dangerous. I need scarcely say that those of us who
> were at work upon it dissected it with special care knowing that the
> slightest scratch might cost us our lives.

Later in the morning he was in the surgical wards when he felt ill
and went out to vomit. Some cold water revived him for a while but
during the afternoon surgery lecture his whole arm and side were
'full of severe pain' and he could not hold his pencil to take notes. By
now he was 'both looking and feeling very ill'. So he consulted the
surgeon demonstrating in the dissecting room. He had no doubts.
'You must have cut yourself in dissecting.' Hudson Taylor denied it,
but then remembered the needle prick the night before. Could that
wound still be unclosed?

> He advised me to get a hansom [cab], drive home as fast as I could, and
> arrange my affairs forthwith. 'For', he said, 'you are a dead man!' My
> first thought was one of sorrow that I could not go to China; but very

soon came the feeling, 'Unless I am greatly mistaken, I have work to do in China, and shall not die.'[16]

To the sceptical surgeon's amazement Hudson Taylor told him that if he was going to die it gave him joy to think of soon being with the Lord, but he did not think he would die as he had work to do in China! All very well, the surgeon answered, but get home as fast as you can, 'You have no time to lose for you will soon be incapable of winding up your affairs!'

A cab was out of the question and Hudson Taylor started to walk. In less than a mile his strength gave out and he climbed on to a bus. He arrived at Soho 'in great suffering', asked the servant for hot water and 'literally as a dying man' exhorted her 'to accept eternal life as the gift of God through Jesus Christ'. Then he struggled up the stairs, 'five nines and a seven' to his top floor room, bathed his throbbing head and 'lanced the finger'. 'The pain was very severe; I fainted away . . .'

When he came to he was in bed. To his alarm his uncle had sent for his own doctor, a surgeon at the Westminster Hospital. Hudson Taylor knew he could never afford it, but Benjamin Hudson undertook to foot the bill.

Hudson Taylor's anxiety was more for his parents than for himself, especially when they found that he was moneyless. If they came to the rescue –

> I must lose the opportunity of seeing how God was going to work for me, now that my money had almost come to an end.

So he made his uncle and Thomas promise not to let them know. He would write himself. Then he waited 'until the crisis was past and the worst of the attack was over', so sure was he that he was not going to die.

Two days later he wrote the understatement of a lifetime.

> I will try to write a few lines, tho' I cannot do them well not being able to use my forefinger. I pricked it on Tuesday but being so small a place never thought of putting a little plaster on it when I went to dissect the next day, and thus I got some matter in it, which brought on inflammation and a little fever, but it (is) much better now and I hope will soon be well, by the blessing of God . . .

This he followed with digressions about George Müller and Thomas Hodson's conversion, and then,

> At the Hospital I am dissecting the head and neck, a most beautiful but difficult dissection . . . My funds are not all expended, I do not expect to be assisted by any London friends, but if I fall short I have the Lord to fly to. They who trust in Him shall never be confounded . . . Excuse more as my arm aches . . .

James Taylor had been suffering from a painful facial neuralgia and Hudson offered to come home in the Christmas recess to give a hand in the pharmacy. But it was several weeks before he himself was fit to leave his room, and in that time two other students died of dissection wounds. The friendly Uncle Benjamin sent him all the tempting food he could manage, from Ruffell's round the corner, and slowly he recovered. Then one day when the surgeon called he found Hudson Taylor dressed. He had walked down the stairs with help, but was tired out by the effort. His money was now exhausted and he needed more.

> I was refraining from making my circumstances known to those who would delight to meet my need, [he wrote] in order that my faith might be strengthened by receiving help from (God) Himself in answer to prayer alone.

As he lay on the sofa praying, he came to the conclusion that he should enquire at the shipping office again. But how was he to get there? It was two miles to Cheapside. He decided he must walk. 'I never took so much interest in shop windows as I did upon that journey.' The shipping clerk looked at him, pale and exhausted, and Hudson Taylor explained what had happened. 'I am so glad you have come,' the clerk said, 'for it turns out that it was an able seaman of the same name [as Finch] that ran away.' So Hudson left with the money he had sent to Mrs Finch refunded, and took the bus home again.

The next day he walked to the surgeon's house, and asked for his bill, lest his uncle settle it first. The surgeon stared at yesterday's ghost now walking and would not dream of charging a medical student. The concession felt like the gift of a fat cheque. But he allowed him to pay for the medicines. So Hudson Taylor told him about the walk to Cheapside and how he had been trusting the Lord to supply his needs, ever since playing off the CES and his father against each other. 'I would give all the world for a faith like yours,' was the surgeon's comment.

A railway ticket to Barnsley was the next thing, and three weeks' convalescence under his mother's care. Of course, the whole story had to come out, and when he returned to London they made him promise to give his experiments with 'faith' a rest. The loss of a few weeks' work mattered little, for he was alive and soon would be well again.

The episode had proved that he had a reserve of stamina that belied any talk of his being a weakling, too frail for the hardships of missionary life in China. For the rest of his life he looked back on those first three months of extreme testing in London as being so valuable to him that the memory of them often renewed his own faith and encouraged others.

Tottenham and Marianne again   *December 1852–April 1853*

From the letter of December 17 to the next on February 6, 1853, there are few records, but later references fill in the story to some extent. Hudson Taylor was back in London near the end of January. During that time his father had launched the Barnsley Permanent Benefit Building Society with the help of some friends, while carrying on his pharmacy. He no longer needed his son's help.

Hudson Taylor seems to have been satisfied by his spiritual experiments, sure now that he could venture alone even to Ili and never fail to be fed and supplied with all necessities by the Lord he trusted in. So from then on he had no need to experiment and no objection to discussing his money matters freely with his father and accepting gifts.

Amelia came over from Dodworth, where she was still mothering her orphaned cousin, and at some point Marianne Vaughan and Elizabeth Sissons, Amelia's two friends, came into the picture again. There is no note that Hudson and Marianne had met in London, but suddenly, after January we find they are already engaged, with her father's approval. We may be allowed to surmise that Hudson Taylor's recovery from his dangerous illness brought them all together more closely than ever, once he confessed to what had happened. But at this time she took his life-work as her own and they were preparing to go to China together.

He arrived back at Soho to find Thomas Hodson very ill with 'Rheumatic Fever' and wrote to Amelia,

> I was not very anxious to have the whole responsibility of his medical treatment on my shoulders – but he seemed to wish it . . . I was much afraid of his having Rheumatism of the heart, and thought I should

have had to bleed him one night, however two strong mustard plasters
made with hot vinegar and kept on half an hour kept it down.

The impecunious art student could afford a doctor's fees no more
than Hudson Taylor could. Loss of sleep from looking after Thomas
at night made life difficult for Hudson and several times he had to
break his long walks to hospital by taking a bus. But even after
Thomas recovered Hudson Taylor was sleeping badly and had to
give up working at anatomy until bedtime. Since his illness he had
been miserable with depression and could not shake it off. Enjoying
the few weeks with his family had made it more difficult to return to
his London life.

> As I was coming home last night [he told Amelia], Passing through
> Finsbury Square, I heard some beautiful singing to the piano, which
> reminded me of old times when you used to play 'Crown Him Lord of
> all' and John and I played the flute . . . I did long to see you. I think
> sometimes I love you too much, but what I should do I suppose is to
> love Jesus still more. Oh! if you were here I could give you such a
> squeeze. But you are not . . .

By February 14 he could tell Amelia that Thomas was 'quite
recovered tho' not very strong' and he himself was 'well and strong'
again. But to his mother he wrote,

> I have been much harassed both by feelings without and fears within,
> but through the restraining mercy of God, poor, weak and unfaithful
> as *I* am, *He* has kept me from anything outwardly disgraceful to my
> Christian character. I do not need to be told you have been praying for
> me – I have felt it – and tho' at times the Heavens have seemed as
> brass and I have felt as tho' left and forsaken and have had by simple
> naked faith (as Father calls it) to cling to the promises, I know He has
> never left me and that that faith itself was the proof of *His present
> sustaining love* . . . I have had plenty of tooth-drawing lately and a
> good deal of Dressing . . .

Returning to London, he went up to Tottenham each Sunday.
Much of the way was past fields and hedgerows, a pleasant change of
scene. A coach ran between the Bank and the sprawling village of
Hackney with the homes and gardens of its city merchants, but there
was the horse-bus for the impecunious. The charming Miss Stacey
saw how tired and pale Hudson Taylor was and made a second home
for him.[17] 'She is a very learned . . . woman and is kind hearted and
truly pious; I am sure you would like her,' he told his parents.
After the meeting the young people in the congregation were

welcomed to her 'open house' but she would ask the others to let Hudson Taylor relax in peace. When the summer came, if he was weary she made sure he could enjoy the garden unobserved. But usually he entered into everything. Often he stayed overnight and went straight back from her home to the hospital.

> Last Sunday I spent at Tottenham at Miss Stacey's again. I spent the afternoon in visiting some poor people and expounding the Word to them, and in the evening some Christians having come in to Miss Stacey's, we had a Prayer Meeting . . . a happy day.

The Lobscheids were just then due to arrive in China and the Tottenham Christians had promised to pray for them.

Sometimes the Howards would have Hudson Taylor over for a meal, or George Pearse would invite him to Hackney. With their wives also running the Ladies' Association of the CES, China was in all their thoughts. Thinking of the Tottenham circle, Hudson Taylor once said he had only happy memories of their friendship. Somewhere out on the high seas on his way to China he wrote in his diary, 'He raised me up kind friends in Tottenham for which I can never sufficiently praise Him. What soul-refreshing communion with Jesus and his people I have met with there!'

Years later George Pearse admitted that they never knew that he was living so frugally in self-imposed privation. He was always neatly dressed as 'a young doctor' had to be. As members of the Committee they were helping him through hospital and hoping he would go to China as their missionary, but otherwise they were simply friends. Even so, they did not know the new distress he was suffering. He shared it with Amelia on March 8.

> I am going through deep waters at present . . . You remind me of the time when at Barton Miss V used to play the piano and we side by side used to sing. Ah! those were happy days – but they are *gone – gone*. I know you love me, and I love you more than all the world besides . . . I trust and know you will not betray my confidence. I have noticed for some time that if ever I proposed going to see my dear Miss V or her meeting me anywhere, she always had some reason which prevented it . . . I know she does not love me as she did . . . She says all her friends are against our union, and they all tell her she is doing very wrong to think of going abroad without her Parents' assent . . . I fear it will have to be broken off. Oh! do pray for me and write soon . . .

That was not all. His funds were exhausted and he did not know what would happen next. Although he was not deliberately experimenting any longer, he was not going to borrow or beg from anyone.

He did not have long to wait this time. God's answer to his prayers was the offer of a resident assistantship to a Dr Brown of St Mary Axe, behind St Helen's, Bishopsgate. He was to have the day free for attendance at The London and only late afternoon and evening duties at Dr Brown's. Above all it would reduce his daily trudge to a mere two miles each way.

He moved at the end of March and wrote his first letter home from 'Corner Camomile Street, St Mary Axe, 5th April/53'. And what a letter. All the cares of the past three years seemed focused on him at one time but he wrote objectively, too busy for the outpouring of Scriptural quotations and deep thoughts so typical of his letters. It was almost a business letter, dealing with each item methodically. The pressures upon him showed heavy imprints step by step across each page. He had no time to write but he must. 'First then I must thank you for the clothes and Louisa for the biscuits.' He was worried about Louisa, dreaming that she was dying of water on the brain, longing for her to show signs of openness to God. Second, his mother had asked him to go to Red Lion Square for her, the offices of CES, but he was too busy that week. Would she please send him certain chemicals he needed. Thirdly, to set her mind at rest, he answered No, he had not made a binding agreement with Dr Brown because he did not know 'what changes the future (might) bring about'. 'If I get any salary, well and good – if not, I get the full value of my services, in my board and lodgings.' Then his daily routine. The London Hospital from 8 am to 3 pm. Then back to St Mary Axe, dine and dispense, visit patients or post entries in the doctor's accounts. More bookkeeping with Dr Brown till supper time. Then reading up his own dissection anatomy, practising chemical analysis instead of paying for a course in it at hospital; or more late visits to patients.

Then he launched into a major problem. To qualify as a member of the Royal College of Surgeons he would need to complete three winter and two summer sessions of hospital lectures and practice. But owing to his illness he had lost attendance time and not even been registered as taking the course, almost insuperable hurdles. Another worrying point was that the Royal College required him to swear to uphold the respectability of the college, and the Word of God said do not swear at all. 'Unless they would dispense with that, the question would be finally settled at once.' The all-or-nothing standards he had set himself would be proof even against a test like that.

But those were passing problems. He was preparing to serve the Lord in China where diplomas would not be necessary. He knew his medicine and surgery and that was enough. The Chinese Evangelization Society, however, were talking of paying another hundred pounds to cover his expenses up to full qualification. He had just had two interviews with Mr Bird at Red Lion Square.

> If I at the expense of the Society pass the College – go out and found a Hospital, I should not feel at liberty if I felt called to go into the Interior and leave all their organisation. [The CES appeared to favour hospital work but Hudson Taylor had his own impressions from his reading of Scripture.] Now it does not appear to be the way most honoured of God in the conversion of sinners. Paul and the Apostles of old, Wesley and Whitefield, etc. in more modern times . . . seem to have been *travelling preachers*, and I do not feel at all convinced that I am justified in . . . binding myself to any particular course of action.

So he asked for his parents' prayers and opinion on these matters.

Still more distressing was the situation affecting Marianne Vaughan. She had met him at Mrs Ruffell's a week or two before, to talk things over. 'I believe our feelings with regard to each other are *unaltered*, at any rate my love to her is no less than it ever was.' But her mother was in a precarious state of health and the prospect of bereavement seemed to be demoralising Mr Vaughan. Hudson Taylor had suggested to Marianne that as her father had given his approval before they became engaged his change of mind ought not to affect them now. But as he and she were both Christians, honouring their parents, they could not continue their engagement, 'without his *full* and *free* consent, so as once and for all to settle that point. With these views she entirely co-incided and so we wrote to Mr V.'

For all his confidence in God's hand on his affairs Hudson Taylor was finding the uncertainty a torture. At the same time he was weighing up the other problems and consulting Mr Bird and Mr Pearse about CES rules and regulations, and the Royal College and London Hospital about theirs. His only hope seemed to be some relaxation on all fronts.

As usual, the news from China month after month was tantalising, coming to him in *The Gleaner* and in conversation with his Tottenham friends. If only he was through his medical training he could go at once. His youthfulness and recent illness seem not to have been obstacles. Bishop Smith of the CMS had made an appeal for missionaries to come without delay. More daily journal accounts of missionary life by Lobscheid, Hamberg and the others made the prospect so real, and Issacher Roberts' reports of the pro-Christian 'patriot army' of Hong Xiu-quan and the Worshippers of Shangdi raised visions of better conditions than ever for the evangelisation of China.[18] The CES scenting victory was pawing the ground with appeals for funds to send out more missionaries and prematurely made reference to someone unnamed as attending hospital 'with the view of becoming an agent of this Society'. For the first time several columns were devoted to 'The Chinese Struggle' and the religious tenets of the rebels.

> Can anyone conceive of the number of preachers and teachers, the amount of Scriptures and tracts that will be needed for T'ien-teh's [Tian De] army just as soon as access can be had to them?

Roberts tended to get carried away but a description of the rebel movement as snowballing was factual. Support for the CES was increasing. The latest name among its contributors was Donald Matheson, a partner and one-time director-designate of Jardine, Matheson and Company who resigned over the opium scandals. And now in April the leading editorial was on 'Encouraging Results from Medical Practice' in many missions around the world. Hudson Taylor found himself in two minds about completing his course.

Taiping break-out   *1850–53*

Serious hostilities between Hong Xiu-quan's rebels and the Manchu government had begun in 1850, and as the contrast between the unscrupulous imperial forces and the friendly people's army became more and more apparent, volunteers flocked to join the rebels. Hong and Zhu Jiu-dao (Chu Chiu-tao), the more militant rebel leader, and their close colleagues began to have visions of power. They were the founders of a new Taiping dynasty, the Heavenly Kingdom of Great Peace.[19] Hong was the emperor, the *Tai Ping Wang*, and his chief officers, princes of the kingdom.

They drew up a religious system of belief, codes of conduct, aims and objects. They would overthrow the Manchus, abolish idols, stamp out the opium vice and set up the Kingdom of God in China. They honoured the Bible, gave prominence to the Ten Commandments, kept Saturday as the Lord's Day, used the Lord's Prayer, held daily meetings and two on the seventh day starting with the doxology and hymns in honour of the Triune God, read Scripture, recited a creed and listened to a sermon. And they baptised adults joining their ranks. Their moral code was in some ways strict: monogamy was for the ranks but concubines were permitted for leaders; opium smoking, drunkenness, theft and sacrifices to ancestors were forbidden. Idols were inexorably destroyed wherever they went. The poor were cared for and private property respected, in the early days. This was the reason for the excitement in the Christian world.

In 1851 they captured the city of Yong'an – Eternal Peace – in the foothills of Guangxi, and controlled most of the province, levying revenue on the Pearl River traffic. But then they were surrounded by the emperor's forces and it was rumoured that Hong himself had been killed. The report was false. Suddenly in 1852 the Taipings, as the rebels were now being called, broke out of Yong'an, descended on the provincial capital Guilin (Kweilin), and ten or twelve thousand strong pressed northward into Hunan province. Several cities fell to them but Changsha held out. While besieging Changsha, Hong Xiu-quan assumed the imperial title, *Wan Sui*, and an emperor's seal. Turning westward they fell upon Yiyang and captured several thousand boats on the Dongting (Tungting) Lake. Swiftly they crossed the lake and seized an almost undefended Yueyang (Yochow), vast military stores and yet more boats. It was December 1852. Yueyang stood on the outlet of the great lake, linked by a river to the great Yangzi and separated from the metropolis of Hanyang, Wuchang and Hankou[20] by an easily crossed plain. As the Taiping hordes approached, all who could of the populace of the three cities, a million souls, took to every available boat, and as far as eye could see the Yangzi was covered with junks and sanpans fleeing to safety. Hanyang was captured and Hankou went up in flames. The governor of Wuchang put up a gallant but unsuccessful defence and after eighty days this city also fell with fearful bloodshed, early in 1853.

Now two options lay before the Taiping Wang and his princes, to go due north through Henan and Zhili (now Hebei) provinces to Tianjin (Tientsin) and Peking, entirely overland, or to turn east and take the whole Yangzi valley, making use of their fleet of boats. They chose the second. Sending the Western Prince's forces westwards to take the province of Sichuan, they swept down the Yangzi. Jiujiang (Kiukiang), Anqing (Anking) and Wuhu fell in rapid

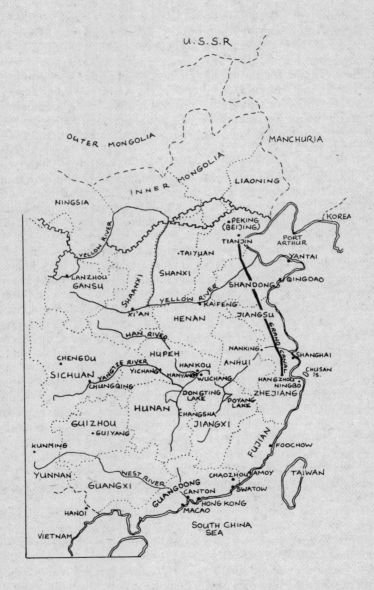

CHINA EAST OF TIBET

succession. In early March they arrived at Nanking, an ancient dynastic capital of all China under the Ming emperors, and put the Manchu garrison to the sword. Nanking was theirs, the heart of the empire and key to the main north-south waterway, the Grand Canal, carrying grain from the fertile south to the dry areas of the north. The Taiping Wang and his retinue set up their court, began to indoctrinate the populace in Taiping ways, recruited reinforcements and set about the wholesale destruction of everything idolatrous within their power. They had cut China in half. The imperial Court at Peking could only communicate with the south by sea or secret courier. Zhenjiang (Chinkiang,) and Yangzhou, where the Grand Canal met the Yangzi, were easy pickings from Nanking.

News of these momentous events was slow to reach Europe. The fastest route was by tea clipper to India and overland by fast relays, taking two months. But word of the Yong'an break-out had arrived and throughout the missionary world news of the Taipings' successes quickened pulses and spurred men to action. While mission committees took note and asked their 'agents' in East Asia for dependable information, Gutzlaff's progeny, the Continental societies and the Chinese Evangelization Society in Britain, could not hide their elation. First to report on the Worshippers of Shangdi as having broken out of Yong'an, the city to which they had been confined, *The Gleaner* now led the way in expressing interest and hope for the future. Hudson Taylor felt all the more strongly drawn to break off his medical course and sail for China. The wishful speculation of foreigners in the Chinese treaty ports knew no bounds. They saw themselves on the threshold of an open empire. The whole country open to trade and travel! A Christian dynasty and the abolition of idolatry and heathenism appeared imminent. Even a million New Testaments would be swallowed up without trace by the allegedly literate majority of China's four hundred million people – a very false illusion in the West.

But the Taipings needed time to consolidate their rapid gains. For two months they halted their advance. In Shanghai there was panic. Refugees told petrifying tales of carnage by both sides in the civil war. The common people were caught, helpless to act in a way acceptable to both sides. The long-haired rebels seized their *bianzi*, rudely known to foreigners as 'pig-tails', a sign of subservience to the Manchus, and cut them off if they had not already done it themselves. But the imperial Manchu troops killed anyone caught without a *bianzi*. The Roman Catholics suffered terribly. Because of their images they fell under the Taipings' wrath and because the Taipings were 'Christian' the Manchus suspected the Catholics of complicity.[21] In Nanking, Zhenjiang (Chinkiang) and Yangzhou where they were strong, many Catholics were captured, killed or victimised by destruction of their homes.

Puritanical Christians?   May–June 1853

Trade practically came to a standstill on the coast. There was nothing to stop the rebels from driving eastwards from the Yangzi along its north-easterly Anqing-Nanking reach and taking Hang-zhou, Ningbo and Shanghai, less than two hundred miles away. Money became very scarce as the Chinese merchants packed up and fled. Sir George Bonham, British plenipotentiary, sent despatches to the Foreign Minister, Lord John Russell. He was proceeding in a warship to Ningbo, the most threatened port. The Shanghai *daotai*, Wu (the prefect), asked Consul Alcock for ships with which to attack the rebels and was referred to Bonham. Bonham was deter-mined not to intervene in Chinese hostilities. Rutherford Alcock, consul in Shanghai, chaired a public meeting of British subjects and formed a volunteer defence force. Late in April the young interpre-ter T T Meadows went out on a long-distance reconnaissance toward Nanking and Yangzhou and reported the presence of thirty to forty thousand long-haired rebels looking, in their Ming dynasty costumes, like spectres from the past.[22] From the garrison at Yang-zhou an advance guard had already started northwards to where the Grand Canal and Yellow River intersected. The rebels were

> Puritanical and even fanatic. The whole army prays regularly before meals. They punish rape, adultery and opium smoking with death and tobacco smoking with the bamboo. The women captured in battle are lodged in separate buildings as well as the children, who are at the same time clothed and educated.[23]

On May 6 and 11 Bonham had more to report. (By then the Earl of Clarendon had succeeded Lord John Russell at the Foreign Office.) Bonham had proceeded up the Yangzi in the steam-sloop *Hermes* as far as Nanking. At Zhenjiang and again at Nanking he was fired on but sent a peaceful message ashore instead of returning the fire. But Manchu forces following closely took the opportunity to attack Zhenjiang with two schooners and twenty-five other ships. Meadows was landed close to the Taipings, hoping to meet the chiefs, and returned safely. He was well received and they in turn now visited *Hermes*. They assured Bonham that the foreign Settlement at Shanghai would be respected. Bonham was not impressed by their Old Testament type of religion because –

> they had superadded thereto a tissue of superstition and nonsense which makes an unprejudiced party almost doubt whether there is any sincerity in their faith, or whether it is not used merely as a political engine of power by the Chiefs . . .

But to the astonishment of the British consuls, naval officers and missionaries, the rebels, denounced by the imperial government, appeared to hold many orthodox Christian doctrines. They were printing and distributing Gutzlaff's *Genesis*, *Exodus* and *Matthew* by thousands and used some admirable liturgies. The Taiping Wang, 'a well-built, handsome, gentlemanly' person, was only 'waiting for a mandate from heaven before taking his departure for Peking'.

Interpreter Meadows had distinguished himself and was sent a message of 'special approval' by Lord Clarendon. It had not all been plain sailing. At first the Taipings had been cold and suspicious. But when they asked him if he worshipped 'God the Heavenly Father' and he replied by reciting the Ten Commandments, the ice was broken. They told him that the Taiping Wang was the True Lord, 'not merely Lord of China; he is not only our Lord, he is your Lord also'.

Bonham and the chiefs exchanged books and pamphlets, and the 'Rev Dr Medhurst' studied and made extracts from the Taiping ones for the information of the British government. Some of them were almost biblical.

A doxology for the Sabbath ran,

> We praise God our Holy and Heavenly Father,
> We praise Jesus, the Holy Lord and Saviour of the World,
> We praise the Holy Spirit, the Sacred Intelligence,
> We praise the Three Persons who united constitute one true God.

And in a pamphlet came this statement,

> But the one great God out of pity to mankind sent His first-born Son to come down into the world. His name is Jesus, the Lord and Saviour of men, who redeems them from sin by the endurance of extreme suffering. Upon the cross they nailed His body, where He shed His

precious blood to save all mankind. Three days after His death He rose from the dead, He discoursed on heavenly things. When He was about to ascend He commanded His disciples to communicate His Gospel and proclaim His revealed will. Those who believe will be saved and ascend up to heaven, but those who do not believe will be the first to be condemned.

What was to be made of all this? Enough was off-key to make caution advisable, but hopes ran high.

On May 18 a revealing new development took place. The port of Amoy (Xiamen) was seized by the Short Sword faction of the Triads, an underground pro-Ming anti-Manchu secret society.[24] They held Amoy until November in spite of a blockade by the imperial fleet. The Taipings were popular so the Triads and other secret societies used their name. But the Taipings disowned them for opium-smoking, idolatry and irreligion. The adulteration and compromising of the Taipings had begun. They themselves left the treaty ports alone and respected foreign neutrality. However, as the confrontation intensified, foreign adventurers began to serve as mercenaries in Taiping, Triad and Manchu armies, and foreign merchants supplied both sides with arms.

In June a Taiping army marched northward, past Kaifeng, in Henan province, to the Yellow River and crossed it into Shanxi province, hotly pursued by the Manchus. The great river, 'China's sorrow', from time to time overflowed its banks and flooded vast areas. Whether by strategic design to impede the rebels or from natural causes this now happened. The river changed its course. But the rebel army was across. Turning east through Zhili they penetrated to Duliu within thirty miles of Tientsin (Tianjin). The imperial Court were preparing for flight while the feeble young Xian (Hsien) Feng emperor made his nine-fold *ketou*[25] and prayed at the Temple of Heaven for deliverance.

This was the zenith, the apogee of Taiping glory, and the world held its breath. Manchu preparedness for such an emergency was negligible. Only a spontaneous emergence of sound generalship and loyalty could avert disaster. For too long, incompetence, corruption and sheer cowardice had been the marks of command in the imperial forces, while Taiping discipline, morals and the power of success carried them forward, against defences weakened by the terror their reputation inspired.

CHAPTER THREE

GOODBYE FOR EVER
1853

Choice of options April–May 1853

K S Latourette, an acknowledged authority on the *History of the Expansion of Christianity* and of *Christian Missions in China* called Hudson Taylor 'one of the four or five most influential foreigners who came to China in the nineteenth century'.[1] This justifies us in turning from the life and death struggle of dynasties to the personal concerns of an insignificant medical student, only now approaching his twenty-first birthday. But on the choice facing him depended his own future and so much besides. A false move, a faithlessness over the issue of marriage or an insistence on the prestige of a medical diploma, and his strength could have been sapped for ever, his insights blinded as surely as Samson was by the betrayal of his secret.

It was after midnight at the end of a heavy day full of stresses when Hudson Taylor wrote across the pages of his long letter home, news of the outcome of his appeal to Marianne's father for final approval of their marriage. The customary practice was for missionaries to marry shortly before sailing and so to start the new life abroad together. Refusal by Mr Vaughan could therefore make all the difference to Hudson Taylor's way of life. There was no missionary wife to be had in China, as far as he could know. China was still no place for single women – the exception being the veteran Miss Aldersey of Ningbo, of whom the Chinese said that even Her Majesty's consul took his orders from her! But Mr Vaughan's reply had come. It said, as Hudson Taylor reported,

> had I been going to remain in England, nothing would have given him more pleasure than to have seen us happily united but that, though he did not forbid our connection, he felt he never could willingly give her up, or even think of her leaving this Country, etc. etc. After which we both felt we could not 'under existing circumstances, consistently continue our engagement'. Consequently it has been both '*mutually* and *honourably*' broken off.

For three years and three months he had loved Marianne and hoped and prayed that she would be called to China. At last they were looking forward to going together, and now this. To Amelia he wrote, referring to Mr Vaughan, 'He could not make up his mind'. But they had told him that unless he would give his 'free and unqualified assent' they could not remain engaged. So,

> we both thought the most Christian thing would be to dissolve our engagement, and this we have done . . . I must say, I think it very wrong of Mr V to countenance our engagement for so long a time, and then not to give his consent. My mind has been so much harassed of late, with that and other things, that I have not felt it so much as I otherwise should have done, and I endeavour to think about it as little as possible . . . I cannot help loving her and believe she loves me. However, it is in the Lord's hands and if He sees fit *He* can remove the obstacles, and if not – His will be done.

Much the same had been Robert Morrison's experience. At seventeen he had proposed marriage and been 'strongly attached' until he was appointed to China. Then the girl of his choice had declined to marry him.

Charles Bird of the CES had asked Hudson Taylor to consider whether the advantage of 'passing the College of Surgeons' would not repay the extra time needed, if the Committee were to bear the expense. But to Hudson Taylor that was not the point.

> Now the advantages would be very great, he told Amelia. But if I did so – and went out under the Society and Founded an Hospital . . . and afterwards felt called to go into the interior, I should not be free to obey that call.

So what did she think it was his duty to do? 'Please write at once as I want to answer Mr Bird.' By the next day, however, his mind was made up and he wrote to Bird, and told his mother in a letter written, he explained, as soon as he reached his room after attending a confinement.

> That the rules I mentioned are both reasonable and necessary for the Society, I do not doubt, and I do not complain of them. I see also, that after 3¾ years, I might be perfectly and *legally* free from them, if I wished to act in a different manner. But I put it to you, would it be honourable, would you like me to act in such a manner? After the Society had borne the expense of my medical education, sent me out, and I had been in China a sufficient time to learn the language and *begin* to be useful; then, as soon as I could legally (it might be) to leave

them . . . Seeing it is my decided opinion that such would be my
course, would it be *honest* of me to accept the offer? (– even if
refunding the expenses). These difficulties are to *me insurmount-
able* . . .

The established pattern of missionary practice was a mission
station, with chapel, school, hospital and perhaps a printing press,
but Hudson Taylor was already convinced that itinerant preaching,
unencumbered by static administrative responsibilities, was God's
intention for him.

The Society, Bird then told him, were prepared to consider
sending him without delay if he chose to go without graduating and
would make a final application to them. If so he must act before
mid-May. They were ready to meet him whatever his wishes. In
acknowledging a donation Charles Bird wrote to Mrs Taylor:

> I saw your son the other day . . . His heart seems fixed on China and I
> doubt not God will find a way for him to go out. I had a very long
> conversation as to his future plans and made a suggestion which I have
> no doubt you will hear of.

Meanwhile the London Hospital were stretching every regulation
to help this unusual youth to qualify.

> I have seen Mr Curling today, with regard to my entering [for the
> MRCS diploma].[2] He says the School Committee decided that if I
> could pay half the fees (£25), the remainder should be left open for an
> indefinite time . . . Then I should get certificates for last session and
> register at the College (of Surgeons) at once. Probably I should find
> some friends to assist me, but if not, it would take me one year after
> departing to pay the 2nd installment. Consequently I should be 24
> before I could go out. – Now is MRCS worth this? [A week later he
> wrote again]: I went down to the College of Surgeons yesterday and
> found that a declaration would do for them instead of an oath, and
> also, that they would *probably* allow me last session [the term inter-
> rupted by his septicaemia], notwithstanding it was not registered for. I
> cannot register without certificates. These I cannot get without paying
> the fees at the hospital . . . I do not know the cost of getting an MD,
> but it cannot be got before the 26th year of age . . .

He would write to Thomas Neatby 'but *have not time*' – this was
his constant refrain all through the summer. His medical duties in
Dr Brown's practice and his medical college studies left no time for
private affairs. No wonder the friends at Tottenham found him ill
and tired on Sundays.

Then he went on in his letter home to set aside the stresses and say,

> May we be found when the Master appears, counting all things as . . . dung and dross, being willing to suffer the loss of all things, that we may win Christ and be found in Him.

MRCS, MD, nothing mattered in comparison with discovering and doing the will of God.

April came to an end and Hudson Taylor began to see the way more clearly through his perplexities. He still had no time, he said, 'to collect my thoughts except on Sundays', but 'May has come in so beautifully'. Whatever his circumstances he always had an eye and a soul for natural beauty. For companionship he was keeping two pet squirrels, and for relaxation he took a stroll in Finsbury Square with the Browns' baby in his arms. These glimpses in the records are as typical of the true Hudson Taylor as all the industry, thought and spirituality revealed by his letters.

'I have written to Mr Bird' he told his mother, 'stating the reasons which I felt as obstacles to my entering [for the MRCS] at their expense.' The Society's rules and regulations were precise. 'Every missionary shall be *subject* to the Board of Management; and also he shall *abide* by the *instructions given him*, etc.' Hudson Taylor underlined the words that he could not accept. 'Also in Bye-law 6 "Every person . . . shall hold himself ready to go to such a place and at such a time as the Board shall decide upon."' This was too much. It involved signing away liberty and conscience. Nine months' notice either way was required, and an obligation to refund all expenses incurred on his behalf if the Board should discharge him within three years. Such rules he saw to be 'reasonable and essential to a Society' but they would –

> remove me from the direct and immediate leadings of God . . . Now it is possible to pay too dearly for even great advantages, and this is more than my conscience allows me to do. If I *am* guided by God, in going out, He will open the way and provide the means; and if a title *be* necessary *He* will provide the means for that also. If *not* necessary – it will be better for the time and money to be otherwise employed. [As for being called by God to go] I never have a doubt on the subject.

Perhaps the influence of George Müller's *Narrative* can be detected here. Müller's separation from the London Society for Promoting Christianity among the Jews had been on the grounds of objection to ordination in Germany by a state church and uncon-

verted men, to being directed by men rather than by the Holy Spirit,
and to a conscientious need to be free to do whatever spiritual work
was indicated, not only among the Jews in Poland to whom he was
assigned.

Slowly some form and order emerged from the uncertainties. Dr
Brown assured Hudson Taylor he could stay on through the summer
and winter sessions, Mr Curling was finding out for him what
minimum sum would satisfy the London Hospital. Benjamin Hudson offered to accept a painting donated by Hudson Taylor's father,
as surety against an advance payment until such time as he could sell
it. If the balance needed were to be forthcoming,

> I shall be, probably, MRCS two years from this time. If not, I must
> continue as I am. My mind is kept at perfect peace in the matter,
> because it is stayed on the Rock of Ages and I am willing either to have
> it or not, as *He* sees fit to order. I thank Father very much for his kind
> promise to assist me, and as I (am) working incessantly, hope it will not
> be thrown away on me . . . The Summer Session commences tomor-
> row morning . . . I finish my Winter Session on Saturday, having been
> dissecting all through the Vacation . . . There is no fear now, you see,
> of dissection wounds for some months to come. Bye the Bye, one
> advantage of passing the College would be a free passage out, which
> alone would repay the cost [of going on to qualify].

As a ship's surgeon he could draw a salary.

So the pros and cons seemed equally weighted. A delay of two or
more years before qualifying was bad enough to contemplate, but
the price in terms of obligations to his parents, the CES and the
hospital was as great. How he would reach a conclusion he could not
tell. He could only look to God and wait for the way to clear.

Go at once?   *May–June 1853*

The Gleaner is not mentioned in the letters of this period, no
doubt because all concerned were taking the magazine and familiar
with its contents. The May issue carried the third annual report of
the Chinese Evangelization Society and spoke of 'cheering success',
'progress . . . steady', 'support by the Christian public highly
encouraging', 'ample funds to supply all our want', and 'We have
two young men in training.' It referred to the deep interior of China
as the Society's 'special field' and its object as being 'to bring the
gospel of God to the mind and heart of every individual in China'.
The Taiping rebellion was paving 'a highway to the utmost limits of

the Empire for the diffusion of the gospel, and it will require courageous and self-denying men, imbued with the love of souls . . .'

There is no record of just how or when Hudson Taylor made his decision, but a note to his mother on a half-sheet of paper scribbled 'at half a dozen times' and at the end dated May 17, 1853, four days before his twenty-first birthday, is in a different key.

> I know you pray for me often, sometimes I feel as if you were praying for me then. My mind has been in great peace lately, and tho' my time is so fully occupied, and my mind is seldom free for meditation, when I am walking or studying and pause for a moment, I often feel the goodness of God in such a manner as the Christian can *conceive* but not *describe*.

He wrote to Amelia and to Louisa on the 22nd without referring to the subject which previously dominated his thoughts. Thirteen-year-old Louisa kept her note for over fifty years. It was only brotherly prattle but with it Hudson enclosed two little tracts which she also kept. He could never forget that he had been reconciled with God through reading a tract. He was writing between midnight and one a m and said,

> – if you knew how much your poor brother has to do and how sleepy and tired he always feels, before he goes to bed, and how often he has to get up in the night and go out to see patients, and then make them some medicine before he can get to bed again, you would think he had plenty to do.

He told her he was 'going to Mr Howard of Tottenham to tea (he is . . . the Great Manufacturing Chemist)' and that he was reading the '2nd Vol. of Huc and Gabet's *Travels in Tartary, Thibet and China*', and he had to stop writing because he was in danger of swallowing the note 'with gaping and yawning'.

June came and with it the month's issue of *The Gleaner*. The name had been changed again, dropping the word *General* it was now simply *The Chinese Missionary Gleaner*, the first English missionary magazine to be devoted to one country only. All the space was needed for news of China. In fact, the whole issue was given to a single article on the origins and conquests of the Taiping rebels.

> The progress of the insurgents is now so rapid [it reported] that unless the foreign powers interfere, Peking will soon most probably fall into their hands . . . Our merchant princes will be ready to seize their

commercial advantages, and we trust that British Christians will . . . eclipse (them) in the race. The light of day is dawning on China . . . We have a prospect of very shortly sending out some medical gentlemen of decided Christian character.'

The reference could only be to Hudson Taylor and a Scotsman, Dr William Parker, who followed him to China.

On June 5 Hudson wrote to his mother that while he was still working at 'The London', he was also attending the Ophthalmic Hospital in Moorfields, near Dr Brown's. A new and urgent matter had arisen however. He had called at the Red Lion Square office of the CES the day before and found that Mr Bird had just written him a note, still unposted. The Committee's attitude had changed, perhaps through fear of losing him. As they discussed it together, 'He seemed very anxious that I should go at once,' was how Hudson expressed it to Amelia, and, elsewhere, that he 'was requested to go out under their auspices'. Bird advised him that if his mind was made up and he was in fact renouncing full medical qualification, there was no time to lose. He should sail by early September if he was to avoid the autumn gales. He could learn ophthalmic surgery as easily in the mission hospital at Canton while he was learning Chinese. If he intended to apply to the CES he should therefore do so at once.

> He assured me that the Committee would impose no obstacle to my progress inland if the way should ever be open, and that if any circumstances should ever take place, in which I could not work happily in connexion with the Society they would not think it dishonourable or unchristian for me to leave them . . . He has thus answered most of the objections and difficulties I felt, and I think I shall probably comply with his suggestion and at once propose myself to the Committee. However, I shall await your answer and hope for your prayers.

In the next sentence he suddenly exposed the deep pain of parting at which he had sometimes hinted but never revealed so pointedly.

> If I should go, would you advise me to come home first? I know you would like to see me, and I long to see you once more, but I almost think it would be easier for us all to be separate than having met to part – for ever – *no*! Only for 'a little while'. . . .
>   Pray for me. It is a very easy thing to *talk* of leaving all for Christ, but when it comes to the proof it is only as we stand 'Complete in Him' that we can overcome . . . God be with you and bless you, my own dear, dear Mother (and) give you so to realize the preciousness of Jesus, that

you may wish for nothing but to 'Know Him and the power of His resurrection, and the fellowship of *His* sufferings . . .'

He could scarcely bring himself to stop writing, as if the thin thread of ink on paper was all that bound him to home.

His mind made up, he asked Charles Bird for the application papers and received them on the Monday before the Committee was to meet. With his days so full he had to complete a lengthy questionnaire and statement of his beliefs and submit it within three days. There was only one way to do it. Two nights in succession he worked from one a m until three a m drafting and copying it out.

I have applied to the Chinese Evangelization Society, [he wrote home on June 19th.] It appears that there is a medical man from Scotland now up in Town, having applied to be sent out, and as soon as his case is decided, my application will be considered.

   In the paper . . . I have stated my views of the most important *points* and *principles* of Doctrine and discipline without reserve . . . After stating my views so freely, I do not expect to be accepted, and my only surprise was that the case was not at once dismissed without further to do . . . From what I gathered from . . . the Clerk, I think that part of my paper stating, I do not believe in the division of the Church into Clergy and Laity – the right of all Christians to preach, baptize and administer the Lord's Supper – the equality of saints, etc., has excited the most astonishment, and no wonder, for the majority of the Committee are Clergymen, Ministers and others holding the opposite views. However, I am determined to cover nothing up now, that might afterwards cause any unpleasantness, especially on that subject, being persuaded that priestcraft has in all ages been the greatest curse to the Church and the world. I have made up my mind *to go*, whether accepted or not, *how* – I must leave. I have given Mr Brown notice . . . Excuse this hasty note as it is nearly twelve and I expect to be called up to a Labour in the night . . . it is very likely we shall both be out . . . I do not feel at all uneasy about the Society so I hope you will not.

What K S Latourette called 'rugged honesty' to describe Hudson Taylor's conduct at this time, surely set a pattern for the future.[3] In one confrontation or crisis after another the same undeviating determination is apparent. Once he knew what he should do, his action was decisive, whatever the opposition. Until then he would not move ahead of the will of God, however indecisive he might appear. The Committee of the CES must be in no uncertainty about the kind of person they were considering. And equally he himself must not be dependent upon men in place of God Himself. He was maturing rapidly as in Hull.

Tenterhooks   *June–July 1853*

For three weeks the Committee kept Hudson Taylor in suspense and uncertainty over the outcome of his application. His parents' approval encouraged him but his mother was anxious about his resignation from Dr Brown's practice before the decision of the CES was known. Now a new test of his determination raised its attractive head. Brown did not want to lose him and, like Hardey in Hull, offered him strong inducements to stay. On June 26 Hudson wrote to his mother again.

> You ask me if I have not been precipitate in giving Mr Brown notice to leave – I think not. If I *am* accepted by the Society, I shall have to go out at the latter end of August or in September. . . . If *not* accepted, it will be still more necessary for me to leave, as I cannot get a ship until I am at liberty. As to where the expense of an outfit and passage will come (from), if I am not accepted, I know not . . . however it will (be) forthcoming when wanted . . . Mr Brown has been trying to persuade me to stay another year and pass the Coll. Surgeons and then go to St Andrew's and pass the MD. . . .

An incomplete and undated note, perhaps a postscript, continued the theme

> As to St Andrew's . . . I think if I was going to stay Mr Brown would give me such perquisites as would pay most of my expenses. Here you see are two powerful obstacles, time and money, and I do not think the advantages arising from the possession of a degree would compensate for them. If in the time and with the expense required to make me MD, MRCS or both, I am made instrumental in leading any poor Chinese to the feet of Jesus – how much better would that appear in eternal ages! Oh! for grace to fully realize that beautiful verse,
>
> > 'I *all* on earth forsake,
> > Its wisdom, fame and power,
> > And *Him* my *only* portion make
> > My shield and tower.'

At last the uncertainty was ended, On July 9 a very hasty note which he dated June 9, on a half-sheet of paper, said,

I have just received a note from Mr Bird informing me that I am
accepted by the Com^tee and that as soon as I can make arrangements for
going out, they are prepared to send me . . . How long would you like
me to be at home? . . . I was at the Ophthalmic Hospital this morning
. . . nearly a score of operations beautifully performed . . .

In his old age Hudson Taylor told his son Howard that one of the
London Hospital teachers suggested that he take the MRCS examination at once 'knowing I was ready'. 'I felt that I knew as much
. . . as I should have done had I waited a short time longer to take
the diploma.' But little time was left for visiting relatives, ordering
drugs and equipment and making all his preparations for leaving
England, perhaps for ever.

July 17 was his last Sunday in London, for a few weeks. The next
he expected to spend in Hull and after a week there to join his family
at home. Writing to Amelia was painful. He spoke of seeing her face
again, 'But we must not set our hearts on this or any other earthly
happiness' – the final parting was so soon to follow.

Adieu!   *September 1853*

If any more was needed to excite the imagination of supporters of
the CES, the July and August issues of *The Gleaner* supplied it. The
Taiping chiefs were incensed against the foreigners at Shanghai, it
reported. But Interpreter Meadows had boldly gone to them, at
Suzhou this time, only fifty miles away, and set their minds at rest.
The missionary Issacher Roberts identified Hong Xiu-quan as the
person he himself had instructed in Canton for two months, and
held out great hopes for China if the insurrection should finally be
successful. He was not alone in this. In an article under the title
'China Open', T Gilfillan, the Presbyterian missionary, held out the
same hope.[4] It was possible now to rent a house on the mainland,
using Chinese clothing 'not as a disguise but as the badge of his
identification with his fellows around'. He urged the Church to
respond to the changes taking place.

Whether the sceptre be wielded by Manchow or Chinese, China can
never again be closed against the West.

The North China Herald also encouraged optimism by reporting
in some detail an account of Meadows' interview with the Taiping
leaders.

The insurgents are Christians of the Protestant form of worship, [it said. The leaders were] practical and spiritual Christians, deeply influenced by the belief that God is always with them . . . they point back to the fact that . . . some four years ago, they numbered but 100 or 200; and that, except for the direct help of their heavenly Father, they could never have done what they have done.

No doubt there were plenty of imposters and hypocrites among the rebels, but among the leaders there were unmistakably good signs. During a ten- or twelve-mile ride through Taiping soldiery on the road to Nanking, Meadows had heard not a word of obscenity or the curses customary among heathen Chinese.

So the atmosphere among the Taylor relatives and friends in Hull and Barnsley was one of expectation even though it meant losing Hudson to the cause. During his week in Hull he was in low spirits. He had been overworking for so long and was feeling the approaching end. But the weeks at home restored his buoyancy. As a family they talked and sang together, and a new composition, *For China's Distant Shore*, with words and music apparently by Mrs Taylor, became their theme song.

> For China's distant shore, embark without delay.
> Behold an open door, 'tis God that leads the way . . .

From subsequent events it is permissible here to conjecture that with Marianne Vaughan finally out of reach though he loved her still, Hudson Taylor was keenly aware of needing someone else as his partner in life. His emotional turmoil as his departure approached is understandable. Of all Hudson Taylor's characteristics his ardent nature, his capacity for loving, is seen to be one of the strongest. The loss of Marianne left him with no prospect of marriage when he was thousands of miles away among strangers. As far as he knew, his only hope of a wife was from among his present acquaintances. When he thought of the Scripture, 'no good thing will he withhold from them that walk uprightly' and applied it to his material needs, he seems not to have thought, or thinking put aside the idea, that God who could spread 'a table in the wilderness' could give him the right wife in far away China. As a matter of fact Maria Dyer, his wife-to-be, had sailed about nine months earlier and was already in Ningbo. So when Hudson Taylor called on Elizabeth Sissons' father in Hull, was it to ask permission to correspond with her? She was not only Amelia's and Marianne's good friend, but

Hudson knew her well through his visits to his aunt's school at Barton. On one occasion she had even said she loved him. He had seen her name in *The Gleaner* as a contributor to the CES. She was interested in China, and perhaps in him.

When Samuel Dyer, the LMS missionary in Singapore, died so tragically in 1843 after the Treaty of Nanking, his wife and children were most lovingly cared for by their Singapore friends, Sir William and Lady Norris. After two years Mrs Dyer married a missionary named Bausum. But before long she herself died. The Dyer children, Samuel, Burella and Maria were taken home to their grandparents the Tarns in London, and in time the girls were sent to Polam Hall in Darlington, where Hudson Taylor's mother had done her Froebel training. The stalwart Miss Aldersey in Ningbo had been a good friend to their mother and invited Burella to come out to China and teach in her school for Chinese girls. So it happened that in September 1852 when Hudson Taylor was starting life in Soho, Burella had sailed with the Rev and Mrs R H Cobbold of the CMS on the *Harriet Humble* to Shanghai and Ningpo, and Maria, only fifteen, went with them. Maria was to become his wife after five more years of waiting.

If Hudson Taylor had seen a notice of their departure he would not have thought twice about them, except perhaps by association with the early history of missions to China. So he was thinking of the only other girl named in the correspondence that survives. Elizabeth was about his own age. But her father reserved his judgement. He wanted time to weigh this unusual proposition before committing his daughter even to considering a correspondence which might take her away to China of all places.

August ended and Hudson Taylor was back in London at St Mary Axe. Dr Brown was a good friend. He let him use his home as a base, while he tore from place to place collecting and packing up the equipment, clothing, household necessities, all he would need when he arrived in Shanghai. An account rendered by C Baker's, 244 High Holborn, lists a 'full and complete Amputating Case, a set of minor Trepany Instruments . . . Cupping Case, Midwifery instruments' and so forth, an ambitious beginning. After only ten years' existence as a foreign settlement, Shanghai with its few shops could supply little more than the day-to-day necessities of foreign residents. Everything else, including furniture, was sent out from their own countries. With political unrest as it was, the Chinese had not yet developed their skilled replicas of foreign goods.

On September 4 Hudson Taylor's friend, Benjamin Broomhall, came to see him at St Mary Axe. Hudson played his concertina, they sang *For China's Distant Shore* together, and parted. Benjamin went back to Barnsley and was there to stand by Hudson's parents after his ship sailed. The next afternoon Hudson Taylor went over to Tottenham and was asked to tell the congregation about himself.

> I just said a few things as to the way I was brought to the Lord – my desire to spread the knowledge of His truth, my prospects etc. . . . I was not very collected in my thoughts . . . However . . . the friends were very hearty in commending me to the Lord and I was very happy . . . Miss Stacey told me to get a warm dressing-gown made . . . and send the bill to her.

On the 6th, he found time to write to Louisa, aged thirteen now. He had given her one of his squirrels, the other to Amelia. It was a link between them.

> I sail from Liverpool for Shanghai, alone, in the *Dumfries* – have a good cabin to myself – and a pleasant Captain. She [the *Dumfries*] has flush decks and good accommodations.[5]

This meant that the *Dumfries* was streamlined in the modern clipper design though built in 1837. She was advertised to sail on the 12th.

> As I have to purchase cabin furniture there [in Liverpool] and get my cabin fitted up, I do not think I can use my return ticket [to Barnsley?] . . . My medicines are ordered . . . I am very busy and very tired but I hope to have nearly done by tomorrow at this time. It is the hardest work I ever did in my life . . .

Dr Parker was unlikely to be ready to sail the same year, but an Arthur Taylor, unrelated, was about to be ordained and married and to follow in another ship soon afterwards. 'I wish he was going with me . . .'

Friday, September 9, came all too soon and at the Red Lion Square office of the CES at seven p m Hudson Taylor was commended 'to the protection and blessing of God' and designated to proceed as soon as possible to Nanking, the headquarters of the Taiping rebels.

From the office he went alone to Euston and took the night train to Liverpool. He needed time to collect his freight, the medical supplies consigned to Liverpool for him, and to meet his mother at Owen's Hotel. His departure and the enthusiasm it aroused, with

Arthur Taylor and Dr Parker also accepted by the Committee, mark the crest of the wave for the Chinese Evangelization Society.

> Nothing is impossible to faith [*The Gleaner* said]. We heartily respond to Dr Gutzlaff's sentiment – 'Money, however needful, is last in order. Let us have the hearts and prayers of the Lord's people; and the Lord will provide the means for accomplishing the good pleasure of his grace, and the work of faith with power.' . . . We do not expect a perfect work, or infallible agents, or operations without obstacles, or progress without reverses, or victories without loss . . . We do not look forward . . . to national conversion . . . We desire to measure all difficulties by his Almightiness – to contemplate all obstacles in the remembrance of the Red Sea deliverance . . . If this be enthusiasm . . . it is apostolic enthusiasm . . . in the same category with Peter and Paul.

George Pearse, as honorary secretary for overseas affairs and personnel, came up to Liverpool on Saturday and on Sunday introduced Hudson Taylor and his mother to some of his Christian friends in Liverpool, including William Collingwood, a leader of the Brethren. They were God's messengers to encourage the family in the ordeal of the next few days. For then came the first of a sequence of delays in the departure of the *Dumfries*, and Mr Pearse had to return to the Stock Exchange in London. Hudson Taylor visited the *Dumfries* and found that his roomy cabin had been newly painted for him. Both captain and steward were out to be friendly. On Monday James Taylor and Aunt Hannah Hardey arrived and joined them in the hotel. Each delay compounded the agony of parting and yet was a bonus of time spent together. Hudson Taylor's freighted drugs and surgical equipment had been delivered to the wrong station and the extra days allowed him to track them down. He caught up on sleep and was on top of life, excited by the start of the great adventure.

After waiting four days James Taylor could be away from his business no longer and they saw him off to Barnsley. Five years later Hudson still felt the agony of that parting from his father. It was traumatic, deeply etched in his memory. With a loud whistle and belching of smoke and steam the train began to move and gather speed. Hudson hung on and ran beside it, till it dragged them apart. Father and son looked long and hungrily into each other's faces in heartbreak and exultation together. They did not expect to meet again until 'in Glory'. But for Christ's sake and China's it was worth it.[6]

In the next two days he wrote letter after letter. Amelia knew him well enough to understand what he had written on the 13th,

> If you should hear from or of Miss Vaughan, write me immediately and let me know how she is – write any time before you hear positively that we *have* sailed, as no one can account for the delays that *may possibly* arise. I should very much have liked to see you once more, if it had been the will of God, but I suppose I *must* submit . . . I enclose a few verses to give Miss Sissons with that brooch . . . [She had wished for a memento.] There is an inheritance, incorruptible and undefiled . . . that fadeth *not* away – till *then farewell* – Fare-thee-well – *Farewell* . . . Give my love to Louisa – tell her I shall pray for her . . . When thousands and thousands of miles intervene, the same God equally near to each – the same prayer-hearing and prayer-answering God, shall hear my prayers for *her* – that we *may* meet again. And the Lord be with *thee* and bless thee, and cause His face to *shine* upon thee and give thee peace . . .

He was very concerned for Louisa, still resisting all their pleas to turn to the Lord. And when it was almost certain that the *Dumfries* would be sailing on the 19th he wrote to his father.

> My soul rejoices in the Lord and I feel very happy, I never was more so in my life . . . Perhaps I shall see (England) and you no more in the body – but I know we shall meet to part no more. . . . The God of *Peace* bless you . . . and use you more than ever in bringing sinners to Jesus . . . I . . . can only conclude by hoping you will forgive me in every respect in which I have acted improperly towards you.

John Hodson, at Mr Hardey's in Hull, was in his thoughts too.

> I write to beseech you, as God's ambassador – to be reconciled to Him . . . Come to Jesus – see all your sins laid on Him . . . I write thus because I love you – but how much more God loves you . . .

Like Louisa, John was probably sated with such exhortations from his relatives, but he kept this and other letters from Hudson to read again and again, until they were worn and tattered. He wrote to Mrs Taylor a few months later on, 'I have often imagined I saw him in the rigging, hat off, long curling hair flowing, a manly face waving his last farewell. What a *noble* and *manly* youth he would look . . . You will excuse (his) last (note) being so dirty. I have had it in my surgery coat pocket from the date of receiving it . . .' John died at twenty-nine after Hudson's prayers for him were answered.

There was a letter to Benjamin Broomhall too, thanking him for the gift of a book. Books were Benjamin's very life.

> My soul is full of the love of God. I am truly raised above and beyond present events. I am *compelled* by the abounding love of God and indwelling of His Holy Spirit to rejoice – to rejoice greatly. I am surrounded by friends and relatives whom I am bound to leave tomorrow – and for ever in all probability.

Finally Hudson wrote at length to Amelia again, rejoicing 'that a dispensation of the Gospel should have been committed to me for the poor Chinese' and pouring out benedictions upon her in the words of Scripture, with much underlining. And then again, 'When you write tell me if you have heard from Miss Vaughan or Miss Sissons.' He knew he needed a wife, yet he was going alone and could scarcely contain his joy.

Bedtime came and Hudson read to his weeping mother from John 14, 'Let not your hearts be troubled' and prayed without difficulty for family and friends and the godless world. His mother was too heart-broken to share his excitement though she was glad to see her only surviving son obey God's call.

So Monday, September 19, 1853, arrived and the *Dumfries* was ready to sail. Hudson Taylor dashed off a note to Mr Sissons, hoping to hear from him in Shanghai, went to breakfast with Arthur Taylor and a friend, and at ten a m met in the stern cabin on board ship with his mother and George Pearse's godly friends. There was the usual strained conversation and then in 'a firm clear voice' he asked if they might sing together 'How sweet the name of Jesus sounds'. He sang it himself 'with the utmost composure'. A few prayers and a psalm, which he himself read, still taking the lead; a break in his voice as he prayed for his loved ones, quickly controlled, and when a warning was sounded and Mrs Taylor was helped ashore, Hudson joined her for a last embrace.

'We had to say goodbye, never expecting to meet on earth again.' He returned to the *Dumfries* and hurried below. In a moment he was back on deck and threw to her on the wharf a pocket Bible. He had written in pencil on the fly-leaf, 'The love of God which passeth knowledge'. A final 'God bless you' and the ship pulled out.

> I stood alone on deck . . . and the separation really commenced . . . Never shall I forget the cry of anguish [from his mother] . . . It went through me like a knife. I never knew so fully, till then, what 'God *so* loved the world' meant.

As the ship moved away into the Mersey Hudson climbed into the rigging, waving his hat until they could no longer see each other.

At last *September 1853*

Then came anti-climax. After they had gone some distance downstream the crew were mustered and one man was missing. By the time they had waited in vain for him to catch them up the tide had turned and they had to anchor until he was found. Hudson Taylor joined the captain in the longboat and returned to shore. 'But when ashore what was I to do with myself?' His reaction had been to be with his mother again, but wisdom prevailed. He could not renew the pain of parting. She had gone to friends in Liverpool so he went to the hotel and wrote a few notes. And with that he made his own way back to the ship.

He did not hear until long afterwards that on this same day the governing body of the British & Foreign Bible Society adopted a resolution in celebration of its jubilee to raise £50,000 to print and distribute a million New Testaments in Chinese.[7] September 19, 1853, was a significant day in the annals of the Church in China.

After a good night's sleep Hudson Taylor began another letter to his parents. The missing man had been retrieved but it was nearly seven p m before they could weigh anchor. When the captain had seen, however, how 'lusty' the sailors were and that the pilot himself was intoxicated, he had anchored again and waited for the morning tide. He was taking no chances in the dark.

A tug took them out into the bay and as the motion of the ship increased Hudson Taylor fastened and arranged the things in his cabin. He was cheerful, playing his concertina, singing and reading Psalms. At last he was on his way to China. All his human props had finally been left behind. From now on it was 'God alone', and the realisation of that was fortifying. But the motion of the ship became 'considerable'. He took a 'Creosote Pill' and fell asleep.

Captain Morris woke him to come and see the bell-buoy, tolling away as it rocked on the waves. He was feeling better and enjoyed watching the cabin lamp –

> swinging in circles, ellipses and nobody knows what other figures – enough to make Faraday give a whole course of lectures on the rotation of the Pendulum. We have three pigs, three dozen fowls, two dozen ducks, two cats and two dogs on board . . . so if animals have souls there are upwards of seven dozen souls in the Dumfries . . .

– including a Chinese boy from Macao with too little English for conversation.

The *Dumfries* was listed by Lloyds as sailing on September 20, 1853, for Shanghai, but with no date of arrival and simply the note 'Lost'.

The doomed 'Dumfries'   1853

Hardly had the pilot gone than the wind freshened and the *Dumfries* headed into the Irish Channel as a gale began to blow. The ship pitched 'fearfully' and in no time Hudson Taylor was *hors de combat*. For three days and nights they tacked to and fro between the Isle of Man and the Welsh coast against west winds and then between Holyhead and the Irish coast making little progress. He quickly found his sea legs and began to enjoy himself. He had no apprehension of danger.

The *Dumfries* was a barque of only 468 tons, three-masted with no mizzen or aftermast topsail. The foremast was square-rigged and her main- and mizzen-masts rigged fore and aft. The crew besides the captain consisted of two mates, a steward, bo's'n, cook and carpenter, nine able and two ordinary seamen, two boys and two apprentices, twenty-three in all. And Hudson Taylor was the only passenger.

On Saturday, the 24th, the gale subsided long enough for them to sight the Isle of Man for a second time, but all day 'the barometer kept falling' as they battled down the Irish Sea and on Sunday morning the captain's customary service of worship for the crew was not held because the men had had a hard night. By noon all possible sail had to be taken in, leaving only enough to steady the ship. Hudson Taylor visited the crew and gave them tracts to read off duty. But the motion was making him sick again and unable to eat. Now what he called 'a fearful hurricane' was blowing. He struggled up on deck in the afternoon for a scene 'beyond description. The sea was lashing itself with fury, and was white with foam . . . like hills on each side'. Already they had stopped trying to continue southward. Survival was all that mattered. They were running northward again before the storm and desperately trying to keep out of Cardigan Bay. A large ship astern was drifting badly but making progress. The *Dumfries* was also drifting 'quickly, irresistibly, about three or four miles towards a lee shore' but making little or no headway.

Hudson Taylor had discovered that Captain Morris was at least a God-fearing man and probably a true Christian. Now the captain could not hide his anxiety and said 'Unless God help us all is up.'

They were still fifteen miles from the coast but closing in towards it. 'It was an *awful time*' Hudson wrote in his journal as soon as he had a chance.

> We can do nothing now, [the captain explained] but carry all possible sail, as the more sail we carry the less we drift. It is for our lives, and God grant that the timbers may bear it.

With two sails set on each mast they made heavy going with seas pouring over their bulwarks. And the sun set with no let-up in the hurricane.

Hudson Taylor became thoroughly scared, thinking of the horrors of dying in the cold water, and the distress of his family. 'Once or twice I thought she was overturning.' They heard a loud crack. The bowsprit was sprung but held. He looked at the fading light and thought he would never seen the sun again –

> unless the Lord works almost miraculously on our behalf, a few broken timbers will be all that is left of us and our ship.

But lest he depend upon material aids rather than on God he gave away his lifebelt.

'The night was cold and the wind was biting' but Hudson Taylor stayed with the captain, wet through by the spray and water they were shipping. At one point he went below and read a hymn or two and some Scripture and snatched an hour of sleep, but then went up again. 'The scene was magnificent – sublime – I could not but admire it.' He found that they were safely past Bardsey Island lighthouse, and the tip of the peninsula (Wales' pointing finger) between Cardigan and Caernarvon Bays. But by all means possible they must clear Holyhead again or they would be wrecked on Anglesey or the Caernarvon coast. It was touch and go.

> I asked the Captain whether we could pass Holyhead or not. He replied 'If we make *no* leeway we could just do it, but if we *do* drift, God help us' – and we did drift.

'Each tack becoming shorter' they came closer and closer to the rocks. First the Holyhead light was ahead of them and then to seaward, they were heading for the shore. 'Our fate now seemed sealed.' Hudson thought of home and felt tearful. But he was never afraid to speak his mind. With death so close he talked about heaven. 'I found the Captain calm, anxious, but trusting for his own salvation; and the Steward said "he knew he was nothing, but Christ was all". I felt thankful for them.'

He told the captain about all the friends who he knew were praying for them and himself prayed earnestly for God to have mercy upon –

> us and spare us. (And) this passage came to my mind, 'Call on *Me* in the day of trouble and I *will* deliver thee, and thou shalt glorify me,' and I pleaded the promise in submission to His will. And now our position was truly awful. [By moonlight they could see land ahead.] I went below . . . took out my pocket-book and wrote my name and friend's address in it in case my body should be found . . .

He tied a few things together in a hamper which he thought might float and help him or someone else to land, and commended his soul and his loved ones to God 'with prayer that if possible this cup might pass from us', and went up on deck again. The futility of it all was almost overwhelming.

> And now Satan tried me much and I had a fearful struggle, but the Lord calmed my mind and after that it was stayed on God and consequently in peace.

This was the end. His sheltered life had been no preparation for this kind of situation. He asked if the ship's boats stood a chance in such a sea and the captain's answer was, No. Nor would there be time to make a raft from loose timbers.

At this point Captain Morris said, 'We cannot live half an hour now; what of your call to labour for the Lord in China?' He must have been surprised by the answer,

> It was a great joy to feel and tell him that I would not for any consideration be in any other position; that I strongly expected to reach China; but that, if otherwise . . . the Master would say it was well that I was found seeking to obey His command.

The water was becoming white and the captain said, 'Now we must turn her . . . or it is all up.' The sea might sweep the deck and wash men and everything overboard but it had to be done. It was three a m on the 26th.

> He gave the word and we tried to turn outwardly [toward open sea] but in vain . . . Then he tried to turn the other way and with God's blessing succeeded, with no other accident than a man's arm badly bruised.

They 'cleared the shore by not more than two ships' lengths'. Within a few minutes of bringing the ship about the wind veered two points and they were able to beat out of Caernarvon Bay. 'Had it veered when we were on the other tack it might have destroyed us.'

From this experience Hudson Taylor learned a lesson which he emphasised decades later in his *Retrospect* account of this storm. It had not struck him as incongruous that instead of using his safety belt he made the floating hamper to help him ashore. When he later thought it out, he saw that every aspect of life depends on external aid and applied the principle to 'faith healing' and the use of drugs.

> The use of means ought not to lessen our faith in God; and our faith in God ought not to hinder our using whatever means He has given us for the accomplishment of His own purposes . . . to me it would appear as presumptuous and wrong to neglect the use of those measures which He Himself has put within our reach, as to neglect to take daily food, and suppose that life and health might be maintained by prayer alone.

Portrait of a personality   *October 1853–January 1854*

Getting dry, checking the damage and making up lost sleep took a few hours but on Monday, September 26, Hudson Taylor wrote it all up in his journal.

> With heartfelt gratitude I record the mercy of God [he began]. *He* alone, has snatched us from the jaws of death. May our spared lives be spent entirely in His service and for His glory.

The only significant damage had been the sprung bowsprit and a few lost spars. They had planned to call in at Milford Haven to repair the bowsprit, but with conditions favourable the captain decided to lose no more time and headed for the Atlantic. Even twelve days from Liverpool to the Bristol Channel was better than Robert Morrison's whole month to reach the Isle of Wight from Gravesend, and Hudson Taylor basked in the goodness of God. The Swedish carpenter, at work on deck, was struck on his right eyebrow and Hudson put a stitch in it for him. So began a warm friendship. He discovered that not only he but the captain and steward were Methodists. In fact the steward had been a class leader in Jamaica. They took to reading the Bible and praying together in Hudson Taylor's cabin.

September ended with the *Dumfries* becalmed beneath clear skies and a bright sun. 'And the Son of Righteousness has been shining into my heart, making it overflow with peace and love and joy.' The wide open sea spoke to him of the love of God, fathomless and unbounded, 'a sea without a shore'. The relief from stress, and gratitude for their deliverance warmed his heart. But when a French brig bound for England came almost but not quite close enough for him to throw a letter across for his parents, his sensitivity out-matched his strength. 'It . . . stirred up my heart . . . I could not refrain from tears.' But he climbed 'to the top of the maintop-gallant-yard before dinner' and 'got a famous appetite'. Captain Morris consented to his holding a meeting in his cabin each night for any who cared to come 'for singing, reading a chapter and prayer'. So they settled down to the long voyage.

For the next three months they were out of sight of land except for Tristan da Cunha and one or two islands in the Indian Ocean. After a gale in the Bay of Biscay the prevailing north-east wind carried them towards South America. Once across the equator they turned south and then eastward to round the Cape of Good Hope on the westerlies and head for Australia on the huge rollers of the southern oceans. The seas in the Biscay gale carried away the fore-skylight and poured in 'causing no little confusion' and flooding every cabin except Hudson Taylor's. So the after-skylight was boarded up as well and below decks became too dark for him to read or work at any time. A boom was carried away and another broken. He did what he could, preparing a chart for the voyage (day by day he entered their compass bearings) and drawing up a plan of study. But he longed for a change of weather.

On October 6 the steward and Hudson Taylor were praying together –

> for a favourable wind and sea for our voyage – for the Lord alone rules the wind and waves – While at prayer heard a good deal of tramping on deck wh. afterwards we found to be the sailors squaring the yards, the wind having veered round suddenly and so now in answer to prayer, we were enabled to keep on our course . . .

Time and again he prayed about weather conditions and was convinced that what happened was a 'striking proof that before we call He can answer us!'

From time to time when animals, fish or birds came his way – a dying ship's cat, a bonito, two albatrosses – he dissected them, impressed by their anatomy, taking measurements and recording comments in his journal. One albatross was ten feet and six inches from wing-tip to wing-tip. The naturalist in him rose to each occasion. 'Dissecting all day' the journal reads on October 13, and 'caught some large sea-nettles' in a basket; on the 21st, 'a kind of gelatinous animal . . . of the genus Pelagia, order Pulmonigrada, class Acalepha (jelly-fish), sub-kingdom Radiata'. But though they tried to catch sharks on several occasions they were 'too wary', until later in the voyage. The phosphorescence, the flying fish, the birds resting in the rigging, everything delighted him. When clear skies showed stars he saw them shining on his family at home and felt homesick. But 'the most magnificent sunset I think I ever witnessed' took him 'up the mast' where he 'sang an hymn of praise to the Maker of this wonderful world'.

His cabin was filled on Sundays and often on weeknights too, when they sang, read and expounded Scripture and then prayed. The steward and carpenter prayed aloud in the presence of the crew. In the tropics they met on deck, under awnings erected to keep the deck cool, when the men were not too busy repairing the weakened mainmast and bowsprit. Sunday, October 23, was

intensely hot. Had prayers on deck after which I gave a short lecture on Genesis 1 . . . Finished Bunyan's *Pilgrim's Progress* this afternoon, and in the evening lectured from Genesis 6 to 22 : . . How I long for the salvation of the crew.

The narrow escape in Caernarvon Bay confirmed for him the uncertainty of life and the necessity of urging on the men the need of decision. Several were 'more concerned about sin and salvation than ever before'. He was longing and praying for conversions.

Doctoring took some of his time. He was still treating the sailor injured in Caernarvon Bay. He opened abscesses in the captain's eyelid, on the cook's arm and hand, and on a sailor's back, and extracted the steward's 'last left lower molar' tooth. And with calm weather he was busy sorting and labelling the chemicals he had ordered. He distilled water and alcohol 'for chemical analysis work and photography', made photographic paper and then a camera using a microscope lens, without much success. His reading included mathematics, astronomy, magnetism and chemistry, Davis's *China*, Paley's *Evidences of Christianity*, Fulloon's lectures on the Holy Spirit, surgery and Piddington's *Law of Storms*. Captain Morris was 'doing algebra' with him and he was teaching the captain to play the concertina and the second mate the flute.

Went on deck when they were washing it, soon after six . . . and had five or six buckets of water thrown over me . . . very warm and pleasant.

This was followed by a row round the ship on a raft with the captain, inspecting it, before a swim, keeping a sharp lookout for sharks. And he sometimes joined the seamen at work.

On December 9 the ship was rolling too much for sleep. So he was up on deck from two to five a m watching the waves washing over the deck continually.

> The wind whistles shrilly through the rigging, the sails roar again with the violence of the wind and rain, the masts crack, the ship reels and lies over, and the seas as they strike her make every timber vibrate. Helped to take in another reef in the topsail. Made 200 miles today. [Again on the 15th] At 8 p m I helped to double-reef fore and main top-sails. Now we are taking a good deal of water . . .

But they were spanking along. When they sighted other ships he hoped to be able to send a message home but was always disappointed.

The Indian Ocean revived Hudson Taylor's homesickness. Benjamin Hudson had gone out to India and was raking in a small fortune from painting rajahs' portraits. Memories of Soho and his near-fatal septicaemia reminded him of his mother. The southern hemisphere felt far from home. They celebrated Christmas by slaughtering their first pig and on Christmas day Hudson Taylor addressed a larger meeting of the men than usual. But it was all very unlike Christmas.

The year ended with the *Dumfries* about five hundred miles from Australia and five thousand from China.[8] They had 'begun to make a little northing' but slow progress in light breezes was distressing to the captain. He promised 'If we reach Shanghai in thirty-three days to give me £5, thinking it so unlikely'. Another distress was the discovery of rot in the main mast. It was 'very deep . . . so men have been putting a "Fish" on it' (a brace), while almost becalmed. Hudson Taylor was blissful and went 'into the main-top to read and enjoy the sun'. He thought back over the eventful year and gave thanks for the 'kind friends of Tottenham'.

By now the long voyage was telling on the crew; the temperature was 85°F in the cabins with skylights and stern windows open. And new anxieties ahead added to the strain. They were making cartridges for the ship's guns to fight off pirates, and putting anchors out over the bows ready for emergency use among the coral reefs and islands. When Hudson Taylor prolonged the Sunday service by forty minutes no one turned up in the evening, to teach him a lesson.

It was not the last time they snubbed or teased him. Some said they were miserable with their sin but miserable also with religion. Only one showed any evidence of responding to his exhortations. Others blamed Hudson Taylor for the storms, the calms, head winds and adverse currents, saying passengers were always unlucky, especially women, but ministers and missionaries were the worst; they caused ships to be lost.[9]

The Swedish carpenter was his good friend. Many a time they were 'out on the bowsprit, the moon shining overhead and the foaming waters beneath and around us, praying and talking together about the Lord'. It was he who rounded up the men for the meetings and helped most in singing and praying. Hudson Taylor's own morale was buoyed up and the nearer to East Asia they drew the more missionary-hearted his journal entries became. When Captain Morris's depression over the calms deepened Hudson Taylor prayed earnestly for some wind 'and felt such confidence that I know my prayer was answered, and we now have a pleasant breeze'.

Among the islands *January 1854*

At two a m on January 13 Captain Morris called Hudson Taylor up to see some islands south of Sumba (Sandalwood Island). 'These islands are not correctly laid down in the chart, which makes the navigation anxious and dangerous,' the captain said. The sight of trees and green fields made them long to be on solid land again. A mountain peak on Timor was visible in the distance the next day as they passed to the north of it, heading for the eastern Moluccas and Dampier Straits, between Papua-New Guinea and Halmahera. In the afternoon of Sunday, January 15, they were in the Ombay Straits and could see the Dutch settlement of Attapopo (Atapupu) on Timor and Alor Island to their north. In the evening Ombay Island's forests and ravines looked beautiful.

> Oh! What work for the missionary! [Hudson wrote in his journal]. Islands almost unknown, some of them densely peopled, but no light, no Jesus, no hope . . . My heart yearns over them. Can it be that Christian men will sit quietly at home and leave these souls to perish? . . . Shall we now think ourselves free from the responsibility of that command, 'Go ye into all the world and preach the gospel to every creature'? Is that word of our Saviour, 'As my Father sent me, even so send I you,' no longer true? Oh! that I could get to them.

As an aid to future navigation he was sketching the islands they passed, from various viewpoints, because the perspective changed so quickly. Day after day it was still and airless. Sometimes they covered as few as seven miles in twenty-four hours with barely enough way on the ship to counteract the currents. On the 16th,

> Captain Morris came to my room almost distracted; there had been no wind. The ship was not under command and we were drifting on Cambing at the rate of four knots . . . So I prayed earnestly for a breeze, and felt assured my prayer was heard and went on deck and told the Mate we should have one soon. And it came directly and has been a steady 7-knotter. Praised be the Lord.

In a letter to his mother, he described another emergency. When they were making good speed one very dark night, a flash of sheet lightning happened to reveal an island only three miles dead ahead of them, unmarked on their chart. They would have sunk in deep

SOUTH-EAST ASIAN APPROACHES TO CHINA

water if holed below its precipitous cliffs. It brought home to him
that they were in the hands of God.

He was learning a great deal about navigation but the wild life of
many kinds which came their way was keeping him busy too. He
recorded the birds and butterflies and fish he saw, 'Boobies and a
solon goose . . . today', noting that the booby was the 'brown
gannet, *Sula Fusca*'. And the tropical nights enchanted him.

> Nothing can be more lovely. The calm quiet, only interrupted by the
> flapping of the sails, and the murmur of the waters as they wash up the
> sides of the vessel. The clear blue sky and few light clouds. The
> occasional illumination from sheet lightning, and here and there the
> splash of the bonito or albicore, and the leap after the unfortunate
> flying fish . . .

His doctoring continued to be often in demand. 'Removed part of
the tonsil of one of the men' runs one journal entry. He was reading
surgery as well as Paley's *Evidences* at the time. On January 25 he
was studying signal flags, man-of-war flags and national flags. But
the ship's progress was depressingly slow as they roasted on a
millpond sea. The men were heaving the lead, and even rowing
ahead of the *Dumfries* to sound for shallows. 'We have now arrived
at the most dangerous part of the passage. The straits are narrow,
the islands numerous, ill known and not properly surveyed; with the
currents variable and sometimes strong.' So as darkness fell the
dangers increased.

A light was seen. 'The sensation it produced was indescribable.'
Three outrigger canoes manned by men and boys came out from
'Waygion' Island. He gave more space to describing them, their
canoes, their food and the plumed birds they were offering for
barter, than anything else on the voyage. But their ignorance of the
gospel moved him most. 'What would not I have given to have been
able to preach the Gospel to them.' Writing to his friend Benjamin
Broomhall he added, 'I longed to go and live among them.'

At last they were through the Straits and thinking they were safe
when on Sunday, the 29th, a new danger threatened them. With no
breeze to keep the ship under way, the strong current began
carrying them on to the hostile Papuan shore, the home of painted
headhunting savages. They had drifted forty miles off course and
were helpless, very close to land. All they could do was to lower a
longboat and turn their head into the current to reduce the drift and
the force of impact.

He however who has protected us so long will not leave us now, I feel confident [Hudson Taylor wrote. And his next journal entry was] On awakening this morning, the cackling of the hen and the chirping of the chickens [bought from a Waygion canoe] reminded me forcibly of England. I fancied myself in the country somewhere, at Tottenham or Dodworth or Barton . . . Then I thought of the chiming Church Bells, of the pealing organs . . . Now there passed before the mind a panorama, shall I say – all the kind acts which love suggests . . . and the sweet communion I have had with friends dear but absent . . . The Carpenter and I prayed for a breeze, and our prayer was heard. One immediately sprang up and by 6 p m we were making 8 knots.

In his *Retrospect* long afterwards Hudson Taylor recalled many details omitted from this brief journal entry. Some of them may belong to the similar emergency two weeks earlier. During the Sunday service Captain Morris kept going over to the side of the ship, checking their distance from some submerged reefs. In the afternoon he said, 'Well, we have done everything that can be done, we can only await the result.' 'I replied, "No, there is one thing we have not done yet. Four of us on board are Christians . . . Let us each retire to his own cabin, and in agreed prayer ask the Lord to give us immediately a breeze. He can send it now as at sunset."' The captain agreed and Hudson Taylor spoke to the steward and carpenter, praying with the carpenter before they went each to their own quarters. But he could not go on asking once he believed God's answer had been given. He went up on deck and asked the first officer, 'a godless man' to let out some sail. He answered 'What would be the good of that?'

I told him we have been asking a wind from God, and it was coming immediately, and we were so near to the reef . . . that there was not a minute to lose. With a look of incredulity and contempt he said with an oath that he would rather see a wind than hear of it! But while he was speaking I watched his eye, and followed it up to the royal [the topmost sail], and there, sure enough, the corner of the sail was beginning to tremble in the coming breeze . . . In another minute the heavy tread of the men on deck brought up the captain from his cabin to see what was the matter . . . We were soon out of danger . . . Thus God encouraged me . . .

Last lap to Shanghai   *February 1854*

They still had a month before them, harder than ever to endure as they toiled northward in open sea past the Palau (Pelew) Islands in the Pacific Ocean east of the Philippines. Hudson Taylor began to pack up his equipment and books, as with the right winds it was possible to reach Shanghai in a few days. Reading the life of Mrs Judson of Burma he felt rebuked.

> Oh! for more of that fervent love, that patient self-denying zeal which characterized her. My coldness and hardness of heart is *so* great, nothing less than the love of *God* could bear with it . . . I *do* love *Him*, but *so* little. Oh! for *more* love. Now we are so near China, how apt I am to become impatient! Is it not more because I hope to receive letters from home than to proclaim to the heathen 'the unspeakable gift'? Alas! I fear it is. What a heap of confusion my mind is . . . Oh! for more steadfastness . . .

Uncertainty of the future was on his mind. By February 15 they were near Taiwan and the Ryukyu islands, only seven hundred and forty miles from Shanghai. The prospect of landing in a strange country with no friends to go to, only letters of introduction to three strangers, was alarming. He comforted himself from Scripture, 'I will never leave thee . . . Lo! I am with you always . . .', but he thought, 'What changes will probably have taken place since we last heard from China! . . . Where shall I go, and how shall I live there at first?' These 'and a thousand other questions' raced through his mind.

A 'nasty confused sea' heralded a cyclone, he deduced from *The Law of Storms* and he went aloft to help reef the sails. A tremendous jumping head sea all night prevented him from sleeping and it was becoming very cold with piercing winds. They lay to among islands north of Fuzhou (Foochow) and on February 22 and 23 snow fell. A two-masted junk, sailing well, came into view but the night of the 24th was dark, thick and wet, as they pressed northwards past the Chusan (Zhoushan) Islands and Hangzhou Bay towards the Yangzi estuary. Early the next morning the mate looked in to tell Hudson Taylor that Gutzlaff Island near the mouth of the estuary was in sight. The water was already green and turbid from the silt of the great river. They anchored off 'Gutzlaff's Isle' on Saturday, February 25, and with a Union Jack at the foremast head to request a pilot, they waited. 'I long to get there,' he wrote, but it was Sunday before three boats turned up, each offering to pilot them in. One had fourteen Chinese on board, the first he had seen. 'How I did long to be able to preach the Gospel to them! After some bargaining they agreed to take us to Shanghai for $30'. But as it turned out they were only fishermen hoping to line their pockets. The third boat to arrive contained an English pilot. The correct fee was five times as much.

This was the moment. They besieged the pilot for news. He told them,

> the Rebels have had possession of Shanghai for 4 months and are marching to Pekin. That, bad as our passage has been we have arrived before a vessel wh. sailed a month previous to us and others we expected to have beaten us have not arrived. That we are too late for this month's (outgoing) mail and much other interesting news respecting Europe, Asia and America.

Russia and Turkey were at war, Britain and France were preparing to invade the Crimea. Commodore Perry and his American ships had reached Japan – and been accepted. The germ of a trade agreement had been concluded. If Japan could open to the West, anything could happen. This was a message of hope. But the *Dumfries* had to drop anchor still twenty-five miles from Wusong, another fifteen miles below Shanghai, and thick rainy weather kept them there for two days. 'Never passed such a Sunday before,' Hudson wrote. 'Men working all day and singing all sorts of songs as they hove up anchor and hauled up topsails, etc.' Everyone was impatient to reach land.

At last on Wednesday, March 1, 1854, they reached Wusong and 'saw an immense no. of junks' both on the Yangzi and its Shanghai tributary the Huangpu, so many that until the flood tide ceased it was unsafe to proceed among them, so strong was the current.

A passing pilot boat took Hudson Taylor up the Huangpu to Shanghai. If he had a thought for England in the exhilaration of arriving in China, he must have been struck by the resemblance of the Huangpu to the Humber, so close to home. But here European sailing vessels shared the stream and primitive jetties with ocean-going junks. A dozen or so foreign business houses, replicas of the two-storeyed 'factories' of Canton, stood shoulder to shoulder with an ornate Chinese temple in use as the Customs house, and other Chinese buildings. A mile and a half further upstream the castellated walls of the ancient city of Shanghai were visible, and between them and the pilot boat he was standing on, British and French men-of-war and, ashore, the banners and panoplied tents of the imperial Manchu army besieging the insurgents in the city (map, p 120).

SHANGHAI 'BUND' AND CUSTOMS HOUSE, 1854

At five p m Hudson Taylor landed at one of the jetties and stood at long last among Chinese people – Chinese merchants, Chinese coolies, Chinese sounds and smells, part of the foreign settlement.

> My feelings on arriving at last among this people cannot be described. My heart felt as tho' it would burst from its place – as tho' there was not room for it.

Simply to stand on dry land again for the first time since September was wonderful, but this was Chinese soil, of which he had dreamed since boyhood. Gratitude for deliverance from 'many and great dangers', elation at having arrived to proclaim the 'glad tidings of great joy', vivid recollections of the distance he was from his dearest friends, a stranger in a strange land – a tumult of emotions swept over him. He could not wait to collect his mail and find the missionaries to whom he had introductions. There should be letters from home and Mr Sissons; perhaps from Elizabeth herself. And credit notes from the CES authorising him to draw cash from the Shanghai merchants, Gibb, Livingstone, & Company. He saw the British and American flags flying over their respective consulates, and made his way to the nearer one, at the junction of the Suzhou river with the Huangpu.

Then came the shock. The office that handled the mail had closed an hour before. He must come again tomorrow. And two of his letters of introduction were useless. Dr Tozer had died of fever five months before. Lewis Shuck, one of the original 1843 'Delegate' translators of the Bible and the first missionary ever to enter Hong Kong, had returned to the States two years ago. What could he do? They directed him to the LMS 'compound' of premises on the opposite side of the settlement, and he set off along the raised bank of the Huangpu called the 'Bund', and a mile of mud tracks that did duty as roads, flanked by deep drainage ditches, to find Walter H Medhurst, DD.

It awed him to have to cast himself upon the hospitality of that person who after Rutherford Alcock, the consul, was the most prestigious in 'the Settlement' as it was called for the next hundred years. Friend of Robert Morrison, Samuel Dyer and Sir Stamford Raffles, Medhurst had already been in Java for ten years before even Charles Gutzlaff arrived as a newcomer to East Asia. Moreover Hudson Taylor's introduction was from a comparative stranger. At Dr Medhurst's house the Chinese who answered his knock could speak not a word of English. What he made clear was that Dr and Mrs Medhurst were away.

PART 2

SHANGHAI UNDER SIEGE
1854–55

CHAPTER FOUR

INITIATION BY FIRE
1854

The China he found   *1843–1854*

To understand the mad-hatter's world into which Hudson Taylor now plunged, we need to glance at events in China during the five and a half months he was at sea, and since the last news he had received.

A great deal had happened in the eleven years since Captain Balfour, the first British consul, arrived with Walter Medhurst, William Lockhart the surgeon and a score of merchants, to act on the Nanking Treaty and establish themselves at this new treaty port, Shanghai. Starting with a makeshift consulate and mission premises in the ancient walled city of Shanghai, they marked out the new Settlement boundaries in the fields outside, and purchased the existing Chinese buildings the perimeter enclosed. Much of the area was flooded at high tide so drainage channels had to be dug and projected roads raised. With realistic vision they laid out the settlement in blocks formed by what were to become intersecting roads, three running north and south, parallel with the river and named after provinces of China, and six east and west, named after capital cities. On the western outskirts, near the old road called the *ma-lu*, later the Nanking Road, future residents were to create a racecourse. In a land with so many mouths to feed, the sheer waste of arable land appalled those Chinese who had no concept of future developments. They even protested against the width of the projected roads, modest by Western standards. Not until 1856 was granite hardcore added to the gradual accumulation of rubble and ships' clinkers used to defeat the mud and ruts of the first few years.

To get about in the Settlement the foreign population rode on Tartar ponies or in sedan chairs, hiring coolies and wheelbarrows for their baggage, but by 1850 horse carriages were common in Shanghai as in Hong Kong among the well-to-do. Rickshaws were not invented until 1870. Business houses, residences, gardens and Chinese quarters were built; and the stinking ditches and stagnant

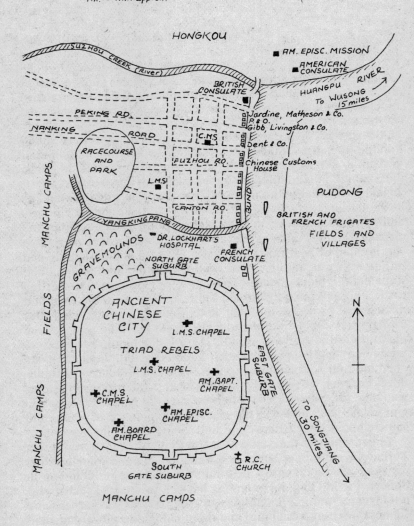

SHANGHAI CITY and FOREIGN
SETTLEMENTS 1854-60

1in. = 1ml. approx.

HONGKOU

SUZHOU CREEK (River)

AM. EPISC. MISSION
AMERICAN CONSULATE

BRITISH CONSULATE

HUANGPU RIVER
To WUSONG
15 miles

PEKING RD.

Jardine, Matheson & Co.
P. & O.
Gibb, Livingston & Co.

NANKING   ROAD

C.M.S.

Dent & Co.

RACECOURSE AND PARK

FUZHOU RD.

Chinese Customs House

PUDONG

L.M.S.

THE BUND

CANTON RD.

BRITISH AND FRENCH FRIGATES
FIELDS AND VILLAGES

YANGKINGPANG

MANCHU CAMPS

GRAVEMOUNDS

DR. LOCKHART'S HOSPITAL

NORTH GATE SUBURB

FRENCH CONSULATE

FIELDS

ANCIENT CHINESE CITY

L.M.S. CHAPEL

TRIAD REBELS

L.M.S. CHAPEL

AM. BAPT. CHAPEL

C.M.S. CHAPEL

AM. EPISC. CHAPEL

EAST GATE SUBURB

AM. BOARD CHAPEL

N

TO SONGJIANG 30 miles

MANCHU CAMPS

SOUTH GATE SUBURB

R.C. CHURCH

MANCHU CAMPS

cesspools of the earliest days gave place to proper drainage, resulting in fewer outbreaks of dysentery, cholera and typhoid. The new
consulate was erected on piles driven deep into the ground, and
modern Shanghai had begun.

The Shanghai of 1854 was an international community of an
unusual kind. The walled city, built in 1554 AD as a bastion against
pirates, had been seized in September 1853 by the Triad insurgents
known as the Short Swords or Red Turbans. Encamped around
them was an imperial Manchu and Chinese army of from forty to
fifty thousand men, 'a much greater source of discomfort and
danger to the little European community than were the rebels
themselves'. Between the city with its suburbs and the southern
boundary of the British Settlement, formed by a creek called the
Yang-king-pang or simply the *pang*, the French had established a
settlement for themselves in 1849, although the Chinese treaty
concessions of 1842–4 allowed only of an international settlement at
Shanghai. The British, first to arrive, had chosen part of the alluvial
flats between the *pang* and the Suzhou river, extended by stages to
include the whole area. The Americans chose to live across the
Suzhou river in Hongkou where rents were lower, and before long
hoisted the Stars and Stripes over their consulate, against the futile
protests of the *daotai* and British consul. Under the pressure of
circumstances, however, it was not long before they combined with
the British to form the International Settlement embracing both
banks, which enjoyed extra-territorial rights until 1943. The Suzhou
river was crossed by ferry until 'St Catherine's Bridge' was built in
1856 (map, p 184, A) so called after William Lockhart's generally
beloved wife. Her 'canonisation' was by public usage.

Into these foreign settlements two miles long by half a mile or
more in width, Chinese merchants and peasants began to pour.
With no more say in how they were treated than they had had under
Manchu government, they accepted foreign rule on Chinese soil
and paid taxes and levies to the barbarians. It was safer there than
outside. Every available house was occupied and new buildings
sprang up everywhere.

Between the racecourse and the Chinese city, near the south-west
corner of the Settlement, the LMS built their 'compound' with
homes and chapel, within half a mile of the city walls. Inside the
walled city they had two preaching halls. After eleven years of work
there were twenty-two church members. The first CMS missionary,
Thomas McClatchie, had also opened chapels in the Chinese city

and during the rebel occupation preaching was still being carried on by both missions in what Hudson Taylor soon found was a truly heroic way. Across the *pang* but outside the French settlement was a no-man's-land of fields and burial grounds, studded as far as eye could see with the mounds of earth, like inverted rice bowls, that were raised over most Chinese graves. Here and there small hamlets or clusters of poor shacks could be seen far out across the otherwise featureless plain. In this region and just off the road between the Settlement and the North Gate of the city, Dr William Lockhart built his hospital in 1846.

The population of the Shanghai Settlement was largely a moving one. The nucleus of officials, merchants, and missionaries reached ninety or a hundred in 1845 when Hong Kong boasted five short of six hundred Europeans, but ten years later Shanghai had its hundreds and the problem of more hundreds of unruly seamen and adventurers. At times they outnumbered the residents by ten to one. Debauched and violent, robbing and being robbed, they and the fall of the city to the Triads forced Consul Rutherford Alcock to call a meeting in 1854, which set up the Shanghai Municipal Council with Dr Medhurst, the doyen of all residents, as its first chairman. Hudson Taylor was in on the early evolution of what is now one of the largest cities in the world.

The *Shanghai Almanac* for 1854 listed two hundred and seventy male residents of whom only forty had families. About a dozen were Parsee merchants. The two dozen missionaries of six or seven societies accounted for a third of all the married residents. Four-fifths of all the men were between nineteen and thirty-five years of age, mostly young assistants in the merchant houses. So the social problems of the community were unusual.

As soon as the major merchant firms started up in Shanghai, the prophesied success of the port was fulfilled and more and more firms moved in. Canton and even Hong Kong became secondary. Chinese merchants cashed in on the booming trade, and for two and a half miles the Huangpu River was flanked by trading junks sometimes thirty deep. With the fall of the city to the rebels, however, and tension between the imperial troops and the foreigners, the junks disappeared.

Opium trading was banned by the Chinese government and the consuls would not allow it near the Settlement, so the old dodge of 'receiving ships' used as depots at Wusong, at the mouth of the Huangpu, saw the transfer of contraband goods to Chinese junks and out of foreign hands. Before 1854 there were ten of these unseaworthy hulks, four of them British, four Jewish and Parsee, and two American. But then, to the chagrin of the merchants, when Shanghai city eventually fell to the Triads and government control was impossible, Alcock and his fellow consuls formed a provisional government and an international board of inspectors which curbed the independence of the smugglers and for a while levied duty on behalf of the Chinese rulers. Even so the sixteen thousand five hundred chests of opium imported in 1847 rose to thirty-two thousand in 1857, a lucrative source of wealth to merchants and Chinese officials alike. The consumer had to pay. Even in 1845 the superior quality of Indian opium meant that twenty-three million dollars-worth was imported into China while the value of other trade was twenty million. And silver to the value of two million pounds sterling was annually being shipped out of China to cover the deficit. These grievances that had provoked the opium war were being perpetuated.

Alcock had a constant aversion to the traffic which he called the 'collusion and connivance' of British subjects and Chinese officials in defiance of Chinese laws. The odium of it fell on the consuls and detracted from the growing reputation for integrity and good faith of law-abiding foreigners in the eyes of the Chinese.

> Whichever way we turn, evil of some kind connected with this monstrous trade and monopoly of large (merchant) houses meets our eye [Alcock wrote] . . . but the cultivation and sale of opium are (still) sanctioned and encouraged for the purposes of revenue in India . . .

The legitimised exploitation of China was being continued by the same outwardly respectable companies. All his life Alcock tried to find a way to break the traffic in a manner which would not drive it into the hands of more unscrupulous people. And all the time he suffered the attacks of the anti-opium front for not taking strong direct action against it.[1]

The social life of the Settlement followed the pattern of the Canton 'factories' for some years.[2] The partners and managers of the merchant firms, often little more than thirty years of age, were called *taipans* (from the Chinese term for manager, literally 'big plank' or boss), and their assistants were 'griffins', named after the half-broken Mongolian ponies which they used for racing at Shanghai. Rank and 'face' demanded that each official kept his servants, essentially a groom, chair-coolie-cum-sweeper, body-servant and teacher. Juniors might make do with one, but *taipans* never fewer than five. A missionary family had to have at least a cook, a water-carrier or outdoor man and a sewing-woman or *amah* for the children. *Taipans* often kept their own tailors and barbers too. Their clerks were usually Portuguese or Eurasians from Macao, and in dealings with the Chinese merchants they employed *compradors*, Chinese intermediaries who in speaking with the foreigner used a semi-English, semi-Portuguese, semi-Chinese trade language.

The social strata were clearly demarcated. Officials, merchants and bankers, the professions and officers of the armed forces had social status. Others, whatever their integrity or ability, never. So Chinese merchants, 'other ranks', clerks, and Eurasians were excluded. Missionaries were misfits. They could seldom attain the approved affluence and broke ranks by being classless among themselves and friendly with the Chinese. Most made no attempt to conform. Therefore a gulf developed between the two types of educated foreigner which was seldom bridged, except by the Christian and liberal members of the élite on the one hand and the incontestably superior like Lockhart and Medhurst on the other. The morals of so many in the merchant community were also a barrier. Many if not most of the unmarried men, debarred from marriage by company rules, had their own 'kept' Chinese women. To Chinese eyes even the unseemly promenading of the foreign womenfolk, arm in arm or pert and coquettish, was a blatant offence against age-old proprieties.

The style of living in the 'collegiate' regime of the merchant houses, carried over from Canton, beggars description. Their existence was a form of exile mitigated only by self-indulgence and the rapid accumulation of wealth. Aesthetic appreciation and creativity seem largely to have been lacking among them. 'If there were no trade, not a single man, except missionaries, would have come there at all,' one of them wrote.[3] They were blind to, and indeed scorned the fabulous wealth of Chinese arts and culture. A visiting doctor described what he found,

> They begin dinner with a rich soup and a glass of sherry; *then* one or two side dishes with champagne; *then* some beef, mutton or fowls and bacon, with *more* champagne, or beer; *then* rice and curry and ham; *afterwards* game; then pudding, pastry, jelly, custard or blancmange and *more* champagne; *then* cheese and salad, and bread and butter and a glass of port wine; *then* (fruit and more wine) . . . and this *awful* repast is finished at last with a cup of strong coffee and cigars![4]

Ice House Street in Hong Kong was named after the warehouse in which blocks of ice from North America and later Japan, were stored for the use of the gourmands. Shanghai enjoyed the same luxury. In vain the physicians advised moderation, as in this example,

> for breakfast a mutton chop, fresh eggs, curry and bread and butter, with coffee or tea or claret and water.[5]

But they were more successful in counselling daily exercise 'to shake up your liver', for 'liver complaints' were almost incessant and due even more than indulgence to the use of human night-soil for fertilising the market gardens, and of river water for cooking and drinking. Both were potent vectors of typhoid, dysentery and cholera. The mortality rate was very high even among consuls, whose self-discipline was exemplary. Exercise at least restored an appetite. Running and wheelbarrow racing were followed by 'griffin' racing, and in 1850 the Shanghai Race Club was formed. Mounted paper chases and drag-hunts and, when politically safe enough, shooting excursions were organised – anything to allay boredom and counteract overeating or to develop an appetite for the next meal.

The learned societies and periodicals of Shanghai, launched very largely by missionaries, had as one of their aims the awakening of these young merchants to better things. But there were also men of the stamp of the botanist Robert Fortune who made long excursions disguised as a Chinese, in 1843–46, 1848–51, 1853–56 and 1861–62, collecting plants and seeds, and enlisting skilled tea-planters for the outside world.[6] And brave missionaries who also travelled in disguise, avoiding recognition as foreigners, as Walter Medhurst did in 1845, reporting his experiences in *A Glance at the Interior of China: obtained during a journey through the Silk and Green Tea Districts*.[7] W C Milne was another, travelling from Ningbo to Hong Kong in 1843. But at the time of Hudson Taylor's arrival in China, shorter journeys of up to one or two hundred miles from the treaty ports were occasionally being made in full European dress.

Taipings and Triads   1853–54

News of the fall of Nanking had reached Britain before Hudson Taylor sailed (*see* pp 78–82). On arrival he was to hear more details of how Hong Xiu-quan and his followers had achieved it. On their victorious passage through Hunan province they recruited coal-miners for use as sappers, and ran a mine beneath the city wall of Nanking. When the mine was sprung on March 19, 1853, and the north-east corner of the defences breached, the Taipings stormed in and slaughtered over twenty thousand Manchus and ten thousand more imperial troops and civilians, in reprisal for the indiscriminate slaughter of Taipings captured in the earlier phases of the campaign.

Wherever they went they recruited both men and women. They were largely an army of the dispossessed with a grudge against the rich and landed classes, reinforced and motivated by the secret societies. Nanking lies in a great plain intersected by waterways. The villas of the mandarins set beautifully on islets in a lake-like widening of the Yangzi river were ravished. The ornately decorated Porcelian Tower beyond the south wall of the city, two hundred and sixty feet tall, in nine storeys, a jewel of Ming art, completed in 1430 AD, was burned out.

At Nanking the insurgents were eighty thousand strong, in five armies, with another hundred thousand non-combatant porters, trench-diggers and artificers. The city became a vast military camp. In November there were four hundred and eighty thousand in the women's labour corps and five hundred thousand men in another sector of the city. A French priest who succeeded in staying there for two days reported that foreigners were referred to as brothers but all enemies as devils.

Four hundred printers supervised by Hong Xiu-quan himself were printing Gutzlaff's Bible, without the alteration of a single character, as Dr Medhurst verified. The religious element of Worshippers of Shangdi was becoming adulterated, however, and used by the pro-Ming dynasty faction. The capture of this original Ming capital (1368–1403) went to the rebels' heads. Hong Xiu-quan declared himself Emperor or *Taiping Wang* of the Dynasty of Great Peace, and Nanking its capital. Then instead of building on his conquests and pressing the Manchus all the way to Peking, he sat back and enjoyed the fruits of victory for two months. It was probably the fatal mistake. Claiming to be the second Son of God, the 'younger brother of Jesus', Hong Xiu-quan required universal obedience to himself. To Sir George Bonham, British plenipotentiary, he sent this message,

Whereas God the Heavenly Father has sent our Sovereign [the *Taiping Wang*] down to earth as the true Sovereign of all nations in the world, all people . . . who wish to appear at his Court must yield obedience to the rules of ceremony.

It was the old concept unchanged. But it was too early to assume that complete conquest of the Manchus would be his.

If the leaders showed a fatal strategic lethargy, their tactical moves added Zhenjiang (Chinkiang) and Yangzhou on the Grand Canal to their kingdom. Even before these key cities fell there was consternation in Shanghai and a great exodus of Chinese merchants. This was the time when it was assumed by Chinese and foreigners alike that the Taipings would drive on to the coast, occupying Suzhou and Hangzhou, the provincial capital of Zhejiang, and the two treaty ports of Shanghai and Ningbo. To effect diplomatic links with the Western powers and secure two ports for foreign trade and the delivery of modern arms was the obvious step, but the Taipings did not attempt it. And this was the moment when the *daotai* of Shanghai requested foreign ships to attack the Taipings; when the residents of the Settlement under Alcock's lead formed a defence force, the Shanghai Volunteer Corps; when Sir George Bonham sailed up the Yangzi in HMS *Hermes* to demonstrate British neutrality, allowing his ship to be fired on without retaliating; and when young interpreter Meadows won high commendation for his face-to-face reconnaissance of the Taipings.

Believing the foreigners to be in danger, William Lockhart's patients forsook his hospital. Happening more than once over the years, this was a sure sign of which way the wind was blowing. With two million dollars-worth of merchandise immobilised by the hostilities, the Settlement was an alluring prize to the covetous. It became an armed camp under the command of the British vice-consul, ex-lieutenant Thomas Francis Wade, with riot gates across its streets until 1856. When *Hermes* returned from Nanking, however, the Shanghai newspaper *North China Herald*, begun in 1850, revealed that the Taipings were scarcely aware of Shanghai's existence, let alone as a port of major significance. Moreover the Taipings were well-disposed towards foreigners and had no intention of clashing with them.

Not only the Taiping advance posed a threat to the treaty ports, however. The independent secret society known as the Triads[8] misjudged the intentions of the Taiping rulers by seizing first Amoy and then Shanghai. So instead of welcoming them as allies the Taipings repudiated them. At Amoy, four thousand Triads with local help expelled the imperial troops on May 18, 1853. But finding themselves blockaded by an imperial fleet the Triads were forced to withdraw six months later. The wrath of the returning Manchus was therefore directed against the inhabitants of the city, although they had had no choice but to collaborate. Scores were beheaded on the water front, and more slashed with swords and thrown into the harbour. Disgusted, the British vice-consul and two naval officers, Captains Fishbourne and Vansittart, cast aside neutrality, commanded the Manchu admiral to stop, fished between two and three hundred mutilated and drowning peasants, coolies and even twelve-year-old boys out of the water and treated their wounds. On land their acts of mercy were repeated by the Scotsman, William C Burns, and the gratitude of the people found expression in an openness to the gospel he preached.

The situation was confused and in both missionary and secular communities opposing views were held as to future prospects for China, for trade and for the gospel. Issacher J Roberts, who had taught Hong Xiu-quan in Canton before the rebel movement began, was attempting to get to Nanking. James Legge read a letter from a Taiping in Nanking to a Hong Kong Chinese exhorting him to go to the missionaries and learn to worship God. 'Surely such a movement', Legge commented, 'in which such letters are going about through all China, must be regarded by us with intense solicitude.' George Smith, the Bishop of Victoria, Hong Kong, reported that the Southern Prince of the Taiping hierarchy had earlier been a member of Charles Gutzlaff's Chinese Union. There were those who saw China soon becoming a Christian nation, and others who were more impressed by the evident madness in the movement.

Then came the Taiping advance northward from Nanking through Henan and Zhili provinces. The Peking Court *Gazette* claimed a great victory for the Tartar cavalry at Yiyang, as hollow a claim as others had been. For seven weeks no *Gazette* reached Shanghai and suspicions were aroused that all was not going well for the dynasty. The Court appealed to the Western powers for help or Peking would fall. The colourful Roman Catholic bishop of Peking and Inner Mongolia, Monsignor Mouly, reported in the *Annals of the Propagation of the Faith* that as the Taipings approached the capital was in panic, for the rebel advance guards boasted of being followed by myriads of soldiers. The effect was that towns and cities fell without a blow being struck. Word spread that while the imperial troops plundered rich and poor indiscriminately, the Taipings took only from the rich. So the common people favoured the rebels. 'The bravery and military skill of the insurgents is incontestable . . . they far exceed the cowardly imperialists,' Mgr Mouly declared.

On October 28, 1853, the Taiping advance guard reached Duliu, not twenty miles from Tianjin (Tientsin) and two days' march from Peking. There they were held. A telegraphic despatch from Trieste (*sic*) to London, the latest development to hasten news brought overland from the East, said 'insurgents marching on Peking'. It was not wholly true, but the *Peking Gazette* carried memorials admitting that the rich were evacuating the capital with their treasures and the army was in disarray, that tribute from the south was cut off but the Taipings had no lack of means.

Now two events occurred which in time altered the whole scene in the Manchus' favour: two new personalities emerged in the imperial ranks; and the Taipings failed to support their northern thrust adequately. The names of Zeng Guo-fan (Tseng Kuo-fan) (1811 –72) and Li Hong-zhang (Li Hung-chang) (1823–1901) were to feature largely in Chinese history through the rest of the century. Zeng was a provincial governor and Li his secretary, a young man of thirty whose wife and children had died tragically near the beginning of the rebellion. Zeng was remarkable as a scholar and administrator, but notable also for the young men he chose and trained. Seeing the imperial forces being pushed back and back by the long-haired rebels, they raised a regiment led by gentry and supported by the literati, the scholar-officials, and joined in. Neither Zeng nor Li was a military man but they were Confucian scholars of high rank.

Li Hong-zhang stood six feet four inches tall, head and shoulders above the average Chinese, an active, athletic man with strikingly large and beautiful eyes. He was said to be as at home in the saddle as a jockey. At Duliu he led his regiment with such success that he was honoured with favourable notice at Court, with promotion and a blue plume, a crow's feather, in his mandarin cap. His path to the highest fame had begun. And the Qing (Ch'ing) monarch began to close in on the *Taiping Wang*.

Meanwhile a French warship, the *Cassini*, steamed up to Nanking, primarily to negotiate the protection of Roman Catholic Chinese, arriving on December 6, 1853. A shot was fired at her by a shore battery but not returned, and when officers went ashore the kind of reception given to Sir George Bonham and *Hermes* was repeated, if less cordially. After a week at anchor receiving visitors, the *Cassini* left again for Shanghai. The intentions of the Taipings towards the foreign community still appeared to be peaceful.

In Shanghai the tension eased when the eastward advance of the Taipings was not continued, but news of Triad militancy in the south became a new cause for alarm. It was a new phenomenon, a rebellion distinct from the Taiping movement but taking advantage of its success. From 1796–1804 a strong reaction against Manchu taxation and oppression had become known as the White Lotus Rebellion, the first of the series of revolts which persisted through the nineteenth century and ended in the downfall of the Qing dynasty.

Significantly, a by-product of the opium traffic also contributed to the unrest of the peasants. The drainage of silver dollars in payment for opium meant that silver became more costly in terms of copper cash, the currency of the poor. These coins lost value, and were actually used as ballast in returning opium ships.

The ancient secret societies, some devoted to the restoration of the Ming dynasty, saw their opportunity, and while one faction

BRASS 'CASH'

under Zhu Jiu-dao made use of the Worshippers of Shangdi to build up the Taiping Tian Guo (Heavenly Kingdom), others recruited strength independently. In 1853 the Triads[9] seized several cities in Guangdong and threatened Canton but failed to consolidate their gains and, as we have seen, the Short Sword faction who were contemporaneous with but entirely distinct from the Taipings, abortively seized Amoy and later Fuzhou.

The fall of Shanghai   September 1853

On September 7, 1853, William Lockhart's servant woke him to say that the city of Shanghai had been seized. It was the birthday of Confucius and crowds from far and near had flocked into the city to witness the celebrations and sacrifices. Among them what is variously stated as six hundred and two thousand Short Sword desperadoes, both Cantonese and Fujianese, took up their positions and in the early hours, armed with only spears, short swords and a few matchlocks, seized the key points, the city gates, the prisons and the government buildings. They attacked the *daotai's yamen*, his official residence, took him and his family prisoner and seized his treasury. They entered the city magistrate's *yamen* and waited while he committed his mother to his brother's care and calmly seated himself on his official dais, before he was stabbed to death.

Criers ran through the streets beating gongs and telling the people they could open their shops without fear. Sympathisers threw bundles of red cloth to the insurgents who decked themselves out with red turbans, caps, jackets and badges. From then on they were known as the *Hong Tou*, Red Heads or Red Turbans. The gaols were opened, and large numbers of the *daotai*'s men defected to the rebels. The city of two hundred thousand had fallen. Lockhart wrote,

> in a state of great delight at their easy conquest (the Triads) issued placards calling the citizens to join them as adherents of the Ming dynasty, and denouncing the Emperor and the Manchus as Tyrants and enemies of China.

Two American missionaries, T P Crawford and the uncouth and eccentric Issacher J Roberts, who were living in the city, heard what had happened and hazarded their lives by going out to see how they would be treated. At the *daotai's yamen* they found the work of destruction going on, but were well received and allowed to go anywhere. Other foreigners followed and were unmolested. Looting of any kind was firmly dealt with, but the Cantonese and Fujian factions quarrelled over the prize money in the treasury, half a million dollars from which the imperial fleet was to have been paid. On the second evening a rumour spread that the Triads were going to attack the foreign Settlement. Dr Lockhart went to the Chief, who assured him that there was nothing to it, and the alarm in the Settlement subsided.

It happened that during the summer when Dr Lockhart had been treating cruelly injured pirates being held as prisoners in the city gaol, he was helped by one young man who could speak some English. When Lockhart arrived at the East Gate of the city after its capture by the Triads, he met this man, now dressed in silks and satins, commanding the Triad guard. He helped to secure the release of some Christians held by the insurgents. A few years later Lockhart visited the gaol in Hong Kong with James Legge, and whom should he find among imprisoned pirates but the same young man. His case was typical of many.

The *daotai*, Wu, had had the good fortune to fall into the hands of Liu Li-chuan, the Short Sword leader, a fellow-Cantonese. So when Colonel Marshall, the American Commissioner, interceded with the Triad chiefs for him, he found an ally. On September 10 an American missionary in the city saw the curtain of a sedan chair lifted slightly and this quick conversation took place.

'Do you know me?' the occupant asked.

'I do.'

'Help me to get out of the city.'

They tried the North Gate, most used by foreigners from the Settlement, but the sedan chair was not allowed to pass. So with the help of another foreigner they let the *daotai* down the wall by ropes [no explanation is given], took him to a missionary's home and later to the more appropriate luxury of a merchant house. Then Dr Lockhart returned to Chief Liu and brought the *daotai*'s family out. Thousands fled the city until its population fell from two hundred thousand to forty thousand.

It was one thing to be free, another for the *daotai* to face the inevitable repercussions from Peking. After events at Amoy and Fuzhou he should have anticipated an attack and watched for infiltrators as was immediately done at Ningbo when the news from Shanghai arrived. He desperately needed to do something to redress the catastrophe. He therefore tried to enlist the help of the Settlement authorities. They declared their neutrality. But surreptitiously some merchants began supplying not the *daotai* but the rebels with arms; and sensing quick wealth and excitement, foreign mercenaries enlisted under the Triads to train them in the use of modern weapons. The *daotai* bought a ship, fitted her out as a warship, and with the war junks on the Huangpu and a large body of imperial troops, newly arrived, attacked the city on September 29, without effect. The river, at that time of year filled with trading junks from north and south China, emptied and was dead except for foreign ships and the imperial fleet.

From then until the city was evacuated in February 1855, eighteen months later, Lockhart's hospital received a constant flow of wounded men. A Manchu general arrived from Peking in November to exterminate the rebels. His troops made camps to the south and west of the city, the river being on the east and the Settlements to the north (map, p 120), and built protective walls and ditches. The Triads burned all houses between them and the camps, cleared away all the debris and bricked up all the city gates except the east gate giving access to the river. Assaults by the Manchus and sorties by the Triads followed daily and the hospital was strewn with the bleeding and dying.

Preposterously, after the daily battle or show of fighting with much noise and display of banners, hundreds of country people would move in to the foot of the walls with baskets of produce and bargain with townsfolk and Triads on the ramparts – until the imperialists took to cutting off the ears and then the heads of the villagers. The injured among these also came to the hospital. Dr Lockhart's reputation soared as he tied off spurting arteries in deep sword cuts, amputated limbs and revived apparently dying men with strong stimulants. On foggy nights he was in greater danger when walking between the Settlement and his hospital or going out to cases than when working there. He took to sleeping at the hospital, his bed barricaded with mattresses against stray cannonballs. But he continued to go into the city to treat the wounded there also. According to the *Church Missionary Intelligencer*, missionaries in the Settlements slept with a bundle of clothes beside them, ready for a night attack – by the imperial forces.

In November the Manchus decided that clandestine supplies of food and ammunition reaching the Triads from the Settlement must stop and three cannon destined for the city must be seized. They launched an attack by three hundred men armed with firepots to burn the Settlement to the ground. The British and American marines and sailors on guard fought them off, supported by members of the civilian community armed with whatever they could lay their hands on. There had been plenty of provocation. Not only were foreign mercenaries fighting with the Triads, but sorties from the city led by 'barbarians' were capturing imperial soldiers, beheading them in the city or cruelly torturing them until they died. When the surgeon-bishop William Boone returned to Shanghai a month after Hudson Taylor's arrival, he was told by Chaplain Hobson of a mercenary known as 'Doctor Martyn' who did his pistol practice on live prisoners.[10]

Early in January, 1854, some Cantonese in the city entered into a plot to sell the city to the imperialists, but the Triads 'learned the signals', waited for the traitors to open the East Gate to the Manchus, seized two hundred of them and beheaded them all. William Lockhart was shown the gory courtyard where it happened. Late in the month even he came in for trouble.

He was attending wounded in his hospital when it was fired on by a cannon on the city wall. After the eleven years he had already worked in Shanghai, William Lockhart's reputation among the Chinese as a surgeon gave him free access wherever he chose to go, in either camp. In theory his hospital was respected as neutral ground. He hurried to the foot of the bastion and called out in protest to the gunner 'saying I would not permit him to fire at my premises!' The Triad gunner laughed and answered that he meant no harm and if Dr Lockhart did not like it he would stop. But Lockhart went into the city to protest in person to the Chief.

'There are imperialist soldiers in the hospital!' the Triad leaders said.

'All are alike to me,' Lockhart answered, 'I treat your wounded too.'

'All right then, "all's fair in battle" but we won't fire on the hospital for the fun of it!'

That was not good enough. Lockhart went to Consul Alcock, a sad and lonely man since the recent death of his wife. At once the consul asked the British naval commander for marines, went to the Triad chiefs and said, as Lockhart described it, 'if by accident or design the hospital should be struck again, they would blow up the North Gate of the city'. The imperialist army would at once make use of the breach. The game was not repeated. But the excitement was still running high when Hudson Taylor arrived in the *Dumfries* on March 1, 1854.

High and dry   *March 1854*

Unsuccessful in finding Dr Medhurst at his house on the evening that he landed, Hudson Taylor looked about, debating what to do, and before long met a young Englishman and introduced himself. Joseph Edkins was an LMS missionary of thirty-one. He welcomed the newcomer and explained that the Medhursts had moved over to the consulate, from which Hudson Taylor had just come. Their son, Walter H Medhurst, Jr. was an interpreter in the consular service, and in any case Dr Medhurst as a right-hand man to the consuls since the treaty ports were opened had the freedom of the premises. The consulate was farther away from the 'almost constant firing' between the opposing camps. Edkins then introduced Hudson Taylor to the other missionaries, including William Lockhart.

Lockhart was in his prime at forty-three, an imposing figure and a fearless missionary. Since 1838 when he arrived in Canton, three years after Dr Peter Parker opened his Ophthalmic Hospital, Lockhart had worked in Macao, twice in the Chusan Islands during the British occupation, then in Hong Kong and finally in Shanghai. In each place he had built a hospital in order to work efficiently as a surgeon. So this was his fourth. His wife Catherine was the first foreign woman to live in Shanghai, elder sister of Rutherford Alcock's promising assistant, Harry Parkes.

Lockhart's welcome to the young medical student was friendly. '(He invited me) to make his home my home for the present,' Hudson Taylor reported. Several of them dined together that evening and, writing home a day or two later, Hudson Taylor said,

> I could hardly refrain from tears of joy when welcomed so cordially among them . . . the very kindness of the missionaries who have received me with open arms makes me fear to be burdensome.

He never lost his sense of indebtedness to the LMS and paid tribute to their kindness in his autobiographical *Retrospect* forty years later.

His first night in China was a strange one. His room faced the Chinese city across no-man's-land, and over to his right was the imperial camp (map, p 120). The city walls were 'covered with lights and sentries' after dark and gunfire continued all night. He managed to sleep, however, and in the morning wrote,

At times the report of cannon shakes the house; and one fired this morning near to us woke us before daybreak, making the windows ring violently.

But he was surprised and delighted to hear birdsong, for the first time since leaving England. The following morning too. 'They are fighting now, and while I write the house shakes again with the noise of the reports.' It was his first experience of war and the thought of men dying while he watched, men unprepared for death and eternity, had 'a great effect' on him.

At the first opportunity he went to the consulate to collect his mail. To his distress there was only one letter for him, from home and written in November, and two copies of *The Gleaner*.

I never paid two shillings in my life more willingly than I did for that letter [he recorded].

But what of the CES and the Sissons? To find no credit notes from the Society placed him in great difficulty, for neither had they given him any to carry with him. They had had time enough to send all he needed. Captain Morris of the *Dumfries* received letters dated January.

Slow mail now took four months each way between Great Britain and China, but by the 'overland' route across Egypt and India, only two months. There was a railway from Alexandria to Cairo with carriages 'like cattle vans', in place of purgatory by camel-back, as a link in the fast P & O shipping service. The Suez Canal was not opened until fifteen years later, 1869. But incredibly, both friends and Society had waited until he reached Shanghai before writing. Their inexperience and lack of imagination left him isolated, largely out of touch until July, four months after arrival in a strange land. Mail ships came roughly twice a month, and time after time he went to the consulate – there was no post office – only to be disappointed.

On March 2, the day after his arrival, the *Dumfries* was towed up the Huangpu to Shanghai. He went with a Chinese guide from the LMS to collect his baggage, and returned entranced by the exotic chanting of the coolies they hired to carry his heavy boxes to the mission. But he also found time to visit the hospital and listened to Dr Medhurst preaching to the waiting patients and their attendant relatives. Medhurst was as cordial as the others, no doubt remembering what it was like, thirty-eight years before, when he himself as a lad of twenty reached Malacca and was welcomed by

William Milne and introduced to learning Chinese. To Hudson Taylor he explained that the choice lay between learning the Shanghai dialect with its restricted local use and the language of the mandarins, used with variations by hundreds of millions all over China. Learn mandarin Chinese, he advised, and offered to find him a teacher.

Walter H Medhurst, Sr, honorary DD of Glasgow University, had himself become 'proficient' (whatever that meant) in eleven or twelve languages and dialects, including Dutch, Javanese and Japanese, which he could also write. And he had to his credit fifty-nine publications in Chinese, six in Malay and twenty-seven in English. But his most valuable work, he believed, was his share in the translation of the Delegates' Version of the Bible, completed in 1855. He was more experienced and knowledgeable about China than any other Protestant missionary. Hudson Taylor took his advice. Later the same evening he attended the missionary prayer meeting held at the consulate, and met more missionaries.

With the Medhursts and William Lockhart the LMS had in Shanghai three other outstanding men. Joseph Edkins was still single and after six years thoroughly at home among the Chinese, whether in the city, the Settlement or the countryside. A graduate of London University and an adventurous pioneer evangelist, he too had an extraordinary gift for languages, had acquired a profound knowledge of Chinese literature, became another of the leading Sinologues of his day, and was awarded a DD by Edinburgh University for oriental research. K S Latourette called him a philologist and expert in Chinese religions. He retired eventually to become translator to the Imperial Maritime Customs, and died in 1905 after serving for fifty-seven years in China. He and Wylie did most to show Hudson Taylor how to live and work among the Chinese.

Alexander Wylie was an unassuming widower of thirty-nine, the printer in charge of the London Mission Press but irrepressibly an evangelist at heart. As a cabinet-maker in his youth he picked up, on a London bookstall, a copy of the Jesuit Prémare's Latin-Chinese Grammar, *Notitiae Linguae Sinicae*, and taught himself Latin in order to learn Chinese. In John 1:1 he looked for the words 'God' used twice and 'Word' three times, and so on, laboriously discovering Chinese characters and their meanings. Then he took up printing as a craft.

When James Legge was on leave from Hong Kong in 1846 he met

A MANDARIN TEACHER

Alexander Wylie and seeing in him a man of character encouraged him to go to China. In 1847 the LMS sent him to superintend their press in Shanghai, until then under Dr Medhurst's control. He set out to master the language and, realising the importance of the classics to the Chinese mind, translated the whole of the *Yi Jing* (*I-Ching*) for himself. At the same time he was learning the Tartar languages, Mongolian and especially Manchurian, wrote scholarly articles in English for the *North China Herald*, and in Chinese on geometry, mathematics, mechanics, astronomy, etc., to awaken Chinese minds 'to more exalted conceptions of Him who hath created these orbs . . . and stretched out the heavens by His understanding . . .' James Legge, the first professor of Chinese at Oxford University (1876–97), regarded Wylie as his superior in some branches of Chinese scholarship, and Latourette described him as 'a distinguished and careful scholar in Chinese literature'. He could himself have been more precise, for 'meticulous' was the word to describe Alexander Wylie's work.

When the North China Branch of the Royal Asiatic Society was formed, with Elijah Bridgman as its first president, Wylie was one of the first contributors, with a paper on 'Coins of the Ch'ing Dynasty'. For years he was a byword for versatility and thoroughness. Above all, he too was a zealous evangelist, taking every opportunity to preach the gospel. Hudson Taylor could have wished for no better companion.

The third LMS missionary whose company Hudson Taylor was now to enjoy was William Muirhead. He and his wife had also been seven years in Shanghai and at thirty-two this tall, erect Scottish Presbyterian with prematurely silvered hair was well on the way to becoming the expert Sinologue he was in later life. He became a master of the Confucian classics to equip himself to be a better evangelist and preacher. He too was honoured with an Edinburgh DD, and became the author of theological works and a geography in Chinese which the Japanese government adopted. To his dying day, in 1900, after fifty-three years based in Shanghai, he was able to hold his audience, Chinese or foreign, by the hour. And he too was 'intrepid' in his pioneering journeys into the 'interior'. 'Intrepid' was the word contemporary reports used frequently for these sorties into the unknown.

Two clergymen of the Church Missionary Society also became Hudson Taylor's friends at this time. John Hobson – to be distinguished from Dr Benjamin Hobson of the LMS in Canton, husband of Morrison's daughter Rebecca – was seconded from the CMS to serve as chaplain to the Shanghai Settlement.[11] And John Shaw Burdon, who with his wife had arrived in Shanghai the previous year, was becoming another adventurous pioneer evangelist. In 1874 he became the third bishop of Victoria, Hong Kong, and twenty-three years later returned to 'station' work.

These then were the men among whom Hudson Taylor found himself cast, completely ignorant of how or where to start and, to his great distress, without the guidance or instructions from his Society he had expected to find waiting for him. He set out to discover where he stood, to take himself off the hands of his kind host, and to become capable of managing his own affairs in as short a time as possible. That meant finding a house, establishing financial arrangements with the Shanghai agents of the CES, and learning enough Chinese language and customs to become independent of the missionaries upon whom he had no claim except as a fellow-Christian.

He wrote a batch of letters, long, descriptive and full of praise to God, about his voyage and arrival in China, to George Pearse and Charles Bird of the CES, to his parents and Amelia, to his friend Benjamin Broomhall and Miss Stacey at Tottenham. Now and for several years to come he signed himself 'James H. Taylor', except in intimate notes to Amelia and his mother, when it was 'Hudson'. He wrote up his journal and copied long excerpts for *The Gleaner* and for the enjoyment of his closest circle in England. 'But I am so cold I can neither think nor write,' he added to more than one. The temperature in his room was 37°F and it was little comfort to be told that in two months' time it would be 100°F.

To his parents Hudson unburdened his anxieties:

> My health is wonderfully improved, and I am quite a different being from what I was – so strong and well. My position here at present is anything but pleasant . . . houses are not to be got for love or money . . . no one can live in the city for they are fighting continually almost . . . While I write the house shakes again . . . If I am to stay here (at Shanghae) [the conventional spelling at that time] – I shall have to build . . . You will see how perplexed I am. It will be four months before I hear [from the CES] in reply . . . The Society should have written . . .

For four months he waited, during which he could not act without formal approval of his intentions, either to rent, if he could find premises, or to start building even the simplest place, if he could not – four months with no alternative but to remain a burden to the LMS. He was embarrassed. To the Secretaries in London he wrote in the same sentence as he described the fighting and his rattling windows,

> – there is not a house to be got here, nor part of one even. The houses not occupied by Europeans are filled with the Chinese merchants who have left the City . . . The missionaries who resided in the City have had to leave and reside with others here . . . so had it not been for the kindness of Dr. Lockhart, I should have been quite non-plussed. As it is I scarcely know how to act. How long the present state of things may last, it is impossible to say. If I am to stay here the only plan will be, Dr. Lockhart says, to buy some land and build a house. The land would probably cost $100 to $150 and the house from $300 to $400 more. If peace was restored I could get a house in the City for $200 to $300 per annum, Dr. L. says, so that in any way the expense must be very great, and I do not know whether it would be any less at Hong Kong, or any other port . . . It is so cold I can scarcely feel either pen or paper . . . Coal costs about $30 per ton . . . Please reply with all possible expedition . . . Continue to pray much for me – and may we all, sure of Jesus' love, when everything else fails – seek to be more like Him . . .'

He acknowledged receipt of *The Gleaner* but said nothing about their failure to write or to make any provision for his arrival and need of funds. He was, after all, still only twenty-one. Nor surprisingly, after recording in the journal he was required by the CES to keep and send to them, 'Pleasant evening with Edkins, Wylie and Muirhead', his next entry, on the 4th, was 'very much cast down and have no liberty in prayer'. But he went on to say he was glad not to be dependent on feelings but upon the Rock of Ages.

He had his first taste of threading his way through the Chinese market in the Settlement, and the next day, Sunday, March 5, went with Alexander Wylie into the beleaguered city to see for himself the state of affairs he had already had described to him in gory detail.

'Imps' and Triads   *March 1854*

How much Hudson Taylor learned in the first few weeks we do not know. He had access to back numbers of the *Chinese Register* but Bridgman had ceased publication in 1851. Mission magazines with accounts of events by his LMS and CMS friends will have been available to him. He subscribed at once to the *North China Herald* and seems to have made friends with the editor, Henry Shearman, for we soon read of his receiving two copies for the price of one, which he sent home and to the CES. Because of this he explained that he would not repeat the secular news in his letters. Instead he confined them to affairs with which he was personally concerned.

His visit to the city on his first Sunday, March 5, he described in a long detailed letter. With a bag of Chinese tracts Alexander Wylie and he walked towards the sealed North Gate and followed round the outside of the city wall (map, p 120), through the devastation of 'rows upon rows of houses . . . some burned down, some blown in', just blackened skeletons telling of 'the misery of hundreds if not thousands of poor Chinese' driven in the cold of winter from home and all they possessed. They saw a ladder against the city wall, being used for taking provisions into the city, and climbed it without opposition. They chatted with Triad soldiers, walked along the wall and down among the damaged and destroyed temples, where Wylie preached about the folly of trusting in idols who could not protect themselves, and told his listeners about Jesus. To Hudson Taylor's delight they were welcomed wherever they went.

They passed a place where the 'Imps', as the imperialist forces seem to have been called, had sprung a mine but failed to take advantage of the breach and waited while the Triads built it up again using tea-chests as sandbags. Hundreds of Red Turbans in high spirits were mustering at the West Gate for a surprise attack on the Manchu camp, and fighting was actually taking place at the South Gate, but the LMS chapel and the street leading to it were crowded with people. Every day Dr Medhurst preached there and distributed food to the hungry townsfolk, although the premises had already been damaged by several 'balls'. They met dead and wounded and a captured cannon being brought into the city and Hudson Taylor examined a rebel whose arm had been broken by another 'ball'. Five prisoners 'in great terror' on the way to decapitation 'looked piteously at us and begged us to save them, but we could do nothing . . . The very thought makes one's blood run cold.'

Joseph Edkins had taken over the preaching when the house alongside the chapel was hit, so Dr Medhurst left the city and waited a while outside the East Gate for Wylie and Hudson Taylor to join him (map, p 184, D). After fifteen minutes he set off for the Settlement, and two coolies happened to come and stand where he had been. When Wylie and Hudson Taylor arrived they chatted with the two men while waiting for a 'companion' (perhaps Edkins) who was behind them. Suddenly some batteries on the far side of the Huangpu opened up and as cannonballs began falling uncomfortably close to them, the missionaries ran for cover (no doubt inside the city gates). When they emerged and passed the same spot again, they saw blood trails – and at the hospital entrance found both the coolies, mortally wounded.

It was Hudson Taylor's fourth day in China. The previous day had been a depressing one for him.

> The cold was so great and sudden, and other things so trying, I scarcely knew what I was doing or saying at first. Then the fact of my distance from home – being at the seat of war – not being able to understand or be understood by the native people was realized. Their utter wretchedness and misery, and my inability to help them, not being even able to point them to Jesus, powerfully affected me. Satan came in as a flood – but . . . *Jesus is here* . . . and precious to His own people . . . pray more than ever for me . . . my position is one of great importance and *very very* difficult to be faithful in. I feel daily more and more unable of myself to sustain it. . . . It makes my heart sad when I reflect how long it will be before I can tell the poor perishing Chinese of Jesus' love to *them*. It is very strange that I do not hear from the Society.

Not learning the local dialect, he knew, would add to his difficulty. But he could not be in better hands. Every evening Lockhart and he prayed together and Walter Medhurst went out of his way to help him.

> On Monday I got Dr. Medhurst's Dictionary. The price of the four vols. is $20, but he let me have it for $10. He gave me his dialogues and Dr. Gutzlaff's Grammar. I also got Mr. Edkins' 'Chinese Conversations' . . . Mr. Edkins then went round with me and introduced me to most of the missionaries I had not previously seen.

He dined with Dr Medhurst before the united prayer meeting at the consulate, and must have heard of the day's new excitement but made no mention of it in his letters: with the strength of their thousands the Manchu forces were becoming scornful of the barbarians; they had boarded an American schooner and removed two sailors. This posed an intolerable threat to the Settlement and challenged the consuls to respond. But how?

Hudson Taylor brought his remaining boxes from the *Dumfries*, ill at ease that all the drugs, equipment and household goods, such as travellers took with them in those days, should have to encumber

Dr Lockhart's premises. And on Wednesday, March 8, his mandarin teacher, a northerner from near the Yellow River, arrived and they began work. From nine to twelve and two to five each day they were to be together.

> My prayer is, that while he is teaching me Chinese . . . the Holy Spirit may influence his heart and bring him to Jesus [Hudson Taylor wrote].

Four days later he was chuckling that they were communicating with each other in monosyllables and Hudson Taylor was supplementing the words he could say by pointing to characters in the dictionary. He tried out some phrases on imperialist soldiers whom he met, and ventured out to the shops in the Settlement 'to see if I could understand and make myself understood at all', with some success.

Again the fortnightly mail arrived and instead of home letters, credit notes and instructions from the CES, and the hoped-for beginning of a correspondence with Elizabeth Sissons, the only one was from Benjamin Broomhall, using his new business address at 20 New Bond Street. Hudson Taylor wished he would come to China, but a letter was enough, he said, to bring 'tears of joy into my eyes. I felt we *are one*, though many, many thousands of miles lie between us'. He sat down to write to his parents and the next day to Benjamin, a long and thoughtful letter about his voyage, arrival and conditions as he was finding them. Memories of his first sight of the Waygion islanders off New Guinea enthused him and he wrote persuasively,

> 'Shall we to men benighted, The lamp of life deny?' No! my dear brother, we *must* not, and by the grace of God we will not . . . Shall house or home – shall ease or comfort – shall worldly considerations or ties of affection, prevent us from treading in *His* steps who left *all* for us? Nay – shall *life* itself be valued in comparison with the work of winning souls to God? No! . . . give yourself up entirely to the work of God. I trust you will. I hope you will. We want more labourers, – . . . men of earnest zeal, yet men of caution and prudence. We want men who will love God supremely, and souls next, we want men willing not only to do but also to *suffer* the will of God, – men of *faith* . . . Oh! that I were such an one! My own utter incompetence and insufficiency for this great, this high, this noble undertaking, I feel more and more . . .

On March 17 a 'small, old, unseaworthy sailing vessel' reached Shanghai from Boston, Nova Scotia, with a young American Presbyterian missionary couple on board. The great strength of the church in Korea today in the twentieth century can justly be attributed to that man.[12] John Livingston Nevius and Helen his bride, about Hudson Taylor's age, had sailed on September 9, the day the *Dumfries* slipped her moorings at Liverpool, and they had been six months on the way. Years later Mrs Nevius recalled meeting him, 'almost the first day of our arrival in China'. 'He seemed very young . . . and we were naturally drawn together by having had such similiar experiences and so much in common.'

For several years they seldom met, while he was in Shanghai and they in Ningbo, or for that matter throughout their very full lives, but those first few days of acquaintance allowed Helen Nevius to say, 'Our friendship was that delightful kind which time and separation never changes.'

Few days passed without some new experience or excitement. Wylie took Hudson Taylor that Sunday on a short country excursion across the uninteresting mudflats near Shanghai, 'twenty miles without a hillock', to preach and distribute tracts. A clump of bamboos was the only attractive feature, and it was nearly a month before he saw 'the only view that might be called pretty'. He had his first taste of piping hot Chinese tea, the courtesy symbol offered by hospitable Chinese, in a Buddhist temple and in homes they visited. 'I long to be able to tell them of the gospel of peace,' he wrote to George Pearse, 'and feel more than ever determined, by the blessing of God, to live and die among them.' On returning home to Dr Lockhart's he found in the hospital a man whose leg had been blown off. The following day he went out with William Muirhead after his language study. But on Wednesday he was personally involved in a tense situation.

Hudson Taylor's language teacher left him at midday and on the way home was seized by Triads and searched. Finding what they called imperialist government papers on him they accused him of being a spy and carried him off to the city. Someone ran to Dr Medhurst, and by the time Hudson Taylor heard of it, Medhurst was chasing after them. With torture and decapitations so commonplace, there was not a moment to be lost. In 'consternation' as Hudson Taylor put it, he followed with Muirhead. Medhurst caught up with the rebels and persuaded them to take the teacher to 'the First Chief' who ordered them to release him. These rebels, however, were 'the Second Chief's' men and unwilling to lose their prey. They insisted on reporting to him. The second chief was incensed that they had gone first to his superior and that Dr Medhurst had

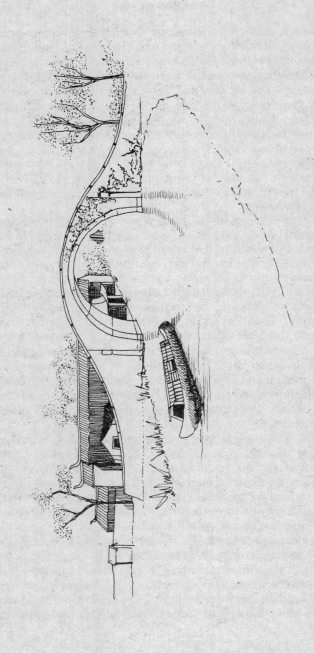

NEAR SHANGHAI: 'THE ONLY VIEW THAT MIGHT BE CALLED PRETTY' (foreground: a 'foot-boat')

pocketed the offending documents. 'In rage' he threatened to have the teacher's head off at once and told Medhurst he could appeal to the consul if he wished. Muirhead and Hudson Taylor arrived while this was going on and one of the Triads led them to Dr Medhurst in the chief's office.

> I never saw such a place before. It reminded me of the den of robbers and tales of banditti I had read of . . . men armed to the teeth kept passing . . . almost enough to make one feel nervous . . . The rebels are very gaily dressed. Long caps richly embroidered, tied on with a red scarf. Rich silk or satin coats with three laps one behind and one each side in red, yellow or both colours, green silk tight trowses (sic) and boots. There are a good many foreigners among them. Some are in Chinese and others in their own costumes. Many rebels are very well armed, having revolvers, double-barreled guns, fowling pieces, etc.

The consul, Rutherford Alcock, acted at once, protesting that the teacher had been 'illegally captured on our ground' and claiming him as under his protection. So he was given up.

Not surprisingly the teacher did not turn up for work the next day, so Hudson Taylor called on Alcock and his vice-consul, T F Wade, to thank them, and went on to visit the *Dumfries*, still in the river and loading bales of tea for the return voyage. Captain Morris was a good friend and had given him the £5 he promised during the voyage. But the seaman of whom Hudson Taylor was most hopeful, 'almost believing' after long talks under the stars, out on the forecastle, was dead. 'I warned him of stopping short of salvation.' He and three others had attended church on March 12. Afterwards they met a friend, went on a drinking spree and, dead drunk, he fell into the Huangpu and was drowned. His was not the only death. The pilot who brought the *Dumfries* into port had been washed overboard and lost.

Hudson Taylor had been unpacking some of his boxes and found 'terrible havoc' among his books and papers, from ink bottles broken in the storms and the heat of the tropics. Salt water had ruined his shoes and some clothing. Only one pair of shoes was now usable. His photographic apparatus was unharmed, however, and as well as using glass he began experimenting with different processes of making photo-sensitive paper. His father's training in chemistry and his uncle Richard Hardey the photographer's skills were to prove useful. Knowing his ability, the CES had instructed him to send photographs for their use in Britain, and in the coming months he was to spend all too much time trying to oblige them, only to find that the climate, especially in the great heat of summer, defeated his attempts again and again. 'I tried to take some collodion views and got some tolerably successful positives, but no negatives that would print,' he explained. It all had to be at the expense of time taken from language study.

Towards the end of March he went into the country at different times with Wylie, Muirhead and Lockhart. He could at least hand out tracts and sell Scripture portions and New Testaments while they preached. The reverence of the Chinese for anything in print or writing drew his admiration; he commented in a home letter on how often in Chinese paintings the subject or a servant in attendance is holding a book. Joseph Edkins returned from a week's visit to the city of Songjiang (Sungkiang), thirty miles away, and told how the people had urged him to come again and to bring a medical man with him. This was just what Hudson Taylor was waiting for. He explained to the Society,

> If I go, I shall therefore take a supply of medicines, and some surgical instruments . . . I do not know whether it may not lead to a more permanent residence, in which case I should probably lay aside *for the present* the study of the Mandarin dialect . . . Unless there is some probability of peace being restored in this place, I shall very likely *try* to reside in some of the villages or towns within a short distance of Shanghai, as it is absolutely necessary to settle somewhere and there is no chance of doing so here, without building . . . Such a step [living in the villages] would, in the present unsettled state of the country, by no means be devoid of danger. But God is able to protect *His* people and there appears no alternative.
>
> Should I go with Mr. Edkins, we shall both adopt the native costume . . . not to deceive them, but merely to avoid the astonishment that foreign clothes always produce; and the continual examination of which is very troublesome, and would frustrate our object, in a great measure.

The initiative in donning Chinese dress must have come from Edkins.

Meanwhile, Wylie and he went out on Sunday, March 26, to the villages and saw at first hand the 'very distressing' plight of the defenceless peasants.

> Wherever we go . . . we find the people lamenting over the devastation committed by the Imperial Soldiers. They rob them of food, clothing and cooking utensils, break up their furniture and make them carry it themselves for them to use as fuel. In many instances . . . they break

what they leave and beat the poor people . . . Unarmed as they are,
they can do nothing against the soldiers, who beat, wound or kill them
and burn their homes . . .

On their way back this time, they met some villagers who were
being plundered but reached the village too late to stop the culprits.
'The poor people were crying and implored us to stay and protect
them.' There was nothing they could do at that stage, but they had
not gone far when another dozen to twenty soldiers came,

> rushing across the fields brandishing their swords. We immediately
> turned back, hoping, as ambassadors of the true Prince of Peace to
> prevent any mischief. Eleven came over; the others seeing us stayed
> behind. The poor people all gathered together like a flock of sheep,
> frightened and not knowing what to do or where to go. After some
> time we induced the eleven to go with us – the others returned the way
> they came.

It was hardly the situation in which a young man without the
language could live alone among the Chinese. He could only stay for
the time being with Dr Lockhart. He went into the city with
Lockhart sometimes – bought Chinese drugs and chemically ana-
lysed them for him (Lockhart was making a large collection of
Chinese materia medica), saw corpses and burning buildings, stopped haemorrhage in wounded men when the doctor was absent, and
quickly increased his self-confidence. His long letter to George
Pearse and Charles Bird ended on the 29th,

> Last night, about 11 p.m., I heard heavier fighting than I had done
> before. The imperialists were attacking the city. They made a great
> noise with shouting, firing, gongs, etc., as usual, and discharged many
> rockets with fire arrows . . .

Unable to sleep, he had stood on the verandah and watched the
battle, a few hundred yards away.

And so his first month in China came to an end, but not his
initiation into life as it was all too often to be, or his anxiety over the
failure of the CES secretaries to write. He protested,

> I have not heard from you . . . I am still in the dark as to the future . . .
> My letter of instructions states I am authorised to draw £80 per annum,
> for my personal expenses, but neither says *how* nor gives the date of
> commencement . . .

It was the beginning of the complaints he was to repeat time and
again in a crescendo of pleas and protests. He was poorer than he

had expected, and still without the means to supplement his dwindling cash in hand.

> The dollars I brought with me are of three kinds: Carolus IIII, Car. III and Ferdinand VII. The first are here called Shanghai Dollars and are well received. The rate of exchange *has been* very high . . . The other two kinds you cannot always pass; they are at 15 to 30 per cent. discount.[13]

For the present his silver was lasting out, but if he did not hear soon from the Society he would be in deep water. On April 26 he had still not heard, but a Mr Skinner of Gibb, Livingstone & Co. 'told me he would always be glad to assist me in any way'. So he lived from mail to mail, two weeks apart, always hopeful but each time disappointed.

The *Dumfries* was delayed a month while one member of the crew recovered from scurvy, repairs were carried out and the cargo of tea was taken on. She then sailed on April 3 and was totally wrecked on the Pescadores on the evening of the 11th; but all aboard were saved, the *China Mail* and London *Times* reported. The hazards were immense. Four times on the voyage out they had come close to disaster, yet here was Hudson Taylor, safely in Shanghai when the ship went down.

The Battle of Muddy Flat[14]   *April 4, 1854*

The Manchu commander-in-chief at Shanghai, Koer-hangar, was faced with an intolerable situation. The city he was meant to be blockading was open on the north to the foreign settlements and they were providing enough food and arms to make the siege a mockery. Large sums were being subscribed by the foreign merchants who hoped for a change of dynasty, and because all trade in the city had been halted and the common people were destitute, rice and meat were being 'plentifully distributed among the poor' by the missionaries. The foreign mercenaries were also adding to Koer-hangar's problems. He decided to tighten his cordon round the city by moving twenty thousand men to Sinza, close to the racecourse and the LMS compound (map, p 184, E). Probably no action against the foreigners was intended. But indiscipline was part of the way of life of his troops, and the presence of so many of them so close to the Settlement was full of potential dangers. Their plundering was brought nearer and bound before long to precipitate trouble. The camp was a fair target for Triad attacks and stray hits on the Settlement had also to be expected. 'Balls often enter the houses of foreign residents.'

The restrictions on the movement of foreigners near Shanghai, due to the fighting, were absent further afield. Joseph Edkins had been able to preach daily to large audiences at Songjiang, at that time a city of higher rank than Shanghai, with a larger population, some thirty miles away. He had found many educated people including women, and was told that he could rent premises without difficulty. Or, as the city was intersected with canals, he could choose to live on a houseboat and move from one part of the city to another. This was what he planned to do. So he hired a boat, Hudson Taylor prepared his medical equipment, and they were ready to start on April 4.

On the 3rd, however, after the *Dumfries* had sailed in the morning for Liverpool, some imperialist soldiers entered a British merchant's warehouse clearly with intent to steal. The merchant ordered them off. They drew their swords and fearing for his life, he shot two of them. Word of the incident spread and several foreigners were caught by surprise and attacked. A Mr and Mrs Aspinall were stoned. A Mr Smith walking with a Mrs Brown received seven severe sword and spear wounds in defending her. Dr Medhurst, returning mounted from the country was accosted by men who tried to seize his horse. Seeing that they were armed with swords and spears and in an ugly mood, he spurred forwards and broke through them.

That afternoon Edkins, Wylie and Hudson Taylor 'were astonished to find the Race Course crowded with Chinese – and to see about fifty (British) marines . . . proceeding towards one of the Impl. camps, and . . . another camp in flames . . .' One account of the day's events spoke of the twenty thousand imperial troops having threatened the international Settlement and begun to plunder property on the perimeter; hyperbole perhaps, but perhaps not. When the marines had been called out they had been fired on, so they had retaliated, shelling and destroying one imperialist camp.

Hudson Taylor woke on the 4th to the 'not unusual sound of guns and musketry, but,' he wrote, 'after the affair of yesterday I wondered what was the cause of it'. He went outside the compound to a group of men among the grave-mounds and learned that only Triad and imperial forces were engaged. 'A ball passing very near me warned me to remove', his letter continued, 'and I came to the Rev. Muirhead's verandah, where I found the bullet had struck the wall of his house, very near him.' His *Retrospect* recalled a bullet passing between them as they stood there on the verandah.

It was six-thirty a m. Together Muirhead and he walked across the Settlement to the riverside Bund, in time to see more action. The Chinese war junks lying off the city were weighing anchor and began to move downstream towards the Settlements and the allies' frigates. Their aim could have been not to get out of danger but to attack, so they were commanded to stop and when some paid no attention and attempted to enter the Suzhou river, a British ship fired on them.

On shore the consuls with the backing of the community agreed to demand the removal of the Manchu camps and cannon from within range of the Settlement. Rutherford Alcock, in his element, sent General Koer-hangar an ultimatum. If he had not begun to move by three p m the marines would be landed again, and if by four p m he had not withdrawn, his men would be driven out and the camps destroyed! The volunteers were mustered outside the English Church (on the site of the present Holy Trinity Cathedral) under vice-consul Thomas Wade and followed the hands of their fob-watches as they crept slowly up to three o'clock. Hudson Taylor described the 'many Gentlemen armed with revolvers, pistols, guns and swords' comprising the corps. The marines and merchant sailors were landed, and all marched under Alcock's command with colours flying and drums beating, along the *ma-lu* to the racecourse.

When the volunteers realised that Koer-hangar had 'refused to budge', 'there was a marked decline in the exuberance which had characterized the march out'. Hawks Pott, a Shanghai man, gave the total force as three hundred and eighty. Other accounts said four hundred, half of them marines and half made up of clerks, merchants and seamen, led by their consuls. In his *Retrospect* Hudson Taylor grouped them as 'a contingent of about three hundred marines and seamen, with a volunteer corps of less than a hundred residents'.

> The officers went forward, and from an eminence viewed the camps. The forces were divided, the Americans taking one side for an attack and the English another. An advanced guard of marines and volunteers prepared to go forward and attack the Camp – and all waited for four o'clock . . . I was startled by the *bang* of the American guns and . . . saw the first shell explode (cf. maps, pp 120, 184, E).

Between them all the Westerners had one field piece, one brass gun and one howitzer, 'the range of our shot and shell making the native artillery useless'. Americans and British alternately shelled the camps and watched the imperialists fleeing in all directions. Then after some time the Americans made a frontal and the British a flanking attack from the north across the flat, open ground. 'It was a moment of breathless anxiety.' Suddenly as the attack began a sea of red turbans appeared among the grave mounds on the south flank. The Triads were seizing their opportunity, uninvited, to join in. The American force quickly ran into difficulties, encountering a deep irrigation channel they were unequipped to cross, and suffered casualties. But the British came to a bridge and crossed over.

J K Fairbank wrote that the allied attack was unexpected. If Koer-hangar had been mistaken in calling what he believed to be Alcock's bluff, he can hardly be blamed, for what could a handful of men do against such an army? But he was to be surprised in another way too. Whatever the reason for the delay, not a shot came from the Chinese until the advance guard were close to the camps. Then, in the words of Hudson Taylor's journal,

> they opened a tremendous fire from the Battery on them. Some of our men fell, and on their again firing our men gave back. I then left my position of observation and went on towards the Camp, to be useful if necessary among the wounded.

But the force rallied and took its objective.

No record states that Hudson Taylor was enlisted as a medical orderly, but it is unlikely that Alcock, the military surgeon, failed to organize available ships' surgeons and civilians in case of need. In the event Hudson Taylor found himself in a maze of water channels and broken bridges, and when he was making for an intact one, met an officer and his men who said the bridge was in the hands of the imperialists and he would be well advised to escape through the water to safety. At that point, he wrote, the war junks in the Suzhou river

> opened fire and the balls passed thickly among us. We took shelter behind a mount and the artillery shelled them . . . In the meantime . . . the two camps were fired, the imps scattered over the country, and all returned home. The number of killed and wounded cannot be accurately told.

– not on that day, perhaps, but it turned out to be an easy victory, for only 'one clerk and one merchant skipper' in the allied force lost their lives.[15] To George Pearse Hudson Taylor added,

> The rebels made a good thing of it and supplied themselves with arms and ammunition from the camps and those which the poor fellows threw away in their flight . . . [– including cannon].

Hudson Taylor's journal continued matter-of-factly, 'Wednesday 5th, Recd. letters, the mail having arrived. Spent 4 hours at Chinese . . .' Whatever else he reported, this was the daily routine – 'at Chinese as usual'.

If he took it all lightheartedly with schoolboy overtones, so did Koer-hangar. The official memorial to the Throne dismissed the incident, explaining that a great wind from the north-east blew smoke from tents ignited by the barbarians' fire-pots, blinding the defending soldiers who prudently withdrew. The memorial may have glossed over the facts, but their rout made the imperial army angry. Not until the autumn was it safe again for foreigners to venture into the countryside, and attempts to settle there were out of the question. Hudson Taylor's hope of an easy solution to his problem of how to get somewhere to live, other than under obligation to another mission, evaporated.

After the battle   *April 1854*

Although the barbarians had surprised the imperial army by their audacity, Rutherford Alcock was no fool. He immediately consulted with his colleagues and community leaders on the defensible boundaries of the Settlement, and built a wall, a stockade and guard posts 'with speed'. The LMS and Lockhart's hospital were outside this perimeter. Hudson Taylor by now had a poor impression of the Manchus' stomach for a fight. He remarked that the new wall would be no obstacle to good soldiers but was possibly enough to discourage 'the Imps'!

> It is difficult to know where it will end [he wrote]. All seems quiet now, but we know not what a day nor an hour may bring forth. Two other ships of war are expected to come here as a further protection for the foreign residents and some of the roads leading to the Settlement are being built up [barricaded] . . . As we are outside the Settlement, [the defences] do not much affect us. We have the Lord, however, a much greater Protector.

The walled area, however, was only an inner enclave. Alcock let it be known to both imperial troops and rebels that infringement of a far wider area would be treated as aggression. The Triads, for instance, must not cross the *pang* or be seen on the racecourse. They would be fired on.

What Hudson Taylor called 'sharp fights' between the Chinese opponents continued daily, as the Triads made the most of the army's disorganisation, but at night there was relative peace and quiet. Feeling secure on the Settlement side of the city the Triads no longer illuminated their north wall and for three weeks Koer-hangar launched no attack.

The wretched villagers scattered over the plain became the victims of the imperial soldiers' chagrin and were ravaged more mercilessly than ever. One fired on a group of people selling food outside the city and hit a woman. His next shot exploded in his gun. When both were brought to the hospital, lying side by side, William Lockhart reckoned that he had attended two thousand wounded since the city fell. But the Triads were little better, torturing the city people to extract money and beheading any suspected of spying. When Hudson Taylor went into the city with Wylie they saw two heads hanging by their *bianzi* (queues). Among the rebels everyone's hair was long. These men had shaved off all but the crown, a sure sign to the Triads that they were about to defect as spies.

On April 19 he 'went for the first time into the city alone and had a long walk there, trying to talk, asking names, etc., all the time'. Three days later he went through the suburbs and –

> looked at the ruins of the temple against the river. Seeing a man's stocking among some stones by the river side . . . I found it to be the half-buried, headless corpse of a man, minus one leg, which had probably been devoured by the dogs . . .

They roamed in packs and wherever he went he had to hold them off with the threat or persuasion of a well-aimed stone. He began to go into the city from time to time, making small purchases and practising the sentences he was learning. Always he was besieged by beggars, 'so glad to receive a few cash, not worth a farthing', and the sight of the headless corpses became familiar to him. But always his refrain was, 'afterwards got to Chinese again'.

If life for Hudson Taylor was gruesome or exciting, it was too much for his teacher, who lived in fear of what might happen to his wife and children in his absence or to himself as he came and went from the LMS premises. Having barely escaped with his life from the rebels, he and a friend were now seized, searched and robbed by imperial soldiers near the racecourse. Hudson Taylor could do little to help him.

He admired the Chinese people. He found the peasants far more polite and forthcoming than their English equivalents, and the educated eager to see his photographic processes or system of chemical analysis. But he was under strain, not only from physical circumstances. In a strictly personal letter in which he exhorted his parents not to repeat what he wrote, lest good missionaries suffer from it, he confessed his disillusionment over the way some others lived.

Towards the end of April he received a formal invitation to a missionary wedding, requesting 'the pleasure of Revd. Mr. Taylor's company at 7½ o'clock on Thursday evening'. Most of the missionary community were present. The band of a ship-of-war was playing, there was a sentimental song about Katey, 'most inappropriate, for Katey was dead and he was kneeling on her grave' – his humour was irrepressible even when he was discouraged. There was a magnificent meal, then prayer and more music!

> The whole affair was most splendid and vastly delighted some of the ladies . . . but to me it was most painful. There is here very little that is not in conformity with the world. The style in which many missionaries live is, I think, scarcely the thing . . . on the other hand some are very *dirty* and vulgar. The Church Missionaries are as far as I have seen them, by far the most pious and consistent . . . I feel very disappointed to see so many missionaries and so little doing, except criticizing, backbiting and sarcastic remarks . . . I long to go into the Country and leave it all . . . We have pious and devoted men in each mission, but they can do little with the example of all the foreign merchants against them . . . I write this to let you see what are really our greatest trials . . . to see unfaithfulness on the part of those who ought to be lights in the world *is* painful . . .

His mother wrote strongly about 'drink and tobacco', afraid that he might indulge in both. He replied, 'As I suppose this is for my edification, . . . the smoking I have given up and wine I take medicinally or at the sacrament. So you need not be alarmed . . .'

The Gleaner was coming to him spasmodically (but still no letters), and some of its contents did not tally with the facts as known in Shanghai. The lapse of months before copies reached China did not help matters. Issacher J Roberts, the visionary, had written of expecting to be in Nanking with the Taiping Wang by October 1, 1853. He was still in Shanghai, not quite in goatskins and girdle but uncouth and prophetic by nature.[16] Hudson Taylor felt he had to warn the secretaries to use Roberts' letters with discretion.

> He seems to be a good man, but is, I fear, deficient in judgement. He is too credulous – believes reports given him . . ., in some instances at any rate, without further authentication – and then is led into error. The newspaper here will not print his letters now . . . I am told, and consequently I do not think it will be desirable for you to place *too* much dependence on information he may send you – I believe him to be a pious man – but wish you to be on your guard.

Word reached Shanghai on April 26 that the *Dumfries* had been lost and before long the details were supplied by the Swedish carpenter who returned to Shanghai on another ship. Hudson Taylor assumed that his journal and other things he was sending home were lost too, but they were salvaged and reached his parents.

The unsettled state of Shanghai drove the rate of exchange higher, and while some advised him to buy at once, others were sure it would fall again. As he had little money Hudson Taylor chose to wait, but the uncertainty added to his anxieties. The American Episcopal bishop, William J Boone, arrived from the States with his party of new missionaries, and wrote that he might have to send the women and children away, but

> my mind is . . . to stand by the work with all the *men* that will cling to me, let what may come . . . Our friends need have no anxiety as to our safety as we can fly to the ships in the case of an emergency . . . I take courage and press on with new force.[17]

But that did not remove his difficulties. The 'high rate of exchange so much against us' ran even his mission heavily into debt, and he was compelled to borrow on personal credit by issuing a promissory note for $1,550 to tide them over. He was a well-known figure. Hudson Taylor was a youth of twenty-one and alone, painfully alone. The LMS missionaries were given adequate allowances in terms of dollars, regardless of the exchange rate from sterling, he told the secretaries. But quite apart from a four-month interval before a reply could come, he might as well whistle for the wind.

Apart from his circumstances he was homesick. He was writing a heart-to-heart letter to Amelia when the mail was delivered with one from his mother. His father never wrote. Reading it brought tears to his eyes, so he went into the privacy of his own bedroom and played his concertina, a close friend. Then he wrote again, 'Pray earnestly for me – you cannot tell how I may be needing (your prayers) when you receive this.'

The letter and his journal mention that he was having considerable trouble with his eyes – severe headaches and inflammation, which made language study and letter-writing difficult. Even so his journal reads, 'managed to learn Chinese for five hours.' And by the way, would they send him a penknife, to sharpen his quills. At last he was making better photographic paper. He would enclose his 'photographic failures'! The successes went to the Society, but none have been preserved.

A little later he was urging his family to write 'as often as possible'. If ships were lost en route it could be a very long time before he heard from home. They often were. 'Now your letters are very precious, you don't know how precious – and you know that I have lost all my friends.' That was a deep heart-cry. If Society and family wrote too seldom, who would expect friends without obligation to do so? When missionaries went away the general feeling was that they were out of reach. So the Hackney and Tottenham friends prayed faithfully but seldom put pen to paper. His cousins and Barnsley friends never. Benjamin had done better. The Sissons – well, he still lived in hope. 'I wish you would give me Father's opinion of Miss Sissons . . . Give her my love.'

CHAPTER FIVE

AMONG THE FORGOTTEN
1854

The wider scene   *1542–1848*

When the Tsar Nicholas I suggested to the British ambassador in January 1853 that the two countries could divide weak Turkey between them, he betrayed the drift of his thinking. He wanted access to the Mediterranean by occupying Constantinople. Britain's traditional policy was to maintain the integrity of Turkey, so when Russia crossed the border and Turkey declared war, Britain followed suit. Napoleon III, looking for prestige and glory, seized on the pretext of a dispute about the holy places in Palestine to join in. So by March 1854 the Crimean War was occupying the full attention of Lord Clarendon, the Foreign Minister under Aberdeen and Palmerston until 1858, and events in East Asia were regarded as less important.

Hong Kong and Singapore, however, were vulnerable to the Russian Pacific fleet. If a few British plums should appear tempting, there was little to prevent their being plucked. While the Shanghai Volunteer Corps was being formed for very different reasons, therefore, similar defence forces began drilling in Hong Kong and Singapore. For missions the Crimean war soon meant the distraction of interest to the plight of the British forces, suffering through mismanagement from cholera, cold, exposure and hunger. Florence Nightingale's departure with her thirty-eight nurses to Scutari caught the public imagination, and support for missions dropped dangerously.

Japan had no current quarrel with Russia, although at intervals Russian ships had attempted to open up trade by force. She was wary of the West in view of Russia's eastward expansion and Britain's opium war with China. Since 1825 Japan's total ban on foreign shipping satisfied her. The *Morrison*[1] had been driven away by gunfire in 1837 and two American ships were rudely rebuffed in 1846, but astute observation of what was going on beyond her shores was changing influential opinion in the country. So when Commodore Perry and his squadron of black ships appeared in Yedo Bay and in the name of the American President proposed opening trade relations, it was a timely move. On July 14, 1853, Perry's four hundred officers and men were met by Japanese officials backed by five thousand and more troops, and his proposition was rejected. Samuel Wells Williams was the Commodore's interpreter, having learnt some Japanese from the shipwrecked sailors he had befriended at the time of the *Morrison* episode. Perry was undismayed. He said he would go away and return for a considered reply. His imposing squadron constituted a threat, and to some extent a decision was forced upon the *shogun*, but in fact his own people were ready for a change. Foreign pressure became the occasion rather than the cause of compliance. When Commodore Perry returned in 1854 Japan was ready to sign a commercial treaty, to be followed by treaties with other powers. So began the rapid conversion of the feudal regime into the monarchical government and modern industrial state of today. The American treaty, signed at Kanagawa, opened the two cities of Hakodate and Sinoda to trade, and ensured human rights for shipwrecked people and general international rights to both parties.

Christianity had been known in Japan since 1542 when Portuguese ships in distress were well received. Seven years later Francis Xavier failed to gain a footing, but other Jesuit missionaries won converts and a church grew up, until knowledge of Spanish and Portuguese conquests by force of arms in other parts of the world, especially the Philippines, aroused Japanese fears. This led to torture, massacre and virtual extermination of the heroic church in 1638. Now, with friendly relationships with the outer world restored, prospects were good. Young Hudson Taylor's comment on hearing in Shanghai of the American treaty was,

> Japan is opened. I trust that soon the name of Jesus will be preached there . . . What a scope there is in the east for missionary operations! [An American marine in Perry's fleet named Jonathan Goble returned to Japan as a missionary.[2]]

One hundred years later Hudson Taylor's own mission was to embark on operations in Japan, after China's 'open century' ended.

The Roman Catholic Church in China was going through the throes of suspicion and persecution by both imperialists and Taipings, but the policy of strict concealment of foreign priests in the interior and proselytising by Chinese converts was still in use and proving effective. Both foreign and Chinese priests were being added (fifty-eight new Jesuits between 1840–57) and in 1851 a far-seeing unofficial synod of vicars-apostolic held in Shanghai recommended to Rome the creation of a hierarchy in China with bishops and archbishops, irrespective of race and elected impartially by Chinese and foreign clergy together. Rome did not accept the proposal, but it was in itself an indication of progress.

In the treaty ports it was a different matter. There was a temple to the Lord of Heaven (the Roman Catholic term for God) and a Cross Street in the city of Shanghai – marks of an ancient Jesuit presence there. The American Episcopalian William Boone had written home in 1845,

> We have several thousand Romanists in this district with whom we shall no doubt come into collision before long. The Romanish (*sic*) bishop, the Count de Bissi . . ., travels about pretty much where he pleases. The Chinese Christians call him 'Da Jen', a title given to the viceroy of the province, and always kneel when they come into his presence.[3]

In comparison, the tally of Protestant missionaries to China was fifty-five, and of communicants in 1853, a total of three hundred and fifty – all too few, but sixty times as many as ten years before (six in 1842) and therefore a significant number.[4] Unlike the Catholics, if only for lack of Christians to hide and escort them, the Protestant missionaries were mostly confined to the five treaty ports and Hong Kong. Adventurous spirits were penetrating beyond the treaty limits without disguise, conspicuous in full Western dress, to test what welcome they might find, but basically schools, hospitals and preaching chapels in the ports were making contact with the Chinese and slowly finding a way for the gospel into the minds and consciences of individuals and communities. In parallel they were translating the Bible and publishing it and Christian books of every description in quantities far beyond what could yet be distributed, and teaching illiterate people, especially Christians, to read.

The Delegates' Committee appointed by the General Missionary Conference at Hong Kong in 1843 had begun work at once, and after setbacks due to deep differences of opinion on the appropriate terms to use for 'God' and 'baptism', had published the New Testament in April 1853 (*see* Appendices 4, 5). Charles Gutzlaff had adapted Medhurst's version to a more colloquial form, and a striking testimony to the purity of its Chinese idiom was the fact that the Taiping rebels reprinted and used it without altering a word (*see* Appendix 6). The CES took it up and Lobscheid proceeded to print an initial ten thousand copies, but as soon as the Delegates' version appeared, educated Chinese showed a preference for it. When Hudson Taylor was in a position to distinguish the differing styles, he favoured a colloquial version for the common people. The story of how he himself undertook to produce one in the Ningbo dialect, and how a colloquial Mandarin version was also sponsored by the Bible Society will be told in its place (1860–65).

A strong foundation was also being laid in knowledge of China, Chinese literature, culture and the language. Missionaries were becoming fluent and correct in its use. Christian leaders were being trained and congregations, still small, being taught how to live and witness together as the family of God. William Boone had ordained his first Chinese minister, Wang Qi, in September, 1851, well ahead of his English counterpart. Latourette judged that the Protestants were making proportionately more progress than the Roman Catholics and potentially much more. But it was all so slow. There was little to be seen for the nearly fifty years of effort since Robert Morrison began. Missionaries of different denominations were crowded side by side in the treaty ports waiting for the opportunity to scatter over the great empire. Not that there were too many of them. Even the LMS had only twelve in China, including the five in Shanghai.

In Hong Kong James Legge and Bishop Smith had their theological college and schools, the American Baptists their church, Wilhelm Lobscheid and Arthur Taylor of the CES theirs, and the Basel Mission pastored a Hakka church while providing a base for the frontline men of the German societies, unbelievably still living unmolested on the mainland. At Canton the LMS, the Wesleyans George Piercy and Josiah Cox going from door to door with New Testaments and being well received, the American Board, essentially Wells Williams, Dr Peter Parker and Dr Benjamin Hobson, and the American Presbyterians all held precariously to their posts. Parker was concurrently US Minister in China. John and Alexander Stronach of the LMS and William C Burns, the Scottish revivalist, now a missionary of the English Presbyterian Mission, were at Amoy. Theirs was the largest Christian congregation of any, a handsome fifty-two, strongly established and outgoing. The CMS, the American Board and Methodist Episcopal Church were struggling against unrelenting opposition at Fuzhou. And at Ningbo the American Presbyterians, American Baptists and the CMS worked in delightful harmony, with the independent veteran Miss Mary Ann Aldersey running her school for girls. In 1851 William J Boone, 'Bishop of Amoy and other parts of China as the Board shall hereafter designate',[5] had opened a school for boys in Shanghai which developed eventually into St John's University. Now in 1854 he was making Shanghai his main centre and laying plans for developing his church in the Yangzi valley.

Gutzlaff's 'solid, continuing missions'[6]   1853–55

George Smith, Bishop of Victoria, and his Hong Kong colleague in the LMS, James Legge, were warm in their admiration of the brave and self-denying German missionaries. If Charles Gutzlaff had achieved nothing else, this group of men and women was a worthy monument to his pioneer spirit. It was immaterial that they were sent and supported by separate 'Chinese Societies' or Associations in Europe. The Rhenish Mission, Basel Mission, Berlin Missionary Association, and the Chinese Evangelization Society formed one team and worked closely together. Following Gutzlaff's method and disregarding treaty restrictions so long as the Chinese officials turned a blind eye, these selfless young men travelled widely on the Guangdong mainland with Christian Chinese companions. Scorning comfort they went on foot or by public passage boats, seldom hiring their own.

Ferdinand Genähr of the Rhenish Mission worked among the Cantonese and married Rudolf Lechler's sister. Lechler of the Basel Mission itinerated for five years among the Haklo of Zhaozhou (Chaochow) near Swatow, without success and then joined Theodore Hamberg in his Hakka work. Hamberg had rented a flight of shops in the market town of Pukak, twelve miles inland from Deep Bay on the Canton estuary, and converted them into a preaching chapel, a school and a home. This was probably the first instance of settled residence by Protestant missionaries outside the treaty ports since W C Milne's Ningbo prelude in 1843. Hamberg spoke Hakka with 'no hesitancy, the words seemed to flow from his lips'. Wilhelm Lobscheid, the first missionary of the CES, was based in Hong Kong but travelled widely among the Cantonese in Guangdong. He was in Canton itself when his new colleagues Arthur Taylor and his bride reached Hong Kong with the two German girls they were escorting.

Hamberg and Genähr happened to be there at the time. They met the party at the ship and took them to Mrs Lobscheid. It was March 4, 1854, three days after Hudson Taylor landed at Shanghai.

On March 17 Rudolf Lechler and his fiancée were married. On the 23rd she, the strongest and healthiest of them all, died dressed in her wedding gown, of the dreaded killer, dysentery. And her friend Miss Poser a few days later. On May 13, after only two years at Pukak, 'loved and respected by everyone', Theodore Hamberg died in Rudolf Lechler's bungalow, also from dysentery. Lechler was left with Hamberg's young widow and 'two fine little boys' to comfort and care for until they returned to Europe.

In an atmosphere of constant disturbances of the peace by robbers and warring villagers he carried on the work, joined soon by a new colleague, Ph. Winnes.[7] Lechler lived into the twentieth century, long enough to see many of the dreams of those brave pioneers fulfilled, but he was the great exception. On August 5 Mrs Lobscheid and her baby died and the Arthur Taylors took two of her other children, although Mrs Taylor herself was ill with dysentery. Five missionaries had died within four months. Within seven months of reaching China Arthur Taylor was writing to George Pearse of the ninth death among South China missionaries in that space of time.

Robert Neumann, Gutzlaff's loyal lieutenant, who continued his work with seven faithful remnants of the ill-fated Chinese Union, kept going only four years before having to return home in broken health. But he in turn handed on Gutzlaff's torch to August Hanspach, who also adopted Gutzlaff's principles and travelled continuously with the Chinese colporteurs, preaching the gospel. They saw their task as being to sow, not necessarily to reap. After the Treaty of Tientsin (Tianjin) in 1858 he penetrated deeply into the interior of China for eleven years, often in danger of his life and more than once severely wounded. Renowned for the speed and extent of his travelling, he created a deep impression on the Chinese. The results of such work he was content to leave with his Master. By 1854 the Basel Mission were able to report two hundred and thirteen baptisms of believers, and in Hong Kong by 1855 there were eighty-seven communicant members of the church Gutzlaff had started. In comparison with most results, these were very striking.

With the example of these men and their success on the forbidden mainland appearing in reports in *The Gleaner*, it is not surprising that the directors of the CES expected Hudson Taylor and other missionaries in the Shanghai area and Arthur Taylor in Hong Kong to emulate them. An indiscreet editorial in May 1855 even took them to task. It recognised that,

> The chief enemies of the truth in China are not the people, but the mandarins; the people generally appear well disposed towards missionaries. It is a cause of regret that a systematic and bold effort has not been made by Protestant missionaries, to penetrate into those parts, where the gospel has never been preached, or the disciples of Loyola have alone dared to go . . .

But the directors were misinformed, remote armchair critics. Every effort was being made and at great risk. Arthur Taylor's wife was ill and had to go on a voyage for her health's sake. In her absence he did go farther afield. He wrote,

> There is room enough in Canton alone for at least 20 more missionaries – I think, however, for a mission at all to prosper in a place where a Foreigner and everything foreign is despised, it must not be independent of the medical missionary principle . . . (The Chinese) crowd around a medical man in China.

The Germans were in the rural areas of Guangdong near Hong Kong. Closer to Canton and northwards up the coast, as Hudson Taylor was to prove, the emperor's ban carried more weight.

Liang A-fa   1826–55

At Canton the leading figure among Protestant Christians was still at work though ageing and infirm. Liang A-fa,[8] the second convert of Morrison and Milne but the first evangelist, the first to be ordained, the first to write Christian tracts and commentaries and without question the most outstanding of his generation, had only a year more to live. His faithfulness and steady growth in maturity had encouraged Robert Morrison back in 1826, when so much was driving him to despair. In a letter to the LMS, A-fa had written,

> Although in the age in which we live we may not see the results (of preaching the gospel), yet we may leave that on record which will transmit the true principles of the gospel to others, in the hope of converting men of succeeding generations.

But in spite of such faith he had wept when saying goodbye to Morrison that he seemed unable to lead his fellow-countrymen to

Christ. Soon afterwards his modest success had begun.

In 1830 Qiu A-gong (Chiu A-kung, Kew A-kang) a young printer at Malacca was converted. Then an incident took place that had vast repercussions, no less than to rock the Qing dynasty on its foundations. It began with the meeting of Liang A-fa with the young Elijah Bridgman and David Abeel on their first arrival in China. Each had separately summed up his impression of A-fa in similar words. 'He bears the image of the Lord Jesus Christ,' Bridgman said. And after A-fa had received the two new missionaries into the infant church in China with a memorable prayer, Abeel described him as 'one in whom appeared so distinctly the image of the Saviour'. But seeing the two intelligent young men drove A-fa to go and say to Robert Morrison, 'I have been a believer in the Saviour for several years but have never yet done anything worthy for God.'

Liang A-fa proceeded to take A-gong aside and together they read through the whole Bible in ten days. Then they printed tracts to take with them, some of them written by A-fa himself, and set out to win young Chinese literati to Christ. Samuel Wells Williams arrived at Canton to find A-fa 'making books as fast as he can' – over seventy thousand tracts and Scriptures yearly.

A-gong had a relative in the Literary Chancellor's retinue, supervising provincial literacy and civil service examinations, so A-fa and A-gong followed the Chancellor for four hundred miles, distributing books and pamphlets in market towns along the way. Through the relative they were authorised to hand books to the candidates as they left the examination halls – thousands of cells on acres of land within high walls. Three literati believed, and the total number of Protestant Chinese Christians rose to ten. Back again in Canton they did the same, hiring coolies to carry the books into the halls and handing them out as fast as they could to twenty-five thousand students as they left. One candidate who took a set of tracts, read and thought about them, was the tall and handsome young village school teacher, Hong Xiu-quan – the future *Taiping Wang* and 'Younger Brother of Jesus', whose revolution was to dominate events in China from 1853 to 1864.

It was almost unbelievable that such liberty as Liang A-fa and Qiu A-gong were enjoying should have been granted, and it was most unlikely to last long. A-fa taught his wife and family from Scripture about persecution being the inseparable accompaniment of preaching the gospel, and Morrison watched in suspense. 'It is as bold a measure as for a tract distributor to go to the townsmen of

Oxford or Cambridge (knowing that the Tower and the block were likely penalties)' he wrote.[9]

Then Lord Napier arrived at Canton and insisted on direct communication with the viceroy. Tempers rose, insults multiplied, Napier posted placards in the city, the insufferable barbarian usurping the prerogative of the emperor's representative. Liang A-fa pressed on while he could. On August 1, 1834, Robert Morrison died. His death drove A-fa to more daring evangelism than ever. For two days he distributed thousands of books without trouble. On the third day a policeman arrested one of A-fa's assistants, but the magistrate ordered him not to be officious over such a small matter. On the following day, however, Liang A-fa himself was taken, with his books. Having his 1820 'criminal record' – for printing two hundred tracts and 'communicating with foreigners and rebels' – and his experience of imprisonment, flogging and fines, his danger was doubly great. He would receive short shrift. He knew what he would do. He broke away from his escort and managed to reach Macao. There he wept bitterly as he told Elijah Bridgman what had happened. It was fear for his family that distressed him. But when a hundred soldiers came to his home, led by a Judas among his converts, the little family had gone. Until he died A-fa was to be held responsible by his own clansmen for the destruction the soldiers then carried out in the village before they left. He could never refund all they demanded.

Again the case against Liang A-fa was his connection with foreigners. His assistants were beaten and the search for him continued. Young John Robert Morrison, acting as an interpreter, learned from the governor of Canton that eight hundred dollars would secure the release of all who had been arrested, but Liang A-fa must be punished. John Morrison paid. And Bridgman hurried A-fa and his twelve-year-old son A-de (A-teh), to whom he was teaching English, Greek and Hebrew, aboard a ship at Lingding (Lintin) Island, sailing for Singapore. On the voyage A-fa recorded this story in full, adding 'My only fear is lest the Chinese officials should injure my wife and daughter.' He returned to the work he had previously been doing in Malacca and lived in exile until the hue and cry at Canton died down. But in 1835, when Walter H Medhurst visited Canton and made his voyage to north China in the *Huron*, A-de was with Elijah Bridgman again and A-fa's wife was safe with A-gong's wife at Huangbo.[10]

In 1839 Liang A-fa was able to return to Canton and for the next twenty years served as evangelist and pastor to the little church in that city, earning a reputation which led to his being cited in both the US Senate and the British Parliament (Appendix 7). But to the end even he saw few results from his efforts and sufferings.

In his last letter to the LMS dated July 15, 1853, he said he was still strong, with good hearing and sight, a strong voice and a healthy body. Less than three years later he lay dying. He exhorted his son to serve the Lord, but A-de subsequently rendered no direct service with the church; commerce and secular importance claimed him. A-fa held his eight-year-old granddaughter's hand and talked about a golden sedan chair coming to carry him to the King's palace.

By April 1855 the Triad rebels in Guangxi and Guangdong provinces around Canton had caused such havoc and suffering among the people that famine was claiming thousands more lives and robbers were everywhere. April was called the 'starving month'. In May the imperial forces gained the upper hand, and so many executions of insurgents and sympathisers took place – about two hundred daily in the last two weeks – that May was called the 'bloody month'. A-fa died on April 12, 1855. To venture out at all was risky, and A-de was a potentially valuable hostage. So Liang A-fa was buried in secret in the early morning, with few kinsmen present. And then he was largely forgotten. In 1905, however, when the Canton Christian College was extending its property on Henan Island, a great-granddaughter of A-fa living in Malaya pointed out that his grave was on the land that had been acquired. So his remains were reinterred at the place of honour in the centre of what became the Lingnan University.

Through a few gallant Chinese Christians and a handful of young Germans, the laborious beginnings by Morrison, Gutzlaff, Bridgman and their colleagues had after nearly fifty years produced a sapling Church in the resistant soil of South China. At Shanghai the soil was barely being ploughed and the vast interior provinces seemed as inaccessible as ever.

Dumb and dependent   *May–August 1854*

With the coming of May 1854 Hudson Taylor had been in Shanghai for two months, still high and dry without instructions from his Society. This strange existence continued and on his twenty-second birthday – his fourth away from home, he pointed out – he was able to say 'I have felt so well and strong lately.' With the spring some beauty had returned to the scene. 'The view from this house is very beautiful – garden, fields of corn, city walls, and showing over the nearer houses, masts and rigging of ships on the river.' And in a few more months autumn anemonies would bathe the scene with colour.[11] But Hudson Taylor was writing before the great heat of summer began. Already the mosquitoes were insufferable; the torments of high summer were only a few weeks away. In saying he felt well he was overlooking his continuing headaches and a prolonged attack of renal colic and haematuria which kept him to his bed. The pain continued periodically for five weeks until the stone was discharged in mid-June. So his letters were thankful, that he did not have to choose between an operation, in the days before anaesthetics and asepsis, and a life of infection and suffering. 'I have seen something of the misery caused by them (the stones) in my surgical course.' Before the spontaneous cure, however, he had some solemn thoughts. Reminded of the deaths in the community around him and the fighting so close at hand, his birthday soliloquy was to wonder whether he would celebrate another and to hope that when his last moment came he might 'hail it with joy'.

If he had felt embarrassed before by being obliged to receive the hospitality of the LMS, by May he was acutely uncomfortable. He could not understand the apparent indifference of his directors to his need for funds and somewhere to live. They neither advised him nor asked the LMS to do so.

> My position is in some respects a very painful one and at times I feel tried almost beyond the power of endurance. But I know it is good for me. *He* who has sent me here sees it to be necessary – and it does reveal the vileness of my own heart to me. Still, it is a painful discipline . . .

Years later George Pearse, the Foreign Secretary of CES admitted that none of them had an inkling of true conditions in Shanghai, or even Hong Kong. Britain and the Continent were their world. But Hudson Taylor was more sensitive than he need have been. His Shanghai friends understood. Alternative accommodation was not to be had. In what has become the universal missionary tradition, they were glad to be hospitable. He wrote of going to Elijah Bridgman for breakfast, to others for a pleasant evening of singing, and enjoyed attending the LMS and CMS chapels. But he could not betray the CES by telling anyone of his plight. His salary was officially £80, to last him a year, and at Dr Lockhart's it was going to be used up in four months.

> I must draw soon, as I have very few Caroline IV Dollars left and Ferdinand VII can seldom be used. My quarter's expenses are large . . . Board $36 Teacher $20 . . .[12]

He must have more, and even then he must live on his own and economise radically; but without enough grasp of Chinese he could not cope – could not even communicate adequately with a Christian cook, let alone unscrupulous shopkeepers. His friends knew this too and welcomed him to stay. It drove him to work hard until he began to say the language was 'not so difficult after all', and 'Time and patience will do wonders . . . You can scarcely tell the pleasure with which one uses a new phrase' – alas, a mood which alternated with despair.

He was not insensitive to the attitudes of his critics, however, when the CES and *The Gleaner* came in for ribaldry and sarcasm:

> last night some of them were . . . speculating on the . . . gullability (*sic*) of the Editors of *Gleaner*; and the quantum of Exaggeration and misrepresentation Mr. Roberts would display in his next letter published in the *Gleaner*.

Before long his own letters were to be edited for publication in such a way as to make him protest indignantly to the CES. In Shanghai some could not understand why he refused to be styled Doctor or Reverend. Did it matter that he was neither, if the courtesy was extended to him? He preferred to do without, whatever people thought.

Shanghai was relatively quiet but rumours abounded and trade was at a standstill. Supplies in the rebel-held city were said to be so low that the Triads were planning to break out and seize another city. The morale of the imperial troops rose accordingly and occasional attacks were launched, but they 'did not venture very near' – so no harm was done!

> Any sudden change *there* (in the city) will not affect our personal safety. But I hope the imperialists will not retake it. The slaughter would be dreadful. Yet if they do not – I fear famine if not plague as well, will make fearful havoc there.

The Triad chiefs let it be known that they were turning Christian, and published a proclamation exhorting everyone to worship God the Heavenly Father. They opened a Temple of the Spirit of Fire in the hope of recognition by the Taiping Wang. But the first Triad chief was an opium smoker, and the rebel leaders took any woman they wanted, threatening torture and death if she was not handed over to them. Nor had the idols in the city temples been removed. So their make-believe was transparent to everyone. They had no understanding of Taiping tenets or Christian teaching, and all was sordid tragedy.

The success of the Taipings was at its zenith however, and the talk was of Peking having already fallen, according to French sources, or of its imminent surrender.

What a Taiping victory, or defeat, would result in, no one could forecast. In April a fracas had taken place near Ningbo between Portuguese and Cantonese smugglers and pirates; sixty miles from Ningbo a local rebellion had ousted the prefect; and Canton was being threatened by thousands of Triads. But uncertainties were wider still. News of the declaration of war by Britain and France against Russia reached Shanghai before the end of May, and Hudson Taylor wondered how it was affecting his parents.

None of these things contributed to his unsettledness so much as his hunger for letters from home. Postage was expensive and his own frequent letters were overwritten at right angles as an economy. Surely they could write more often. He walked the mile or more to the consulate on a broiling day, waited nearly two hours, thereby missing 'tiffin', the midday meal and had the pleasure of bringing letters for everyone at the LMS, but none for himself. He 'felt quite sick and faint and could scarcely walk home . . .' and then added, 'Well a truce to this!' And he began to count his blessings.

Late in June he went to the consulate again and waited for three hours for the mail to be brought ashore and sorted. But again there was nothing for him. Instead of a feast of reading he had to write,

> Is it kind to disappoint me – five minutes writing would tell me you are well? But it has always been so with me. Whatever I set my heart on I lose. I thought Miss V. would prove an exception, but it was not so . . . Do write please. I have no letters, no *Gleaners* – no papers – no companions . . . [At another time it was,] Oh! I wish I could tell you how much I love you all. The love I have in my composition is nearly all pent up, and so it lets me feel its force. I never knew how much I loved you all before . . . You would (write by every mail) I know if you saw how disappointed I am when a mail comes and no letter.

Yet another time only a bill of lading came for him. Surely Charles Bird of the CES could have put in at least a few friendly lines with it. But his longings went further, as he confided to his mother,

> I am glad to hear any news of Miss Vaughan you may have. She may get a richer and handsomer husband – but I question whether she will get one more devoted than I should have been. But I see she is not fit for a missionary's wife. It is very improbable that I shall meet with one here . . . a good wife – one who could sympathize with me and assist me . . . would be an inestimable prize. But I have not one and must wait and hope as you say. Yet I do trust Miss Sissons would come out if her parents' assent were gained . . . I only fear someone else seeking her first. But the Lord knows best. . . . I am a dull scholar and slow to learn to leave myself *altogether* in His hand. . . . One idol after another has been removed, and yet I have not learned to set my affection wholly on things above.

Then he heard from home, but not the Society, that Dr and Mrs William Parker and children had sailed, to join him in Shanghai. But when? In March or April? When would they arrive and how without funds could he prepare a house in which to receive them? In fact, they sailed on June 6. So in his letter to the secretaries he politely wrote, 'I shall no doubt hear positively [about Parker] before he arrives.' It was unbelievable that they could fail him in that too.

Settling in   *June–July 1854*

The heat and humidity in June were insufferable. 'We have been in a sort of vapour bath.' At 98°F it was most 'oppressive' but the temperature was often higher. They were all 'sweating like bakers', too bound by convention to adapt their clothing adequately to such conditions. He found it hard to breathe and almost impossible to study or write letters. In July it was worse. When the thermometer registered 98°F the water they drank was so tepid as to be 'just the temperature to use as an emetic'. He was covered from head to foot 'with an eruption of lichen caused by the heat' and felt 'as if I must tear myself to pieces'. It was his first experience of prickly heat. Even in these conditions he ground on at the language, putting in five hours daily. 'Gutzlaff's Grammar', he purred, 'contains in a small space, a vast and invaluable amount of information (with) examples innumerable.' Always given to writing at night, he took advantage of the semi-coolness to go on with his letters until one a m or later.

Sitting still indoors with a hand fan might be cooler than going out in the roasting sun, but somehow it was more tolerable to be doing something, even in coat and cravat. Out on the canals in a boat would actually be cooler. So from time to time, with John Burdon or Alexander Wylie or both, when hostilities permitted, Hudson Taylor would load up with tracts, Bibles and medical bag and venture into the countryside. While the others preached he would examine and treat people, even to doing a simple pterygium or entropion operation on trachoma patients with inturned eyelids. 'We were everywhere welcomed by the people' was his comment after one expedition in June. When they reached home again he stayed the evening with the Burdons, playing his concertina and singing. At last he could write,

> I think I may say I have one friend now – but I do not want to go too often, as I am only one of his circle, and he has a wife too for company. I feel the want of a companion very much.

Apart from the five or six hours with his Chinese teacher an average day would hold for him many hours alone, reading and writing or pursuing the hobbies he developed. Increasingly he helped in Dr Lockhart's hospital, mentioning in his letters an amputation of the arm one day and the removal of a small tumour from his teacher's scalp on another, but busy though William Lockhart was, he knew that fluency in Chinese came first, and spared Hudson Taylor to study. He had strong views on doctors dividing their time between two occupations.

> A man attempts to follow two professions and always fails signally in one, sometimes in both . . . as a layman he can do all the teaching and preaching that he has opportunity and ability for . . .[13]

– but medicals should concentrate on doctoring while others preached. It worked well in his hospital. Hudson Taylor meanwhile was thinking, 'besides learning Chinese I do not want to lose sight of my late studies . . .', so he distilled ether, read chemistry, watched or assisted at operations and took a close interest in Lockhart's large collection of Chinese materia medica, for all of which the Royal College of Surgeons gave Hudson Taylor full credit in due course.

One day he visited a temple in the city and watched a woman worshipping the idols. It stirred him deeply. He had to speak. Calling on all the Chinese he had learned in three months he protested – idols cannot hear or help, only the true God. To his delight he saw that the temple attendant understood, laughed and supplied words when he came to a halt.

He began to go shopping on his own. There were bargains to be had in the increasingly deserted and derelict city as people sold their possessions, even whole libraries, to buy food – for a song he picked up bottles to hold the chemicals he was preparing, books, musical instruments, a musical stone. It all gave him opportunities to use the language, and a new pastime – transcribing tunes from Chinese to Western notation.

> The weather is now too hot to take photos by the Collodion or Calotype processes [he wrote], and I have not yet found a suitable wax for the wax-paper process.

Daguerrotypes (of 1837) were still in vogue and wet collodion photography was only five years old. Dry plates were not available until 1874, twenty years in the future, so do-it-yourself photography was the only way. But there were more than enough other interests. With Wylie he watched Chinese printers at work and commented,

> Really the Chinese are a most ingenious people, and do everything in the most simple, but at the same time effective manner.

The Chinese charitable institutions in the city pleased him. In spite of the siege there were a foundling hospital, sixteen free schools for children of the poor with five hundred attending, aid for the very old, coffins for the destitute and reverent preservation of books and writing of any kind. He began collecting insects and botanical specimens, and saw his first swallowtail butterfly. 'When it lit on a tree I saw the splendid thing and it quite paralysed me for a second, it was so fine.' But he could not catch it. On another occasion he left the Settlement to hunt insects after dark – the fireflies with light generators in their tails intrigued him – and found himself shut out and being challenged by the sentries. In his journal and letters he sometimes devoted a full page to commenting on the plants, flowers, fruit and crops. In two months the maize had grown shoulder high, the first of three crops in the year.

Nevertheless as the weeks wore on Hudson Taylor became increasingly conscious of being the odd-man-out, different from most and unattached to any.

'Harassed' *August 1854*

The baking heat of summer dragged slowly on through July and August, and with it the unremitting tensions of the stop-go war, just over the Settlement wall and the *pang*. T P Crawford reported that all the missionaries were in 'more than usual health' but 'very much harassed by the unsettled state of things' and longing for the return of peace. Under Rutherford Alcock's influence and Walter Medhurst's chairmanship the Municipal Council, like a small parliament, set up an administrative system with Land Regulations which they submitted to a folk-moot of tenants and owners and to the *daotai*. Poor man, his life had been saved by two foreigners, and he could hardly object when they were assigned to securing his approval of this strengthening of foreign control. As a plot of land conceded to the barbarians by the emperor, the Settlement was kept in the hands of the foreign residents and they governed it and the Chinese refugees who were allowed to rent and build in it. Naturally the merchant *taipans*' voice carried most weight. A police force of thirty-two armed men was set up, to deal with the drifting population of sailors and adventurers, and at long last a post office was opened. Because of the complexity of differing laws in the national legal systems of the nations involved, including China, the consuls retained judicial powers. In course of time a voluntary fire brigade, a health department to cope with epidemics, and a licensing system for opium shops and dens followed.

In the Chinese city morale was falling. The common people lost faith in the idols and some gave their own idols away. Missionaries were treated as true friends and the chapels were filled. But skirmishes and cannon duels continued almost daily. A cannonball fell within ten or twenty yards of Hudson Taylor, and one night the fighting was so noisy that he thought the city must have been taken. Three mines, tunnelled at a cost of two thousand taels each,[14] were sprung, breaching the south wall but killing many imperial soldiers. The hundred or so who succeeded in entering the city were not supported. The Triads made a sortie, repulsed the imperialists and repaired the walls 'with astonishing alacrity'.

The first northern army of Taiping rebels was still being held at Duliu, near Tianjin, and the second army had failed to join up with it. Encouraged by the prospects, an independent revolt sprang up in Shandong and Henan provinces, coming to be called the Nian rebellion. Swollen later by the addition of Taiping troops, it developed into another serious threat to the dynasty. By their hold on Nanking and Zhenjiang (Chinkiang) the Taipings controlled its main artery, the Yangzi River, and the imperial fleet of seventy vessels lay helpless while the normally vast trade stagnated. In June Elijah Bridgman and another missionary reached Nanking as interpreters in an American embassy but on their return had little new to add to what was already known. Because it was a political mission, they explained, they neither gave away Christian books nor received any from the rebels. They watched the Taipings' religious ceremonies but 'took note of no details'. Knowledge of the true nature of the movement was advanced very little, though so much depended upon it.

Zhenjiang at the junction of the Grand Canal with the Yangzi was, they reported, no more than a fort, deserted except by the rebels and vendors of food. The beautiful pagodas and temples, the pride of all China, had been destroyed and their stones used for fortifications. Nanking was a vast camp, or two camps of men and women separately, well-dressed in red and yellow, well-fed and well-regimented, with provisions in abundance, but under fanatical despots with blasphemous ideas. Admittedly, in their documents the Taiping Wang's name was raised one space above the rest, the imperial privilege, while the name of God and the Bible were raised three places. But the powerful 'Eastern King' of the Taiping hierarchy had assumed the title of Holy Spirit, using Morrison's term, a ploy as it turned out to filch power from the Taiping Wang, Hong Xiu-quan, who only boasted of being the Younger Brother of Jesus.

> They declared that God had sent them to subdue China, and that they were *not only to have China but the whole world under them . . .* one Kingdom on earth as there is one in heaven

– and expected foreign visitors to bring tribute with them.

The American plenipotentiary brought discouraging reports for those who hoped that the rebellion might lead to a Christian China, and when the steamships HMS *Styx* and HMS *Rattler* went up to Nanking they were 'snubbed' by the Taipings. Many missionaries were studying the situation carefully, led by their doyen, Dr Medhurst. Both he and the Bishop of Victoria, Hong Kong, detected two competing elements in the movement, a good and a bad. One of the Taiping princes was Hong Ren (Hung Jen), cousin of Hong Xiu-quan, and at one time a good evangelist. From him

Theodore Hamberg, before his death, had learned all he could and wrote what was perhaps the best account of the Taipings' history and beliefs. But the Eastern and Western Kings were schemers, introducing fantastic ideas and behaviour. 'Every well-wisher of China,' the bishop wrote, 'will ardently desire that Taiping Wang and the Southern King may regain the religious control and direction of the movement.' It was not to be.[15] Hudson Taylor in writing to his parents echoed the general fear,

> The struggle will probably last 10 to 20 years – and thousands of lives be lost before peace and tranquility are regained . . . all parties are filling the people with fear and the country with cruelty . . . Nothing seems certain but that the people must suffer.

He was right. It was 1864 before the rebellion ended. The Taipings were in fact getting 'worse and worse'. A month later he commented,

> You will probably have heard what a *dreadful* set the (Taipings) are . . . They are meeting with many reverses in the north now – and may possibly be put down after all.

To George Pearse he had written,

> I hear that they do not want and will not permit, the residence of foreign missionaries among them . . . their object is to expel a dynasty, because it is a foreign one and they can scarcely be expected to desire still greater foreigners among them . . . each successive mission of enquiry is worse treated; and should they ultimately succeed and continue their present policy, collision with some of the foreign powers may be anticipated . . . They seem to be boxed in at Nankin . . . as the imps. have 50,000 troops, and the steamers on their return met 50 junks on their way to attack. There seems to be every reason to fear, that there is more evil mixed up with them than we hoped was the case . . . But the *Word of God* is there . . . They do not like our ships to go up – it is evidently part of their policy to avoid contact with the foreign powers at present . . .

If that was indeed the Taiping policy, it was certainly reciprocated by the new plenipotentiary for Britain, Sir John Bowring, who arrived at Shanghai with the admiral commanding the eastern fleet. Their main concern was to sound out the Peking government on a revision of the twelve-year-old Treaty of Nanking, unsatisfactory in many points to merchants, missionaries and British government alike. They were also keeping a watch on the Russian fleet, provocatively cruising unnecessarily far south. But a first-hand look at the Triad and Taiping situation came a close third.

Sir John Bowring (1792–1872) was an eminent orientalist, better known to the Asian scene as Dr Bowring, HBM Consul in Siam and Canton, an experienced diplomat and a Chinese scholar of note. He was notable as a linguist in twelve European languages, Arabic and Chinese, and in 1855 wrote *The Kingdom and People of Siam*. Very different from his predecessor, the stolid Sir George Bonham, Bowring was full of energy and zeal. While on leave in Britain he had been knighted, and returned to Hong Kong in April, 1854, accredited as Minister Plenipotentiary to 'China, Japan, Siam, Cochin China and Corea', no less. The inaccessibility of all but two of these countries explained the title in prophetic rather than practical terms. Where Rutherford Alcock was a master administrator, Bowring was a reformer, J K Fairbank observes.[16]

To Christians he was familiar as the author of the hymn, 'In the cross of Christ I glory, Towering o'er the wrecks of time.' The legend that he wrote it after seeing the cross on top of the burning St Paul's Church at Macao, wreathed in smoke and flames, is unlikely to be true, for the hymn was written in 1825, when he was thirty-three, before his tour of duty in China. Whatever his religious beliefs at that time, in 1854, while he believed in the inevitable triumph of 'commerce and Christianity in natural and necessary alliance to promote the progress of the pacific principle', he was a Unitarian, according to W A P Martin. Sir Henry Parkes called him 'a man of considerable ability but full of self-conceit'. He was the most unpopular of governors of Hong Kong, but this was perhaps because he tried, unsuccessfully, to bring aesthetic and practical order out of the chaos of a town that had been allowed to grow unplanned; and to create a waterfront. The mighty merchants had put down roots and could not be dislodged.

So now in Shanghai, when the British and American plenipotentiaries insisted on their merchants paying the customs dues not collected during the upheavals of the rebellion, the merchants resisted them – and established the nicety that the treaty put the onus on the Chinese to *collect* the dues, not on the merchants to pay them.

Judging that the highly specialised nature of dealings with the Chinese required intimately knowledgeable diplomats to represent the British Crown, Sir John Bowring initiated a system of young diplomatic cadets. They began by learning the customs, culture and

language of China and by working as interpreters, later to rise by
stages as assistant consuls, vice-consuls and acting consuls to full
consular and ministerial dignity.

Sir John formed his own opinion of the Taiping movement, a view
so strongly critical of the rebels that he favoured not only the
Manchus, but active aid for them. The Jesuits and French minister
supported him in this so when the French openly sided with the
imperialists against the Triads at Shanghai and against the Taipings
along the Yangzi, Bowring approved. He also revealed a bias
against Protestant missionaries, which Lord Clarendon at the
Foreign Office was to remark upon. When Bowring refused to allow
Walter Medhurst, the acknowledged authority on things Chinese,
to accompany the British treaty delegation, this prompted an
editorial protest in the secular *North China Herald* denouncing the
'strange fraternization' between 'liberalism and Romanism'.

The fourth Annual Report of the Chinese Evangelization Society
presented in May 1854 was still sanguine. Two missionaries had
already been sent to China with the aim of making Nanking the
'chief mission station' of the Society, it claimed. Presumably Hudson Taylor and Arthur Taylor who sailed on October 14, 1853, were
referred to, as Lobscheid was the only other. Dr William Parker was
waiting to leave with his family very shortly. Hudson Taylor, the
report said, was 'well known to many members of the Board and
greatly esteemed'. 'It is intended that he should remain at
(Shanghai) until an opening at some large town presents itself. He
. . . has taken a large supply of instruments and medicines.' When
this reached him in July or August he at last knew what they were
thinking, for the Society still had not sent him any but disciplinary
instructions.

The CMS report for the same year aired the Bishop of Victoria's
optimism.[17] 'We have the means to send out twenty additional
missionaries to China. But where are the men?' A reserve fund of
ten thousand pounds had been in hand for three years already. And
in the universities, the chief source of personnel, the interest among
Christians was becoming directed to China. The bishop's hopes of a
pro-Christian victory in China were tempered, however, by the
prospect of a wild rush to the choicest locations. 'The representatives of every sect will then probably hasten to the head quarters of
the new dynasty.' Disunity could wreck things at the outset. At least
the Chinese Evangelization Society had its eyes on Nanking and not
Peking.

Hudson Taylor waited and prayed as he watched his meagre supply of Spanish dollars dwindle, but still in vain. A letter dated May 6 came from Mr Pearse acknowledging his of March, but failed to answer his queries. He was stretching his pittance to cover all his expenses, personal and missionary. Could they possibly mean that eighty pounds per annum was to house, feed and clothe him, pay for his language teacher, his travelling expenses, his subscription to the *Herald* for the Society and incidentally to supply them with photographs and curios, and pay costly postage on his journals and the Chinese books they asked him to send them? They did. It was the figure Lobscheid had given them in an unthinking moment.

With the Taiping advance, and talk in *The Gleaner* of a new Christian dynasty, donations to the CES multiplied. From ninety pounds in their second year, receipts had risen to seven hundred and sixty in the third and two thousand pounds in the financial year just completed. But instead of consolidating commitments already undertaken they extended their responsibilities to support more missionaries and Chinese workers in China and Penang.

What, then, was Hudson Taylor to do about preparing for the Parkers' arrival? They were well on the way when he wrote on July 7, and again on the 14th, but he only knew of it by hearsay;

> . . . where they are to go, I cannot at present foresee – for houses in Shanghai are neither to be had for love or money. To sleep on a ground floor here, is only one step removed from suicide [inviting fever and death]. The only plan will be to build if Dr. P and family make Shanghai their station. This is a very bad time for building because all the land within the limits [of the Settlement] is felt to be more valuable and secure, and is consequently dearer than formerly.

Eight hundred to a thousand pounds would be needed for a small house but the only alternative was to abandon Shanghai. No wonder he added,

> I have been much tried since I arrived here, almost 'pressed beyond measure' sometimes. But the goodness of God is never-failing . . . the last few days I have enjoyed . . . such a personal application of some of the promises, as tho' they were written and spoken directly to me . . . [And to his parents, about the Parkers, there was] nowhere for them to go . . . and I suppose (the CES) will expect me to provide him with a residence.

It was suffocatingly hot, 98°F and not a breath of air stirring. When the temperature dropped to 85° he remarked that it was refreshingly cool. But the daily round continued. His journal and letters were peppered with odds and ends. He had at last mastered a thousand Chinese characters, but Bishop Boone's party of new missionaries had arrived knowing a thousand two hundred already – the CES must provide new missionaries with books for the voyage. He had translated a tract into simple mandarin for practice and his teacher told him the result was unintelligible. Never mind, study was 'now getting very interesting'. He was reading Aesop's Fables in Chinese and was keeping up his five to six hours of study daily, as well as reading medicine, natural history, chemistry, theology, Greek, Hebrew and much else.

But he wished he was learning the local dialect. On an evening stroll in the Settlement he 'met multitudes of Chinese and felt very sad at not . . . being able to speak to them of Jesus' dying love'. Still, there were several baptisms at the LMS chapel and this was always a delight to him. On a jaunt to the ruins of a temple he had found eight or ten idols rotting away. Only two were in good condition, six to eight feet high. 'I should very much like to see them grace your committee rooms', but the freight on them would be prohibitive 'so I left them to rot' too. There was an epidemic of dysentery in the Settlement. It was dragging him down. 'I think the water has something to do with it.' If he had acted on that hunch and insisted on the unfailing use of only boiled water in the kitchen he could have made history. But it was not to be.

Then, suddenly, nothing venture, nothing win, he resolved his perplexities by deciding to leave the comfort and comparative safety of Dr Lockhart's home and house-hunt in the city suburb, the no-man's-land between rebel and Manchu forces, outside the North gate (map, p 184, c). Premises were available there. The owners had moved into the Settlement to escape hostilities. Hudson Taylor heard of a place and on Saturday, August 12, Alexander Wylie went with him to see it, an empty Chinese house half a mile beyond the *pang* and Lockhart's hospital, and beyond protection by the foreign guards. Dirty and dilapidated but large and useful, it could be repaired and cleaned up for use as a dispensary, a schoolroom and a chapel. He himself could live upstairs.

On Monday he had 'a most harassing day' negotiating with the suspicious Chinese owners. Why, after all, should a foreigner want their house so close to the rebel bastion? They demanded a deposit of a hundred and eighty dollars and ten dollars a month in rent. So 'that settled the matter'. But on Thursday he found another house nearby and his offer of eight dollars and no deposit was accepted, with vacant possession on Monday, August 21. He signed the agreement. Now he was committed to going there, though 'ill and very weak'. The prospect alone was enough to make a veteran quail, and he had not been in China six months.

CHAPTER SIX

TRIAL BY FIRE
1854

'Nothing venture, nothing win'　　　　　　　*August–September 1854*

The North Gate suburb was a straggling mass of battered shops and houses, reaching nearly to the *pang* but clustered more closely towards the bricked-up city gate. Barricades and barred gates closed the roads at night and the main houses backed on to moats or creeks of foul water, little more than stagnant sewers. Occupied by neither imperial nor rebel soldiers this no-man's land was accessible to each and vulnerable to musket or cannon fire from both the imperial camps and rebels on the city wall. Desperate men and women remained there with their children, to protect their property if they could or for lack of an alternative.

Monday, August 21, came and the house was Hudson Taylor's. It was culturally essential for him to employ a cook and a water-carrier if he was to have 'face' among the Chinese as a teacher, and for the sake of some privacy he decided to remove a set of stairs and unnecessary doorways before moving in, so he hired some men and, to keep them at work, sat learning Chinese and writing letters while hammering and whitewashing went on around him. To George Pearse he explained,

> The house I have taken is in a very dangerous neighbourhood, exposed to injury from both rebels and imperialists – but I take it for several reasons. 1st. I must go somewhere. 2nd. I cannot pay a high rent, and in the settlement houses are not procurable for $100 to $200 per annum. Consequently, as this is the best situated of two or three unoccupied . . . it is quite a boon . . . Tho' there seems no prospect of getting up country for several years, I wish to be ready for any opening that may offer . . . If Mr. Parker and family dare come and live in the same house, or can come, (for if there should be fighting in the street – as there has been before – or if the premises were set on fire, ladies or children could not escape as men perhaps might) the items of rent and servants and fuel for cooking would be unaltered. [Listing the barest costs he went on,] Therefore, tho' this is an expensive mission, it will not be rendered unnecessarily so by me – and I think compared

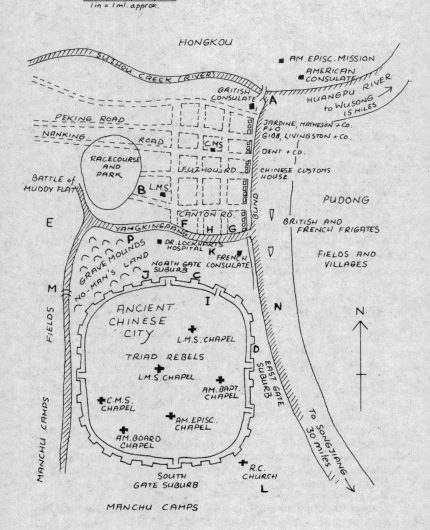

SHANGHAI CITY and FOREIGN
SETTLEMENTS   1854~60

1 in = 1 ml. approx.

HONGKOU

SUZHOU CREEK (RIVER)

AM. EPISC. MISSION
AMERICAN CONSULATE

BRITISH CONSULATE   A   HUANGPU RIVER
to WUSONG 15 MILES

PEKING ROAD
NANKING   ROAD
C.M.S.
FUZHOU RD.

JARDINE, MATHESON + CO.
P.+O.
GIBB, LIVINGSTON + CO.
DENT + CO.
CHINESE CUSTOMS HOUSE

RACECOURSE AND PARK

BATTLE of MUDDY FLAT   B L.M.S.

PUDONG

BUND

E   CANTON RD.   F H G
YANGKINGPANG   BRITISH AND FRENCH FRIGATES

P   FIELDS AND VILLAGES
GRAVE MOUNDS   DR. LOCKHART'S HOSPITAL
K FRENCH CONSULATE
NO-MAN'S LAND   NORTH GATE SUBURB
J   C

M   I

ANCIENT CHINESE CITY   N

L.M.S. CHAPEL

TRIAD REBELS   D
L.M.S. CHAPEL   EAST GATE SUBURB

FIELDS   AM. BAPT. CHAPEL

C.M.S. CHAPEL   AM. EPISC. CHAPEL

AM. BOARD CHAPEL   To SONGJIANG 30 miles

MANCHU CAMPS

R.C. CHURCH
SOUTH GATE SUBURB   L

MANCHU CAMPS

N

with other missions will be very economical. If my house proves uninhabitable or unsafe, I do not know what Dr. Parker and family are to do – and in any way, building here will be the cheapest and only plan if you intend a permanent mission . . . What am I to do as regards a chapel in the city when I am able to preach in this dialect?

His directors must think realistically about the cost of developing the work if they wanted to keep a rein on expenses. They had left little to his own discretion.

After his mandarin teacher's brushes with both Triads and imperialists, to venture into the suburb would be unsafe, so Hudson Taylor employed a local Christian named Si to teach him the dialect, and asked approval of the CES to employ a mandarin teacher as well. On the Saturday evening he wrote up his journal,

> 25th. Cool and pleasant, the thermometer at noon being 90°F 26th Took a walk in the evening, and found on the bridge leading to the French Quarter, a man weltering in blood, cold, and scarcely conscious. I got some men to carry him to my new house, and gave him some medicine, after which the pulse, at first barely perceptible, regained its power. He had four gashes in the scalp . . . and several severe contusions. After he was revived and his wounds dressed, he began to thank me in true Chinese style, going down on his knees and bowing to the ground, but I told him to rise, and the teacher who is to instruct me in Shanghai Dialect, coming in at the time, I got him to tell him (not) to thank men, but to worship the only true God·, . . .

At last the house was ready for Hudson Taylor to move in, and in spite of high tides, flooding the roads inches deep in some places, he began to move his possessions. John Burdon showed him how to check his cook's daily purchases and avoid being overcharged, and went with him to buy furniture. The price of everything appalled him. Then on a Wednesday, August 30, after six months as Dr Lockhart's paying guest, he made this journal entry,

> Removed my bed and other things to new house, and having determined to sleep here from tonight, dined for the first time in it. Having resolved to have family prayers in Chinese twice a day, with my servants and neighbours, collected them this evening, got teacher 'Si' to read a portion of Luke and pray with them. Afterwards felt great liberty and confidence in God, while commending myself to His kind care, and Fatherly protection.

It was a moment for bunting and bugles, the inauguration of independent missionary work by the second missionary of the

Chinese Evangelization Society, and Lockhart had the right sense
of occasion. Before breakfast a messenger came from him with two
precious bottles of chutney, followed later in the day by a gift of two
bottles of wine.

Now Hudson Taylor was on his own and gaining experience the
hard way. Very soon, after an evening at Dr Medhurst's, he set off
for 'home', a ten minute walk at most, with his servant carrying a
lantern. The Settlement gates were closed and he was challenged by
the American guard, but the corporal opened them to let him
through.

> I imagined all my troubles were over (having already been in some
> tolerably deep puddles), but never was a poor fellow more deceived;
> for when I came to the . . . bridge, [over the *pang*], I found it had
> disappeared (map, p 184, F).

Failing to find a boat they slithered about in the mud, making for
another bridge in the French quarter to the east (map, p 184, G).
Getting past the French sentries with a mixture of languages was
'truly laughable', but wherever he tried after that he found walls or
closed gates or guards who refused to let them pass. So back to the
American guards he had to go again, made another fruitless search
for a boat and then went westwards to find a third bridge (map, p
184, H). The candle in the lantern had long since burnt out and both
he and his man were 'tired and wet and dirty'. 'In silence, for fear of
rebel guns' they clambered over a barricade and across the third
bridge, to wander 'through water and mud and grass', taking wrong
turnings until brought to a standstill by an impassable pool of water.
Retracing their steps once more they tried again and were congratu-
lating themselves on being near home when they found the suburb
gates barred and bolted. A pack of dogs 'soon put an end to our
scruples' about noise. But no one would open them. Then he
remembered that the first empty house he had inspected had a low
window in the outer wall which could be used as a way through. Like
burglars they broke in, found their way to the street, and before
long were thumping at their own front door – at midnight, three
hours after leaving Dr Medhurst's.

Such a curiosity as a young foreigner coming to live among them
brought neighbours flocking in to see him and Hudson Taylor's first
few days were busy with entertaining and trying to use mandarin
Chinese to talk with them. He treated a few patients, opened an
abscess, performed some chemical experiments for an old man who

wanted 'to see something of the Foreign System' and 'seemed greatly surprised and pleased, but when I showed him the heat produced by diluting cold sulphuric acid with cold water, his surprise was boundless almost.' 'This is indeed the day of small things', he commented early on, 'but small seeds oftentimes have much fruit and must not be despised.'

After a week, with half a dozen attending his meetings, he decided to adopt Joseph Edkins' suggestion to start a small school for the neighbours' children with Mr Si as their teacher. As his mandarin language teacher he employed 'a B.A.', a Mr Dzien from Songjiang, a city Hudson Taylor was to know well before long. Whenever free from callers he worked at the dialect, taking his turn with the rest at household prayers to read a verse of Scripture, with the teacher to prompt or correct him; '. . . it encourages others who are no great scholars to try, by finding they are not alone'. When he went with Si into the besieged city to distribute leaflets, he found it a great help to listen to him reading and explaining the contents to people. And it gave him an idea. Here was a man with a gift for colportage and evangelism. Would the CES support him in such work, under supervision? It would be a proper application of Gutzlaff's principle.

By nightfall he was always tired but it was his only opportunity to study and to write up his journal and the detailed records the CES required of him, of patients treated, New Testaments and tracts distributed, and congregations at his meetings. The Bible Society had made him a grant of three thousand Testaments to distribute selectively. With letters to write too, it was one, two or even four o'clock before he went to sleep. How could he supply statistics, he protested to the Society, when people wandered freely in and out during meetings? But after two weeks the numbers attending had doubled, and by October quadrupled. Twenty-seven people were coming twice daily to hear the gospel. To his delight he found that adaptation from mandarin Chinese to the local dialect was easier than expected and by being less among foreigners he was beginning to use Chinese more freely. 'Every day will increase my capability.' And treating patients was swelling his vocabulary of Chinese medical terms.

The school opened with ten boys and five girls and gave him great pleasure. 'I hear their dear little voices chanting their lessons . . . (it) prevents any thoughts of loneliness,' he wrote. A few weeks later he took to questioning them on what they learned, good practice for himself and the highlight of his day. But to deny loneliness was no more than euphemism, for in the same letter of September 20 he confessed to very mixed feelings about his situation. His house was in a more dangerous location than he had realised, but 'one gets accustomed to it . . . If I feel lonely or timid at night, I recall some of the sweet promises of Divine Protection, and plead them in prayer, and invariably find they compose my mind and keep it in peace.' For 'the Imps' and rebels were no less at each other's throats.

He was not neglecting any possible precautions, he assured his mother, keeping a guarded light burning all night and the swimming belt she had given him ready inflated so that if driven to it he could at a moment's notice make for the *pang* and plunge through it if the bridge planks had been withdrawn. He had discovered that as a young man alone his reputation was at risk. Deprived of a livelihood, the young women and girls in his desperately poor neighbourhood were notoriously opportunist, so 'if I want to go out after dark . . . I never go alone, but take a servant and a lantern'.

His friends in the Settlement supported him in his adventure, so far as their own busy lives allowed. Dr Medhurst welcomed him to tea before each weekly community prayer meeting. Joseph Edkins and John Burdon called on him or invited him to go with them on short expeditions. And he made the acquaintance of a young bachelor from Ningbo, John Quarterman, a colleague of the Neviuses in the American Presbyterian Mission.

In mid-September Edkins, Quarterman and Hudson Taylor hired a boat and went down the Huangpu to distribute Testaments and tracts on the big junks from the far north and south of China. Strategically this was as good a way of sending Scripture to the inaccessible northern provinces as any, and in the tradition of Gutzlaff at Bangkok in 1828. 'In every instance we were well received,' Hudson Taylor reported with his statistics. But on the way back after dark they had to pass the imperial war junks, guarding the river against Triad sorties, and over-ready to shoot if their suspicions were aroused. The 'griffins' called it the 'mosquito fleet', more nuisance than menace, but not to be trifled with. To avoid being fired on,

> Mr. Edkins . . . proposed that we should sing as we passed them, and then they would hear we were foreigners. The boatmen were delighted . . . we approached some ships we took for the fleet, and sang away and passed them very well, but when we (were) prepared to crow over

our success, the boatmen told us we had nearly arrived at the fleet . . .
So again we sang . . . but unfortunately we finished the last verse just
opposite the largest ship . . . 'What next?' cried Mr. Edkins, 'there is
not a moment to lose' but we could not think of a tune and the gong was
going on board the ship.

Each began a different tune, the war-junks' sailors began to
shout, and the boatmen too. 'I began to laugh, for the whole affair
was so irresistibly ludicrous, if it had cost me my life I could not have
refrained.' To the challenge, 'Who are you?' Edkins and Hudson
Taylor shouted 'Englishmen!', Quarterman cried 'American!', and
the boatmen, 'White Devils!' They were allowed to pass.

Cholera was now rife in both city and Settlements. John Burdon
was nursing his wife who had been ill since her confinement three
months before and was getting worse. On September 18 her condition was desperate and 'she was scarcely expected to see the
morning'. But John Burdon was ill too. So although Hudson Taylor
himself was seldom free from dysentery, he went over to them, to let
John get some sleep. Until she died on the 26th he divided his time
between his house and theirs, staying the night when needed, and
after her death he remained with John until midnight, when his
colleague, John Hobson the chaplain, came to be with him. All the
next day Hudson Taylor was making arrangements for the funeral,
until John Burdon locked up and moved over to the Hobsons. And
he joined him again through the agony of packing up his wife's
possessions. Then in John's desolation they went for walks
together.

All this time Hudson Taylor was fighting not only his own
dysentery, but toothache and a pain in his back – that betokened
another kidney stone? At his house in the North Gate suburb all the
water came from the Huangpu. With his carrying-pole and two
buckets the outdoor servant would bring it up from the river to a
butt in the yard and, after solids in it had settled, the cook would use
alum to precipitate organic matter still in suspension, to make it 'fit
for use'. The water in their well was unfit for anything but washing
floors – and to cool bottles of cleansed water to something below
room temperature in the nineties. In the ignorance of the medical
world that dysentery, cholera and typhoid were water-borne, they
blamed exposure to the sun for much of the prevalent illness.

However, that was less worrying than the turn his financial affairs
were taking. The CES at last had acted to meet the situation in
Shanghai, but in rigid committee resolutions – a new source of

confusion. Hudson Taylor pointed out in reply that while they authorised him to draw sixty pounds each quarter, they qualified it as being 'merely a provision against contingencies'. What did they mean? How much was for current expenses? And having said sixty in their letter to him, why did the letter of credit to Gibb, Livingstone & Co., the merchant agents in Shanghai, say forty pounds? (There were as yet no banks in Shanghai.) Again, for their own convenience they instructed him to draw only once a quarter.[1]

He could point out the absurdities and suggest improvements in his instructions, but it would be fully four months before he could hear from them again. Meanwhile he had no idea when the Parker family would arrive – complete strangers depending on him for everything. At least they would have their own funds. He was anxious about the amount of money he had already drawn. 'What the Committee will say, I don't know,' he confided to his mother, 'I hope they will not refuse to accept my bills – I don't think they can.' At any time the revolution could get out of hand leaving him penniless in major emergencies.

Bad news was reaching Shanghai from the south. After the Triads plundered a city near the Bogue, the fortified mouth of the Pearl River, Canton itself came under threat and the pirates in the estuary had a heyday intercepting wealthy refugees fleeing to Macao and Hong Kong. The missionaries at Canton and Huangbo ran the gauntlet to safety, and Dr Bettelheim of the Loochoo Medical Mission had a narrow escape. Pirates had begun their attack on his boat when a foreign ship came in sight and they fled. There was anarchy in Guangxi farther upstream, and in Guangdong the Continental missionaries reported confusion and lawlessness. Bands of dissolute men were pillaging the people. Wilhelm Lobscheid wrote, '"If they are victorious", said a soldier to me, "all the people join them; but when defeated, they throw away their arms, take a basket of earth . . . on their shoulders, and are at once converted into peaceful peasants . . ."'

Lobscheid himself had been robbed of almost everything he had up-country and so was able, empty-handed, to travel through bandit-infested country, some of the time in the company of bandits. He returned to Hong Kong via Pukak and Saiheng, where the Genähr family and Rudolf Lechler were at the time, and found the Genährs in a deplorable state, pitifully ill and 'nearly skeletons', unable to travel to safety. They had fearful tales to tell of rebels, including women, being caught and crucified, taking up to six days

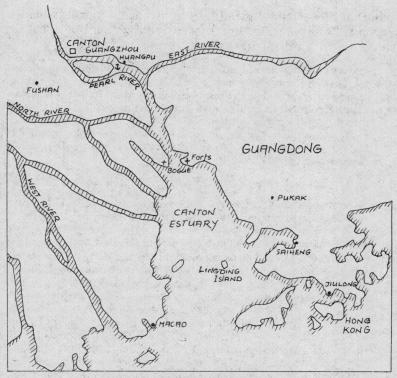

CANTON ESTUARY

to die.[2] Just over the water from Hong Kong Island, Triad insurgents seized Kowloon (Jiulong) and drove the mandarins out. Arthur Taylor wrote that several of them had been rogue members of Gutzlaff's ill-starred Chinese Union. In the southern provinces every man seemed a 'law unto himself'.

During the days after John Burdon's bereavement, Hudson Taylor's own circumstances were difficult.

> (There had been) a good deal of firing about here lately [his journal reads] much nearer than is pleasant, but the Lord, Who is both the *strength* and *shield* of His own people, has mercifully preserved me from harm.

In a letter he said, 'too close to be desirable'. Remarkably, he had made no entry about it during the previous days. It was part and parcel of his new life. Instead he recorded that a friendly Chinese presented him with a singing cricket, to be fed on two grains of newly boiled rice daily. But to his mother he confessed,

> I never passed a more anxious or trying month in my life, but I never *felt* God so present with me. I begin to enjoy the sweet, peaceful resting on Jesus and on the promises I enjoyed in Hull – for that was the brightest part of my Christian career (and how dull at best). Since then I have been in a declining state, but the Lord has brought me back, and as there is no standing still in religion, I trust to experience heights and depths and lengths and breadths of love Divine far exceeding anything I have yet attained to.

On September 30 he wrote to Mr Pearse,

> As to my position, it certainly is one of great peril and risk. For on two successive nights bullets struck the roof just over my head . . . But I feel I am where the Lord has placed me . . . When I hear the great guns near me discharged and the whiz of the balls as they fly over head or pass near the house, I do sometimes feel a little afraid . . . Awakened suddenly by the loud report of the guns from the North Gate Bastion, which shake the house, and hearing the gongs sounding and the discharge of fire arms in the stillness of the night, I have felt lonely, and my heart has palpitated painfully for a few moments, not knowing where these sounds were, nor whether my own home might be the object of attack . . . One night I awoke and found the rooms full of smoke and a strong smell of burning and . . . I was not a little alarmed, for I knew the threat of the imperialists (which I see has got into Saturday's paper) to burn the suburbs as far as the *pang*. But it was only some stubble burning in the field near (by) . . .

'Too hot to be healthy'   *October–November 1854*

Shanghai is in the same latitude as the southern tip of Japan and shares its changeable climate. October ushered in swings of temperature between 89°F and the 50's in twenty-four hours, and in his wretched state of health Hudson Taylor found it a trial. Walks with John Burdon were a cheer to both of them but Hudson Taylor was depressed.

> I have now been in China seven months and am almost useless as a missionary. I long for the time when I shall be able freely to speak of the *love* of *Jesus*.

But stress of a new kind began on October 3.

This morning as I was reading Chinese with my teacher . . . one of Dr. Medhurst's teachers came in in a great fright, saying there was a number of rebels in the house of one of his relatives, doing I know not what.

At this point he was interrupted, mislaid the letter and did not find it again until June the following year. But his journal continued the story. He hurried to the house, five doors away, and found Chaplain Hobson already there. The Triads had packed up the family's possessions, even furniture, ready to carry it all off, but 'took to their heels' when the missionary appeared. '. . . The sight of one foreigner was sufficient to make them . . . run like lamp-lighters,' Hudson Taylor chuckled. The things could not be left or they would return for them, so some were taken to Hobson's house, some to another missionary's, also in the Settlement – and some to Hudson Taylor's; but a house in the same street was another matter.

By allowing this I have not only irritated the Rebels . . . but have given them an additional inducement to break open my own house and take the things, or in revenge fire the premises. However I trust the Lord, Who has the hearts of men at *his* command will not suffer them to come – for *He* is our *only* protector here.

He prepared himself for the worst, even to losing his life.

Felt a good deal of uneasiness, lest the result of my own imprudence should come upon me; but the promises of God set my soul at peace . . .

The night passed without incident, and in the morning he sent most of the teacher's possessions away. But he heard that the Triads were 'a good deal irritated against' him, and the same evening thought he was deliberately fired at twice by men concealed in brushwood between him and the city wall. Both times they missed. Later the same evening more than a dozen bullets passed close to the house and two hit the tiles while he was reading, 'so near as to painfully startle me, knowing there is no escape if an attack is made on the house, nor hope of assistance' . . . 'it makes me feel lonely and nervous'.

Even in these circumstances he carried on his work and although he kept a score of the neighbours' chairs to furnish his large guest-hall, they were not enough to seat his congregations. When dark-ness fell, he went on, '(I) felt very timid and did not sleep soundly, the least noise awakening and startling me. Oh! for more faith.'

Nor did it help his state of mind to find that his teacher, Dzien, was deceiving and stealing from him and had to be dismissed. Hudson Taylor still had Si to help him, but an educated man and especially a *xiu cai* (*hsiu tsai*) or BA, legally immune from physical punishment by the mandarins, had been a great asset.

Then, over the roof-tops of the French quarter and intervening no-man's-land, there drifted to him the very un-Chinese sound of the French naval band. 'The tunes remind me most vividly and painfully of those dear ones (now doubly dear)', he wrote, . . . 'and of the 20,000 miles between us' [by sailing ship round the Cape of Good Hope]. It was just over a year since he had parted from his mother at the Mersey dock. 'But, thank God, I have no desire to go back.'

Armed rebels were going about the suburb now. Attendance at Hudson Taylor's meetings and dispensary dropped, but some eight persisted in coming and the little school and his language study went on as if all was well. Then the cook fell ill with 'typhus', but possibly typhoid, and Hudson Taylor's dysentery worsened. For Sunday, October 8, his journal reads,

> Very poorly . . . but . . . I am in the hands of God, let Him do as seemeth Him best. He can protect me and bring me thro' it, or He can give me a new inheritance among the sanctified. I feel very lonely now, but still am happy and feel I am not alone while Jesus is with me . . . the least noise in the night causes me to awake and my heart palpitates most painfully and I feel so terrified for a few minutes, that I don't know what to do. This, I think is caused by weakness, induced by repeated attacks of diarrhoea.

If the thought occurred to him, he did not record that being involuntarily forced to lie low he was giving the Triads' tempers time to cool off. By the 11th, however, he felt well enough to want a change of scene and planned another boat trip to the Shandong junks at Wusong with another missionary and Si. To his delight the northerners could understand his mandarin speech and when he 'found it impossible to help mixing mandarin with Toopah', the Shanghai dialect, they did not hesitate to call out '*bu dong*' – 'Don't understand!' But it was too much, he relapsed and had to spend most of the weekend in bed, 'very ill all night and today'. Even so he wrote letters and worked at Chinese. He got his March to September accounts balanced and written up for the CES and made a summary for his parents. The exchange rate was swinging between three and eight Spanish dollars to the pound sterling.

Income		Expenses	
provided by G. Pearse	$185	Private: furniture, rent	
from Capt. Morris (£5)	$ 18	wages, fuel, food etc	
drawn from Agents	$261	to June	$165
		Same, July-Sept + school	
		& dispensary + teacher	$238
		Balance in hand	$ 61
	$464		$464

He had subsisted on little more than $150 (about £30), but sixty-one dollars could not see him through to the new year.

> I don't know whether I can get credit (to draw again before the end of the year) and if my agents knew that I had just received a copy of a resolution stating they [the CES] would not accept bills for more than we were authorized to draw – of course it would be refused . . . You will not wonder that the anxiety about my expenses, and as to whether my bills will be honoured or not, added to those of my present position, have been too great a burden for my health to stand against . . . I don't think that less than £200 per annum will cover my expenses . . . The Church Missionary Society allow single men $700 besides paying (rent, medical expenses, teacher, books etc.) . . . To married men they give $1000, besides expenses.

After another week of increasing excitement he added that the cold, below freezing on the 16th, had forced him to buy an old wood-burning stove for ten dollars, instead of a new one for thirty, leaving him only twelve dollars to live on. On the 20th, he was wearing all his clothes including his top coat, indoors.

> What can I do? I must draw soon, and if I can get a bill discounted here I am in terror of its not being accepted by the Committee. I think and study night and day and don't know what to do.

To George Pearse and Charles Bird, even then he did not confess his greatest fears but made his situation as plain to apparently deaf ears as he could.

> I wish (Dr Parker) would come, so that we could consult about the future. I am very much afraid you will find this a much more expensive mission than you expected . . . I shall have to draw again next month

and with *all possible economy cannot alter the present high rate of prices*. I fear the expenses of my first year will be little under £200.0.0: and at that I feel confident there will be no missionary here who will not cost considerably more . . . Do not refuse to accept my bills for I cannot help drawing them – pray for me, for I am almost pressed beyond measure, and were it not that I find the Word of God increasingly precious, and feel *He is* with me, I don't know what I should do.

These problems were worrying enough, but the aggressiveness of both the Triads and Imperialists was increasingly alarming. Men dressed as imperial soldiers were holding up civilians in the country and robbing them as never before. One of Hudson Taylor's patients had been stabbed in the thigh and robbed. Appeal to the mandarins was useless, for the bribes demanded by officials and underlings would only cost more money. The Triads on the other hand were terrorising the suburb. 'They have been firing down the street and over the houses in a very unpleasant promiscuous manner.'

On October 16 a four- or five-pound cannonball fired from the North Gate bastion, just behind them, struck the roof and fell into the courtyard of Hudson Taylor's house two feet from Mr Si's son as he was standing in the doorway holding an infant. Hudson Taylor sent the ball home to his mother in his next box of gifts. On the 17th several musket balls hit the house, but he enlarged in his journal on the four-inch centipedes and ugly flat lizards that infested the place, 'better than scorpions or venomous snakes, neither of which I have seen here yet'.

Drawing freely from his home letters and journal a clear picture of his next experience emerges. On the night of the 18th –

a fire that seemed near alarmed me about ¼ to 3 – I had not been in bed an hour when I awoke and saw a very unusual light to the SE . . . It was an anxious moment. I dressed with all possible speed, prayed God to protect me – and having my swimming belt, watch and purse ready, climbed on to the house top to see if it was coming this way. Chinese houses being made of wood, on a windy night only want 5 minutes each [to catch fire and burn down] . . . I thought it would be here directly. At that moment it began to rain, for which I was more thankful than words can express . . . for I fancied it was not more than four or five doors off – but it got less and less. – [Crouching behind the roof ridge] I heard several bullets strike the houses around me and two or three on my own tiles – When a ball of about a pound's weight struck the ridge of the roof (on the opposite side of the courtyard and) flew off

IN THE NORTH GATE SUBURB
'A ball . . struck the ridge'

obliquely . . . some (fragments of tiles) falling just at my feet, – You
may be sure I did not stop up there for another – After being kept in
suspense till five a.m. I ventured to bed (for an hour or two) . . . I may
have to leave here suddenly – I might even be killed – but whatever
happens I do not rue coming here and would do it again . . . But our
Society must provide for its missionaries as others have to do.

To his surprise he found the next morning that the fire had been
on the other side of the city wall, several hundred yards away (map,
p 184, 1). He had been over there the previous day with Alexander
Wylie and met the Christian mate of a newly-arrived ship. Mr

Farnie came almost daily during his week in port, and stayed late.
There was little Hudson Taylor would have chosen at that time in
preference to the spiritual fellowship they enjoyed. To avoid empty
conversation he proposed that they study together 'the 2nd Coming
of Jesus in His glory'. One night they left Farnie's return too late and
wasted an hour arguing with the Settlement guards before they
would put a plank across the ditch and open the gates for him to
rejoin his ship. Farnie stayed with Hudson Taylor the following
night. 'I never saw a man so drink in the Word of truth. When he
went, I felt it most acutely, if he had been my own brother I could
not have felt it more.'

On October 23 (after a preaching visit to the city with Joseph
Edkins, when he managed to read a chapter from Matthew's Gospel
and comment on it in dialect) Hudson Taylor heard that an American Southern Baptist missionary was dying of cholera. He went
over to Hongkou, the American quarter, two miles away, and
agreed to take turns on duty with him. On the evening of parting
from Farnie he sat up with Mr Pearcy the patient until three a m. At
least it was quieter in Hongkou. [His eye for spelling was never
good, but in a day of haphazard variations in surnames he rang the
changes on this Mr George Pearcy's name, confusing it with George
Piercy, the Wesleyan at Canton, and George Pearse, the CES
secretary.]

Following his night up he snatched what sleep he could and spent
a normal day seeing patients, attending meetings, distributing tracts
in the city and doing some 'practical chemistry' for good measure.
But in the evening some rebels entered another neighbour's house
to plunder, and the old man and his daughter and grandchild fled
through the back door and took refuge with Hudson Taylor. The
next morning they dared not go back, so he went with them – to find
the home ransacked and bereft of almost every movable object. He
stayed while they removed and tried to sell the pathetic relics to
cover the cost of travelling to relatives in the country. And after
another full day's work he took night duty with Pearcy again.

Until mid-November he kept this up, two or three times a week.
Once or twice he went to Alexander Wylie to get some sleep – on
one occasion because, after he had gone into the city with him, a
fracas between the French and rebels prevented his returning home.
He reached 'home' next day by crossing no-man's-land between the
imperialist camp and Triads while a cannon duel was going on
overhead. Pearcy had a long fight for his life but survived. It was no

sinecure nursing him, for he was delirious with 'brain fever' part of the time, and getting to him in all weathers was difficult. Once, in a gale, no boat would cross the Suzhou river and Hudson Taylor had to return home drenched.

On Sundays he questioned his school-children, as on October 29. 'Their little eyes sparkled with delight when I said "Hao! Good!" . . . I believe I felt fully as delighted as they seemed to be.' Then in the afternoon he crossed the Huangpu river with Wylie and they spent four or five hours in the villages telling people the gospel. A group of Buddhist nuns entertained them with tea and of one Hudson Taylor told his parents, '(she was) the only Chinese I have ever seen serious on a religious subject.' He was still a beginner.

October 30 was a red-letter day. John Burdon had decided to relinquish his house in the LMS compound next door to Wylie's, and Hudson Taylor was asked if he would like it. With the Parker family due any day, this was wonderful. But the son of his North Gate Street landlord also came with a proposition. They had seen what was happening to other houses and that occupation by a foreigner was the best insurance they could hope for. So they offered him the place rent-free with liberty to make any alterations he wished. He accepted.

Then a neighbour said his brother was being tortured by the rebels and pleaded for Hudson Taylor to help. The victim was being hoisted from the ground by his hands behind his back and left dangling until he fainted, only to be revived by a dousing with water for the process to begin again. Hudson Taylor went into the city to intervene but there was nothing he could do in the new climate of relations with the Triads. He walked to Hongkou and sat up with George Pearcy all night.

Suddenly fighting flared between the imperialists and rebels. It 'rather startled me,' his Sunday home-letter said. As usual cannon duels meant balls flying over the house from both directions. The Triad guns on the city wall shook the house, but the imperialists let fly indiscriminately, and so were 'most dreaded', especially at eleven p m this night. The French were moving towards a policy of open collaboration with the government, whether or not the British and Americans remained neutral, and a French 'stir' against the rebels in the city prevented Wylie and Hudson Taylor making another of their visits on November 4.

The next day they succeeded. Like the apostle Paul in Athens, Hudson Taylor was so distressed to see a woman burning incense and worshipping idols that he expostulated. Turning to an old man in a knot of people, to his own surprise he poured out, in very stumbling dialect, Were they not all in distress and misery? What was the cause of it? Why, sin! the sin of forsaking the true Creator God to worship false gods. But God sent Jesus to save them from sin and misery. They must repent and turn to Him. It was the longest speech he had attempted. To his delight he saw that they were understanding and answering him. At last he was beginning to get through to them, no longer wholly dependent on Si or a missionary companion. He wrote to Amelia and his parents wishing they were in Shanghai too! Why, if he could do it, so could they. 'In less than eight months Father would be preaching in Chinese I know,' Mother could have a meeting for women, so neglected, and Amelia a school for girls.

The North Gate suburb was 'too hot to be healthy' he had to admit, and becoming uninhabitable – 'I gave up attempting to sleep except in the daytime' – but the LMS might need John Burdon's house before long. So he began discussing with his friends the prospect of some journeys to test the possibility of residence inland. Joseph Edkins was the most experienced traveller so far, and always ready for another 'excursion to the interior'. As a favour the LMS rent for the house was no more than a nominal thirty pounds a quarter, nearly all of Hudson Taylor's income at the 'contingency' level, but for the Parkers' sake it was imperative to take the house, looking to them to pay their share when they arrived, even if for the present he would be left penniless. It was a quandary whichever way he looked at it, except that at this moment he heard of a vacancy in a merchant's office for two hours daily after six p m, with a salary of two hundred pounds per annum. It looked 'very inviting', he eventually told his Society, and the Committee's resolution not to honour irregular bills nearly drove him to it. But to accept would be to lower his standards and take time from his primary occupation, so he let the chance go by.

On November 2 and 3, under pressure of so many kinds he at last gave vent to his feelings. The Society's resolution had been rankling for weeks. Later he apologised for using strong expressions when he was 'nervous and irritable', but they form a useful window on his circumstances and exasperation. The Board of Management had ordered that full particulars of purposes for which money was drawn should be reported in advance – but it was impossible to know in advance! He *must* keep money in hand. So he demanded, must he really consult them about everything, benches for his meeting room, the hire of a boat, and wait four months for a reply? Why, the opportunities would be lost and requests for authorisation be irrelevant.

> If I had heard of those resolutions from another quarter, I should have believed either there were no lay members on the committee, or if there were they were asleep or absent at the time it was passed.

Parsons only! Such resolutions involved –

> forgetfulness that we cannot spend the money before we get it, and a great thoughtlessness as to the kind of merchants we have to deal with; but would seem to be drawn up by men who did not know there was such a thing as fluctuation of exchange . . .

The tensions in his circumstances were telling on him. By way of apology he explained that he was entirely isolated from missionary companionship and 'these things, and sickness, and spiritual conflicts . . . are at times almost more than I can bear . . . I would give anything for one Christian *Friend* – acquaintances there is no lack of.' He meant friendship without restraints. His brand of pietism was different from the devotional experience of his LMS and CMS friends. Their prayers were more formal, their conversation less larded with the language of Scripture, and he could not lay bare his soul to them in the affectionate, confiding way he had known hitherto. The Society could not help him in *this* situation, but surely they could trust his integrity? He was financially embarrassed and anxious as well as being in great danger.

> Your missionaries are sent to a country in a state of revolution . . . they should be well provided against contingencies before you adopt such an *ultra* measure (as to refuse to honour bills drawn) – a measure that would *at once* and *for ever* destroy their credit if any they have – a measure compared with which their dismissal by the Society would not be severe. At any rate, if not accepted, such bills should not be positively refused, before you hear the reasons which led to their being drawn. PS. I have only one dollar left, and so shall have to draw, probably tomorrow.

He postponed his visit to Gibb, Livingstone & Company for his pathetic amount of cash, and wrote home instead, despondently and critically, expressing youthful censure of the missionary community. Only the LMS and half a dozen others in Shanghai, were worth their salt. One or two were very fluent, spoke like Chinese, but preached only once a week. How did they pass their time? Before long he learned to appreciate the achievements of the Sinologues, but for the present he could not understand. Then he caught sight of himself and added, to Amelia,

> I don't think I am the same Hudson 'I used to was' as you say, at any rate my laughing humours do not often make their appearance now . . .

Three days later he had to act on his option on the LMS house. Another client wanted it. To let it go would leave him without provision of any kind for the Parkers. He drew twenty pounds from the agents and paid a first instalment of the rent. It was his until the end of the year. After that the LMS would prolong the agreement only month by month. A new missionary, the young Welshman Griffith John, and his bride were about to sail.

That night Hudson Taylor 'slept once more on the South side [beyond the *pang*, the limit of safety] but determined it should be the last time . . .' He took possession of the LMS house the next day and sub-let half of it to the other applicant, the Rev Dr Jenkins, an American in the same predicament as himself, bravely hanging on, with his family, to his house near the Chinese city, but at last forced to withdraw. As refugees they would not grumble about close quarters in makeshift conditions. But how would Dr William Parker like living in the two remaining rooms and sharing the kitchen and other facilities?

Hudson Taylor had no intention of changing his daytime pattern of work. It was only the freedom to sleep safely at night that he wanted. As safe, that is, as he used to be when Dr Lockhart's windows shook and stray shot struck the houses. He stayed at his North Gate suburb for the evening meeting with the fourteen or so neighbours and his own employees who formed its nucleus, went to the LMS house to sleep and was back for the morning meeting and breakfast the next day. By then patients would be waiting to be seen, if all was quiet, and between interruptions he and Mr Si would work at the dialect. After lunch they would go into the rebel-held city and walk through the streets giving out tracts and talking with people or preaching to larger groups, especially if Wylie or another missionary were there too. That was the pattern, but only three weeks remained in which to carry it out, and they were turbulent.

He told his parents that with the Russian war in the Crimea and the alarming increase in piracy in Asian waters 'everything seems to be in doubt and uncertainty'. They had apparently rebuked him for inquiring about Marianne and Elizabeth. 'If only you knew how lonely it was . . . neither to hear one word of English, nor see one English face you would not wonder at me,' he pleaded. Shivering beside a little fire, for fuel was so expensive, he thought of the beggars in the city without even clothes or food and was ashamed of his self-pity. But where was the Parkers' ship, the *Swiftsure*? It was long overdue. He was getting anxious. He judged that he needed a change such as a country preaching trip would provide, 'to know what opportunity there may be for residence in the interior'. But a little sense of the ridiculous had survived. 'I should not be inclined to sneeze at a pair of warm worsted stockings now as I once did – but there is no danger, as I have none to sneeze at . . . All my clothes are so shabby I am ashamed to go out . . . my topcoat alone excepted.'

An end and a beginning   *November–December 1854*

On his first morning after sleeping at the LMS, November 8, Hudson Taylor was hurrying to the North Gate suburb for breakfast when he found a company of American guards at the bridge over the *pang* (map, p 184, F) and on the other side a company of Triads withdrawing. A confrontation had just ended without violence. He asked what had happened and the guards said some rebels had come into the Settlement and were being driven out. Were they allowed in at all, he asked? Yes, but only in small unarmed groups, to buy provisions. So Hudson Taylor caught up with the Triads, explained in Chinese what the guards had said, and advised that two or three civilians be sent instead. They were very grateful and followed his advice at once.

As he reached his house in the suburbs he saw hundreds of rebels streaming down the city wall at the North Gate bastion (map, p 184, J) to make a flanking attack on the imperialists at the West Gate. Because some would be going to their death, he talked with them, saying 'how happy they would be if believing in Jesus', necessity spurring him on to use what language he had learned. Soon afterwards he heard the battle in progress. It went against the Triads and some, retreating, tried to get into the Settlement for sanctuary. Imperial troops followed and fired on the resisting foreign guards. The whole force of American marines was then landed to repel the imperialists and the French prepared to join in against the Triads;

but a timely withdrawal by both Chinese factions forestalled a major incident. Hostilities had cut Hudson Taylor off from the Settlement, but when all was quiet he returned to the LMS. It was late that evening that he tried unsuccessfully to get to George Pearcy, 'suffering an attack of brain fever'. 'After getting wet through, my umbrella blown to pieces and my lantern blown out, I had to give up in despair . . .' (re. map, p 184, A).

He reported the trends to his Society, expecting the Western powers to become seriously embroiled before long with one faction or other. The French were already preventing supplies from reaching the rebels from the Settlement side, the only route open, and that last relatively quiet corner of no-man's-land outside the walled city (map, K) was becoming a battlefield. Even in the Settlement food was costly and difficult to procure, but the plight of the common people in the besieged city was desperate. As Hudson Taylor saw for himself when Wylie and he walked six miles to preach and distribute Scripture at Jiangwan, halfway to Wusong, the fields were rich with a succession of crops on the alluvial soil. Green shoots and golden grain side by side prompted long notes in his journal on what was growing and at what stage. But the abundance so near at hand was in stark contrast with the misery of Shanghai.

At four a m the Triads attacked the imperial camp again, but even so there were seventeen Chinese at the morning meeting when Hudson Taylor arrived at his North Gate house. They kept coming daily as long as he was able to reach them.

Then the bridge over the *pang* began to be taken up at an earlier hour each evening, until one day he was almost too late to cross. It was not difficult to read the signs. He began to pack up and remove his possessions from the suburb, 'as I expect before the middle of the week there will be an outbreak among the French who, like tigers in human form, appear to thirst for blood, for the mere pleasure of drawing it.'

In broad daylight three French soldiers raped a woman in the street behind Hudson Taylor's house, holding the Chinese off at bayonet point. His neighbours asked his advice and he sent Mr Si with them to the French consul. But 'being very pleased with their men, they wanted to hear no complaints'.

Asked to protect a man while he dismantled and removed his possessions, he obliged and went with them. All he had left was his doors and window frames. It was these he wanted to save. Even so

Hudson Taylor installed a chimney and windows for his own school-room, hoping to carry on.

On November 18 some 'alarming news' reached him – he does not say what. But the next day, Sunday, the house next door was set on fire at two places. His own was saved only by the strenuous efforts of servants and neighbours eager to keep a foreigner among them. Something was afoot, but he could not find out what, and stayed out of the walled city.

On the 21st he had breakfast in the Settlement for the first time but went over to the suburb as usual. People were selling their valuables and he bought a fine book of Chinese materia medica and began studying it – an indication of his progress in academic Chinese. But on the 23rd the Americans followed the French example and began to build a wall which would finally preclude access to the suburb (map, p 184, F–G). There was nothing left but to close the school on the 25th, say goodbye to Mr Si and move everything over to the Settlement.

> When the scholars left, they came upstairs and thanked me, but my heart was too full to reply, and it was with difficulty I could refrain from tears at seeing (the good work) broken up by the officiousness of a set of men, like the French here have proved themselves.

He was seen off by thirty or forty people lamenting his departure and their own inability to escape the threatening dangers. While he was there they felt safer. He stood and talked with them, explaining the world's miseries as the product of sin for which there was a cure. As he went on to tell them of hope in the life to come, through faith in Jesus Christ, 'in Whom alone true safety is to be found', the audience grew bigger. But the problem of how to get food was dominating their thoughts, and he 'went away sad at heart'.

The next day was Sunday again and after morning worship Alexander Wylie and Hudson Taylor crossed no-man's-land to the south of the city (map, p 184, L) to visit the Longhua (Dragon) pagoda and preach. Cannonballs hurtling overhead 'startled' them but all was well. On Monday, November 27, the way to the North Gate house was still open, so he went across to visit his friends. While he was there an urgent message came from Dr Lockhart asking him to return at once, but not saying why. Was he in danger of being shut out of the Settlement? Or had Lockhart heard of an impending attack? In fact William Lockhart simply had the measure of Hudson Taylor's sense of humour. 'Wondering whatever could

THE PAGODA AT LONGHUA

be the cause of so unusual a summons, I lost no time in obeying it, and on arriving there was no less surprised and pleased to find Dr. Parker at tiffin with him.'[3]

He was caught unprepared. If the *Swiftsure* had been delayed into the new month or the Society had not imposed its tight regulations, he could have drawn more cash and furnished the house, however frugally, to receive the Parkers. But here they were, Mrs Parker and the children still on board in the river off the Bund but impatient to touch terra-firma again – with almost empty rooms awaiting them.

Red dawn on the Parker period   *November–December 1854*

William Parker, MD Glasgow, was a no-nonsense Scotsman, mature, experienced, sent out by the Chinese Evangelization Society but supported entirely by its Glasgow auxiliary. From the start he felt independent of the main Society. When they urged him to go, at the height of Taiping hopes, he said No, he was not ready. He needed to be a self-sufficient surgeon if he was going to work many miles from any other. When he arrived at Shanghai he quietly formed his opinions, made his plans and looked for the means to carry them out. He was a man after the veteran William Lockhart's own heart and could have had as notable a missionary career. Hudson Taylor and he knew little of each other and had never met. Their oneness in the missionary cause as members of the same society brought them together and helped them to live harmoniously in spite of strong differences. Parker was a Presbyterian, Hudson Taylor by choice unlabelled and wishing denominational barriers could be demolished. His links with the Methodist reformers were tenuous and although favouring 'believer's baptism', he belonged neither to the Baptists nor the Brethren.

His very openness gave ammunition to his critics. After the Parkers moved in with him and the Jenkins family, sharing kitchen and toilet facilities, only one slight hint of friction appeared in their accounts of months of exasperation ahead.

Dr Lockhart was 'very kind and attentive'. When it became known that young Hudson Taylor was not ready to receive his colleagues, Dr and Mrs Medhurst opened their home to the Parkers while the deficiencies were made good. Eyebrows were raised and tongues wagged, as Hudson Taylor knew they would, but he made his explanations only to the Parkers and, again very frankly, to George Pearse and Charles Bird in London. For he had been caught still without credit or authorisation to provide housing, furniture, fuel or food for them, and no means of his own.

> I have had no *official* notice of the departure of Dr. P. and family, nor been authorized to go to any expense in preparing for them, nor have had a line from Dr. P. himself on that or any other subject.

It was nine months since he had written about his own predicament on arrival, the first of many reminders. Yet Parker revealed that he himself had little cash, no credit notes and no authorisation to draw from Gibb, Livingstone & Company. He had been assured that he would find them waiting for him in Shanghai. To his 'great astonishment', instead of many letters for him there was only one, from Charles Bird of the CES conveying nothing but a copy of the regrettable resolutions for the restriction of their missionaries, 'necessary no doubt'.

When they called on the agents together Parker found they had received nothing either. This was 'a nice fix' he told his journal, but Mr Skinner at the agents' office 'who stated that he was no friend of missions' offered to cash a bill if Hudson Taylor would endorse it. 'As for Mr. Taylor, he was passing rich with *three* dollars in his pocket'. Mr Skinner agreed to advance twenty pounds if Hudson Taylor would write a letter asking him to do so, quoting the CES official letter which authorised him to draw sixty pounds per quarter, instead of the £40 notified to them, and would get the extract signed by two merchants.

This was humiliation upon humiliation. However, when Hudson Taylor and Parker went back with the document, the firm was too busy to deal with it. Not until several days after their arrival did they have money to pay for the beds, furniture, coal and food William Parker ordered (while with the Medhursts) in the belief that he would draw cash the next day. 'Though he has said little, I am sure he has felt it,' Hudson Taylor noted. He gave a fuller account of the episode when he wrote to George Pearse. The godly and well-meaning but overworked stockbroker and honorary Foreign Secretary of the CES took the brunt of rebukes from all and sundry for the ineptness of the Board and Managing Committee, the indiscretion of *The Gleaner*'s editor and the inefficiency of the salaried Charles Bird. Pearse's copy of the resolutions came into Hudson Taylor's hands years afterwards, showing that his own wiser views had not prevailed. At the end he had scrawled, 'Law, law, all law . . . withdraw' the whole document.

In early December 1854, Hudson Taylor had another serious matter to bring to the attention of the Society. Its publications were again criticising other missions, especially the LMS, their generous hosts in Shanghai. So he pleaded that,

> irrational statements such as that . . . we want the Bible and not Chinese classics, would be better avoided for the credit of the Society and *Gleaner* . . . You should not voluntarily irritate those who are more *thoughtful* for the *shelter* and *support* of your missionaries, than the Society which sends them out, seems to be . . . [But that was not all; they would lose good missionaries if they did not make provision for them on their arrival in China.] Of course, the (community), when they found I had made no preparation, blamed me very much. Could I tell them that having paid nearly $20 rent I had only $3 in the world – a sum not sufficient to pay my own week's provisions bill at the present rate of prices? . . .

All the Parkers wrote was, 'It is not very pleasant to be in a house almost empty, with scarcely the means of buying coals to warm our dear little ones.' If they were uncomplaining, it was because of what they had endured on the *Swiftsure*, during six months at sea. In the first week smallpox had appeared among the crew. On the giant rollers of the Indian Ocean Mrs Parker had given birth to a son and a week later they were becalmed for six weeks in the oven-like heat of the equator. Then they had run into a typhoon and received such a battering that they had little hope of survival. While two men had stayed lashed to the helm and sailors stood ready to cut away the masts, the captain had sent the passengers into the forecastle, believing the poop would be carried away. Yet here they were.

Safe from the sea the Parkers lost no time in receiving their baptism of fire on land. On their third day, while they were still with the Medhursts, a cannon or musket 'ball' fell close to the Medhursts' daughter while she walking in front of the house. 'I am not a little surprised', Parker's journal reads for that day, 'that the people here are so little annoyed at the sound of war close by. The Mission grounds are so near the City walls.' (map, p 184, B).

On the next day, November 30, however, he went into the city with Hudson Taylor and saw how 'ill-fed' the people were. This time he was impressed that God was 'opening the hearts and country', when he saw how they gathered round and listened attentively while Hudson Taylor spoke to them. He thought he was in good health 'and has made considerable progress in the Chinese language'. This was the day when the Parker family moved into the little house with the Jenkins family and Hudson Taylor. There were 'only three habitable rooms' in their half, and domestic life with small children made the Parkers' two rooms impossible for doing language study, so Hudson Taylor's bedroom had to be the classroom by day. No shred of privacy remained for him until night fell. They shared the fourth, the dining-room, for receiving guests and holding family prayers. With them on the voyage had been a Chinese youth from near Shanghai and William Parker arrived able 'to converse a little with him'.

By the weekend they were more or less settled in and on Sunday, December 3, Parker joined Wylie and Hudson Taylor on his first preaching expedition into the country. As usual it involved crossing no-man's-land between the city and the imperial camps (map, p 184, P and M), but this time they went up to an observation post, talked mandarin with the pickets and left gospels with them. Their return journey naturally lay across the same territory. They had come to the remains of a half-dismantled bridge when to their dismay they saw a body of Triads coming out of the city to attack the outpost where they had just been. 'We were in the interesting position of being between the two batteries,' was how Hudson Taylor put it. Scrambling across the debris for all they were worth, they fled towards the Settlement and five minutes later watched the rebels firing at 'the Imps' from that very bridge.

On the 6th more history was made.[4] At last the French threw off any pretence of neutrality and without regard for their allies, the

AN 'IMP' OUTPOST

British and Americans, openly sided with the imperial government against the Triads, a move which led on perceptibly to co-operation against the Taipings also, and the involvement of Britain on their side. Dr Lockhart got wind of a French ultimatum to the Triads and preparations for a dawn attack on the city and acted at once. At eleven p m he secured a promise from the French admiral not to fire or attack before five a m, to give him time to go to the rebel chiefs and persuade them to yield to the demand of unconditional submission to the French. Wylie went with him and at two am they succeeded in reaching the Triad top command. Doing their best to convince the chiefs that the odds were too great and that they would be starved out if not defeated in battle, with untold suffering for the thousands of civilians in the city with them, the two missionaries expostulated until close on five am without effect. The Triads deliberated, could not trust the French not to hand them over to the Manchus, and decided to fight it out.

The battle went on late into the afternoon of the second day before the imperial and French command called a halt. The city was unbroken, but the French had suffered sixty-four casualties and the imperial army twelve hundred killed and a thousand wounded. As a reflection of the bizarre element in all these events, young Hudson Taylor then proceeded to visit the city. He did not say how – whether by passing the French outposts near the East Gate and being admitted on the river side, or by scaling the wall by a rebel ladder from the suburb. Nor did he explain why he was not afraid of being seized as a spy. He wrote in his journal, 'The number of killed and wounded must have been very considerable. I went into the City afterwards, but could not ascertain the number, as they try to conceal that now.'

It is possible that he went to give medical aid, for Dr Lockhart was never slow to be involved, yet he does not mention Dr Parker in this connection except that they collected his last boxes of medical supplies from the *Swiftsure*. The obvious was understandably omitted from reports.

On December 9 shooting began again while they were at breakfast, and by the sound of it the French were involved. 'From (a) verandah . . . I saw the French displaying their national agility by skipping round the graves and scampering off in quick style . . . The French, now Imperialists to the backbone, would not lose a chance of annoying the Rebels . . .'

His scorn for France echoed the tenor of contemporary Victorian journalism, including a gratuitously anti-papist overtone typical of the period. But he was not going to miss anything. When the French ships shelled the city he was impressed and went to the Bund to get a closer view.

Sunday's evangelism this time had to be in the Chinese market area of the Settlement, but on Monday, December 11, his friend Mr Si asked him to try to get his wife's sisters out of the city. After the morning bombardment by the French the two of them climbed the city wall and called on the Triad second in command, Qin A-lin. To their delight he consented, but said it was too late for the women to leave that day, they must come for them the next day.

> While I was in his office a letter came in from the English and American Consuls and was read aloud in English, offering to try and make some arrangements with the French, if they would promise to capitulate on such terms as they [the consuls] might offer; but without naming the conditions. These they stated were the only terms on which they would interfere, to save the lives of the men under him [Qin A-lin] and those of the innocent people of the City. On reading this he seemed to become desperate, said he never would agree to a step the consequences of which he did not know, and that he would fight and die in the city, but not die alone. There appeared no means of influencing him, and as it was getting dusk, I left him and returned home . . . I had a great deal of conversation with him and endeavoured to persuade him to accept the terms, or to write and ask if *their* lives would be spared in the event of their acceding.

The next day Si went in alone to fetch his relatives and did not return, so before breakfast on the 13th Hudson Taylor went again to find him. The French guns opened up as he climbed into the city and he had to 'descend the city wall' and 'withdraw'. While the French marines landed, took the rebels' battery at the waterside, spiked the guns, fired the post and departed, Hudson Taylor took Parker on a round of introductions to American missionaries and then tried again. Si and his sisters-in-law were at Qin A-lin's office. This time all was well and Hudson Taylor brought them out safely. Yet he went in to the city again on the two following days.

He learned on the 14th that Qin was trying to persuade the first chief Liu to capitulate, and saw the Jenkins' old home in flames. On the 15th he found the rebels full of confidence and 'bent on holding out'. Back at the Settlement he was told 'the French are giving notice that the City is in a state of siege'. So, 'thinking it would probably be for the last time before the city is taken . . .' he went in yet again. 'I got several curiosities and some things for use, very cheaply. . . . The poor people are daily getting worse off, tho' provisions are not yet entirely kept out.'

A few weeks later he sent home a trunk full of gifts for family and friends for the purpose 'that God may cause some to pray more for China' – the 'ball' which struck his house and fell at the feet of Si's son, fans, necklaces of carved peach-stone beads, chessmen, buddhas, Chinese puzzles and padlocks, tea caddies and chopsticks, Chinese books and medicines, pots and pictures; for Elizabeth Sissons, a folding fan and carved ivory abacus, books and Scriptures in the new translation. His letter about them expressed the jocular hope that –

> you may enjoy the fruits of that 'exalted benevolence which, high as heaven, and boundless as the ocean, has induced me to remember even you poor outside barbarians, who by the grace of Heaven's Son, are permitted to eke out a miserable existence in some barren isle in the remotest corner of the earth'.

So that was that – the end of the North Gate suburb and city adventures for the time being. Lockhart's hospital was now in the front line and hostilities were closer than ever to the Settlement. Hudson Taylor had seen it coming and during the last few days when Joseph Edkins planned another extended journey into what was called the 'interior', well beyond the limits permitted by the Nanking Treaty, he gladly agreed to go with him. There were too many missionaries working among the hardened Chinese community in the Settlement, so now was the time for the journey thwarted by the Battle of Muddy Flat.

Apprentice to Edkins   December 1854

Joseph Edkins had the apostolic urge to carry the gospel to places where it had not been preached before, and was no novice in the type of work they intended to do. His aim was to test the feasibility of travelling about a hundred miles from Shanghai in the present disturbed state of affairs. That meant seeing what the reaction of the mandarins would be – whether they would despatch them in custody back to Shanghai – and whether the populace and any troops encountered would be antagonistic. He hired a junk about forty or fifty feet in length, with a crew of three men and a boy. In the centre was a covered cabin 'capable of giving us a *good deal* of shelter from the wind and rain . . .'

LIFE ON A CANAL BOAT
(After a sketch in *The Graphic* 1889)

It provided just enough living space in two sections separated by a partition, for the crew and Edkins' cook and the missionaries, and had a mast, sail and oars to be used according to the winds and currents in the tidal streams and canals they were to follow. Their destination was Jiaxing (Kiahsing), the home of a teacher once employed by the LMS. And on the way through the city of Song-jiang and many towns and markets, they planned to distribute as many of the Bible Society's million New Testaments and other pamphlets as they could. In the manner of the merchants they dressed as Englishmen, eating their English meals with knife, fork and spoon. It was called travelling without disguise, and not for some months was Hudson Taylor to discover the pleasures and advantages of an alternative way.

After an early breakfast on Saturday, December 16, they boarded the junk, hoisted the sail and 'the British Flag' and with the tide in their favour sailed up the Huangpu, past the French frigate and steamer blockading the city, and the new Roman Catholic cathedral (map, p 184, L), and by ten am were out of the war zone and near the Longhua pagoda. 'We met with plenty of proof that trade was not annihilated, in the number of junks passing in all directions.' Bends in the river brought them at times head on to the wind and ebbing tidal current, and progress became impossible, so they tied up and shouldering bags of books visited hamlets along the banks, looking for people able to read, and preaching the gospel. In the eight months and more since this journey had first been pro-jected, Hudson Taylor had become capable of at least talking in both mandarin and the Shanghai dialect, and set himself the goal of preaching in both by the anniversary of his arrival in China, on March 4.

With the turn of the tide in their favour after dark they got under way again and woke on Sunday morning riding at anchor near Songjiang, the prefectural city of the region in which Shanghai lay. What happened to them here would indicate what they could expect in other places.

Songjiang dated from AD 250 and in its present form from the thirtieth year of the first Ming emperor, AD 1398. Its two pagodas were pre-Ming. Hudson Taylor was fascinated and recorded it all with much detail in his journal. To be here at last, over the treaty wall, even if only just, and seeing ancient China for himself, was ample compensation for the frustrations of Shanghai.

Edkins and he walked ahead of their boat and entered the city,

SHANGHAI HINTERLAND
SHOWING THE MAIN WATERWAYS

SHANGHAI HINTERLAND
The immediate 'interior'

making for one of its temples, the conventional place for public gatherings. By then their extraordinary appearance was drawing crowds of excited people who followed them into the temple yard shouting, 'the foreign teachers have come to burn incense'. Edkins preached and Hudson Taylor handed out leaflets until the excitement subsided and they were able to go and talk with a hermit, bricked into his cell, and leave a tract with him.

Going on through the city they were jostled by a rabble of men and boys, so Edkins turned down a side street to what he thought was a ferry pier. But it was a private wharf. They were trapped. The mob whooped with glee at the prospect of seeing some sport with these barbarian devils, closed in behind them and shut the gates to prevent escape. There were plenty of boats passing along the narrow stream but none would stop to take them off, so Hudson Taylor leaped into a moving one. With a roar the rabble opened the wharf gates and rushed towards the water's edge. Hudson Taylor pulled the boat to the bank and Edkins jumped in.

The boatmen were then only too glad to put them ashore on the far side where they made for the rendezvous with their own junk. It was to be waiting for them at a certain bridge. But the mob of young hooligans had seen what happened, and they soon had the whole pack after them in full cry. At the critical moment when they reached the bridge and their boat had not arrived, they saw Dzien, the teacher Hudson Taylor had dismissed. As one of the city's respected literati he quieted the mob and escorted the missionaries away. They were learning what to expect, if not how to meet it.

Nothing daunted, they returned to their boat and after lunch traversed the city with a new stock of books from west gate to east gate and then the south, trying a new technique. Walking at top speed in a most un-Chinese manner, without pausing to talk to people as they handed out their booklets, but picking out those they judged could read, they kept ahead of the curious crowd who wanted a better look at them. Eventually they climbed one of the pagodas to survey the city and countryside. With Hudson Taylor's characteristic precision he counted the steps up the nine storeys with fourteen steps per flight. Looking out over the city, and its suburbs housing as large a population again, they thought how 'few knew anything of Christianity and perhaps none believed', and took note of the city wall, 'about 19½ feet in height and more than nine *li* [three miles] in circumference, and surrounded by a moat of considerable width'.

Nightfall found them in a lonely, robber-infested stretch of country near the provincial border on the way to Jiaxing so they lowered the conspicuous sail and cast anchor in midstream. The border regions were always most lawless because of the ease with which offenders could escape from pursuing mandarins. Moving on, at the small town of Jiashan they found that co-operation between neighbouring areas did exist. A passenger they welcomed to travel with them turned out to be an officer of the Songjiang magistrate, keeping an eye on them and carrying a message to the Jiashan magistrate about them. Hoping to get into the town to distribute books before being intercepted, Edkins and Hudson Taylor left the boat to walk ahead. Sure enough, the 'shadow' came with them, and although they walked fast, kept up 'puffing away famously'.

They climbed the Tang dynasty pagoda – AD 784, seven storeys, one hundred and twenty-six steps, considerably older than the town itself, built in 1554 – with some of a crowd following them up and others congregating at the bottom, and came down again to address them. This time their audience was very attentive. But as they left the premises, to their surprise they –

> saw an imposing cavalcade entering the gates, and at our approach stopping. First came two men with gongs, then men followed with immense red cloth caps, bearing flags, etc., then came a man with a large umbrella and he was followed by a huge sedan chair carried by four bearers.

Edkins and Hudson Taylor went up to the chair as the chief magistrate dismounted, a mild but prepossessing, handsome man of fifty. He questioned them politely as to their intentions, saying he had read some of their literature, and tried to dissuade them from going on to the prefectural city of Jiaxing but, when they stood firm, said he would send an escort. So when they rejoined their boat, the escort followed them in another and they were 'watched by thousands of people from the doors, windows, wharves, bridges and every available position', as the river passed right through the suburb and town. Coming to a more open area they went ashore but were so thronged that Hudson Taylor was glad his clothes were not torn in shreds in the eagerness of the people to be given a tract. There was nothing for it but to go back on board and distribute them to people who came out by boat and could be spoken to. Edkins and later Hudson Taylor joined the escort boat and as they travelled had a long conversation, delighting in the official's beautiful northern accent.

Jiaxing fascinated them. The wall – twelve *li* long and sixteen feet thick, with a twenty-four-foot moat – had been built, as it still stood, in AD 888; but the history of the place, Hudson Taylor recorded, went back to the Xia (Hsia) dynasty, 2000 BC. He described the trade in silk and copper goods, cotton materials and books. Mulberry plantations, for feeding the silkworms, grew everywhere.

Again they took their carpet-bag of tracts and books, traversed the Six Li Street and made a 'flying excursion' on the other side of the river. They were such curiosities everywhere they went that noisy crowds collected, always a threat of disorder, so they directed their boat out to an island in a lake, where the Qian Long (Ch'ien Lung) emperor had built a summer residence and there was a pagoda – a hundred and seventy-two steps. Even there the crowds followed them and the ferrymen did a thriving business as Hudson Taylor treated patients while Edkins preached. Several mandarins came to talk with them, and a man from the far north-western province of Gansu who had seen the Nestorian tablet at Xi'an. A mandarin with a crystal globe on his cap, higher in rank than the chief magistrate of the district (*see* Appendix 3), lowered his voice and said, 'Your books are true, your words are truth.' It was worth every discomfort to hear such a comment.

The last two days were spent travelling back to Shanghai where they arrived 'after hard work [against the tide], about an hour after sunset – when we little regretted exchanging a cold boat for a warm fireside'. Hudson Taylor's first sally into 'the interior' had given him plenty of food for thought.

In reporting to the LMS on this eight-day journey, Joseph Edkins highlighted their dealings and interviews with government officials and that none suggested that they had 'wandered too far from home', beyond the treaty limit of about thirty miles from Shanghai. This augured well and encouraged them to attempt more journeys.

The festering sore that was Shanghai appeared not to be a gauge of the country as a whole. It happened that at Ningbo around the same time a French merchant made a distant journey into the province and was well received. The American Presbyterian, H V Rankin, wrote, 'for us it will be still safer, for he knew nothing of the language, and yet experienced no harm'. And so it proved, though Rankin and his companions stayed together until sure of what reception they would receive.

The effect on Hudson Taylor was that he bought an old boat

'complete with its furniture' for twelve pounds, 'less than one third of its true value', determined to exploit this promising situation. He could not afford the expense of hiring boats and did not foresee problems from being tied to his own. While Shanghai simmered, the 'interior' held great hopes.

'A ravelled maze'   *December 1854–January 1855*

With Hudson Taylor away the Parkers had enjoyed a little more elbow-room and were coping as comfortably as might be. Language study was all but impossible. The Jenkins' children and their own together with many visitors were too distracting. And even at night the noise of fighting continued for hours on end. But Dr Parker had been out with tracts and found the Settlement Chinese welcoming, even if few could read. At a bridge over the *pang* he came across four heads dangling by their *bianzi* (queues), each with an indictment of guilt. The *pang* was the Settlement boundary, so this choice of location for displaying them was menacing in itself. One man had done nothing worse than sell rice to people in the city. Impatient to start work, the threat of having nowhere else to live weighed on Parker's mind; should the LMS need their house in a few weeks' time, what could he do?

A wise condition imposed by the LMS on the use of the house was that no missionary work should be done at it. The compound had its chapel and guest-rooms. Activities of the same nature by another mission, even if not competitive, would be confusing. The only way left for Hudson Taylor and William Parker was to go out on the streets of the Settlement or at risk to the surrounding villages, or to establish a 'station' of their own, with premises to suit their purposes. This was what everyone else did, and what other missionaries had probably been telling Parker he should do.

When Hudson Taylor arrived home they pooled their thinking on the subject. They saw it from two different angles but agreed on what was needed. Hudson Taylor wanted, and had already advocated to the Society, a base from which to penetrate the interior, in the Gutzlaff tradition favoured by the CES. He could not always be away travelling, so a continuing activity such as a school and preaching chapel with Chinese Christians in charge, would provide work to return to and a nucleus for developments.

Parker saw little value in peripatetic medical or evangelistic work. A firm establishment with hospital, schools, chapel and missionaries' homes, the accepted pattern, was to him ideal. This would achieve more than occasional visits to places and people who might never be seen again. The people of China must be taught to read if Scriptures were to do their work. It did not worry him that missionaries were thick on the ground and overlapping their efforts in Shanghai. As far as he could see there was room for all among the hundreds of thousands right here.

Both knew that they must, above all, be independent of other missions, not depending on their hospitality and help. They saw no reason why each should not follow his own plan, one scattering seed, as it were, while the other planted fruit trees, making a co-ordinated whole. So both wrote setting out these convictions, trying to break through the mistaken ideas of their directors on immediate penetration of inland China.

Word was coming from Hong Kong through LMS missionaries of Arthur Taylor's plight. His first letter to the directors after arrival reported renting accommodation in which to start learning the language. To his alarm, the first he received from them was a reply censuring him for what he had done. He should have gone on to the mainland, like the Germans, they said. But at the time it was impossible to live there, let alone without the language. A tangle of misunderstanding and neglect had begun, which quickly led to rebukes for exceeding his financial credit, as inadequate as Hudson Taylor's, and a demand for his resignation. He demurred. Then in March 1855 they dismissed him. The LMS would gladly have taken him on, and Hudson Taylor wrote, before the dismissal, asking that he might join him at Shanghai, warning that the reputation of the Society would suffer if he were to be dismissed on such grounds alone. It was too late. By the time his letter reached London the deed was done. Arthur Taylor found employment in Hong Kong and continued his missionary work.

The plan Hudson Taylor and William Parker submitted was for a hospital, school and 'mission buildings' costing a thousand pounds, three or four village schools with attached dispensaries, to be visited weekly on the Wesleyan pattern, each costing only seven dollars a month, and the employment of two colporteurs under Hudson Taylor's supervision to be his companions in travel. Chinese and foreigners must be in it together. Again the Gutzlaff pattern is discernible. The only reason for not immediately embarking on the less costly features of the plan was their lack of funds.

I think nothing would be so likely to improve the position of our Society as the establishment of an efficient mission here . . . Having such a mission to point to when asked, What are you doing? would be followed by a large increase in funds . . . headquarters are *absolutely indispensable* . . . We would require one or two other missionaries . . . I trust no time will be lost in enabling us to carry (it) out . . . As to the purchase of *land* for building on, the sooner we are empowered to do so the better, for all the land (in the Settlement) is being bought up; and its price, in all places rapidly rising, is in many places double . . . what it was three months since.

Unfortunately there were two crippling obstacles to this proposal. They did not know their directors well enough, or the diversion of interest from China following upon the sufferings of the army at Sebastopol, Balaclava and Inkerman in October and November 1854, and the departure of Florence Nightingale and her nurses to Scutari. Loss of interest again meant loss of funds. Neither did they know by more than hearsay of the potential in Ningbo or one of the other treaty ports. Ningbo was a relatively small place, with fourteen missionaries already. Why think of going there? The strategic importance of Shanghai on the Yangzi and near the Grand Canal, was acknowledged by everyone, missionary and merchant, diplomat and soldier. Yet the overriding consideration for Parker and Hudson Taylor was 'Until we get settled we can do little.'

For Hudson Taylor public opinion began to weigh more and more. How long could he withstand the criticism without revealing to his critics in the community that he was being immobilised only by the Society that had sent him? But the Society, while approving of schools and medical work, not only lacked the funds but would agree to nothing short of establishing them in forbidden territory beyond the treaty ports. They were insisting on the impossible. But in so doing they were spurring Hudson Taylor on to scorn the treaty wall and penetrate the interior.

Christmas came and went and was almost overlooked in the correspondence. The joy was lacking while the guns roared and the battle gongs resounded and the children wailed. Hudson Taylor's long, affectionate letters, written after midnight when the house was relatively quiet, betray a bleakness, but not without his usual tilt at himself.

Dr. Parker is an excellent man – (but his wife peculiar, putting some oil of peppermint in a Christmas cake, for instance). She took it into her head to mend two pairs of my trousers and spoil the beautiful fringe round the bottom of them both . . . (But the children's crying and the parents' scolding were) very discordant to me. I often think of Martyn's saying, 'The power of gentleness is great.'

Home letters seem to have contained distressing things that called for comment. Yes, mails in and out were haphazard, he replied, according to the ship that brought them, and costly, depending on the whims of the crews delivering or the officials handling them at Shanghai. Every resident knew he was overcharged and 'done in Exchange' but 'put up with it quietly'. Any complaints risked letters not even being delivered in future, 'so for goodness sake, don't meddle with it'. News of a certain unmannered acquaintance proposing to come to China was alarming. 'There is nothing scarcely I should dread more – here people stick to etiquette in the most freezing way, and he would do great injury both to his society and his colleagues.'

His mother had written regularly, so his complaints of getting too few letters grieved her – and now he grieved to have caused her any sadness. But she must change her ideas of the Taipings, fostered by *The Gleaner*. 'I am afraid their success would do more harm than their destruction. Their errors are great and their impostures so numerous.' The CMS *Intelligencer* for November 1854 reflected the same opinion.

> Recent letters show that the religious aspect of the insurgent section of the Chinese is perilous, and that there is a danger of its degenerating into a startling fanaticism.

No letter of credit for the Parkers had arrived by the year's end, and Dr Parker was making his own protests to Charles Bird in London. But once again Mr Skinner of Gibb, Livingstone & Co advanced ninety pounds on the strength of an endorsement by Hudson Taylor who told his parents,

> If they make any nonsense with (Parker), he will resign . . . It is shameful to send a man and family here, and tho' promising, not to send any credit for him, and *now* above all times . . . do not send us funds to carry on our work, I am sure they will lose Dr. Parker . . . If we three retired the Society would be ruined, and to prevent this we daily make it a matter of prayer that we and they may be directed aright.

His mother had commented on Elizabeth Sissons, but why not Marianne Vaughan? 'You never mention her.' That she could not marry him did not mean the end of his friendship. 'I am glad to hear your opinions of Miss Sissons, they just co-incide with mine . . . and to find that she is at present dis-engaged.' Already more than a year had passed since he had asked Mr Sissons for permission to court her, without an answer, so he had written to her direct. In January, his mother wrote to his sister Amelia. 'I think as she has written a *favourable* reply to him, and your letter explaining what might be misunderstood will probably reach him about the same time, it may be unnecessary for her to write again to *him* till his reply reaches England . . . When Hudson's *next* letter comes to her, (her parents) must certainly be consulted.' So while his mother and sister were both doing all they could for Hudson in his loneliness, his correspondence with his second choice of a wife had only just begun.

On December 31 Hudson Taylor and Parker went out to the racecourse together, distributing leaflets.

There, to their surprise, was the provincial governor, the *Futai*, with an opaque red globe on his cap and peacock's feathers, attended by one dignitary, a judge or treasurer, with a blue stone, one or two departmental chiefs with crystal globes, several district magistrates with opaque white ones and other inferior officials with gold cap buttons (*see* Appendix 3). Some were wearing fox-tail honours as well. Undeterred, Hudson Taylor and Dr Parker went up and offered leaflets to them all. The *Futai* asked what they were and on being told turned away, but some were more forthcoming. Once again Hudson Taylor happened to be at the scene of a historic happening. As before the Battle of Muddy Flat the officials were in the act of challenging the foreigners by choosing the site of a new army camp, provocatively close to the Settlement (map, p 184, E).

On New Year's Day, 1855, Taylor and Parker attempted to reach Wusong at the mouth of the Huangpu but the tide was flowing fast and they could make no headway. Instead they were carried past two French frigates, newly arrived to bombard the city, and landed on the far bank, Pudong (map, p 184). They came upon an imperial armoury where the men were casting musket balls, and the captain in command received them warmly, presenting them in return for the books they offered him with six of his own on filial piety. While they were there the frigates opened fire, disregarding protests from the British and American consuls, and bombarded the rebel bastions – ostensibly because they posed a threat to the French settlement and shipping. What damage they did to the walls was quickly repaired, but as the rebels refused to allow civilians or their property out of the city, casualties were heavy.

In spite of hostilities the two men were hard at language study for the next two days. Hudson Taylor was studying Chinese chronology from the *Book of Ten Thousand Years*. But on January 4, while they were out distributing books along the *ma-lu*, the old road near the racecourse, they found rooms for rent which would do admirably for a small school, and took them at once. The area had become densely populated, a good place to begin new work. Better still would be a boarding school, Parker thought, costing a mere six pounds a year for each boy, to separate them from idolatry and bring them up under Christian instruction. While there they heard that three men occupying Hudson Taylor's old house in the North Gate suburb had been arrested by imperialist soldiers as rebel supporters. He went out to the imperial camp to secure their release, and was promised their freedom the next day, but not until February 4 did he succeed, after many importunate visits.

That night and the next day, 'the bloodiest fighting I have ever witnessed, or wish to, . . . an affair as disgraceful and wicked, as it has been bloody', raged between the beleaguered Triads and the imperial troops with their new allies, the French. The heaviest cannonade since he came to China woke Hudson Taylor at six a m, leaving no doubt it was from the French. He and Parker had planned another visit to Wusong but discarded it and watched the battle.

The city wall was breached and with a loud shout one thousand five hundred picked imperial and French assault troops together poured in by the breach and scaling ladders. Everyone expected the city to fall. Reports had it that the imperialists began to kill and to behead men, women, children and dead bodies indiscriminately for the glory of having bloodied swords, and that the French killed imperial soldiers they saw doing so. The Triads fought back 'like lions', however, and drove the attackers from the wall, taking prisoners and hurling others on top of the men heaped below with arms, legs and necks broken in jumping for their lives. The imperialists then retreated, leaving the French to end the battle, and they too were forced to withdraw.

It was all over by noon. Hudson Taylor watched the killed and wounded being evacuated, about five hundred dead and many more 'mangled and mutilated in every possible way'. In the afternoon a great conflagration was seen in the city, and soon Dr Lockhart reported it to be the burning of a temple into which sixty imperial prisoners had been herded. The brutality was no less on one side than the other. A survivor brought into Lockhart's hospital had with him a wallet filled with ears and a scalp. As a result of witnessing so much bestiality, an awareness never left Hudson Taylor of what might happen to him if mobs, soldiers or bandits should be so disposed, when throughout that year, 1855, he went on journey after journey, sometimes alone, far from Shanghai.

An immediate effect of the defeat of the French was their loss of prestige among Manchus and Chinese of all complexions. That they were not invincible meant that they were no longer to be feared. 'The failure will probably affect the safety of foreigners here . . . and now the rebels who were formerly friendly are unwilling that foreigners should come into the City,' Parker told George Pearse. The residents of the Settlement, indeed, had no real power to protect themselves, had the Chinese challenged their defiance. A second Battle of Muddy Flat was out of the question. Nor was it ever impossible for Christians, Chinese or foreign, to be cruelly persecuted again.

During January the school near the racecourse began classes with twenty pupils, more intelligent and responsive than those in the city, involving daily visits to supervise the teaching, until it was running smoothly. It was the severest winter for several years and writing home Hudson Taylor said he was so cold he could hardly hold his pen. Fuel was too expensive. The temperature was 25°F at night. He piled everything, dressing gown, top-coat and even scarf on top of him, and took to using Chinese brass fire-baskets.

> And when I began to have two fires *in* bed with me . . . I was not at all too hot . . . powdered charcoal and salt-petre is made into cakes, . . . heated redhot and buried in a brass pan [with a lid] full of wood-ashes . . . the requisite oxygen being supplied by the nitre. By increasing or diminishing the size of the cake you can regulate the amount of heat . . . The comfort of having one under your feet at home, at chapel, in your boat or sedan-chair . . . is very great.

To his delight he found he could combine evangelistic outings in his boat with foraging for food and fuel in the country, saving a full third of the costs. He was quite at ease now in carrying on a conversation in mandarin or the dialect, and planned a week's journey with Dr Parker. On the 16th the best batch of mail ever to reach him brought letters not only from home but from the Howards and Miss Stacey in Tottenham and even from Dr Brown of St Mary

Axe. But still nothing from the CES, not even the Parkers' letter of credit.

With only one day's warning, the imperial commanders suddenly acted to establish their new camp – on a site where many new houses had already been erected close to the Settlement and LMS compound (map, p 184, P). On the following day all houses not already being dismantled were set on fire. Dr Parker wrote,

> The poor people were running about with their furniture, saving as much as they could from the flames and also from the soldiers, who are great thieves. The mission hospital was thrown open to them . . . (and) a supply of rice was provided by some of the merchants. (The camp lies) in front of our house (almost a stone's throw from it) . . . We are now in considerable danger . . . Everything between the camp and the city walls was razed to the ground, in effect the whole north suburb.

Then Rutherford Alcock notified the foreign community of the imperialists' intention to build a wall between the city and the Settlement, finally sealing off the Triads from any hope of supplies, and to site a battery close to Lockhart's hospital. No sooner said than it was done. Not content with that, they deliberately displayed their flags in such a way as to draw the Triads' fire towards the Settlement, hoping to provoke the British and Americans to retaliatory action against the rebels. Inevitably the hospital and LMS compound were hit. A cannonball struck the house behind the Parkers' and pierced its stone wall. Dr Lockhart was walking with his servant past Alexander Wylie's house one day, when a gingall ball (heavier and of higher velocity than the musket balls of the day) passed between them and 'shattered to splinters the arm of the chair' from which Wylie 'had just risen' after lunch.[5]

The *North China Herald* described the position of the LMS as one of the most dangerous.

> This is no exaggeration, [Hudson Taylor commented]. But we trust to be preserved from all evil . . . You will not forget however, we do need the prayers of the saints, for ourselves and for those who are suffering the effects of war . . . [And in a later letter, to the Society,] (the North Gate house) was totally destroyed – not one brick now stands on another on its site. From this you will see how necessary it is to leave us a discretionary power of acting, without having to consult you on minor matters . . .

When Dr Lockhart opened the hospital grounds to the helpless Chinese as their homes were burned, he quickly had two hundred looking for protection. But a British marine deserter was teaching the Triads to make explosive brass shells. One 'came smashing through the roof of the hospital,' Lockhart recalled. It fell among a crowd of people in the hall, 'tore up the floors, shattered the furniture, and flew in all directions; but to our surprise, no one was hurt.' The huddled refugees in the yard behind the building were untouched. Soon afterwards a French howitzer put the offending battery out of action, and Dr Lockhart was admitted to the city to treat wounded Triads.

With all this unrest, criticism and not even the certainty of a home in Shanghai until the Society made funds available, Hudson Taylor was fighting against 'melancholy'. When the temperature was twelve degrees below freezing and the children were miserable, and a man he had given up many hours to help had proved to be no more than a confidence trickster, he saw his concertina and began to play. 'Music produces a singular effect on me . . . and always acts like oil on troubled waters.' But in an incomplete, undated letter written at this time to his mother he revealed a deeper tranquillity.

> . . . I acted as well as I could, under the circumstances, and those who seek only to know the will of God, and to do it, need not fear missing their providential path. The future is a ravelled maze and my path(s) have ever been made plain one step at a time. I must wait on God and trust in Him, and all will be well. I think I do love *Him* more than ever, and long to serve Him as He directs, more than ever.

He and Parker were about to start on the week's journey into the country when the imperialists began their incendiary onslaught on the suburbs. Anything could be about to happen, so Parker stayed with his family. 'I thought it prudent to forego the pleasure and remain', he wrote, 'to see how things got on.' But Hudson Taylor set off in his boat, alone but for his cook and the boatmen. He did not know that Joseph Edkins and William Aitchison, a new missionary of the American Board, were under arrest at Suzhou and about to be delivered under escort to their consuls.

PART 3

URGE TO GO INLAND
1855

CHAPTER SEVEN

BEYOND THE TREATY WALL
1855

China at the crossroads   *1854–55*

The cauldron of destiny was not only simmering for the ancient city of Shanghai and for the weak handful of foreigners in the International and French Settlements, but for the whole of China. At Shanghai Triads, imperial troops and French all had old wounds to avenge. At last the encirclement of the city was complete and the few thousand desperate rebels were debating their best moves. Most of them were Cantonese and there were substantial numbers of Cantonese in the Settlements. If sheer numbers made the imperial troops impenetrable perhaps an alliance against the foreigners, with a Cantonese rising inside their defences, would provide a route for escape through the Settlements and down to Wusong with its abundance of junks. The city could hold out for a month at most.

The rest of China was as unstable. The Taiping success had already gone stale but the strength of the Manchu dynasty was seeping away at many points. Hong Xiu-quan's rebellion was the disruptive opportunity for men with other aims and grievances to take up arms. The Nian rebellion in the north was gaining strength. The 'Mohammedans' in the far south-west and north-west were ready to rise. The Hakkas and Triads in Guangxi and Guangdong had Canton by the throat and other cities in their power (map, pp 80, 191). At Fushan, just south of Canton, because the populace supported the government the Triads blocked all exits and razed the city to the ground. Two hundred thousand of its inhabitants perished in the flames. A large British and American naval force was stationed at Canton to protect the foreign community. In Guizhou the warlike Miao tribes needed many garrisons to restrain them.

Piracy on the coast was more formidable than at any time. Ships, not only junks, were being seized and plundered, until British naval power called a halt by destroying fifty pirate vessels. But the

Chinese government was itself employing pirates to protect its grain fleet and they were openly levying protection money.

In Manchuria, by the device of a treaty allowing navigation on the Amur river, the Russians were taking complete control along the whole course of the river over an area one thousand miles in length by five hundred wide and extracting its gold and silver. China was too deeply embroiled elsewhere to be able to restrain them. Above all, Court intrigue and perfidy were moving towards those events which signalled the exploitation of China by the foreign powers and the dissolution of the dynasty itself.

In some ways it was already touch and go. The first northern army of the Taipings, held at Duliu near Tianjin, was short of ammunition. The second relieving army and the massive fleet of barges bringing supplies from Nanking were making slow progress. In the west beleaguered Wuchang fell at last to the rebels and the governor was killed. The annual report of the American Board spoke of –

> the approaching downfall of the reigning dynasty . . . Everything augurs that the empire of China will soon be open to missionary efforts.

And *The Gleaner* exulted in similar vein.[1]

The common people in the northern provinces pressed on with their busy lives and the Roman Church hoped for better things. Monsignor Mouly, the bishop of Peking and Inner Mongolia, came out of hiding to plead for greater toleration for his members and, to his surprise, instead of arrest and expulsion was asked to mediate for foreign aid to the government. In the *Annals of the Propagation of the Faith* he described how, 'After my voluntary tradition[2] to the Chinese government, for the salvation of my Christians', he travelled overland through imperial and Taiping territory from Peking to Shanghai, impressed by the large number of travellers seen on the way. On arrival 'I met with the most honourable reception of anyone, not excepting the *Futai*, the Governor of the province. May the Lord be praised for it!' He asked M. Lagréné, the French plenipotentiary, to negotiate for the restoration to him of the cathedral and other property in Peking, confiscated decades before.

He was not alone. *The Gleaner*, though always strongly critical of Rome, was on the same tack. While Lord Palmerston, prime minister again until 1858, put pressure on Sir John Bowring to obtain the unobtainable – unrestricted access to the Chinese authorities, and at the same time a review of the terms of the Treaty of Nanking and better co-operation in the treaty ports – the Chinese Evangelization Society in an editorial brought to the attention of the Christian public a striking omission from the treaty of 1842 and supplementary treaty of 1843. The wording of both documents provided rights in China for merchants but not missionaries. Only in a subsidiary penal article were the missionaries included.[3]

> It is agreed that English merchants and others residing at or resorting to the five ports to be opened shall not go into the surrounding country beyond certain short distances, to be named by the local authorities in concert with the British Consul . . . and should any person whatever infringe the stipulations of this article . . . they shall be seized and handed over to the British Consul for suitable punishment.

This was the article being disregarded by merchants, botanists, missionaries, consuls and mandarins alike. In October of the following year, 1844, however, the French treaty specified the right to establish Christian institutions in the treaty ports, and under the Chinese 'most favoured nation' clause the same right was automatically extended to the British, and acted upon. For on December 28, 1844, the Chinese plenipotentiary, Qi Ying, had issued a proclamation in the spirit of the 'diplomatic honeymoon' (see Book One) and the fruit of his own observation of true Christians. Previous imperial edicts against religion were directed against evil done under the cloak of religion, he said, not against the religion itself. Therefore,

> henceforth all nations and foreigners without distinction, who learn and practise the religion of the Lord of heaven and do not excite trouble by improper conduct, be exempted from criminality.[4]

When M. Lagréné discovered that the term, *Tian Zhu Jiao* (T'ien Chu Chiao) 'Lord of Heaven Religion' in the Chinese text implied only the Roman Catholics, he personally negotiated a complementary proclamation by Qi Ying to include all Christians under the same toleration.

The privilege of Protestant worship in China was thus granted owing to the efforts of the French minister and not the British. In due course these edicts were ratified by the emperor. But limitation to the treaty ports still held, with the onus upon the mandarins to deliver offenders to the consuls for restraint and correction. The principle that all share whatever privilege might be accorded to any one nation was very soon to affect Hudson Taylor personally, to his disadvantage.

Meanwhile *The Gleaner* of December 1854 called upon the British government to ensure that discrimination by Sir Henry Pottinger against missionaries would not be repeated – incidentally a warning to Sir John Bowring – but that the debt of commerce and indeed of the nation to missionaries from Robert Morrison onwards be acknowledged. The editorial appealed to all missionary societies to approach the government that,

> whenever such revision does take place, the interests of religion may be fully considered and entire liberty obtained for its promulgation in any part of that vast Empire.

This could have been an empty effervescence by the visionary directors of the CES. Having survived the disintegration of Gutzlaff's Chinese Union, and taxed the loyalty of their supporters by over-optimism about the Taiping rebellion, this flight into international diplomacy might justifiably have been scorned. But the thinking of the directors was sound, in political terms, even if dismally at fault in principle and in the tactical application of policy. This editorial led to action at the highest levels of government and contributed strongly to the penetration by missionaries to the deepest recesses of the empire, with unforeseen consequences.

Even before its publication the CES invited the treasurers and secretaries of several missionary societies and the Bible and Tract societies to two consultations, on November 10 and December 8, to obtain the concurrence of all in a representation to the government, to obtain,

> in the revision of the treaties or foundation of new treaties with China, full privileges for missionaries, and for their residence in China, and for the liberty and protection of Christians generally.[5]

The delegates agreed to memorialise the Earl of Clarendon, Foreign Minister, on the subject. On January 10, 1855, a deputation of members of the CES Committee led by Sir John Dean Paul, the treasurer, was received by Lord Clarendon, although he was fully occupied with the Crimean War. They pointed out that the treaties of 1842–43 secured rights for merchants but not equally for other British subjects; that the treaty between France and China of October 1844 made concessions favouring French subjects and their Chinese converts; and that although British subjects already enjoyed the same privileges by virtue of the 'most favoured nation' clause, they remained subject to the revision of the British treaties now pending. The British plenipotentiary, Sir John Bowring, and the American minister had in fact already left Shanghai for the Beihe (Peiho, now Hai He), the river of access to Tianjin and Peking (map, p 80), and were expecting the appointment of an imperial commission to treat with them and the French. The societies' petition to Lord Clarendon read,

> . . . Your memorialists do most earnestly press on your Lordship's notice, in the event of such revision taking place, the importance of securing to those engaged in China, in teaching and preaching the Gospel, distributing the holy scriptures, and otherwise promoting Christian knowledge, not only protection for life and property, but privileges of residence for themselves and families, and liberty to prosecute, without molestation, their christian undertakings, and the right of erecting churches and chapels.

Lord Clarendon could hardly believe the facts alleged, until he re-read the treaty himself. He was even more surprised to learn that there were eight-six Protestant missionaries in China, apart from wives and families, of whom thirty-two were British. 'One reason for the little regard paid to the interests of missionaries in China was, he believed, the circumstance that Sir John Bowring, the English Plenipotentiary, is a Unitarian, and cared little or nothing for the Gospel,' the annual meeting of the CES was told.[6] Lord Clarendon promised that the subject would be 'fully attended to'. A memorial from the dean of Bristol, a score and more of clergymen and several influential Bristol merchants was presented at the same time, and others were to be delivered by the CMS, LMS and Religious Tract Society.

The earl was as good as his word, and saw to it that the protracted negotiations eventually resulting in the Treaty of Tientsin (Tianjin) and the Peking Convention of 1858–60 did not lose sight of the interests of missions. In view of subsequent developments it cannot but be suspected that the older societies deliberately avoided closer association with the CES in this petition.

The Gleaner broke down the total of eighty-six missionaries as: LMS, ten and two en route, CMS six, Baptist Missionary Society one, Presbyterians three, CES four, Wesleyans three and three en route, Americans forty-six and Dutch and Germans three (probably a misprint for eight). In July Samuel Wells Williams published a list which threw more light on these figures. Of one hundred and eighty-eight missionaries to China since Morrison's arrival in 1807, including twenty-five physicians, the eighty-six were still there and seven temporarily absent, thirty-two had died with an average of five years' service, three by violence on land and four by drowning at sea; fifty-eight had retired, mostly from ill-health; thirty-three had lost their wives, and twenty-four were unmarried women. The mortality rate was 17% for men and 27% for women. It was right that such people should be provided for in the treaties to be negotiated.

The British and American plenipotentiaries duly presented themselves at Dagu (Taku), the fortified mouth of the Beihe below Tientsin, hoping to go on to Peking. To their amazement they were rebuffed. The American president's letter to the emperor was returned with the seal broken and a curt message that it should have come through Canton, to receive attention. The court at Peking were even now living in the past, blind to the lessons of the 1840–42 war. Uncomprehending regents were acting for the child emperor.

For China these were the crossroads. She could accept the necessity of adaptation to the West as Japan was doing, or go on in a dream-world of her own. And the Western nations could still choose to attain their ends by peaceful statesmanship, or resort again to belligerence. Each chose the hard alternative, China to be the immovable mass and the Western powers the irresistible force.

In January 1855 the American Commission was preparing to go to Japan to ratify the commercial treaty made the previous year but could find no interpreter. It happened that Wilhelm Lobscheid was also contemplating a voyage, for the sake of his health. He was intending to ask if he might join the steam frigate *Powhattan*, when he received an invitation to serve as 'Dutch' interpreter. Like Wells Williams, he also had picked up some Japanese from the marooned sailors in Hong Kong and to some extent could use Chinese in Japan.

The Japanese officials were cordial and the ratifications were exchanged at Simoda on February 21. Provision had been made for peaceful trading relations at two ports, not for the admission of missionaries, but the groundwork for that was also laid. Lobscheid duly reported on his experiences and urgently appealed for the churches in Europe to send a missionary to the Japanese. The *Powhattan* then sailed for Shanghai and arrived to find a dead Chinese city and Lobscheid's two CES colleagues, Hudson Taylor and William Parker, champing at the bit to get on with their planned campaign, but moneyless and to all appearances forgotten.

At last 'the interior' *January–February 1855*

The letter of the Nanking Treaty placed the onus upon the mandarins to arrest any foreigners who 'strayed into the country' in breach of agreements between the local authorities and consuls. Whatever the spirit of the treaty, however, sportsmen ventured out undisguised in pursuit of the abounding game, merchants to size up the potentials for trade, smugglers to establish their contacts, and missionaries to distribute Scripture and preach.[7] As we have seen, Walter Medhurst, Alexander Wylie, Joseph Edkins, William Muirhead, John Burdon and others deliberately tested the tolerance of the mandarins and the welcome of the people and found them satisfactory. The LMS *Chronicle* quoted Dr Medhurst as saying,

> We have liberty of action and of locomotion. Even the interior is not closed against us; and large cities nearly a hundred miles from Shanghai are within the reach of our missionaries, going without disguise, and in their own proper character, as ministers of the gospel.

At Canton foreigners could scarcely live in the city, let alone outside, but the mandarins were shutting their eyes to the harmless Continental missionaries in the east Guangdong countryside. At Amoy (Xiamen) William Burns found he also could travel freely. Ever since the slaughter when the British ships' captains saved two hundred mutilated men and boys from drowning, and Burns rescued others on shore, he was hailed everywhere as a friend and father-figure among the Chinese. For six months he lived at the up-river city of Zhangzhou (Changchow) unquestioned by mandarins or consul. At Fuzhou the CMS doctor, W Welton, wrote of freedom to travel unmolested. The great barrier to acceptance of the gospel, he said, was the association of the opium traffic with a nominally Christian nation.

> How lamentable that England should have given twenty millions sterling to emancipate her slaves, and yet pocket annually six millions sterling by the opium contraband traffic.[8]

From Ningbo too, the Americans Henry Rankin and W A P Martin were the first missionaries to visit Hangzhou, the heavenly thirteenth-century capital city of the Song dynasty.[9] And R H Cobbold of the CMS began, with Rankin, to make extensive tours in Zhejiang province. So when Edkins and Aitchison were arrested and held for two days before being escorted to their consuls at Shanghai, it was because they met with mandarins of a different stamp. Their brush with the authorities was explicable by the fact that Suzhou was a hundred miles to the west of Shanghai and only a hundred and fifty miles from the enemy Taipings at Zhenjiang (Chinkiang). Rutherford Alcock of course knew all the missionaries socially, for the foreign community was small, but his duty was to administer a reprimand using whatever tone of voice he chose.

When Hudson Taylor set off in his house-boat on his first journey alone, his expressed purpose was, as well as preaching the gospel and distributing books, to test the reaction of Chinese officials and the public to his presence in foreign clothing, and to find a place to live and work. He was putting himself to the test as well. With ten months in China and one expedition with Edkins to prime him, how would he fare? It was to be the first of ten such journeys (*see* Appendix 9) alone or with a missionary companion. As an introduction to Chinese life and culture these travels built upon his experience in the North Gate suburb, and weaned him from the ugly foreign-ness that could offend and isolate him from the people he loved and wanted to influence. Between the first few journeys he worked with Dr Parker at Shanghai. While the CES withheld the funds for developing their work nothing more could be done than to help other missions and find their own niche in a modest way.

It was the depth of winter and cold in the draughty little house-boat when Hudson Taylor and his crew slipped their moorings at four p m and set off, up the Huangpu on the rising tide. They passed the French and imperial warships without trouble and after darkness fell kept going with sail and oars to leave the area of hostilities well behind. When they tied up after midnight in a side-stream they had covered sixty *li* (twenty miles) south-eastwards, a very good start. Daylight revealed that they were surrounded by ice but they rowed on, breaking it as they went. Hudson Taylor went ashore at hamlets on the river and canal banks, trying to find people able to read his books. The illiterate would only use them to make shoe soles. At a sadly derelict town, Chuansha, he worked systematically through the suburb to the east gate, up and down the main streets and then the poorer ones, and out again to the south, west, and north gate suburbs. He climbed up on to the defensive wall for a better view of the town and made for the principal temples, preaching as best he could to the curious crowds who followed him. All went well, without opposition, and he arrived back at his boat at dusk, thoroughly tired but followed by twelve patients wanting treatment (map, p 216).

The next morning the ice was thick. Three men were needed to break it as they made slow progress, until the sun came up and other boats helped to clear a way through. Hudson Taylor walked to get warm and called at several villages. At another town when he went ashore he was 'never more thoroughly mobbed' by a rabble of noisy followers and had to walk fast to keep ahead of them, in an attempt to escape more rough handling. Rushing to where the boat had been, he saw it had gone. And when he asked bystanders which way it went and started in that direction, he judged from the way they laughed that the opposite direction was the way he should go, and sure enough soon found it.

That night they stopped at Nanhui and his presence was reported to the authorities. They ordered that the east gate be closed against him, but Hudson Taylor had gone to the west gate and started work. When they discovered that he was doing no worse than distributing religious books and leaflets, and the official who attempted to remonstrate with him was disarmed by the gift of a book, they left him alone. Hudson Taylor stood on a hump-back bridge and tried to address a noisy crowd but could not make himself heard. So he made his way back to the boat and allowed only two or three visitors aboard at a time, trying to divert their inquiries from the subject of his clothing or his spectacles to the gospel he came to tell them. A young Catholic stayed for three hours, insisting that Hudson Taylor's theology was deficient, he ought to worship the Virgin Mary, for 'no mother, no son – no Virgin Mary, no Jesus'.

Men came from the magistrate's office and politely chatted with him before warning him not to stay longer – for fear of robbers in the area. He thought he saw through their motives and stayed. And on Monday morning he toured the city wall looking nostalgically through his pocket telescope at foreign ships out on the China sea, and making friends by letting the inevitable onlookers have a turn with it. He preached to crowds of four and five hundred in the temples (a measure of his fluency), and a man took him by sedan chair to see his sick wife. All the people in the neighbourhood seemed to gather round to see and listen to him, but there was nothing he could do for her without a hospital. The importance of medical work as the key to a friendly welcome seemed obvious. Back at the boat he was told that three robbers had been executed during the day.

Undeterred they passed on, travelling thirty miles, until at midnight they could move no farther because of the thickening ice. With daybreak he was besieged by patients, mostly with malaria and eye disease, and could not leave until three p m, but at last he reached Zhapu on the coast at the mouth of the Hangzhou Bay, a very large moated city, fortified against pirates and filled with Chinese merchant refugees from Shanghai. Within the past year it had been attacked from the sea by pirates with cannon, although, or because, one quarter of the city was a Manchu garrison with five thousand men. Wherever he went he and his books were welcomed, for he spoke the people's own dialect and they were eager for the latest news.

By now he had been away as long as he had planned, so he stocked the boat with food and fuel, so much cheaper than at Shanghai, and headed for home. Stopping for nothing except five hours' sleep they kept going until they reached the Settlement on February 1, eight days since leaving and with his boat sadly the worse for wear from battling with the ice. In every way his maiden venture had been a success, and looking back upon it from the vantage point of time we see an unfolding of his lifework.

Dr Parker had been getting anxious for Hudson Taylor's safety, for the 'Chinese authorities are now very suspicious of foreigners, believing that they are favourable to the rebellion'. But after his safe return the next two weeks were more tense and fraught with danger than his week away had been. They went out preaching together, treated such patients as they met, and took the boat down to Wusong to distribute books. On their way back the guard on one of the *daotai*'s war junks fired at them and missed. In the LMS compound life was noisy and hazardous all the time, with the imperial cannon now so close and rebel 'ball and shell' landing among the houses. Missionaries' children playing in the open brought home a 'ball' which fell among them without injury to any. Mrs Parker, out for a stroll, came upon a little girl dying in a ditch, left unpitied by passers-by. They took her to hospital where she died.

At long last they secured the three North Gate men's release from prison, and it was on the way home from the imperial camp that they watched as one or two hundred men dragged a massive new cannon over a track of greased bamboos into position provocatively close to the mission and 'in front of our house'. In one Shanghai account, denied by Lockhart, the soldiers were 'urging them on with whips, sticks, etc. as if they were horses'. Desperate as the state of the beleaguered city had become, Hudson Taylor still thought it could hold out for another month.

On Sunday, February 11, unusual activity on the city walls during the night and among the Cantonese in the Settlement itself alerted the community to the possibility of treachery. Rumours spread that both 'Canton and Fukien men' were going to attack and plunder first the foreigners, then the mandarins and then the imperial camps, to raise the siege and capture Suzhou, a big stride towards linking up with the Taipings. Dr Parker wrote that he was 'much annoyed' at the idea.

Every day brought more information, and excitement among the foreigners rose to a high pitch. Why should the Cantonese be buying such large quantities of red cloth if not for rebel badges and turbans? Everyone was sure that something was in the air. The camps were illuminated, the American marines were landed to strengthen the Settlement guards, missionary vigilantes including Elijah Bridgman joined the night patrols, the English searched some houses, found hidden arms and made arrests. The daily sorties and fighting between imperialists and Triads intensified.

Hudson Taylor wrote laconically in his journal that language study was difficult in such circumstances. There was little else to do. Hundreds of starving people left the Chinese city and reported that all horses, dogs, cats, frogs and rats, leather and insects had been eaten, and they had been reduced to living on grass and weeds. The French let them through, but those who went out to the imperial camps were killed or robbed of whatever they were carrying.

After the arrests in the Settlement, tension subsided, but without dependants, Wylie, Burdon and Hudson Taylor did not wait to know that outcome. With difficulty they obtained permits from Consul Alcock to see them past the French warships, and left Shanghai on Friday, February 16, for another week of evangelism. This time they headed south-west for Qingpu (Tsingpu), where Medhurst, Muirhead and Lockhart had been so badly mauled six years before, and for the city of Songjiang preaching and distributing Scriptures along the way. They were 'exceedingly glad to escape from a very rude mob' on the 17th and kept going until after midnight. On Sunday morning they climbed a hill to a ruined pagoda on its summit and there sat singing hymns and reading Scripture 'with great pleasure and profit'. And there, from the hilltop they saw far away in the direction of Shanghai what they realised was a great pall of smoke (map, p 216).

VILLAGE TEMPLE AND PAGODA

The end of the siege[10]   *February 1855*

'Early in the morning', William Parker wrote on that Sunday,
February 18, after a day of strange experiences,

> my servant came and told me the rebels had set fire to the City and fled.
> I rose and looking from my window saw that a great portion of it was on
> fire . . . I hurried out, for the news seemed too good to be depended
> on. The first place I visited was the American guard house, which was
> filled with rebels getting their heads shaved and their tails dressed. The
> third in command of the rebels was there, severely wounded on the
> right knee joint by a musket ball . . .

The first and second chiefs had fought their way through the
imperial lines and escaped for the time being.

Parker crossed the *pang* and went through several hamlets to the
imperial camp. Soldiers were streaming from the city laden with
loot, even to the coverlets from people's beds. He was treated with
respect and taken into a mandarin's presence to see 'justice' dispensed, and from there into the city itself over the ruins of the North
Gate suburb. Headless corpses everywhere littered the streets
among the ruins and desolation. Crowds of Settlement Chinese
were trying to get into the city with food for their relatives and to
guard what was left of their property, or simply to join in the
looting. The *daotai's yamen*, which had been the Triad chiefs'
headquarters, was in ruins, with the charred bodies of some horses
still in the stables – no doubt saved for an escape instead of being
eaten, but useless at the end. He met a high-ranking mandarin with

a procession of attendants, who stopped and chatted pleasantly with him. A little later he saw soldiers dragging a wretched prisoner along and followed them into the same mandarin's presence. There was nothing he could do. Before Parker's eyes 'they had him down on his face, hacking at his head with a sword like a butcher's knife, and after much ado the head was severed from the body.'

Dr Lockhart got into the city as soon as he could, to go to the help of the Christians and to see how the LMS property had fared. During the night he had heard strange explosions and seen fires spreading on the city walls. It was the night of the Chinese New Year, but this was no celebration. He learned that the rebel chiefs had made their own escape secretly, leaving their men in the lurch, and as soon as this was known a mass breakout had begun. At once the imperialists had touched off a mine near the South Gate and swarmed in, cornering hundreds of rebels. Lockhart searched for civilians among the beheaded bodies but saw not one. All were Triads.

On Tuesday, the 20th, Parker went into a different part of the city and found human heads littering the ground, suspended by their hair or heaped in hundreds. 'It is reported that from one *thousand* to *eighteen hundred* heads have been *cut off since Sabbath morning*,' he wrote. Chaplain Hobson also reported seeing hundreds of heads at the Manchu general's headquarters near the racecourse.

Hudson Taylor and his friends reached Qingpu that day and found that several escaped rebels had been caught and beheaded there. The city was in a state of alarm. When the missionaries' boat was seen approaching, the gates were closed to keep them out but they hurried on to the next gate, 'leaped on shore, and before the news could have passed to them, rushed to the gate. As I gained the gate they were just closing it and I only just got the end of my stick in . . .' Hudson Taylor said.

Boldly they pushed the outer gate open, then the inner gate and were inside the city. No further attempt was made to hinder them. They preached in the temple and were followed back to their boat by crowds wanting tracts. A 'military mandarin' came on board and shared their lunch, telling them the news about Shanghai. At Songjiang they saw a placard about the fall of the city and the slaughter of the chiefs and their families. But in his journal Hudson Taylor showed more interest in the Muslim mosque and burial ground with Arabic inscriptions, and a Confucian temple with Mongol script of the Yuan dynasty, as well as Manchu and different styles of Chinese engravings. A year of destruction and horror had inured them to the news, however frightful, of what after all meant peace and quiet returning to Shanghai.

On Thursday, February 22, they returned home. Now the impact of the tragedy struck Hudson Taylor with full force.

> Here such a scene of desolation met my eye, as I never before witnessed. The outside of the city was full of ruins – the little south gate, by which I entered, had evidently been blown up – . . . and the city itself was a mass of smoking ruins. I . . . saw bodies without heads, ripped open, . . . broken coffins (that the corpses might be beheaded) . . . places with which I had been most familiar were so altered I was unable to recognize them. I returned home quite sick of the sight.

If civilians were spared on the first day, they were soon disillusioned. By March vengeance against the rebels and their collaborators extended to their families. In the mud near the ruins of Hudson Taylor's north suburb home Dr Parker saw about two hundred heads where there had been none before. That day his journal betrayed his disgust. Who could do language study in such an atmosphere? 'Today I did a little Chinese and visited some of the other missionaries . . . When these cruelties will come to an end, I know not . . .'

What then followed is too gruesome to be reproduced verbatim, but because the memory of such things bore directly upon Hudson Taylor's later adventures it is right to include the facts they recorded. As he and Parker were returning from the city they came upon the still warm body of a handsome young man, beheaded, naked and eviscerated. As they looked, two soldiers came up and hacked out the testicles, each going off with one. Parker retreated in horror. Hudson Taylor stood rooted to the ground. Into the mid-twentieth century this practice of cannibalising the heart, liver and testicles of brave and virile men continued, in the belief that the one who ate them would (by what is known as 'sympathetic magic') receive those qualities. But this young man was only the brother of a rebel. On another day they saw 'a large quantity of blood' and came upon forty heads, several of them women's and children's, half eaten by dogs. The next day it was twenty-six.

Day after day the two of them went out with their books, even to the camps, preaching and distributing to any who would listen. The imperial troops were packing up to join in the siege of Nanking, now invested by land and water, Hudson Taylor noted. 'We may not have another opportunity of supplying them. The people (from at least five provinces) . . . were uniformly civil and polite and received our books willingly.'

Shanghai was experiencing such peace as it had not known for a year and a half, but the peace of death. The tally of executions now stood at eighteen hundred to two thousand since the siege of the city ended, but barbarous tortures were going on and on as the mandarins tried to track down every collaborator. Women as well as men were stripped stark naked before being executed, and left lying where they fell or tossed away for the dog packs to find. Hudson Taylor was becoming accustomed to it all and yet was appalled.

> These awful and disgusting sights are now so common that they do not produce the effect on the mind, they did at first. But it is impossible to see these things without unutterable disgust and aversion to that government which perpetrates such disgusting and barbarous atrocities . . . I have seen the most disgusting liberties taken with the dead.

Trying to be forward-looking   March–April 1855

As soon as the Triads had gone and the fires in the city were under control, rebuilding began. The Chinese genius for recovery without self-pity amazed the foreigners. Such resilience deserved the success it earned. Trade began to spring to life. Land was sold to raise money to rebuild whole streets destroyed in the fighting. For Hudson Taylor and Parker this was the moment to buy a site and build the hospital and other premises of their planned headquarters. Their little school near the racecourse had a regular twenty-one pupils, a nucleus for development. March 1 had come and gone, and Hudson Taylor had reached his goal of being able to preach in both mandarin and the Shanghai dialect after one year in China.

To his father he said, 'In my goings about the country I am seeking to find the most suitable place for an attempt at a branch station – but till we have headquarters we can do little good.'

Realism and vision had to go hand in hand. He was neither planning in terms of the impracticable, the 'interior' at all costs, nor dreaming of better days and waiting for them to dawn. In his opinion Shanghai was no place for yet more missions to rub shoulders, let alone compete, but until it was possible to live securely inland, only visits to the country could be made, and that still meant the need of a roof under which to live and work between times. With the Griffith Johns coming nearer, the LMS might need their house at short notice. Where then could the Parkers and Hudson Taylor go?

He longed to get immersed in work that left no time for the frivolous social life of Shanghai which shocked him by its blindness to the sufferings of the Chinese, and wrote censoriously of some of his acquaintances, not allowing that it could be their emotional escape from the proximity of death and distress. Surely the CES would respond to his and William Parker's appeal for funds. Or were they bankrupt? By April a response to their appeal could be expected. Or could it? After more than three months in China Parker had to say that he had received not a single letter from his family or friends and only one impersonal message from the Society. His first arrived in April and the second in August – to report the deaths of his wife's and then of his own mother. Nor, so late in the day, had any credit notes arrived.

> Is not such treatment too bad? [he asked Charles Bird]. It is now nearly a year since I left home and friends, and have not yet received a single letter . . . except your own. This seems to agree with a quaint statement made by a gentleman here, viz. that young societies tumble men into the field, careless whether they fall on their head or feet.

In fact, the latest business letter to reach Hudson Taylor gave him permission to buy benches for the preaching chapel in his North Gate suburb house which had been a heap of rubble for weeks already. It asked him to buy and send more Chinese curios, charging the Society, but said not a word about operating expenses. It was an intolerable situation, yet the two young men tolerated it loyally, making shift on their inadequate personal allowances. Hudson Taylor, the twenty-two year-old, sent meticulous statements of what sums he drew from the agents, and again went as far as he dared in advising his superiors on how to manage their affairs – without success.[11]

But if these promptings were necessary to stir the Society to action, the earliest he could hope for a reply would be in July. It was a recurring theme. Unfortunately *The Gleaner* was having to admit that 'unless considerable funds are soon forthcoming, the Board will be embarrassed in its proceedings'. So Dr Parker's message to George Pearse, that his immediate missionary neighbours were provided with a house and three hundred pounds a year in addition, was foredoomed to fall on deaf ears.

Hudson Taylor reached the nadir of his morale. 'We are in a

shocking position now,' he told his parents. If the CES would not take up the plan for developing the work at Shanghai, 'we mean to try to carry it out without them'. But if the directors opposed their ideas in principle and would not change their insistence on an impracticable policy of residence inland, he and Parker would be forced to a choice between either the Society or their only hope of 'usefulness'. Couldn't a bazaar be got up? he asked. Only a trifling sum was involved. Bondage to an organisation seemed to be sapping his dependence on God. Lack of privacy from morning to night, and sleeping next to the Parker children's room had undermined his vigilance. He soon recovered.

A significant new development took place at this time, whether evidence or not of waning confidence in the CES among its friends and supporters. W T Berger of Hackney in contributing ten pounds specified that it was to be forwarded to Hudson Taylor and the Parkers for use at their discretion. He was as wise and godly a man as any they knew. Rather than allow it to be swallowed up in general expenses they decided to devote it to the support and education of a single Chinese boy in need, and began to look for the right one. And hopefully they began touring the city and neighbourhood, looking for a site or vacant house for them to occupy if the authorisation should come in the next mail.

On March 8 the *Powhattan* arrived at Shanghai with Wilhelm Lobscheid aboard. He 'found this once flourishing city in ruins'. Having come in the service of the United States, he was received with great hospitality by William Boone, the American bishop. Hudson Taylor and Parker went over the Suzhou river to Hongkou and stayed talking with them until nearly midnight. News of the expedition to Japan had to be shared, and the latest reports of the Arthur Taylors and Continental missionaries in the south. They spent all the next day together and much of Lobscheid's time until he sailed for Hong Kong on the 14th. Membership of the CES was common ground.

When Lobscheid reached Hong Kong he found a rebuke for not being at work on the mainland and, worse still, the Society had asked another missionary to report on him. He answered hotly. Why, he had barely escaped to Hong Kong with his life; he was not afraid to expose himself to danger; and he had stayed in Hong Kong to complete the printing of the Bible while the mainland was so disturbed. He issued an ultimatum: trust him or accept his resignation, for he had a challenging alternative.

It is my earnest prayer and endeavour to get up a mission (to the Japanese) and I recommend them to your prayer. The (Americans) offered the Consulate to me but I would not accept of a secular appointment.

In April Hudson Taylor heard from Arthur Taylor that his infant son had died and he had left the CES. Lobscheid had gone to Japan again, this time with the British expedition. The *Occasional Papers* of the Loochoo Naval Mission reported that the bishop of Victoria, Hong Kong, had published parallel Chinese–Japanese volumes of the four Gospels and Acts, and it may be surmised that Lobscheid took copies with him. Then after his return Lobscheid lost his own wife and child and for a time he was content to let other things take their course.

These random indications of the impossibility of administering from Europe the work of missionaries so far from home, formed strong impressions in Hudson Taylor's mind. In years to come, when he became the leader of a growing mission, nothing would shake his conviction that the final direction of missionaries and their work must always be close to where they are located. Otherwise they must be allowed to act on their own discretion under the guidance of God. For the present he endured the inefficiency: George Pearse's humility and courtesy were always disarming and he enjoyed a deepening friendship with him. From 'Dear Sir' and 'Dear Mr Pearse' even official letters in both directions now began, 'My dear Brother'. That this could happen was remarkable, for Hudson did not mince matters. On April 7 he rebuked Richard Ball, the editor of *The Gleaner*, for publishing –

> (a) monstrous mass of absurdities printed as my communication . . . Better have no *Gleaner* at all than send out such a tissue of nonsense to make the Society and its agents a laughing stock to all who see it, and justify the statement of our Agent here, 'the management, or rather mismanagement of your Society is very bad.'

Ball's confusion of place names and dates was unpardonable.

A turn of the medical key   March–April 1855

Dr William Parker had missed two inland journeys through new dangers forcing him to stay with his family, and Hudson Taylor had come back from Zhapu convinced of the value of medical work to ensure a welcome. So they tried again, this time successfully.

On March 19 they set off together in their boat, 'wet and miserable', travelling westwards at first, making for Jiading and then Qingpu. The waterways were crowded with commandeered boats returning from conveying the imperial army to Nanking, but they covered thirty miles the first day (map, p 216).

In the hamlets and southern suburb of Jiading crowds of curious spectators surrounded them, trampling over the wares spread out for sale at the shop doors, for these apparitions in their outlandish dress were a sight to behold. Others, men, women and children fled at their approach, showing considerable fear, and shut their doors until the 'foreign devils' had passed. But when they began preaching and seeing patients at the boat and going to the homes of the more daring ones, the very people who had fled came to invite them to call. Early, before breakfast, the people began to collect on the banks near the boat. Hudson Taylor went ashore, referring the more serious cases to Parker on the boat. They learned that a Catholic priest visited the town every twenty days and voted it 'an admirable plan', for systematic working would clearly have great advantages. But at Jiading, Parker's case of surgical instruments vanished; they had no clue how it happened.

When they arrived at Qingpu on the 23rd, a new kind of surprise greeted them. 'Respectable and intelligent people' accepted their books 'in a pleasant manner', and when they came upon a Chinese concert in progress, with most of the audience standing, a seat was quickly brought for them. They visited the temples, the approved place to preach, and as usual gave New Testaments to the priests. But the attitude of the bystanders struck them most, for some laughed, agreeing that their idols were inert and useless, and another even took a stick and beat one to prove his point.

At the granary city of Changzhong near Songjiang 'uproar' greeted them. So crowded and crushed were they that had they risked a free-for-all by starting to distribute books they could not even have opened their bags. Instead they stood off on their boat and let those have books who came by boat to get them, learning from this that students and people of rank would not demean themselves by pressing through the crowds, but gladly came if they could do so with dignity. When the pressure of visitors became too great they moved along close to the banks and handed thousands of leaflets to men who reached out for them. There was no doubt of the scope for missionary work, with 'scarcely-to-be-exaggerated' illustrations of the value of doctoring – if only the authorities would permit them to settle and get on with it.

On the way back to Shanghai they had a 'narrow escape' but gave no details of it, and reached home between one and two a m, to write their reports and urge again 'the crying necessity for a hospital'.

A few days later Hudson Taylor wrote to George Pearse,

> I hope you have taken up our proposal for an hospital with the vigour that its importance demands. We have already had an offer, entirely unsolicited, of $50 from Revd. J. Hobson, British chaplain, towards it if we can procure a suitable site at the southern part of the City, and from this I think you may see that the importance of the object is apparent to those on the spot . . .

He hoped the Society would lose no time in providing funds, and had enough income to double and treble the number of missionaries.

> For we are . . . longing to be at work . . . but in our present position we cannot be so . . . The door is opened wide . . .; there is a great harvest but few ready to reap.

This journey seemed to do something for both of them and through them for John Burdon and the chaplain. For the next fortnight they worked hard together. Burdon was discouraged by the poor attendance at his chapel in the city, until Parker offered to help. In the *Church Missionary Record* a letter was published in which he said,

> Dr. Parker of the Chinese Evangelization Society . . . has come forward in a very noble, unsectarian spirit to help me . . . A medical missionary has the advantage of the mere evangelist at first.

Parker suggested that three times a week they should run a dispensary, and visit patients in their homes. He still had language study to work at on the other days. They saw the effect immediately. John Burdon's hearers increased to a hundred daily, only half of them patients.

The recovery of the city and its inhabitants was a typically Chinese phenomenon. Rebuilding was gaining pace, trade returning and ocean-going junks were back in the river. A huge idolatrous procession to the temple of the city god drew thousands. The city god was the spiritual counterpart of the chief magistrate of the county. Idols were carried through the streets to the din of percussion bands and wind instruments, and many men bore brass chains, to Hudson Taylor 'fit emblem of the bondage they are in to sin and Satan and superstition'. When he walked out to the Longhua pagoda, distributing tracts, the cemeteries were full of people prostrating themselves and burning paper money at the graves. But the city still teemed with destitute people scavenging and sleeping where they could, and many more finding it difficult to make ends meet.

To help a widowed woman, Hudson Taylor began to teach her grown son, Guihua, and adopted her ten-year-old Hanban, using William Berger's gift of ten pounds to provide for him.

> Hanban was placed under my care, for board, clothing and education, for five years . . . I sincerely trust that he may be early influenced by the Spirit of God, thoroughly converted, and made extremely useful to his own countrymen.'

He also supervised the little school near the racecourse, examining the children and teaching them from the Bible, and was pleased with their progress.

At a general meeting of Shanghai missionaries an unnamed gentleman proposed a united effort to reach all of Shanghai by house-to-house visits, dividing the task between all the societies and meeting to report and pray together. The cool way the proposal was received deeply disappointed William Parker. The rebellion and siege were over, the imperial army and war junks had gone, but a habit of inactivity seemed to have gripped the community. Writing to George Pearse to press his own plan of action Parker said, 'I have no desire to be added to the already great numbers of almost idle missionaries at this port . . .' thereby confirming Hudson Taylor's lament.

Parker himself was certainly not idle. In March he asked Charles Bird to send him books on chemistry, business methods and science, including Humboldt's *Cosmos* in four volumes. And in April Hudson Taylor wrote home for a three-volume tome of *Natural Philosophy and Astronomy* for Parker. With John Burdon, Parker planned to open an outstation, a country dispensary and preaching point, oblivious to the fact that his company meant so much to his primary colleague, Hudson Taylor, and that the new arrangements left him not only to find his own work but lonely at heart.

All the time they were on their recent journey together, Hudson Taylor's thoughts had been straying to his apparent inability to win a wife. At home again, he sat down and wrote two long letters, to Elizabeth Sissons and her father, repeating his proposals to her, and pleading with him not to oppose her coming.

> We have plenty of ladies here who have so many calls to make, so much crochet work and fancy knitting to do, that they have no time to seek out the poor neglected females around them.

He sent home a Chinese Grammar, to be passed on to Elizabeth if she decided to come to him, to get her started on the language.

He was being cynical, but the fact remained that Chinese propriety forbade a man to look at or speak with a woman except in carefully controlled situations. The women kept their distance, and patients were well chaperoned. Devoted women missionaries had access and opportunities among their own sex denied to men. He was longing for a wife. He also wanted Chinese women to have the gospel given to them. He did not then know that Elizabeth had at last written to him; or that he was sailing into some very choppy water.

John Burdon had no thought of leaving Hudson Taylor out. On April 11 when Hobson and Burdon dined with the Parkers they all enjoyed 'a profitable evening'. It was no mere cliché. Future plans must have featured largely in their conversation, for as a result Hobson doubled his offer to a hundred dollars in the hope of encouraging other donations to swell the fund for launching Parker's hospital. They thought three to four hundred pounds could be raised in Shanghai. And Burdon and Hudson Taylor resolved on an adventurous journey to Chongming (Tsungming) Island in the Yangzi estuary and to part of the north shore where they knew no Protestant missionary had ever been.[12] Only one other point had been touched at in passing, on an unsuccessful attempt by Ningbo missionaries to go up the Yangzi to Nanking. This was not only unevangelised territory, it was unknown and from the point of view of foreigners, remote. Anything could happen (map, p 216).

Taken for rebels[13]   *April 1855*

On Monday, April 16, Hudson Taylor and John Burdon, 'an excellent and devoted man', engaged two sea-going Yangzi junks for their journey and arranged for two Chinese teachers to go with them. Packing up books and medicines, provisions and bedding took them most of the day and until five am the next morning.

Hudson Taylor's custom was to compound some of his medicines from Chinese sources. His own little boat was far too small for the great estuary. The Yangzi was thirty miles wide where they planned to go and could be very stormy. They knew the risks. He told George Pearse,

> The rebellion (and more especially since foreigners have enlisted themselves on both sides), makes access to the interior no *easy* matter now. But the Word of God must go, and we must not be hindered by the slight obstacles . . .

Apart from preaching the gospel, his purpose was always to find a place to live and work –

> and of course it is impossible to say whether the attempt when made, will be successful or not.

At nine am on the 17th they set off with the ebbing tide down the Huangpu to Wusong where enquiries about the wind and visibility were customarily made. 'The great number of opium shops was here what we most noticed; in one we saw a young girl of not more than twelve years smoking the noxious drug . . .' Then out on to the estuary and northward until after dark they reached Chongming Island and pulled into the mouth of a creek for shelter. The island was sixty or seventy miles long by fifteen or twenty broad, with a population of a million. With daylight the next day they worked up another stream to the city of Chongming itself, and a circuit of the walls and visits to the temples quickly drew 'uncommonly attentive crowds' who jostled them for books without any evidence of ill-feeling. This was a good start.

Hudson Taylor saw a tablet in honour of Guandi, a general of the late Han dynasty who was elevated to deity as the god of war, so to gain the interest of the crowd he launched into a sketch of Guandi's history, going on to tell them about Jesus, who also lived at the time of the Han dynasty; how he healed the sick, raised the dead and 'laid down his life for the good . . . of the whole world . . .' They listened until he could go on no longer and had to tell them to come to the boat if they wanted more books. To accomplish so much meant he had made considerable progress in the language.

From there they went to the temple of the city god and while Hudson Taylor doctored, John Burdon preached, until the yard was filled with five or six hundred people and he was exhausted. The clamour became deafening and the pulling and pushing so violent that Hudson Taylor climbed on to a large incense urn and at the top of his voice called for quiet. The extraordinary spectacle of this young barbarian in Victorian garb created great excitement, but hearing him speak in mandarin and not even a southern dialect, brought silence (*see* p 323).

They listened well, calling out '*bu cuo*' (*pu ts'o*), 'quite right' until it began to rain. Then a young humorist pulled him down, snatching at his bag of books and instruments. He tried to get away and took refuge in a sedan chair, but the chair was smashed and he had to walk the mile to the boat. It was all good-natured horseplay, but hands grabbed at his bag, broke the handle and took things from it. They laughed when he managed to shut it again. In the mêlée he lost his hat and spectacles. The hat was picked up and returned to him but the spectacles, so necessary to prevent his headaches, had gone irretrievably. It was nearly dark by the time he reached the boat, wet and exhausted. That was the prelude.

On Monday, April 23, they moved north-westwards along the coast of Chongming, working through several towns on the way, and were well received on the prosperous island of Dushan. But when they came on to the alluvial island of Haimen (completely joined to the mainland by the end of the century) some 'uncommonly rude men' crowded round them. While Burdon was preaching in dialect, however, he happened to say that he and his companion were foreigners. At once 'the people seemed quite astonished and remarked to one another, "They are foreigners, they are foreigners!"' They had mistaken them for Fujianese.

Travellers up the Yangzi river pass between Fu Shan, Happy Mountain, on the south side, and Lang Shan, Wolf Mountain, on the north mainland. Hudson Taylor and John Burdon headed for Lang Shan and because their voices were so hoarse, decided to take the day off and climb the mountain to survey the area. For a week they had shown the feasibility and value of the kind of work they were doing. 'The scene became beautiful beyond description' as they walked. Lang Shan stood in the centre of five hills, crowned by a five-storey pagoda, newly repaired and painted. Around it stood a temple and a monastery so extensive that they thought they were coming to a village. In his journal Hudson Taylor became lyrical in his descriptions. But here the idolatry was by no means the dead or dying observance in dilapidated buildings they were accustomed to seeing near Shanghai.

Here was an institution, swarming with priests, and those under training . . . The idols were hundreds in number and varied from those of gigantic size, to those of not more than a few inches in height. They were richly painted (as indeed was the whole establishment), and gilding in profusion was lavished on them and it.

Not only so, it was a festival day, with thousands of every age, rich and poor visiting the temples. Bowing, burning incense, throwing cash into the coffers, the worshippers went from room to room, shrine to shrine, level to level up the hillside, with the heavy odour of burning incense, the clinking of coins, the pleasant religious music and the voices of the vast multitude creating an unforgettable effect.

Together they climbed to the summit of the hill and the very top of the pagoda. The view brought 'involuntary exclamations of surprise and delight . . .' Hudson Taylor wrote. 'No language can adequately describe it.' The day was wonderfully crisp and only the horizon limited the clear view in all directions through his pocket telescope. The 'magnificent Yangtzekiang, here 15–20 miles broad' in an arc with its concavity towards them, Fu Shan and other hills with their temples and pagodas far away on the other shore, lakes to

IDOLS BY THE HUNDRED

the westward reflecting the sky, and to their north-west the city of Tongzhou.[14] The wheat was already in the ear, and orchards of peach, apricot, plums, apples, cherries and other fruit in blossom.

Well-educated Chinese, many with the gilt buttons of lower-ranking mandarins collected round them, and beautiful ladies came and went in their Buddhist worship. Hudson Taylor's heart became fuller and fuller. On the way downhill again, while he was passing through a courtyard named the Pool of Tranquillity, a priest invited him to burn incense and bow to the Buddha. He could restrain himself no longer. Disregarding priest and idol he stood on a raised platform and began to preach in mandarin. John Burdon reported that he was well understood by the crowd. He decried the folly and sin of idolatry as a substitute for worship of the true God and told them of his love and provision of an acceptable sacrifice for sin 'theirs and ours'. 'I asked . . . if these remarks were not true and they acknowledged they were.' Then John Burdon followed in the Shanghai dialect. But on the way back to their boat they witnessed the other side of the festival, polluting scenes 'the very mention of which would outrage propriety'.

Tongzhou, the neighbouring city, was notorious for its belligerent militia and people, 'Satan's seat', and bound to give foreign missionaries a hot reception.

Their companions, the Chinese teachers, did their best to dissuade them from going on, so Burdon and Taylor told them to stay with the boats and, if they did not return, to find out all they could and hurry back to Shanghai with the news. The second boat was to wait in case the missionaries succeeded after all in getting back.

> We felt persuaded that Satan would not allow us to assail his kingdom . . . without raising serious opposition; but we were also fully assured that it was the will of God that we should preach Christ in this city, and distribute the Word of Truth among its people.
>
> After breakfast [on Thursday, April 26] we commended ourselves to the care of our Heavenly Father, and sought His blessing . . . packed some books into two bags with a servant to carry them and set off on the seven miles to Tongzhou.

It was a dull, wet day and the road was rough and muddy, so they hired passenger wheelbarrows, the only available transport. They had not gone far when the servant asked permission to return, he was too afraid. They relieved him of the book-bags and let him go.

At this point a respectable man came up, and earnestly warned us against proceeding, saying that if we did we should find to our sorrow what the Tungchow militia were like. We thanked him for his kindly counsel, but could not act upon it, as our hearts were fixed.

Hearing this, Hudson Taylor's wheelbarrow man would go no farther, but another was found and they ploughed on through the mud and rain encouraging one another with the words of Scripture and fitting hymns. 'Now, Lord, behold their threatenings; and grant unto thy servants, that with all boldness they may speak thy word . . .' felt most appropriate. Passing through a small market town they preached outside a tea-shop and Hudson Taylor was so 'filled with joy and peace' that he 'was able to speak with unusual freedom'. Afterwards he heard a bystander repeating correctly to another what he had been saying, 'That one moment repaid me for all the trials we had passed through . . .'

Coming to the suburb of Tongzhou they made their plans. The wheelbarrow men were to wait where they would not be involved in any trouble, and taking the bags the missionaries prayed together and started to walk. At first they were unmolested and found it amusing to be called 'black devils', a comment on their clothes. Several soldiers let them go by.

Long before we reached the gate, however, a tall powerful man, made tenfold fiercer by partial intoxication, let us know that all the militia were not so peaceably inclined, by seizing Mr. Burdon by the shoulders.

In John Burdon's own words, 'with a tremendous shout (he) attacked me.'[15]

Burdon tried to shake him off, and as Hudson Taylor turned to see what was happening,

we were surrounded by a dozen or more brutal men, who hurried us on to the city at a fearful pace. My bag now began to feel very heavy, and I could not change hands . . . I was soon in a profuse perspiration, and was scarcely able to keep pace with them. We demanded to be taken before the chief magistrate, but were told they knew where to take us, and what to do with such persons as we were, with the most insulting epithets.

The big man left Burdon and became Hudson Taylor's 'chief tormentor'.

TAKEN FOR REBELS

He all but knocked me down again and again, seized me by the hair, took hold of my collar so as almost to choke me, and grasped my arms and shoulders, making them black and blue. [As John Burdon saw it] My friend was most terribly mauled and dragged along at a fearful rate.[16]

In spite of everything Burdon tried to pass books to the jostling crowd, not knowing whether there would be another opportunity to do so,

but the fearful rage of the soldier, and the way he insisted on manacles being brought . . . convinced us that in our present position we could do no good . . . There was nothing to be done but . . . go along with our captors. Once or twice a quarrel arose as to how we should be dealt with . . .

Some of the soldiers were for killing them out of hand, but others said they should be taken to the magistrate's *yamen*. They had mistaken them for Taiping rebels, not even recognising their clothes as foreign. So now it was touch and go. Writing later to George Pearse, Hudson Taylor said, 'We had such a narrow escape from death.' But to his mother he revealed the insistent fears he had been suppressing.

> Knowing the atrocities perpetrated . . . on the unfortunate Rebels who fall into their hands – our feelings were well expressed by those beautiful lines quoted to me by Mr. Burdon (at that moment . . .), 'calm amidst tumultuous motion, knowing that the Lord is nigh', and by a passage of Scripture which I quoted to him, 'rejoicing that they were counted *worthy* to suffer in the cause of Christ'.

But the more moderate men in the militia had their way.

At last Hudson Taylor somehow managed to get a hand into his pocket and produced an identity card, a sheet of red paper bearing his name. At once they were treated with respect – and taken to the office of a minor mandarin. Exhausted and bathed in perspiration, with his tongue clinging to the roof of his mouth, Hudson Taylor leaned against a wall as soon as they stopped. John Burdon was little better off. They asked for a drink and to be allowed to sit, and were told to wait. A crowd gathered, and Burdon mustered strength to preach to them.

The official decided they must be taken to a mandarin of higher rank, but nothing would make either of them budge until sedan chairs were brought. So relieved and even cheerful did they then look that they heard people say that they 'did not look like bad men, while others seemed to pity' them. They were carried through great gateways into what they feared was a prison, until a large tablet with the characters 'Father and Mother of the People' put them at ease. It was the chief magistrate's *yamen* at last.

Suddenly things took a dramatic change. They were ushered into the presence of a higher dignitary than they had expected. Wearer of the opaque blue button of a lieutenant-governor he was addressed as Great Venerable Father. The attendants tried to make them *ketou* as everyone else began to do. But this magistrate had in the past been *daotai* of Shanghai and was at home with foreigners

Incredibly, he came forward to meet them, showed them 'every possible token of respect' and took them into an inner room. There he shared refreshments with them and accepted copies of the New Testament and some books of the Old. They told him that they exonerated the soldiers, who knew no better, but they would like with his approval to continue distributing books and preaching, if he would kindly direct that they should not be molested again. As if they were honoured friends he escorted them to the door of his residence and sent them off like notables in sedan chairs with an escort of *yamen* runners to see that they were treated respectfully.

Crowds filled the streets, but the runners cleared a way through by flailing with their *bianzi* (queues) and, when all the books were exhausted, saw them out of the city 'quite in state'. Apart from John Burdon's supply, Hudson Taylor had distributed five hundred and thirty-three New Testaments and other Scriptures, and one thousand three hundred and sixty-two books and tracts. In the suburbs they paid off the chair-bearers, mounted their humble wheelbarrows and headed back to the boats, escorted half the way by a representative of the chief magistrate.

The story could end there but needs a postscript. Just as Hudson Taylor a few days before had entered in his journal not that there was a slight earthquake but with characteristic punctilio, that it occurred 'at 2 h. 57′ 30″ and lasted 40‴', so now he settled down to record the day's events and details of books distributed, and to name the crops and fruit trees he had seen, that the grave mounds were lower than elsewhere, and that well-to-do homes had private cemeteries hedged by cypresses. At the height of their adventure he had observed to John Burdon that the experience would make good copy for their journals, and both men wrote it up fully. The following day they crossed the Yangzi and turned for home, reaching Shanghai late at night on Saturday, April 28. Altogether they had travelled nearly three hundred miles.

Yangzi reconnaissance   *May 1855*

During the week after the Tongzhou adventure Hudson Taylor house-hunted with Dr Parker for a dispensary in the city and joined in the routine evangelism. Already the adventure was a thing of the past. He met Hong Ren, the one-time evangelist and now a Taiping prince, who gave him a copy of Theodore Hamberg's booklet on the Taipings, 'the best account of the rise of the rebellion I have yet

seen'. (Hong Ren, the *Taiping Wang*'s cousin, had been the verbatim source of most of its information.) But the journey with Burdon
had whetted Hudson Taylor's appetite for pioneering. Undaunted
by the danger and without a companion free to go with him, for John
Burdon still had his motherless child to care for, he decided to
return to the Yangzi at once and to go as far up as he could – to
Nanking if the way was open to do so, and to be in no hurry to return.
It would leave more room for the Parkers in their little house, and
lead, he hoped, to finding fertile soil where he could put down roots.

To meet a wretch on Sunday, May 6, whose *tendo achilles* of both
heels had been severed for his association with the rebels, was not a
good start, but on Monday Hudson Taylor hired a junk, a better,
rainproof one this time, and prepared his equipment and provisions
for the journey. The next day he sailed down to the junction of the
Huangpu and Yangzi and worked first through Wusong and then at
Baoshan, two or three miles inland, distributing booklets and
commending their contents. While he preached the gospel he was
given a good hearing, but when he started on the folly and sin of
worshipping idols, a maker of incense and paper money raised a
clamour and drove the audience away. (It was customary at that
time for missionaries to use this approach, like the apostle Paul at
Athens and Ephesus, until the resentment aroused by its negative
nature taught its own lesson.) After that Hudson Taylor could get
no one to listen.

It was late in the afternoon, but the tide and wind were in their
favour, so in spite of their protests that the estuary would be too
rough, he urged the boatmen to sail without delay. No sooner had
they left the shelter of the Huangpu than he ate the words he had
just written: 'the Chinese are an astonishing people . . . No matter
what it be you propose, the first thing they do is to prove its utter
impracticability.' For the boatmen's protests had been more astute
than he had realised. With the folk-wisdom of centuries they had
deftly placed the onus of risk-taking on their employer before
setting out. Very soon the rudder was disabled and the motion
became so great that he was 'afraid the mast would work the bottom
out of the boat'. They succeeded, however, in repairing the rudder,
and reached another river-mouth by nightfall.

Then began a systematic search for literate people in the villages
and towns on the south shore of the Yangzi to whom to offer books,
and he saw patients at the boat. His journal listed his itineraries:
May 9th, to Qianjing (Tsuenking) by wheelbarrow; 10th, Liuhe old

city, 40,000; 11th, Liuhezhen, 20,000 – and so on. Foreign sportsmen had been to Liuhezhen on a shooting expedition, and he was
'pestered' by a mob. As far as he knew missionaries had never been
to this region.

> As usual, the demand for books from the mob was very great, and
> when I refused to give them to those who were unable to read, not a
> few tried to snatch them from me, but they were not successful.

On he went to Huangjing and a very different reception (map, p
216):

> . . . they ran away from me as if I was going to eat them. . . . As I went
> along I could not help feeling sad and cast down. Wherever you go
> towns and villages are teeming with inhabitants and few of them have
> ever heard of the true God, or of His Word. And just to visit them, give
> them portions of Scripture and tracts, and then pass on, seems almost
> like doing nothing for them (except that it is the Word of God and will
> do its own work), but we see no fruit at present and it requires strong
> faith to keep one's spirits from sinking. Besides which, I have felt a
> degree of nervousness since I was so roughly handled at Tungchow . . .
> and one feels this the more when alone . . . Faint and weary (having
> eaten nothing since breakfast but a few sour plums) we arrived at four
> pm and I prayed God to enable me to distribute my books to the best
> advantage, and to give me a word to speak to this people.

In the event he could have distributed to readers four times the
number of books he took with him. They brought him a stool to
stand on and he 'preached Jesus Christ and him crucified', while
they listened 'with utmost attention', wanted books about what he
said, 'and eagerly asked when I should return and bring them
more?'

The next day too, the hottest of the year, at four more places
alarm and shyness evaporated and they were 'hugely delighted' to
find he could understand and talk with them. His spare spectacles,
watch and *leather* shoes aroused great curiosity and speculation, a
conversation about them reflecting the naivety he had to contend
with. 'My watch . . . was stated to be . . . a small clock, announcing
the time by the striking of a bell.'

Then he visited an eighty-year-old mandarin in his home, 'a rich
and intelligent old gentleman'. Outside the reception room was a
large lacquered and gilded inscription, 'Act morally and you will
have happiness.' In return for Hudson Taylor's gift of books the old
man presented ten volumes by himself. He believed that the earth
moved on an axis round a stationary sun. And for Hudson Taylor he

wrote out a list of climbing plants which twist clockwise or anti-clockwise as they grow.[17] Hudson Taylor so enjoyed the old gentleman's company, and wanted to talk with him again, when he had read some of the Christian booklets, that the following day, after preaching to two hundred in another town and laying open two carbuncles, he returned to the old mandarin. It gave him a more restful Sunday.

On Monday, May 14, it was a very different story. He had to abandon the next place he visited, when he was driven out by noisy villagers and half-drunk sailors who pelted him with mud. He dropped downstream to the Yangzi again and waited at the mouth for the tide to carry him up to Fushan. The hill, Fu Shan, was the one he and John Burdon had seen far in the distance from the pagoda at Lang Shan. So he first climbed it and surveyed the area before entering the town. To his surprise he learned that Joseph Edkins and a colleague had been there only two days before. The intricate river and canal network of the whole area, over hundreds of miles, made access possible from inland, and their absence from Shanghai would explain his ignorance of their intentions. Plainly the whole region was being worked through, however cursorily.

On May 16 Hudson Taylor was so preoccupied with his work that darkness fell before he could reach his boat at Changshu and its semi-foreign comforts.

> (Without) plates, dishes, cups, saucers, knives, forks, spoons, bedding nor any provisions, I had therefore to turn to a basin of rice and one or two (duck's) eggs fried in oil, with the chopsticks, which had been in the mouths of I know not how many Chinamen before.

As he had had nothing else since breakfast, the simple meal was 'a scrumptious repast'. He slept rough and, waking long before meals would be served in the foodshops, went for a six-mile walk in the mist and rain, climbing up through low cloud to some temples, counting four hundred and eighty-three idols between one and twelve feet high in one temple hall, and enjoying the beauty of trees and streams through the haze.

> The air in the valley was laden with the perfumes of the rose and honeysuckle; and I noticed that the wild-roses here were fragrant, whereas those near Shanghai (are not).

By the time he got back to the boat he was soaked through, but hunger made him 'very proficient with the chopsticks'. The local women reminded him of Amelia by the way they parted their hair in the current English fashion, bringing it down over their temples and up again to a knot at the back. Then he found parts of the town not visited by Edkins, distributed his books and instead of reverting to English ways, 'had a chopstick dinner'. This was the weaning process he needed, and he began to enjoy emancipation from the fussy clutter of foreign implements and conventions. 'Sculling along' he wrote letters. The boatmen and other Chinese were delighted by his adaptation to their ways, and recommended him to get his head shaved and to change into Chinese clothes – 'till one suggested I could not change my eyes and nose'. Ten miles farther on he was pelted again, in a village with two hundred Roman Catholic families, when they 'discovered I was no Romanist. I determined not to be driven away', but stayed to treat patients and break down prejudice, 'besides which I felt unwell'.

His twenty-third birthday, May 21, found him on an island out in the Yangzi, seven miles from shore, peopled from the north and therefore mandarin-speaking. There too he preached 'with ease' and gave out books and tracts discriminatingly to reading people. Always, in his journal, are notes of whether literati were few or many, and whether there were 'respectable people' who would value the books. 'I had to treat between forty and fifty patients before I could dine.' Then back to the mainland, from town to town. At one place he removed a tumour from the back of a young man's neck, but such doctoring as he did was mostly for the ever-present 'ague', and eye and skin disease. Then followed a day feeling ill but badgered by troublesome people. He was tiring.

> Today while walking, bathed in perspiration and weary, it was a refreshing thought, that Jesus doubtless often felt the same, for he went about in a hot country.

In fact, his daily journal entries tended to finish with the refrain, 'returned to the boat as it was getting dark and I was tired and hungry'. Yet he wrote up his experiences, conducted evening prayers with his servant and crew, and after dark had a refreshing bathe in the river before turning in for the night.

Then more stormy weather and a rough crossing to another island, the discovery of 'two or three insects' new to him, an intensely hot day on the 28th, and a visit to Jiangyin, a town with higher walls than most,

. . . the next city to Chinkiangfu [Zhenjiang], where the rebels are; so you see I am gradually getting up the river. My present object is the distribution of the Word of God, and I am trying to learn all I can of the geography of the country, and to get as well known as possible, lest the remark often made, that I am one of the foreigners in the service of the Rebels, come to spy out the land, should be thought correct.

Medical work was proving most effective in creating confidence and a welcome wherever he went. But his supplies were nearly exhausted, and he was nearing the Manchu defence line. So on the 30th, after pressing on westwards for twenty more miles, to two smaller towns about sixty miles short of Zhenjiang (Chinkiang) and two hundred miles from Shanghai, he turned and crossed the Yangzi to Jingjiang (Tsingkiang) on the north shore as his last objective before returning to base. The people were 'rough and boisterous but not unfriendly'. It was an antagonistic magistrate who was soon to be his downfall. With the end of May he started for Shanghai again, on a rough and stormy Yangzi so that he was very sick and the junk was shipping water, and on June 1 they reached Wusong and covered the last fifteen miles to make Shanghai at midnight.

In the twenty-five days away he had been to seven walled cities and fifty towns and villages. Never before had anyone taken the gospel to two of the cities or forty-nine of the other places. Of fifteen hundred books and leaflets and twelve hundred Scriptures, he had given out two hundred and twenty New Testaments, seven hundred and forty quarter- or part-Testaments, and two hundred and fifty part-Old Testaments.

On that same day Parker was writing to George Pearse that Hudson Taylor had left three weeks ago and not returned, while the Taipings had won a great victory at Zhenjiang over the besieging imperialists. He could not have gone farther if he had tried. At more than one place the people had mistaken him for a long-haired Fujian man, so ignorant were they of the appearance of their own people in another province.

The manhandling at Tungzhou had never been far from his thoughts. As for the rebellion, he told his parents and Amelia in long letters from the boat, he thought it could go on for ten or twenty more years, with little possibility or desirability of the rebels' success. It did not matter that he had had to return before making contact with them. In the event the Taiping revolt ended after nine more years, but concurrent insurrections went on for many more.

Shanghai was much as he had left it. The rats at home had been so bad, eating his candles and jumping on to his bed while he was in it, that he had bought a cat and two kittens during his journey, expecting Shanghai to be his base for a long time to come. But he found Parker more disillusioned than ever with the CES, and he himself had been mulling over problems while he travelled. How could he marry if his society, the CES, was so unreliable in supporting him? he asked in a letter home.

> I wish that when I was in England, I had been able to procure a medical diploma, *independent of them*, as then I could easily have got a position of £300 or more per annum, without preventing my doing missionary work . . .

The CES were in danger of losing Dr Parker and had little hold left on Lobscheid, but the family must not think Hudson's own position was in that way altered or endangered. Had he been medically qualified he could by now have been taken on by the British residents in Ningbo. Six merchants and three missionary families would have guaranteed his salary. But he was not, and that was that.

This was his first mention of Ningbo as a possible place to work in. Plans were afoot for an evangelistic journey there and back, preaching along the way, and Burdon and Parker were waiting for him to join them. They too had heard of possibilities in Ningbo, and Parker wanted to make more enquiries. If the Society would not finance his hospital in Shanghai, Ningbo was an alternative place and source of funds. So after just a week to rest and stock up with drugs and books Hudson Taylor was off again.

CHAPTER EIGHT

A PARTING OF THE WAYS
1855

'City of Tranquil Waves'   *June 1855*

On Friday, June 8, John Burdon, William Parker and Hudson Taylor set out from Shanghai by canal boat, heading southwards towards the Hangzhou Bay. For five days they preached and dispensed their books and tracts in four walled cities and fourteen towns and villages, but found them largely depopulated. With the garrisons depleted by the need to send all available men against the Taipings, pirates were having a heyday, pillaging town after town along the coast. And not all were Chinese. At Jinshan on the Jiangsu-Zhejiang provincial border, desolated by the pirates, where they preached the gospel in the *yamen* itself, they met an armed American who told them he was in the salt trade. He could have been a guard or pirate or both. At another place they met other missionaries working as they were. Bit by bit the area was being covered. Finally they approached Zhapu, the Manchu garrison city at the mouth of Hangzhou Bay where Hudson Taylor had been in icy January (map, p. 216).

There he left the others to make their way to an agreed rendezvous, and himself went out along a sea dyke to give books to the men in a coastal fort. He preached in mandarin to soldiers from distant provinces, visited the temple of the sailors' goddess in Zhapu city, and then tried to find a sea-going junk to cross the bay. When he came to the city gates to rejoin Burdon and Parker outside, they were already locked. As a measure of what foreigners could do, despite the treaty limitations, he sent a messenger to the mandarin for permission to leave, and while the key was being fetched, preached to the inevitable bystanders. But outside, his friends were not at the rendezvous.

Darkness fell and they had not turned up. A friendly housewife took pity on him and gave him food and a bed for the night.[1] In his accounts of the journey he said nothing as previously about knives and forks. He was fully at home with bowl and chopsticks among the hospitable Chinese. Early in the morning he arranged for messengers to go east, north and west to search for his friends, while he himself went down to the harbour to hire a junk for the crossing. 'Astonished to see my lost companions', he recorded, giving no explanation.

The boat duly hired, a deposit paid and a departure time agreed (at night to avoid the pirates), they spent the day working through the town and preaching. Then after dark they took their essentials with them, leaving the canal boat and other things to wait for their return, and made their way to the junk. To their surprise it was already dangerously full with cargo and twenty passengers. Over and above the sum agreed with the foreigners, the skipper had taken fares from all these men, thinking he held the trump card. But the 'foreign devils' refused to let him leave until most of the 'yellow fish' had disembarked – insisting on his finding them another junk. It was midnight before they sailed, straight into rough seas and *mal de mer*, and still so crowded that there was not enough room for all to lie down on the deck planks. 'We should have been in a pretty mess had we not been firm and refused to be imposed upon,' Hudson Taylor commented. He learned from this experience that in agreeing a price with a skipper he must distinguish clearly between chartering the junk for his sole use, and paying simply his own and his companions' fares.

The crossing was made safely, without a sign of pirates, and

A DEFENCE AGAINST PIRATES

transferring to a canal boat with more haggling and delay they reached Ningbo after dark and unannounced. Unexpected arrivals were commonplace at a time of unrest, and the Ningbo missionaries rose to the occasion. The travellers were entertained in different homes, made the acquaintance of the Americans, met the translators of the Ningbo dialect New Testament, went on an evangelistic expedition with some of the Englishmen, watched tea-picking in this source of the choicest green tea in China, and Hudson Taylor saw but failed to catch more unfamiliar insects. The visit was over in a week, and he was immobilised by dysentery much of the time, but all unknowingly he was having his introduction to the environment that would most strongly shape his future life.

According to the Sinologue, W A P Martin, the meaning of the name Ningbo, like *pax vobiscum*, 'peace be with you', is 'Peace to the Waves' or 'the city that gives peace to the open sea', a historical allusion. For centuries piracy, Chinese and foreign, had plagued the coasts, and from its position near the mouth of Hangzhou Bay this city provided what protection the emperor could give to his subjects. Its almost impregnable position and construction made it the envy of less fortunate cities, for it lay in the angle between two tributaries where they joined to form the navigable river Yong, twelve miles from the coast. There at its mouth where it narrowed to a mere one hundred yards, stood a rocky island and the fortified town of Zhenhai (Chinhai). 'An extensive artificial sea-beach of hewn granite' was used by 'an enormous fleet of junks', and trade flourished, with ocean access to northern and southern ports and, since 1842, Europe and America. Not far away, at Hangzhou, the head of the bay, began the Grand Canal, the arterial trade route all the way to Tianjin at the portals of Peking, thirteen hundred miles to the north (map, p 80).[2]

At the imposing city of Ningbo itself the river formed a moat from the north to the south gate.[3] A ring of hills a few hundred to three thousand feet high formed an outer bastion to the amphitheatre in which the city lay. Castellated granite-faced city walls extending for five miles in circuit, with a fifteen- to twenty-foot road on its summit, formed its inner line of defence, strong enough to withstand the British bombardment in 1841. Six gates with guard houses above them and a garrison of three thousand troops were there for the protection of its four hundred thousand inhabitants. Besides the north, south, east and west gates Ningbo had a Salt Gate on the north-east fronting one tributary, and a Bridge Gate near the east gate, so named from a pontoon bridge linking it with the largest suburb.

After Hangzhou, Ningbo was the most important town in Zhejiang and in the words of the bishop of Victoria, Hong Kong, 'one of the finest and largest cities of the Empire' with many beautiful temples, gardens and spacious mansions. Its 'superior population' made it one of the most literary cities, inferior only to Suzhou and Hangzhou in refinement; one fifth of its people were said to be literati. Its main streets, spanned by ornamental arches, were broad and clean. Canals honeycombed the densely-built areas, and at its centre lay a moon-lake.

This city was about a thousand years old. Even so its place in this 'Glorious Kingdom' was one among many. The viceroy of the two provinces of Fujian and Zhejiang had his palace at Fuzhou. The lieutenant-governor of Zhejiang and the provincial treasurer and judge were at Hangzhou. Four *daotai*, of whom one was at Ningbo, presided over eleven prefectures, including three cities and sixty-three county towns, all walled. As a missionary sphere it was superb. Six or seven million people spoke the distinctive Ningbo dialect, as mellifluous, according to W A P Martin, as some were harsh, but in the words of the sage, 'I'd rather take a scolding at Suzhou than listen to a love-song at Xiaoshan' – not far from Ningbo.

Surrounding the city, on both sides of each tributary and the main river, lay populous suburbs, Chinese shipyards and docks. And in a loop of the river largely given over to rice-fields, cemeteries and a few villages, the foreign merchant community and consulates had become established. A Portuguese settlement had been tolerated there since as long ago as 1530, and British merchant houses had sprung up beside the main anchorage for foreign shipping. A loose-living, drifting community of seafarers was the outcome – English, American, Indian, German, Spanish and Portuguese – 'living in a state of fearful and open wickedness'.

W C Milne of the LMS had succeeded in living briefly at Ningbo before the Treaty of Nanking and making his daring, or foolhardy, overland journey in disguise to Hong Kong for the first missionary conference, but in 1855 he was no longer there. The rest of the missionary community were to become Hudson Taylor's close associates. For five years after the treaty, and the opening of Ningbo as one of the five treaty ports, the American Baptists and American Presbyterians were the only missions, represented by two medical

GRANITE WALLS FOR FIVE MILES (Ningbo)

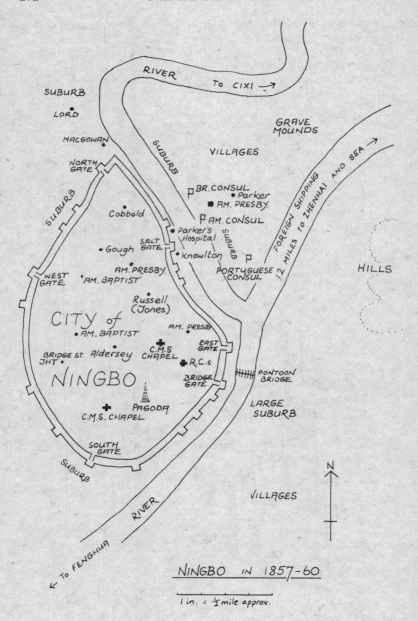

RIVER

To CIXI →

SUBURB
LORD

GRAVE
MOUNDS

MACGOWAN

SUBURB

VILLAGES

NORTH
GATE

SUBURB

SUBURB

FOREIGN SHIPPING

Cobbold

BR. CONSUL
Parker
AM. PRESBY.
AM. CONSUL
Parker's
Hospital
Knowlton
PORTUGUESE
CONSUL

12 MILES TO ZHENHAI AND SEA →

HILLS

Gough

SALT
GATE

SUBURB

WEST
GATE

AM. PRESBY.
AM. BAPTIST

Russell
(Jones)

CITY of
AM. BAPTIST

AM. PRESBY

EAST
GATE

BRIDGE ST.
JHT

Aldersey

C.M.S
CHAPEL

R.C.s

PONTOON
BRIDGE

NINGBO

BRIDGE
GATE

PAGODA

LARGE
SUBURB

C.M.S. CHAPEL

SOUTH
GATE

N ↑

SUBURB

VILLAGES

RIVER

To FENGHUA →

NINGBO IN 1857-60

1 in. = ½ mile approx.

men, Dr D J Macgowan using a temple as a temporary hospital, and Dr D B McCartee, soon joined by ministerial colleagues and an independent English Baptist, T H Hudson. Miss Mary Ann Aldersey arrived from Jakarta and started her school; E C Lord joined Macgowan in 1847 and was still there thirty years later; Josiah Goddard came from Bangkok in the same year; R Q Way and William (Walter) M Lowrie, the senator's son who was killed by pirates, and Henry V Rankin joined McCartee, followed in 1847 by John W Quarterman, Mrs Way's brother, and in 1850 by the two Martin brothers, William and Samuel. J L Nevius, the American Presbyterian whom Hudson Taylor had met in Shanghai two weeks after his own arrival, was also there and becoming a fluent and adventurous pioneer – laying the foundations of his missionary strategy for indigenous Chinese and Korean churches, for which he remains notable to this day. Three Anglicans, W H Russell, R H Cobbold and F F Gough formed the CMS contingent. So diverse a collection of missionaries might have found co-operation difficult, but not at Ningbo.

William A P Martin, a tall, spare American five years older than Hudson Taylor, had had a colourful introduction to China. When he and his brother arrived at Hong Kong on April 10, 1850, the only steamer on the China coast was the memorable side-wheel steamer *Lady Mary Wood*, serving Shanghai. In spite of his first acquaintance with mainland Chinese at Canton where 'a hooting crowd' bayed 'Foreign devils! Cut off their heads!', they chose to go by *lorcha*, a hundred-ton foreign-hulled but Chinese-rigged vessel, and visited the ports up the coast as far as Ningbo.

On their arrival it happened that they were left to sink or swim, with little help from other missionaries. By force of circumstances, while learning Chinese, William Martin evolved a phonetic system using romanised equivalents for each Chinese sound, and his teacher took to it so quickly that Martin demonstrated its usefulness to Russell, Cobbold and Gough, and with their co-operation launched a major project for printing books and publishing the New Testament in romanised Ningbo vernacular. To the amazement of the Chinese they saw their children learning to read in only a few days, and their illiterate servants and an old woman of seventy 'read in their own tongue the wonderful works of God'. Instead of cries for the blood of foreign devils, the Martins met friendliness from the Chinese, because as they said, they had experienced kind treatment at the hands of the British during the war (of 1840–42) . . . After a battle at the mouth of the river, the inhabitants (of Ningbo) were astonished to be protected instead of pillaged. Before the battle they were in mortal terror – in dread of the 'red-haired barbarians' and . . . of their own soldiers. They were never tired of telling how Dr. Gutzlaff . . . had been installed in the *yamen* of the prefect, and how careful he was to see justice done, so that if a soldier bagged a fowl it had to be brought back or paid for. Not only did this state of feeling make it safe and pleasant for us to promenade the streets [Martin commented] – it opened to us the doors of many families (*see* Appendix 8).

To anticipate, in due course W A P Martin wrote a book in Chinese on *Christian Evidences*, which had 'an enormous circulation over many years in China and Japan'. He also translated into Chinese a tome on international law, became head of the Chinese government's institution for training diplomats in international law, and was appointed first President of the Imperial University of Peking with official rank in the Chinese hierarchy, one of the Chinese government's most valued foreign friends.[4] In Hudson Taylor's early days, Martin made a habit of riding a pony up the long, easy flight of steps to the top of the city wall and taking his exercise there. He was not the only missionary to use it for a daily constitutional – but thereby hangs a tale, to be told in its right place. When he arrived in China the average life expectancy of missionaries, merchants and consuls was seven years, but he lived until 1916 and the age of eighty-nine.

The different missions were well deployed in Ningbo. Macgowan and Lord, the Baptists, lived and worked in the north suburb, with chapels in the city near the west gate. The CMS missionaries and their chapels were spaced like stepping stones across the city from north to south, and the American Presbyterians east and west. The independent Miss Aldersey and her school were near the centre. With her as teachers were Samuel Dyer's two daughters, Burella and Maria. Another Baptist, M J Knowlton, lived outside the Salt Gate, on the river bank, and the Presbyterians had boarding school premises across the water, between the British and American consulates.

When Burdon, Parker and Hudson Taylor arrived after dark on June 15, 1855, the city gates had long been shut, so Hudson Taylor certainly and probably the others too were taken in by Dr Macgowan. The next day they moved to the Cobbolds, visited the city with Gough while Hudson Taylor, suffering from dysentery, stayed at the Russells for some hours. When they went out preaching the party was made up without regard to national or sectarian differences between them. This spirit impressed the three from Shanghai.

On June 21 they said goodbye and started back, intending to take their time and preach from town to town along another route, but they had not gone far when a messenger overtook them with an urgent message from Shanghai for John Burdon. His child was desperately ill and might not live until he reached there. Once again Hudson Taylor was able to support John Burdon in his distress. He did not say in either journal or letters how they passed the time as they hurried without stopping day or night towards Shanghai, but from similar occasions it is clear that his habit was to draw upon his fund of memorised Scripture to comfort his friends and support their faith. At Hangzhou Bay they transferred to a sea-going junk in 'a tremendous hustle' and were content to huddle with some matting over them for the three and a half hour crossing, as there was no cabin.

At Zhapu on the north shore they landed in darkness at low tide and struggled ashore with their baggage. They trans-shipped at once to a canal boat, had to resort to porterage where the water was too low for boats to pass and rejoined their own boat at one-thirty am. At last they could lie down. But with first light at four am they set off again with tides and wind behind them, and with full sail reached Shanghai at dusk on Sunday, June 24.

The big decision   *July 1855*

John Burdon's child was still alive but hung between life and death for two or three weeks before succumbing. Hudson Taylor's dysentery returned to incapacitate him and the demands of work, the school, reports, letter writing and language study made recuperation difficult. The detailed statistics required by the CES, like a disciplinary check on his diligence, again took too much of his time. In April, May and June he alone had distributed nine thousand books, treated eleven hundred and forty-six patients and 'preached salvation through Christ on 49 occasions'. It was all an expression of his devotional life. While confined to his room he 'enjoyed reading the Word, and communion with God exceedingly' so that Jesus again 'felt . . . more precious than of late'. And being more at home in the dialect he ventured upon extempore prayer with the household servants.

Meanwhile at Ningbo a proposition was being debated. Having met Dr Parker, the missionary and merchant body together invited him formally to move there as community surgeon. His first reaction was to decline. And when in a letter to Hudson Taylor the CES suggested that if Shanghai presented too many problems they should consider Ningbo, Fuzhou or Amoy, Parker would not entertain the thought. He replied to Ningbo that he would not be justified leaving Shanghai unless he could develop and support a hospital, but that would cost eight hundred dollars a year. A rule of the CES read, 'every missionary shall practise without receiving fee or reward of any kind from any person whatsoever'. For this reason the Parkers, who were entitled to two hundred pounds per annum from the Society, regarded anything they might receive in Shanghai or Ningbo as a source of building funds, not personal salary. On further thoughts, with no equivalent scope in Shanghai, a firm proposal from Ningbo began to look attractive.

On July 3 Hudson Taylor began a letter to his mother, adding to it from time to time until the mail-boat left on the 24th. Writing in bed and longing for replies from Elizabeth Sissons and her father, he told his mother about the Ningbo journey and what they had observed.

> We were much profited by the example we there saw of missionary work, and missionary zeal, and missionary success. There is a great want of a medical man there, and of a missionary Hospital, and I think it is more than probable that Dr. Parker will go down there and take some practice and devote the funds to the support of a hospital for Chinese, as our Society have neither the means, nor the desire, to aid us in getting one. My own mind is not made up as to the course I shall pursue . . . for while many reasons make me desirous to go to Ningpo, there are many also against it. There are already 14 missionaries there, able and willing to work, and to work in peace and unity – and they are working the field well.

Shanghai, he went on to say, was not nearly as well worked by more than double the number. Moreover, learning another dialect held no attractions for him; it would be a useful acquisition, but confusing. But the fact that living would be less expensive at Ningbo made him think twice, for the Jenkins who shared his LMS house were building a new home and would soon be moving into it. If the

Parkers also left, he could not possibly carry the rental alone, even if the Griffith Johns' arrival was delayed.

> So you see I am as unsettled as I was the first day I landed in China, as to my future prospects. I am looking to the Lord for guidance and direction . . . I shall for the present stay at Shanghai if I can . . . but perhaps eventually go down, if my efforts to gain a footing in the interior should fail in this neighbourhood. It seems as if I never was to be settled. I do wish I had a pious companion, with whom there would be some sympathy of mind, and feeling, with whom I could take counsel, and that I was somewhere or other, settled in a good regular work.

This was the nearest he came to saying that Parker and he were not kindred spirits. His longing to marry was another matter. He also recognised his need for a colleague in his exacting work, and his words are a revealing comment. Parker knew his own mind and went his own way, now and in the years ahead, co-operating pleasantly with others in so far as doing so coincided with his own ideas. If Parker went to Ningbo and Hudson Taylor stayed, he would be back in his solitude.

Then, out of nowhere, a new problem arose. A message reached him from the consul, Rutherford Alcock, 'stating he was anxious to show me some letters which appeared to have a reference to me'. So the next day he went over to the consulate. The Chinese magistrate of Jingjiang (Tsingkiang), the last place he had visited on his Yangzi reconnaissance, had reported him as 'violating the treaty'.

> (They) had complained of my visit there, and the Consul had endeavoured not to know who it was but the Chinese authorities had clearly identified me. The Consul informed me if I broke the treaty he had no option but to punish me as he would do if a merchant did so, etc; tho' he had no desire to restrain my missionary labours.

For a week Hudson Taylor gave the matter his solemn thought, without any change of mind. Alcock was doing his duty by the letter of the 1842 accord, without regard to broader concessions in the French and other treaties, and being pleasant enough about it. His warning was a formality, for he knew full well that none of the travellers in his community would change their ways, nor did he want them to. Acceptance by the Chinese of the foreign presence was his own diplomatic aim, and growing familiarity with harmless missionaries would prepare the Chinese for freer dealings with merchants and others. The 'most favoured nation' clause could always be invoked, but relations with Peking had been strained since the rebuff at the Beihe (p 236) in the past year, and sooner or later a revision of the treaty must be broached again. It was politic to tread softly. The youngest member of the missionary community need not be made a *cause célèbre*.

On the day after his interview, Hudson Taylor preached to congregations of thirty and forty at the school, about to be moved from the *ma-lu* to near the South Gate, and between the services stayed to explain the gospel to others who came and went. On some days he preached five or six times. It was the occupation he enjoyed above all others – unless question-time with the school-children could claim first place. At the end of the day he wrote, 'Enjoyed the evening very much, and was much melted by the love of God . . . I earnestly and pointedly . . . exhorted them to seek salvation, thro' the blood of Him Who loved them.' When a neighbour died of cholera, Hudson Taylor talked with his audience about death and the hereafter. A day or two later he asked 'whether *they* had prayed God to pardon their sins, because Jesus had died for them and atoned for their guilt . . . when before them all (one) said "I have" . . .' He was Guihua, Hanban's elder brother. Hudson Taylor was elated.

It was not always so. The hottest months of July and August made travelling inadvisable. Cramped quarters with the Parkers and Jenkins in the house, and continuing illness hardly helped as he faced three crucial problems. Should he go with the Parkers or stay? Should he disregard the consul's warning and quietly take up residence in a country place? And should he adopt Chinese clothing to make himself less conspicuous? In such circumstances he observed, 'Godliness' needed to be cultivated. So now he added, 'My heart felt so hard and the heavens were as brass, but in the goodness of God, it has been melted by His love.'

At some point, now or earlier, the doyen of all missionaries in East Asia, Walter H Medhurst, Sr, advised Hudson Taylor to use Chinese dress for travelling into the country.[5] In 1845 he himself had adopted it, on his exploratory journey to the green tea district, but as an essential disguise. The Catholic priests habitually did so. Robert Fortune, the botanist, also. Whether Hudson Taylor went to consult Dr Medhurst, or after the consular rebuke he was offered some avuncular advice when they met at the weekly 'concert' of missionaries, is not recorded. He probably possessed a copy of the great man's *Glance at the Interior of China*, published anonymously in Shanghai six years previously, but if not, it was easy to come by. It provided not only a narrative of his adventures but detailed instructions for transforming one's appearance into that of a Chinese. It told how to avoid detection by meticulous mimicry of Chinese ways on those few occasions when the traveller could not remain stowed out of sight in a boat or emerge under cover of darkness. At just such a moment Medhurst himself had had the misfortune to encounter a fortune teller, a physionomist who, staring at him had said to his companions, 'That fellow has a most unusual face!' Imagining floggings and imprisonment Medhurst's guide had been hard put to it to lure the man away.

Since the Yangzi journey Hudson Taylor's thoughts had already been moving in the direction of adopting Chinese clothes. So in considering this advice his intention was not to disguise himself but to do the Chinese the courtesy of dressing, speaking and living like them all the time, and so to win greater freedom for his work. He did not think of dressing up for isolated journeys and reverting to foreign clothes betweentimes, but of living openly like a Chinese outside the treaty limits. But should he or should he not? The merchant community would flay him if he so demeaned his 'superior race'. And many in the missionary circle shared that view.

On Friday, July 27, six days after the consular rebuke, Hudson Taylor made his big decision: if he must be 'a homeless wanderer by necessity, not choice', he would stay in the Shanghai area and take a calculated risk, renting a house in the country and starting regular medical and evangelistic work – and he would do it in Chinese clothes, complete with the conventional *bianzi*, the hair queue. If the experiment failed he could rejoin the Parkers at Ningbo later on. That was a bridge to be crossed when he reached it. For the present his course was clear. No sooner said than done, he ordered a set of Chinese clothes and began preparations for wearing them.

Perhaps it was the fact that he had been reported *as a foreigner* two hundred miles away from the treaty port, that decided him, or simply that experience had shown what a foreign appearance did to excite the people. Whatever the criticisms and ridicule, he was going to be a Chinese to the Chinese, not a rabble-drawing barbarian in outlandish European costume. As the boatmen had told him, with nose and eyes like his he would never be mistaken for a Chinese, but at the lowest reckoning, by dressing and living like them he might spare himself rough handling. With the moral

IN *BIANZI* AND CAP, A HOUSEHOLDER AT HIS SHRINE

courage increasingly natural to him he discounted the social price he
would have to pay, telling his mother,

> . . . as soon as circumstances permit (I) shall make an attempt [to rent
> premises and live in the forbidden interior] . . . Don't speak of this till
> we see what comes of it – it is as the Chinese say 'van ih' – a myriad to
> one. While a successful attempt proves an 'enterprising fellow' a
> failure never shows the impracticability of an undertaking, it only
> proves one 'an incompetent ass'. At any rate this is the way in which
> persons here speak. There is little doubt as to the possibility of sitting
> down, if the object were philosophical, botanical, geological – or
> 'pen-siang' (pleasure); but when an earnest zeal for the salvation of
> sinners is the impelling motive, their native prejudice, Catholic in-
> terference, and all the power of Satan is at once arrayed against you.
> How the *Lord* will have it remains to be proved.

He knew the odds and was doing it with his eyes open. Wearing
Chinese clothes was a small matter in comparison with courting

trouble by deliberately defying the strict interpretation of the Nanking Treaty. He had an idea where he would attempt it but, like Edkins, Wylie, Aitchison and others, had not yet met with an undoubted welcome from influential Chinese. While many were biding their time, the policy of the CES, their veto on developing commitments in Shanghai itself, his personal need to live frugally, and pure zeal all drove him to make the experiment against the odds he called '10,000 to 1'. Acting creatively and carrying it off could pave the way farther into the 'interior'. Antagonism from the Jesuits was in his reckoning, but in the event he omitted, whether intentionally or by default, to allow for it in his choice of location. Nor did he wait to obtain from the CES an assurance that should things go wrong they would take the responsibility. Letters took too long. Not until September did he belatedly receive the categorical answer he anticipated to his and Parker's plea for a base in Shanghai, 'our professed intentions (are) *not* to work in free ports, but in the *interior*. . . . We don't want to spend money in Shanghai.'

Were they being blind and stubborn? Must he muddle along as before, or be carried along by Parker's institutional bent? Or could they possibly be right after all? Were the CES going to succeed through strong faith and determination where others in Shanghai were convinced it was impossible? He would settle the matter one way or the other. He would make the attempt.

On the Sunday, July 29, instead of the usual preaching expedition he stayed at home to 'wait upon God'. His journal reads, 'In the afternoon had a very profitable time in my own room, and felt that Jesus was able to fill my every void, to supply *all* my need.' Work, wife, colleagues, funds, health, protection, 'fruit' – the proof of effective service – everything that filled his mind lay in that emphasis.

Monday was an intensely hot day and they stayed indoors. Parker was writing to George Pearse, another letter of protest. While residence in the interior was impossible, were missionaries surrounded by Chinese dying 'unpardoned' to be idle, without regular work? Other societies had the same aim as the CES, he begged to point out. Hudson Taylor, Edkins and Aitchison were not the only ones reprimanded for venturing too far afield, others had been 'similarly dealt with'. Reprimands and fines would not deter them from making such sorties, but was it not plain to the directors that settled residence in the interior was quite out of the question in this part of China?

How can persons at the distance of many thousand miles judge as well as those on the spot as to the state of the country or what is the best course to pursue?

And he went on to describe the visit to Ningbo.

While Parker wrote, Hudson Taylor began making up medicines and concocting a dye to blacken his fair hair as soon as he had grown it enough to be able to have a Chinese *bianzi* plaited firmly into it at the back. The alchemy involved using 'litharge and newly slaked lime'. His journal and a letter to Amelia tell what happened. He took down a two-quart bottle of ammonia, often used before, and because of the great heat loosened the cork with special care. But he underestimated the pressure that had built up inside. It blew the cork out of his hand. Both gas and liquid ammonia gushed out. Frantically trying to stop the waste he pressed his hand down on the bottle mouth – and ammonia spurted into his eyes, nose, mouth, hair and over his clothes. The fumes were asphyxiating. He could not breathe.

> I . . . had to run for my life. I could see nothing, but got out of the house I know not how . . . I felt if I fell before I got to some water I should be suffocated . . . Instinctively I made for the Kitchen . . . Tho' I staggered about I fortunately got in and at the door was a large water jar full of water. . . . I immediately plunged . . . head and shoulders and arms into it and it saved me . . . Time after time did I continue to do this, for tho' scarcely conscious, I felt like one on fire . . . As soon as I could speak I told the (servants) [in English] to call Dr. Parker and it was a second or two, which seemed an age to me, e'er I could tell them in Chinese.

But Parker had heard the commotion, leapt up from his letter and run to help.

> He states my face was so much swelled that I should scarcely have been known. Without any delay Castor Oil was put in my eyes and over my face, and a very large dose of opium given me, which was difficult to swallow. Then my feet were put in hot water, iced water applied to my face, ice to my eyes, and a powerful saline purgative given. As soon as possible I was got to bed and the applications incessantly applied, so that by night I was much relieved.

Hudson Taylor had a letter for Amelia's twentieth birthday lying unfinished, so the next day with his right eye opening just enough for him to see, he defiantly finished it, and another to his mother on the following day. Most of the time he lay with eyes closed and ice packs on his face.

Notice to quit   *August 1855*

Five days after the accident Hudson Taylor could say that apart from a still very painful nose he was back in action. He went out for a walk and for the first time since coming to China saw with his own eyes evidence of the widely practised custom of infanticide. Lying dead in a stagnant pool was a newly-born female infant. Only the girls were unwanted. They were mouths to feed until married off for paltry bride money. The sight confirmed his strong conviction. Cost him what it might, China needed and must have the gospel.

The box he had sent home full of curios arrived back, packed with delights to cheer him on his way. His father had sent him Wesley's hymn-book to replace one that he had given to the *Dumfries* carpenter. 'I do not like to be without a copy of Wesley's hymns' he wrote in gratitude, but he had no need to say so. He and his parents sang them so much in their private devotions that to quote a phrase was to convey a wealth of meaning. And a bunch of periodicals brought more pleasure, especially the *Photographic Journal*. But he was most glad of the apparatus and materials for chemical analysis in his study of Chinese materia medica. News from home was good.

Then the sword of Damocles fell. They received notice to be out of the LMS house by October 1. The Griffith Johns were expected. In normal times, if ever there was anything normal about Shanghai, a house could be bought, built or rented, but in 1855 the face of Shanghai was changing at a startling rate. In February all was desolation between the Settlements and the Chinese city. By the end of the year maps of Shanghai showed the whole area laid out in streets with French names, and the racecourse and Muddy Flat now an expansive recreation park surrounded by new building developments. Sites and building costs were prohibitive. The only hope was to find an old house inside the city walls.

Parker was feeling more strongly drawn to Ningbo, but loth to leave Hudson Taylor at Shanghai alone. He started house-hunting with him. They had just seven weeks to find a place and move. On August 7 Hudson Taylor told his father, 'We are quite unsettled as to our future movements.' He thought that if the Parkers left, he himself would at once don Chinese clothes, move into the city, 'and live Chinese style for a time at least, but we are so harassed by being continually unsettled, that we scarcely know what to do, and have to throw ourselves by prayer on the Almighty Arm, Who alone can support us.'

Their funds were inadequate to do anything about premises and staff for a reasonable strategy of work, and the Society's veto on work or premises in Shanghai was doubly inhibiting. Even so, country travel must always end in a return to a base of some sort, however small, so this was the object of their search. The extreme summer heat made it no easier. Writing at eight pm with the windows wide open Hudson Taylor was bathed in perspiration. He was feeling it far more than the previous year. Not until September did it begin to abate.

He was entering upon what he described to George Pearse as a month 'of considerable anxiety and trial'. For two weeks they plodded to and fro, from area to area and street to street without finding anything. Chinese houses were either unsuitable or the rents exorbitant and 'key-money' deposits too great. Foreign houses were unobtainable. Then the awaited reply from Ningbo arrived. They would guarantee eight hundred dollars or two hundred and sixty pounds a year for running a hospital, and support Dr Parker while in charge.

By mid-August, therefore, William Parker's mind was made up. The Society had given him liberty to go to another treaty port and approved of his opening a dispensary or hospital if funds came in; the Ningbo community had promised his working expenses; Ningbo was the only port without even one hospital; and finally, in spite of so much effort they had failed to find a house at Shanghai.

> I have resolved to go and to do so at once . . . This will not prevent my taking an occasional visit, or being the first to plant the standard of the cross in some important place in the interior, on the country being opened.[6]

His policy was to do solid medical work until that happened. Let others do the preaching. He planned first to rent Chinese premises at Ningbo and then to build. Writing to George Pearse, Hudson Taylor commented,

> Dr. Parker's way was very clearly opened to go to Ningpo, but I could not feel myself called to go there. I had made it a matter of prayer and deliberation for some time, and finally was led to believe that my duty (was) to remain here – for the present at least.

Parker, however, revealed that Hudson Taylor had been thinking of returning to England 'for his own good as well as the Society's'. This could only mean to get medically qualified, perhaps to meet

Elizabeth again and to do some plain speaking with the CES Committee and Board. If he could find no house at Shanghai, perhaps it would after all mean that he should go. 'It is a great pity I left home without a more thorough medical education and a degree . . .' he confessed to his mother.

Now house-hunting in Shanghai was for Hudson Taylor and some Chinese companions alone, and memories of his solitude and difficulties at the North Gate suburb returned to depress him. Still nothing turned up. 'I thought I must be homeless.' He would have to send most of his possessions with the Parkers, and live in a boat moored at Shanghai or wherever he could in the country. William Burns, the Scottish evangelist, was doing this. On July 26 he had been in to visit them, talking about the thriving church in Amoy and his current attempts to reach the Taipings at Nanking. But by now Hudson Taylor had sold his own boat as being too foreign in appearance and too costly to repair since the journey through the ice and winter gales.

On August 23 Parker asked him to go part of the way to Ningbo with him, and he changed from house-hunting to quick preparations for the journey. They decided to make the best use of it for preaching and book distribution, as usual. While Parker went on across the Hangzhou Bay to find a home for his family in Ningbo, Hudson Taylor would continue preaching on his solitary way back to Shanghai.

This was the moment he had been preparing for. He had a month's growth of hair to plait into his false *bianzi*, and his Chinese clothes were ready to wear. The journey would provide a good proving time, to see how he fared in them and how the Chinese reacted. Yet he was tense and anxious, knowing what to expect from his fellow-Europeans. Hard work and close quarters in a bad climate were undermining his health.

Feeling very unwell he went out to hire a boat – and while making enquiries he heard of a vacant four-roomed house in the Chinese city. Its owner had run out of money and could not finish it. If Hudson Taylor would advance six months' rent he could have it for his own use in only ten days' time. He agreed at once, arranged for a contract to be signed, found a boat and brought it to the jetty.

At eleven that night he called the Chinese barber. Shops were open and life went on into the early hours and there was no extra charge for being served at your home. Hudson Taylor, however, hired the barber to travel with him and daily attend to the precarious attachment. Having his head shaved, all but the tuft to be plaited with the queue, was painful enough with his prickly heat, but when he applied his lime and litharge dye, his scalp was on fire. The next morning the barber came again and plaited the tail of true Chinese hair into position, complete with an extension of black silk cord hanging far down the back.

Then Hudson Taylor donned his clothes.[7] First the *han san*, a cotton shirt fastened under the right arm and down the right side, and the *han ku*, voluminous cotton or calico trousers fastened with a girdle. Sitting in them he wrote to Amelia a few days later '(the breeks) have a graceful fulness before and behind, in which, as Dr. Parker remarks, a fortnight's provisions might be stored.'

Over these he put on his ankle-length gown of blue cotton or coarse silk with full sleeves inconveniently long. In the winter one padded with cotton or silk for warmth would take its place. Then a collar and shoulder tippet with tails tied under the armpits, and over them all a waist-length outer jacket or *ma gua* buttoned down the front and in cold weather wadded or lined with fur. His stockings were of calico with thickened soles stitched through and through, and shapeless cylindrical legs pulled up over the trousers and tied below the knee with green, blue or yellow garters. Satin or cloth shoes with upcurled toes, and large enough to accommodate the bulky stockings, were most uncomfortable until his feet were toughened. For the past month he had been wearing them two hours daily for this reason. Because the cloth soles absorbed water, travellers carried a spare pair. Finally, a skullcap with a knot or button of twisted silk, worn indoors and out, or a crown-shaped cap with an upturned brim all round. In hot weather out of doors a cool conical straw hat might be used instead. And because foreigners' eyes looked so strange to the Chinese, tinted spectacles with black Chinese frames tied on with string were an advantage. 'Unfortunately', he wrote to Amelia, 'no cap or hat is worn now, except on state occasions' – during the great heat of summer, that is.

As soon as he was ready, Parker and he went down to the jetty, a frock-coated foreigner and a very self-conscious 'Chinese'. The barber attendant and their servants were on board with the crew, and their provisions and books safely stowed – when a hundred dollars were handed to Parker with this note,

For founding an hospital in Ningpo, from a friend, per Rev. J. Hobson. This is the money promised to assist in opening one at Shanghai.

The friend in fact was Hobson himself.

They cast off at eleven am and headed south. It was Friday, August 24, 1855, historic for Hudson Taylor and for hundreds, thousands of Westerners who in time would follow his example. Like the Catholic priests for centuries, he had exchanged 'barbarian' for Chinese clothes, not simply for the journey but for constant use.

A Chinese to the Chinese   *August–September 1855*

In spite of the laziest and most insolent boatmen they had so far encountered, and only by badgering them continually, they reached Hangzhou Bay in four days. At each town they preached and gave away Scripture and tracts as usual, and Dr Parker saw patients at the boat. On Sunday they climbed a pagoda and 'in the top sang the praises of God, and engaged in prayer', before conducting a Chinese service for their companions and preaching to the usual crowds on the canal bank. In one town Parker 'raised his voice very loudly against opium and promised medicine to its victims if they would come to the boat'. Many did. But what made the journey a success was the discovery that until Hudson Taylor spoke to Parker in English he was taken to be his Chinese companion and overheard many comments about him. 'Some said a white devil had come (and) was giving away good books; he did not come from the country that sent opium for he was exhorting people to give it up.' Others called him a 'red devil'.

At Ganpu on the bay Hudson Taylor overheard another conversation which was water to a thirsty man. They were negotiating with a sea-going junk captain who insisted on receiving payment in advance. Hudson Taylor on the other hand knew the skipper might take advantage of Parker's inexperience once he had parted with a substantial sum of money. So there was deadlock. Then he heard him say to Parker's man, 'How can I be sure of my money when you have reached the other side?' and the servant answered, 'We three . . . are disciples of Jesus. Disciples of Jesus do not cheat or lie and defraud. What he *says* he will do.' It was the first they knew of his faith in Jesus. The deal was struck, and Parker sailed away, reaching Ningbo in good time.

Then came the real test of Hudson Taylor's Chinese clothing. Without a foreigner in his company would he be free from those excited, pestering crowds and free to talk with people interested in

A DEAL AND A SNACK AT THE WHARFSIDE

the gospel? First he paid off his insolent Shanghai boatmen, and hiring others made good time to Haiyan, a larger town up the coast (map, p 216). Now for the moment of truth. He went ashore and walked through the town. Not a soul paid any attention to him. When he wrote to Amelia later in the day he was cheerful if blunt –

> I was always discovered when with (Parker), for I had to speak to him in English, but today I went about in Haiyen city and no one ever guessed a Foreigner was near. It was not till I began to distribute books, and see patients I was known . . . One is not so much respected as a Chinese as a Foreigner in a crowd, but medicine soon puts all right – it is evidently to be one's chief help in the interior. I fancied that the women and children manifested more readiness to come for medical aid than before . . .

He climbed the pagoda and could see right across Hangzhou Bay to the mainland beyond, east to the Zhapu hills, and to the north the Pinghu pagoda. When alone he seemed more receptive to beauty. Orchards of mulberry trees in full leaf impressed him, and he noted in his journal that when the silkworms finished feeding and began to spin their cocoons, the leaves were used to feed sheep. Then on again in the afternoon to Pinghu and another walk about with the same result. He visited two large temples 'without anyone remarking that I was a foreigner', except people who remembered seeing him with Parker.

As they sailed on and Hudson Taylor chatted with his companions, he studied their dialect differences. The barber was a Nanking man with the characteristics of his area, and to Hudson Taylor's delight he revealed that Nanking people always used the term '*ai mei*' for a 'beloved sister'.

> I could at once pick out a Shantung man, a Shanghai man, a Ningpo man, Fokien man, and Cantonese, as readily as you would a Scotch man, an Irishman, a Frenchman . . .

Shanghai was reached at midnight on the last day of August. The agreement for his little house in the city, near the South Gate, had been completed for him, and in a week or so he could take possession. Reports and correspondence kept him busy. Commenting to his directors on his change of life style and the prospects before him he said,

> It is premature yet to offer an opinion as to which is likely to prove most successful. Time must show – and if, by becoming all things to all

men, we can win any to Christ, who would regret the little sacrifice it costs? I believe it would be an easy thing to *live* in the country – but whether it be possible to *work* there or not is another question. I believe that the Catholic missionaries keep themselves very quiet . . . My soul has been greatly drawn out in prayer for the conversion . . . of sinners of late . . . I think I can say the one intense desire of my heart is to be made useful, and I have been enabled to plead the promises of God . . . with great confidence.

But the arrival of the mail ship gave him more to write home about. A wait of three hours 'in no small state of excitement' was at long last rewarded by letters from Elizabeth Sissons and her parents. Elizabeth's 'was very satisfactory'. A month later, however, another came from her father and, worse than silence, a seesaw of prevarication began. Inarticulately Hudson told his sympathising parents, '. . . he does not speak positively, but says, if it *is* to be it is not now – that he *wishes* to do the Lord's will – is more favourable than Mrs S. but adds, but remember, she is her *mother* . . . had I been labouring in or near England, he thinks there would have been little or no objection – thinks it savors something of romance etc. Thank God! It is in His hands. *There* I would have it . . . tho' not *my* will, I cannot complain.'

His affectionate nature was tormented. For two years he had had no one nearer than months of travel and thousands of miles away to love or show love to. His emotions burst forth in an outpouring to Amelia like those from Hull and London. She had curled her hair, and warning her against a seductive world, he said,

> I love you with a love so intense, that the very possibility of your love to the Saviour, or communion with God being in the slightest degree weakened causes me to pray and almost to weep . . . No words can tell the intense fervency of my love to thee my sister. I love you more than life . . . I long for your growth in grace and advancement in holiness more even than for my own . . .

The South Gate house was ready, two small rooms upstairs and two down, with an outside kitchen across a little yard (safer in the event of fire), all cramped and comfortless. The floor of beaten earth and rubble was damp, the walls were of planks nailed on to a rough framework with cracks through which the wind whistled, and the roof was of thin tiles lying exposed from below. But it was in a good position and all he could afford. To avoid creating the impression of having many possessions, he started moving a few at a time from the Settlement, and on September 17 first slept in the city, to guard his stock of medicines. At once he began meetings for Guihua and other Chinese who joined them, an enquirer named Tsien and the Christian teacher, Si. To be back in this kind of situation was bliss. He wrote that while teaching the others his own heart was melted by the love of God. And after preaching on Sunday till his throat was hoarse, he enjoyed the comfort of easing it with some of his mother's blackcurrant jam from her wonderful gift hamper.

At Ningbo Dr Parker had no difficulty in renting premises large enough to allow for taking a few in-patients. By choice it was a place outside the city, not far from the consulates, across the river and among rice-fields bordering a Chinese cemetery, where it was relatively quiet and healthy – except for a risk of 'ague' (map, p 272). On the 14th he was back in Shanghai packing up and arranging to take his family, probably by merchant ship down the coast. Hudson Taylor joined them for a farewell meal on September 24 – the very day the long-expected new LMS missionaries arrived, two who were to become both famous and formidable as missionary pioneers in the years ahead, with their brides. When the Parkers had gone, Hudson Taylor removed the remaining furniture he had left for their use, and was out on his own once again.

Alexander Williamson,[8] one of the new arrivals, tall, handsome and commanding in appearance, was three years older than Hudson Taylor. After only two years his health failed and he returned home. But recovering he came back under the National Bible Society of Scotland following the second opium war, to make many epic journeys through North China, Manchuria and Mongolia.

Griffith John[9] was physically very different. Five months older than Hudson Taylor, he was no taller or less youthful in appearance. They were to become good friends. He had begun preaching at sixteen and after theological training offered himself to the London Missionary Society to go to Madagascar. His Welsh college principal commended him to the Society with deep regret, reluctant that Wales should lose him.

> He is a strangely winning and affectionate little creature, overflowing with kindness and sociableness, and a universal favourite . . . beyond comparison the most popular preacher in Welsh we ever heard . . . In intellectual power he is far, very far above the average of young men . . .[10]

Wales' loss was to become China's great gain.

Williamson and Griffith John arrived together at the Mission House in London for a farewell luncheon. The imposing Scotsman led the way in. The little Welshman following on his heels was grabbed by the beadle with a 'No you don't!' and had to be rescued by his friend. As they went on they heard the beadle say, 'So it has come to this, sending children to convert the Chinese.' But Madagascar had become impenetrable since gruesome massacres of Christians, so to China he went, three weeks after marrying the daughter of an exiled Madagascar missionary. He quickly became as fluent in Chinese, and as adventurous as Hudson Taylor in his travelling.

Looking back after nearly fifty years in China, Griffith John recalled 'a very enthusiastic welcome' by the twenty-five or thirty missionaries in Shanghai. (With so much coming and going it was impossible to be more precise.) Of his LMS colleagues he wrote,

> The venerable and venerated Dr. Medhurst (was) still busy at work on the Delegates' Version of the Scriptures . . . a very prince among the missionaries . . . very genial, very accessible and very helpful . . . His wish was law to us, for the simple reason that we trusted his judgment and felt the warmth of his heart . . . but he never tried to rule.

> (William Lockhart) was looked upon . . . as a sort of marvel, and (people) were never tired of talking about the wonders of his art. He was the soul of kindness, a tremendous worker, and one of the social pillars of the Shanghai community.

> (Alexander Wylie) the famous Chinese scholar yet so modest that, while others were sounding his praises, he himself was profoundly unconscious of his fame . . . any verbal compliment he treated as an insult . . . one of the most remarkable men I have ever met.

> (Joseph Edkins) was diving into the deep depths of Buddhism, unfolding the mysteries of the Chinese language and literature . . . Between Edkins and myself the closest friendship sprang up at once . . .

Griffith John arrived with a library of books on chemistry and mechanics, astronomy and mathematics, as well as theology, and a microscope and chemical and electrical apparatus to show the Chinese people. He found the Chinese city of Shanghai 'one of the filthiest in the world', not yet cleaned of its 'dirt and filth' since the end of the siege in February. Hudson Taylor was no longer mentioning such things, so accustomed to them had he become.

The newcomers stayed with the Medhursts until the house was ready for them, and saw the preaching chapels in action. Two or three times every day audiences of fifty to two hundred were gathering. It would have been possible to preach from morning to night and have plenty of hearers. In the countryside too, his impression was that 'a wide door is opening in China for the preaching of the Gospel'.

Within a week Griffith John had memorised some simple Chinese phrases, enough to say, 'Do you believe in the Lord Jesus? Believing in Him is the best thing you can do.' And six months later he was out in the temples and streets talking, distributing tracts and beginning to preach. After nine months he was preaching in the chapels for half an hour or more 'with considerable ease and fluency', well understood by his hearers. The average foreigner took two, three or even five years to attain the same skill. All his life evangelism was his aim and weapon. His biographer summed up his life in terms of 'amazing and tireless industry and thoroughness' and 'magnificent optimism'. The 'magnetism of his faith and enthusiasm' influenced all who came in contact with him. It was fitting that a month before Hudson Taylor's death in 1905, these two and W A P Martin of Ningbo and Peking should meet and be photographed together.[11]

But in September 1855 Hudson Taylor was the talk of the Settlement and the butt of ridicule, scorn and anger. He was using what was ineptly called 'disguise' – for he made no attempt to conceal his identity. Medhurst's book had set out to describe both disguise and concealment, how to hide, to walk with a Chinese gait, to avoid detection. Robert Fortune had disguised himself like the adventurers of the Indian *raj* when collecting for the Royal Horticultural Society.[12] But Hudson Taylor's adoption of Chinese clothes and mode of living had none of that glamour or mystique. As George Woodcock put it in *The British in the Far East*,

> A belief in the equality of all men before God, too literally acted upon, can produce patterns of behaviour which no imperial society can accept with equanimity. [And Shanghai's foreign community was just that.] To the *taipans* and all the other people who believed that the white man's dignity rested in strict adherence to British dress and British habits, his [Hudson Taylor's] action was deeply shocking. He had gone native. He had lost face. He had broken the magic ring of white solidarity. The word *traitor* was not too harsh to describe him.[13]

It was *de rigeur* to dress in tight-fitting coat, waistcoat and trousers, cravat and hat. No gentleman would be seen otherwise. The women could take advantage of fashionable muslins and lace to keep cool, but to the men the drenching perspiration and prickly heat were tolerable for the sake of the conventions. Brazenly dressed as a Chinese when he attended community functions, when he called at Gibb, Livingstone & Co. to cash credit notes, and even at the consulate, young Hudson Taylor was affronting the very people to whom he owed his security. Even Issacher J Roberts, unkempt but Western in appearance, was less despicable. This nobody, this pauper without degree or title, neither flotsam of the mercantile and seafaring world nor accredited representative of any church, hatless and 'pigtailed', was disgracing the respectable community he had entered. Chinese respect for the dominant Westerner would be eroded. What might it not lead to? Even missionaries were among his detractors. Decorum mattered supremely to some. Adaptability had not yet occurred to them as being a qualification for becoming a missionary. To pay this small compliment to the Chinese people by adopting their culture was too revolutionary, however often it had been done by others down the centuries.[14]

Then there were three   *October 1855*

Hudson Taylor accepted the opprobrium with resignation. It was no more than he had bargained for. Yet even he could not foresee that the courage to take that step paved the way to far greater innovations in the years ahead. Working hard from morning to night, he was tired out by bedtime. Daily he was giving time to teaching Si, Tsien and Guihua before going out to preach in the highways and byways. On Sunday, September 30, after prayer and exposition of Scripture with the whole household, he taught Tsien alone, then Si and, after a brief rest, 'preached to 40 or 50 persons, on the importance of seeking the salvation of their precious, never-dying souls, by faith in Christ'. The house would hold no more. Most were standing. 'Were the room larger more than twice the number would come in.'

The *North China Herald* described conditions in Shanghai at the time. Refugees from the devastated areas of neighbouring provinces had flooded into the city and Settlement and the administration was failing to keep abreast of the situation. The neighbourhood of the CMS school swarmed with brothels, gambling houses, opium dens and 'fences' for stolen goods. After 'rebel-robbers in the city and imperialist-robbers in the camps' why should the foreign Settlement become a sanctuary for the protection of thieves and vagabonds? the *Herald* asked. It was time for the consuls to act. And, Hudson Taylor realised, time for the messengers of the One who came to call 'not the righteous but sinners to repentance' to spend themselves for these unfortunates.

After four o'clock that Sunday afternoon he again opened the doors and invited people in to hear Si preach. Then three hours of reading with Tsien and Si led finally to prayers with the servants before going upstairs to write, 'tired but happy I retired for the night'. But Monday was much the same apart from a visit from William Burns and a colporteur, and having to collect his mail from John Burdon. 'At 5 p.m. sang a hymn, read a portion of Scripture, prayed for Divine aid, then opened the doors, and preached to between 30 and 40, some of whom were very attentive, while others came and went.'

His thinking was clear on this point. Shanghai was only his base. When he was there he would work as he was doing, but as soon as possible he would try to put down roots in the precarious 'interior'. He was constantly praying about this, he told George Pearse. The men he was teaching were the only companions he would have for such a venture, and he was training them with that in mind. His own grasp of the Shanghai dialect improved in the process. Unable to sleep with a heavy cold, he composed a dialect hymn, suitable for uneducated local people, and began translating Matthew's Gospel into the patois.

Tuesday, Wednesday, Thursday, Friday were the same, with up to sixty at a time standing silently while he prayed and preached. Then on October 6 his heart was bursting as he wrote when the day was already over,

'Kweihua [Guihua] has asked to be admitted into church membership by baptism. I have felt little doubt as to his conversion for some time . . .'

But pride was Guihua's besetting sin. Tsien asked if he too could be baptised, and then another, a Ningbo man, very fluent about sin and salvation, but how genuine? The difficulty of seeing through men's motives was always there. Even Liang A-fa had been hoodwinked and eventually betrayed by a false convert.

Referring to another generous gift of fifty pounds from Mr Berger, Hudson Taylor wrote to his mother,

> I rise between six and seven, sing a hymn, read a portion of Scripture and pray to Him who feeds the young ravens *when they cry*, to feed me . . . Then I wash, dress and have my tail looked after . . . [and about Guihua's conversion] – I cannot tell you the joy I have experienced – I could say with Mary, 'My soul doth magnify *the Lord*, and my spirit rejoiceth in God my Saviour' . . . If one soul is worth worlds, am I not abundantly repaid – and *are not you* too?

Let the critics scoff, he was 'walking with God'! About another enquirer he added, echoing William Berger's thought,

> May our united prayers be heard. It needs great faith – but the Lord says, 'Open thy mouth wide, and I will fill it! It honors God to ask great things.' [To George Pearse also] I can only write one or two lines more, as the mail is closing, to tell you how joyful my heart is . . . I feel deeply humbled by it. It is *all* of the Lord's doing . . . that He should use me . . . May he be the firstfruits of many who shall be gathered *by* the Lord, *to* the Lord, through my instrumentality. But were my mission now to be closed, I feel I am abundantly rewarded, and honored beyond worldly honor, by the goodness of God. May I be enabled . . . to *live* the Gospel before him for Jesus' sake . . .

With mutual confidence and understanding at the deepest level growing between Hudson Taylor and George Pearse, he felt free to write as objectively as he saw necessary about everything, including the Society's affairs.

Charles Bird, the General Secretary, in failing mental health had written offensive letters to one and another and, laughably, to Hudson Taylor he said, 'for want of better matter, your journey to Kiating [Jiading] occupies a good part of this month's *Gleaner*'. Gibb, Livingstone and Co. had shown Hudson Taylor and Parker an 'underhand' letter from Bird to their disadvantage, which nearly precipitated their resignation. Charles Bird's condition deteriorated until he finally had to leave, but not before the damage was done.[15]

William Berger's practice of sending funds exclusively for Hudson Taylor's use, begun during this year, implies that he like so many had lost confidence in the Society and the General Secretary in particular. As well as such gifts he also undertook to send ten pounds twice yearly for the adopted refugee Hanban's care and education. Hudson Taylor received them with the words, 'I am filled with gratitude for Mr Berger's liberality to Him who disposes the hearts of his people,' a recognition of Divine provision through human stewardship.

No sooner had Guihua and Tsien declared their faith and intention to confess it openly, than it was tested. Trouble struck each of them. Guihua had been betrothed for five years to a heathen girl and betrothal in China was as binding as marriage. In asking for baptism he revealed he was soon to be married. When Hudson Taylor pointed out that now he could not follow idolatrous wedding practices, he determined to avoid them and to tell the family that idols and ancestral tablets would not be allowed in his home. So Hudson Taylor had a Christian form of marriage copied in Chinese for him to discuss with his bride's family. A week later Guihua returned – the laughing stock of his whole village. When he would not yield, the betrothal had been broken off and his future prospects of finding a wife became very slender. So concerned was Hudson Taylor about this that he wrote again to the Society urging that women missionaries be sent, to take the gospel into Chinese homes, and to Amelia, wishing she could go and speak to Guihua's betrothed. How could he teach marriage 'only in the Lord' if young Chinese men were to become Christians without Christian girls to marry?

Tsien took a supply of Christian books to relatives at Songjiang and returned with a friend so interested in the gospel as to want to hear more. But two days later Hudson Taylor found him in tears. News had come that Tsien's little girl was dead. Faithfully Hudson Taylor urged that no heathen rites should be used at the funeral, but now he had two chastened companions to share his own suffering for the cause of Christ. Confiding to his mother that if he had been medically qualified he himself would have been able to take the position in Ningbo that Dr Parker had accepted, he went on,

> I must give up all hope of that. Well, the Lord knows best – my will must be to do His will; and as it seems to be my lot, I must labor alone, and look more to the Lord, and less to circumstances, for aid and blessing.

Tsien's family home was at Jiading, the 'middle-sized walled city some thirty or more miles' away, at which on Hudson Taylor's first country journey with Parker the people had fled to hide in their homes, only to invite them in the next day. Tsien wanted his Christian friends to come with him and tell his family the gospel.

Hudson Taylor agreed at once. If the time seemed ripe when they were there, he might baptise Tsien publicly. And, as always, he would be ready to stay if welcomed to do so – to make it his first firm stepping stone into the interior. Si was to stay in Shanghai and keep up the daily meetings.

Then a strange thing happened. Hudson Taylor sent a servant to hire a boat, 'but while the man was away,' he wrote, 'my mind was powerfully impressed *not* to go to Kiating [Jiading], but to go to Tsungming [Chongming], the island in the mouth of the Yangtze . . . So strong was this impression, that when he returned, having engaged a boat [suitable for going inland only] I paid one day's fare . . . as a rue-bargain, and called another, to proceed to Tsungming.'

With books and tracts from Alexander Wylie, his medical equipment and their bedding, Hudson Taylor, Tsien and Guihua set sail from the Great East Gate, no doubt still scarred from the French and imperialist attack on the Triads, on a journey which was to have repercussions in international history. Tsien's reaction to this reversal of plans is not recorded, but to Hudson Taylor's great interest, when he returned to Shanghai for fresh supplies, he learned that John Burdon and William Aitchison, British Anglican and American Congregationalist, had just been to Jiading with thoughts of settling there.

Chongming experiment   mid-October–November 1855

There was much to be said for choosing Chongming Island to settle in with its quiet, progressive community of a million farming people, isolated from the tidal bores of revolution and counter-revolution that surged unpredictably through the mainland (map, p 216). The mandarin Chinese of the Yangzi north shore and the Shanghai dialect of the south shore were both used or understood. On Hudson Taylor's visit with John Burdon they had been well received. The young chief magistrate of Chongming city had accepted a New Testament and welcomed their offer to return with the Old Testament when its translation was completed. To head straight for the island's capital might not be wise, however. A quiet start in a strategic but less sensitive place could be more prudent.

A good crossing on October 19 brought them to the creek leading up to Xinkaihe (now Xinhezhen), the largest town after Chongming city. Thirty other towns and countless villages were to be visited in the course of their work. The night was spent on board and the next day they set out with books and tracts, preaching when the people gathered round them. At once to his distress Hudson Taylor found himself addressed as 'spiritual father' and realised that the Jesuits must have a chapel not far away. This meant prejudices to overcome in the minds of the Chinese, and perhaps more trouble. But without difficulty, through the customary middleman they succeeded in renting two floors with six rooms, above a shop facing on to the street, and on the fourth day paid a month's rent and moved in. Such a good beginning was beyond their fondest hopes.

For the next two days an incessant stream of visitors meant endless, tiring conversations. Hudson Taylor's Chinese clothes and manners led to his being accepted on equal terms, without unnatural deference or rudeness of any kind. Gentlemen in full formal dress called on him, and orderly crowds attended an evening meeting. Some were amused but there were plenty who were genuinely interested, and an invitation from a senior mandarin to visit his home at Hainan on the mainland may have shown that not all the social calls were idle.

Xinkaihe, a long straggling town of about twenty thousand inhabitants reminded him nostalgically of Dodworth, near Barnsley, and therefore of Amelia and Elizabeth. 'I wish I had a portrait of her (and you too),' he wrote to his sister, 'but I suppose I must wait for a while longer . . .' A bad attack of malaria laid him low with a crippling headache for two days, and to be ill with only unappetising food was a trial. He wished Amelia were there to prepare something tasty for him. But never mind, the rooms had been cleaned and whitewashed and, 'Fortunately for me, I am at home anywhere by the second day . . . the novelty of my coming is passing away . . .'

The second Sunday came round and he left his sick bed to preach to a room full of people. 'Suppose you die in the night?' he asked them, and went on from there. They listened solemnly and stood while he prayed for them. Never had they met such ideas and they seemed impressed. Two hundred thronged to hear him on Monday, and he had thirty-nine patients and an eye operation to perform. Day after day patients came until, on November 1, he had fifty including twelve women, and his medical supplies were running low. For settled work like this he needed more, and cash for a long stay.

He wound up his letters, to post them in Shanghai. 'I wish you could pop in and see how snug I am, in the midst of these people,' he told his mother. They were poor but very industrious. The island

was 'cultivated like a garden' through sheer hard work, men pulling
the plough for lack of buffaloes. This life among them was all he
could want. He would go over to Shanghai for a week, have wadded
winter clothing made, and come back for a long unbroken spell of
work. Tsien, a mature man, was showing himself to be gifted as a
public speaker. He would stay and continue preaching – but not
without some anxiety on Hudson Taylor's part. 'I hardly liked to
leave so young a Believer in such a position, but what could I do? I
have no colporteur to assist me . . . Pray God to enlighten his mind,
keep him faithful and humble, make him a fit instrument . . .'

After a busy Friday, November 2, he and Guihua boarded a junk
at dusk and set sail across the Yangzi. Soon it was so dark that the

AT THE HELM ACROSS THE YANGZI (30 miles)

boatmen turned back unable to see stars or land to steer by. When he realised what was happening, without sailing experience except in the *Dumfries*, Hudson Taylor took the helm and put the junk about again. Steering by wind direction only, and praying it would not change, he took them safely to the other side. Then by daylight they went up the Huangpu on the rising tide.

It was good to be back among friends. He called at Dr Lockhart's for his mail, found another fifty pounds from William Berger, and heard that three ladies in the little community had died during his absence, including Mrs Kloekers of the Netherlands Chinese Evangelization Society. Typically he went to comfort the bereaved husband, and then dropped in on William Burns and his nearest missionary neighbours, Reuben and Mrs Lowrie of the American Presbyterians, outside the South Gate. (When his brother had been killed by pirates, Reuben had immediately volunteered to take his place.) John Burdon and William Aitchison were back from their travels, so Hudson Taylor called on them too and, hearing of their hope of starting settled work in Jiading, understood why he himself had been diverted to Chongming.

After the night in the open boat he went down with a heavy cold. But many Chinese homes were too crowded for all to stay indoors day and night, so when he saw people drifting aimlessly about in the streets he flung his doors open to welcome them in, and 'preached Jesus' till he felt 'suffocated' by his cold. At Songjiang he could buy winter clothes more cheaply than in Shanghai, and wanted to visit Tsien's friend who was interested in the gospel, so as soon as he had recovered he set off again.

One of William Burns' great achievements had been a translation of *Pilgrim's Progress* into Chinese. For decades it continued to be in demand, embellished with Chinese illustrations.[16] As Hudson Taylor travelled he read through this translation for the first time.

Reaching Shanghai again on November 14 he found a rude welcome awaiting him – a writ by the chief magistrate of Chongming against him and all associated in his rental of the house at Xinkaihe. Tsien had brought this copy of the writ to Shanghai, but finding him away had left two notes and returned at once to the island.

If his heart sank, Hudson Taylor was calm when he committed the news to his journal as,

> . . . a mandarin's writ, against me and all concerned in giving me shelter, which made me feel a little uneasy about the success of this

mission. But remembering I had not gone on warfare on my own charges, I cast my care on Him Whose servant I am . . .

In fact, he was anxious. The worst that would happen to him would be a few days' detention by the magistrate, an armed escort to the consul and a fine. But Tsien, Guihua, the landlord and middlemen once in the power of unscrupulous *yamen* underlings might be bled of all they owned and punished most painfully.

Waiting in Shanghai for his return was the retainer of a white jade mandarin of county rank, retired to Dasha Island near Hainan on the Yangzi north shore, who with his brother had read books brought to them from Chongming. They were inviting Hudson Taylor to come and live with them, to tell them more, and were influential enough to protect him from trouble if he did so. It was the kind of invitation he had been waiting for. But it had come too late! He had trouble on his hands and could not involve them. A letter of explanation and a parcel of books carried by the manservant were all he could manage.

The next morning he sanguinely collected more books from Wylie, cash from the agents, and medical supplies. He needed an adviser, so a Christian teacher named Deng bravely agreed to go with him. Si came in to pray with them about the situation before they started, and John Burdon and Aitchison happening to pass joined in. Then Hudson Taylor, Deng, Guihua and the mandarin's manservant boarded their junk and dropped down the river to Wusong.

Emergency or none, the journey was a matter of hours and tides could not be altered. So on the junk Hudson Taylor preached to the crew and taught his companions, and the mandarin's servant said he believed it all. When they reached Xinkaihe, Tsien told them of a blacksmith and a grocer's assistant who were also believing, the blacksmith sincere enough to have closed his shop on Sunday. If they were genuine, God was honouring the Chongming venture, and opposition was to be expected. 'May His almighty power break down the Strongholds of sin and Satan,' Hudson Taylor wrote in his journal, defiantly.

If the Dasha mandarin's story had a touch of Cornelius about it, the Xinkaihe drama was Ephesus over again. It transpired that four druggists and two 'doctors', afraid that Hudson Taylor's medical work would harm their reputation and takings, sent twelve dollars to the chief magistrate's *yamen*, asking that the foreigner be expelled. Whether it reached the great man could not be known. But *yamen* underlings, scenting business, came to Tsien and told him it was not only unlawful for a Chinese to let his house to a Western barbarian, but also for Tsien to accompany the barbarian, and 'unless he made friends with them (he also) would have to suffer for it'.

Tsien was too wise to yield at once to extortion, so the underlings went away, only to return with a writ sealed with the magistrate's seal. Whether he had issued it, again could not then be known. The writ accused Hudson Taylor of having brought Canton and Fujian men who would be sure to breed disturbances, such was their reputation. This was demonstrably false, but the writ went on to say that the middleman, witnesses and *dipan* (a local elder over a number of houses) were culpable for not informing the magistrate of the deal. All these were to be taken to the city for 'examination', implying torture, and the *daotai* and consul were to examine and punish the foreigner.

The underlings were full of stories about the depravity of foreign religions, echoes of old imperial edicts and folk-tales, but Tsien had shown them Hudson Taylor's notices posted at the entrance, that women would be attended separately from men patients and only if accompanied. Finally the underlings declared that as his intentions were benevolent, for thirteen more dollars they would hush up the whole affair. This was the message Tsien had taken to Shanghai.

On enquiry Hudson Taylor found nothing from the magistrate. The writ had been shown but not actually served. It could well be a forgery for corrupt purposes. He at once let it be known that they need not expect a copper cash from him. His motives were only good. The demand was then reduced to ten dollars and finally to three. Still finding him resolute they transferred their attentions to the unfortunate druggists and extorted the thirteen dollars in full. Then for a week no more was heard from the *yamen*. 'All seemed over.'

On Sunday November 18 the blacksmith and grocer joined with Hudson Taylor, his companions and several others in worship, and he, Deng and Tsien each preached to fifty very attentive people. At the local temple the doorkeeper opened the gates and brought seats, and there too they preached the gospel; and unhindered through the week they alternated medical work in the town with evangelism in the villages. While Hudson Taylor saw patients upstairs, Deng and Tsien preached to a room full of people below.

Without doubt it was a responsive population and they hoped and prayed for no repetition of the *yamen* threat.

On Monday, 26th, however, they were at breakfast when the sound of a mandarin's procession with gongs and shouting came nearer and nearer. Alarmed, the whole house waited apprehensively, but the procession passed by. On their way the underlings told the people that the chief magistrate was going to another town to seize some pirates, but on his return would have all connected with the foreigner's presence there dragged before him and flogged with '300 to 1000 blows' if their replies were unsatisfactory.

'As may be supposed, I felt very anxious all day, but I preached and saw patients as usual,' and his companions held their ground. Repeating to himself as a prayer and comfort 'times without number' the words, 'Call upon me in the day of trouble. I will deliver thee, and thou shalt glorify me,' he got through two days of 'intense anxiety'. Tsien and Guihua he kept at home with him, determined to go with them if they should be arrested.

On the second evening the magistrate's procession was heard coming again. Hudson Taylor was just finishing a delicate cataract operation on an old woman. 'It was fortunate that the operation was over . . . for I quite trembled with excitement . . . My anxiety was intense.' But the procession went by. Not until nearly two hours later did he learn that the magistrate had gone straight through Xinkaihe and on to Chongming city without stopping. 'My prayers were changed into praise . . . and thankfulness took the place of fear. Most likely the report was an attempt to extort money, by his followers . . .' And still no official communication came.

> I determined if there was any enquiry, to go myself before the Mandarin, and point out the inconsistency of annoying me, while my neighbours the Catholics had a chapel built and two resident priests there. But we had no message of any kind. . . .

So back to work and the same routine they went. At one village of four hundred they could find not one person literate enough to understand what he read. 'The truth is, China must be evangelized . . . by the *preached* word. So we need more men, willing to deny themselves . . . and live among and spread the Gospel among this people.'

'Take arms against a sea of troubles?'   *December 1855*

On November 30, two days after writing so hopefully, Hudson Taylor made another twelve-hour journey to Shanghai for yet more medicines. Rowing all the fifteen miles up the Huangpu, he tied up soon after daybreak and dropped in on Dr Lockhart for breakfast. Robert Fortune the botanist called in again while he was there. Then home to the South Gate – and another shock. Another summons already a week old lay waiting for him.

'November 23, 1855

Sir,

I am directed by Her Majesty's Consul to inform you that an information has been lodged at this office by His Excellency the Intendant of Circuit [the *daotai*] to the effect that you have rented a house . . . at a place called Sinkaiho . . . and opened this house as a physician's establishment . . . His Excellency refers to a former complaint lodged against you for visiting Tsingkiang [Jingjiang], upon which subject you appeared before her Majesty's Consul. His Excellency also reports that (the Chinese involved) have been arrested. Her Majesty's Consul has therefore to call upon you to appear at this office without delay, in order that we may investigate the matter . . .

I am, Sir, Your most obedient Servant,
Frederick Harvey, Vice Consul'[17]

The facts were otherwise; not one of them had been arrested; but at least he knew now that more than extortion was involved.

Hudson Taylor's letter home the next day gave a fuller picture than his journal.

Sunday, December 2nd . . . my heart is sad, sad, sad, . . . I lost no time in seeing him, and have been prohibited from residing on Tsungming. I do not know what to do. If I disobey, I incur a fine of $500. All I can do is to give up the house, or I shall bring many Chinese into trouble – and pray over my future course. I think I shall appeal to Sir Jno. Bowring, the Plenipo: stating that I feel it a hardship that my consul should prohibit me from residing on Tsungming, while two French missionaries not only reside there but have built a Catholic Chapel, and that within 6 miles of the town in which I was . . . I leave tonight at 1.00 a.m. for Tsungming . . . Thank God my health is very good and the Chinese costume much warmer than yours . . . Pray for me, I need more *Grace*, and live far below my privilege. Oh! to feel more as Moses did . . . 'forgive their sin . . . and if not, blot me, I pray Thee, out of

Thy book' or as Paul did when he could wish himself accursed from Christ for his brethren; – and as Christ felt when he said 'I lay down my life for the sheep'. I do not want to be as one of the hirelings who flee when the wolf comes – neither do I wish to run into danger, when much may be done in safety. I want to know the Lord's will, and grace to do it, even if it results in expatriation. 'Now is my soul troubled and what shall I say? *Father*, glorify Thy name . . .'

His problem was not that he feared the consul or his judgment, but that this ended the Chongming venture, for lack of the five hundred dollars. Reporting to George Pearse he added that the Frenchmen had actually bought land,

> But I, an Englishman, am forbidden by my consul from doing so, and told that if I disobey I shall be bound over under heavy penalties to keep the treaty. This is most distressing.[18]

Rutherford Alcock told him he could appeal to Sir John Bowring and he, the consul, would be glad to forward the appeal, or he could wait to see Sir John personally when he came to Shanghai. He was expected soon. Several fellow-missionaries advised him to appeal and he thought he would, but there were several reasons for not doing so. It would be very easy for the consul to plead the 'most favoured nation clause' and reply to the mandarins that the British should enjoy the same privileges as the French. If they claimed that the French were there without their knowledge, they could be told that if they overlooked the one they should overlook the other.

> Wherever we go we find the Catholic Priests [Hudson Taylor reported], often flying the French flag over their houses. And it is very unjust that our Consuls should unite with the Mandarins to prevent our enjoying the same privileges of residing in the country . . . Excuse this rough letter . . . penned in the boat.[19]

At the same time Hudson Taylor wrote privately to George Pearse as a friend and not primarily as the Foreign Secretary of the CES. Did he think the Society would carry the responsibility for paying the fine if he were to go on as before in spite of the consular prohibition? And if by giving up the protection of the consul he were to go inland as he had opportunity, would Mr Pearse advise him to do so, or leave the choice to him, or object to his doing so? He wondered if Lord Clarendon would direct the consuls to allow Britons to do as the French were doing, if the facts were put before him.

On Chongming island itself the results of this matter could be serious in the extreme, in Hudson Taylor's absence, even if nothing was done in his presence. The *yamen* underlings could extract their last pound of flesh and drop of blood from the landlord, the go-between and others. A consular representation to the *daotai* and chief magistrate on Chongming would forestall action against them and thwart the underlings' schemes, Hudson Taylor suggested. But Alcock would not hear of it. International friction was not going to be set off by a novice missionary.

> All I can do is to pray God to protect them [Hudson Taylor told George Pearse.] . . . I do not want to be one of the hirelings who flee . . . nor do I wish to tempt providence . . . I need more of the spirit of my Master, more *entire* resignation to the will of God, and more boldness too. These Mandarins are cruel, rapacious liars . . . It will need no slight faith in God and resignation to His will and trust in Him, to enable me to go among them without any hope of protection from any but Him who has all power.

If his aim and his method of going about it were clear to him and already proving successful, this consular obstruction no less positively brought him to a halt. Now the problem was how to get round it. At no point did he contemplate accepting defeat. On the contrary, his reaction was to be resentful, belligerent, and because of that to feel his need of Christlikeness. It awoke in him a sense of need to be able to take this injustice humbly, not realising that humility clearly shone through the lines he was writing. He saw himself as unforgiving and unfaithful while he contemplated compliance lest his Chinese landlord, middleman and colleagues should suffer. Concern for them prompted retreat, but retreat smacked of the hireling. What should he do? Appeal to Sir John Bowring was the superficially obvious course. But Bowring was pro-Manchu and critical of missionaries. *The Gleaner* in reporting the success of the Societies' deputation to Lord Clarendon at the Foreign Office had held out hope of his intervention. Could this be the moment for him to take action?

> The Chinese had permitted a foreign firm to build a silk factory some distance inland, with the proviso that the style of building must be purely Chinese, and that there should be nothing external to suggest that it was foreign.

This fact had moved Dr Medhurst to suggest to Hudson Taylor the experiment with Chinese clothes. This and the Chinese blind eye to the Jesuits inland were enough precedent to secure with-drawal of the ban on him. How was it, moreover, that Cobbold and Rankin were able to travel for three weeks in foreign clothes from Ningbo to Fuzhou, both consular stations, with five carriers for their bedding, baggage and books, without protest from anyone? Logic seemed alien to this matter.

This time it was Hudson Taylor's turn to receive the sympathy and support of the brave men he knew, especially John Burdon. He 'dined and slept' at Joseph Edkins' home on the night of the interview with Alcock, for he had no bedding at the South Gate house. And after preaching in the city the next day, Sunday, he spent that evening with the Lowries, intending to leave on the one am tide for Chongming again. His hired boatmen, however, were nowhere to be found. So the Lowries gave him a bed, and breakfast at six-thirty before he combed the waterfront again for them. They had sailed without him and without their pay. Only news of the trouble he was in at Xinkaihe could have made them do that. He hired another junk, reached the island at eight pm and walked to Xinkaihe.

To his relief there had been no fresh developments, but his news kept him and his team talking in distress until after midnight. It gave substance to the *yamen* underlings' threats. They slept, but he 'woke with a sad heart and feeling very unwell' while they prepared to leave. Naturally the landlord and the middleman were highly alarmed, until they knew that he proposed to call on the chief mandarin himself to inform him of his departure and plead their case.

Together Deng, Tsien, Guihua and Hudson Taylor sadly headed for the boat. The townspeople standing at their doors and others in the street called out 'Come again soon! Come again soon!', but they could not know whether they would ever be able to return. Leaving the blacksmith and grocer was most painful. Who could teach them now? They headed up the coast to Chongming city and went to the *yamen*, only to find that the annual examinations of the literati were in progress and the magistrate was invigilating. He sent a message telling Hudson Taylor to come and see him in a month's time. So there was nothing to do but to return on the two am ebb-tide to Wusong and up the Huangpu when it turned.

His first priority on reaching Shanghai again was to tell his friends and enlist their prayers. He called on Burdon and Aitchison, Edkins and Hobson, and went on to the missionary prayer meeting at the

Lowries. Then at last to his South Gate house and his Chinese companions again. Living with and like them, he was soaking up their way of life and way of thinking. By seeing how he met each crisis, prayerfully depending on God at every stage, and by sharing in the experience with him they were learning more than any number of sermons could teach them. That night they worshipped and prayed together, and the next day took up their old pattern of teaching and preaching.

There were letters for him and one was from Elizabeth. Nothing seemed to happen by halves. It reversed what she had said before.

> I had just been compelled to leave Tsungming [he told his mother later on, thanking her for urging him not to despair] and had received Miss Sissons last letter, telling me she feared she did not love me; and between one thing and another was quite knocked down, and had scarcely heart to read my other letters. I have written (her) a long letter, to prove to her that her fears are groundless, and to plead my cause, and that of the heathen . . . if she did not love me she would not be tormented with the fear that she did not love me . . . I trust this cup may pass from me; if not, may He give me strength to drink it to the dregs . . . how difficult to keep a *single* eye to God's glory – how easy it is to follow God when our own leadings go the same way . . . As Mr. Burns says, . . . if you see a dog following two men on a road, it is not easy to tell which of them is its master, but wait till the road divides . . .!

Expulsion and rejection coming together were hard to take. He knew his Master and went on trusting and following him though the road became no easier. He wrote his reports and letters home, and filled his days with work in the city. John Burdon called to see him, and he himself visited William Muirhead, Chaplain Hobson, Dr Lockhart, the veteran Elijah Bridgman, and William Burns on his houseboat. 'What should be done?' was the great debate. It affected all of them, for their own hopes hung upon the outcome, and important principles were at stake. Then he wrote to George Pearse,

> Sir J. Bowring is expected up at Shanghai by the mail steamer – today, tomorrow or Monday. I shall appeal to him against the Consul's decision . . . I feel the importance of this case in many respects. It will show the footing in which Protestant missionaries are in China, and if I am still forbidden will prevent some of our officials from saying that while Romish missionaries are willing to deny themselves the pleasures of society etc, and go amongst the Chinese, we are not so. The

Gospel *must* be preached among the Chinese, and if owned by God, the opposition of Satan will be sure to be roused. May God give us grace and at the same time give us wisdom and caution to avoid all unnecessary difficulties and dangers.

Word came from Miss Stacey, after the news reached England, that W C Milne, the adventurous missionary son of William Milne, and others thought Hudson Taylor should have disregarded the threats,

(saying) you would have done the best to remain there, and like the Apostle have made them fetch you out . . . I cannot see but you did right to act upon the words 'If they persecute you in one city, flee ye to another.'

Reminding him that it was the experience of missionaries everywhere that success and encouragement were followed by Satan's attacks, she continued,

God has given you, dear brother, a remarkable place amongst us at Tottenham in not being forgotten in our prayers; no name comes in so often . . . Farewell dear brother in Jesus and fellow partaker in the hope of glory . . . Rich the promises to him that *overcometh*!

To Amelia he admitted that he had no great hope of success with his appeal, but some of his Shanghai friends were for making the most of the occasion to establish their rights. They did not know that the CES had already started a ball rolling which was to result in more than they imagined. In time *The Gleaner* carried this statement, slanted to make their point:[20]

Interference of British Consul
    The Board recently received from Mr. J. H. Taylor a detailed account of the conduct of the British Consul at Shanghai . . . The Consul . . . ordered Mr. Taylor not to reside [on Chongming island] and also that, if he persisted, he would be subject to a heavy penalty. This course the Board believes to be contrary to the law, as by residing in Tsungming Mr. Taylor was beyond the British jurisdiction; and if he chose to expose himself to the dangers, the Consul had no authority to interfere . . . any British subject is, according to treaty, to be allowed to do the same (as the French priests do). The matter is so important that . . . it will be duly brought before the British Government.

Nor was this the bleating of an uninfluential body. On its General Committee sat the Rt Hon the Earl of Cavan, two other Members of

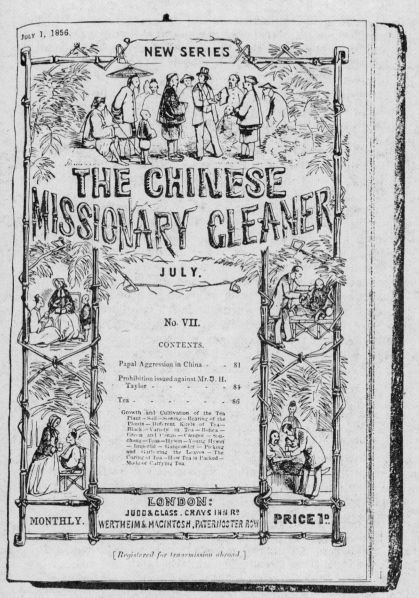

THE GLEANER TAKES UP THE CUDGELS

Parliament, including the Hon. A Kinnaird, as well as a baronet and Robert Bickersteth, soon to become bishop of Ripon; and the archbishop of Dublin was among the Society's donors – an adequate constellation of luminaries to catch the eye of Lord Clarendon.[21]

Sunday, December 9, was a good day, good in that after two hours of studying the Scriptures and praying with his household, Hudson Taylor, Deng and Si preached to successive audiences totalling two to three hundred people. And after an evening with William Aitchison, he spent more time with his four Chinese companions, noting that all four prayed aloud. 'Truly', he told his journal '(prayer is) "the Christian's vital breath, the Christian's native air". Oh! that some of this seed may be found fruitful . . .'

William Burns and he were seeing more of each other, and in Latourette's phrase 'each found in the other a kindred spirit'.[22] On December 12 Hudson Taylor visited him on the boat he called home, and he came to preach at the South Gate house. A man in their audience said that several at the town he came from were interested in the gospel, and another invited Hudson Taylor to his home town where it had never yet been preached. Burns and he thereupon agreed to go together, each in his own boat, and started studying maps of the area. Far from being deterred, both took Hudson Taylor's setback as an indication to try in another direction. 'When will the Gospel be preached throughout the length and breadth of the land?' The tactics could be varied. What mattered was the strategy and outcome. As for waiting for the CES to reply about responsibility for the fine and what attitude he should adopt, Hudson Taylor felt so inhibited by obligation to refer things to them and wait four months for an answer, that he made his own decision, to scorn the treaty restrictions, and from then on seriously considered resigning from the Society.

As for the Chongming affair, little more was heard of it locally. The chief magistrate of the island made a proclamation accusing him of opening a medicine shop and deluding the people,

> thus infringing the treaty stipulations with the most determined intention. The substance of this representation has been communicated to the Barbarian Consul that he might take the said barbarian, and . . . severely bind him down and reprimand him.[23]

It also said that the Chinese involved, 'traitors in concert with the barbarians', had been arrested and rigorously dealt with, and exhorted all under his jurisdiction to co-operate in sending foreigners back to be punished. But in January Tsien and Guihua went to Dasha to visit the mandarins who had invited Hudson Taylor to come. One had died and his brother was away, so the two Christians preached in thirteen towns and many villages before returning safely.

In no letter of Hudson Taylor's is there any reference to direct involvement of the Jesuits in this expulsion, as on another occasion in 1868, but a memorial by Monsignor Mouly, Vicar-Apostolic in Peking, to the Court in 1854 reveals the climate of Catholic-Protestant relations. Appealing to history and the Kang Xi emperor's use of Catholic 'western scholars' in public office, he offered their services again. And then in a deliberately misleading passage he equated Protestants with the Taiping rebels from whom he was at pains to dissociate the Catholics.

> For instance [a translation runs] in the South of China, at the five ports, there has recently been disseminated a religion, called the religion of Shangdi and the religion of Jesus. [Here the Taiping term and the Protestant term were set side by side.] Now, although the adherents of these religions do, with us, worship the Lord of Heaven, honour Jesus and venerate the cross, yet because they err in numerous instances from the true doctrines of the Roman Catholics, they have therefore lost the essential elements of truth; and . . . belong to the class of those who delude themselves and deceive others, and are therefore . . . heretics. The western scholars . . . although they associate with such in common things, would not dare to worship God in the same temple, deeming them to be defiled and transgressors against the Lord of Heaven, for whom no intercession can be made . . . the western scholars of the present day are willing to become the arms and legs, the ears and eyes of the Government . . . and to exert their energies in behalf of the emperors of the Tartar dynasty.[24]

There is no knowing how this memorial may have influenced future developments, but as a ruse to blacken the Protestants as a whole it would appear to have failed. Certainly Hudson Taylor had no evidence of the French priests on Chongming instigating the move to oust him from Xinkaihe.

Sir John Bowring did not come to Shanghai, and when William Burns 'thought no good would arise out of it and it seemed so to me too', Hudson Taylor dropped all thought of appealing against Alcock's ruling. Wilhelm Lobscheid threw a little light on the situation a few weeks later. As interpreter to the British expedition to Japan he knew Sir John personally and could have heard him express his views. He wrote to the CES,

> Sir John Bowring is opposed to English missionaries going into the interior, and I should therefore like you to send a German to assist me . . . I have no doubt but that Sir John Bowring wishes to approach the Court of China without being subject to blame for having allowed English subjects to violate the treaty stipulations, and, so far as I am acquainted with his views, he intends nothing but to open China, also, for the missionaries.[25]

In Britain the CES took up the matter, asking Hudson Taylor for more particulars of the French practice of flying their flag, and he replied,

> As to the French Flag over the houses of Catholic missionaries, . . . I certainly have seen it more than a hundred miles from Shanghai – and nearer to the City (perhaps 4 miles from it) on both sides of the Whangpu it is now flying.[26]

It was not as if Britain or the administration in Hong Kong were abiding by the Nanking Treaty. Hong Kong, the seat of Sir John Bowring's government, was a huge warehouse for the opium traffic. Even smuggling was carried on under the protection of the British flag with ever increasing daring and success. And this in the face of the 1843 supplementary treaty which bound British consuls at the ports –

> to discourage all smuggling trade and instantly to inform the Chinese authorities of any such transactions coming to their knowledge.

How then, asked *The Gleaner*, could twenty-five heavily-armed merchant vessels be allowed to carry the British flag and Hong Kong itself be 'legally the established depot for a retail opium trade and for which the British government receive a regular tax'? The agreement had been still-born. But this being the case, in fairness to Hudson Taylor his *legal* rights should have been upheld and his Chinese friends and landlord shown to be within their own law. As a test case the incident could have been used to induce the Manchu court in Peking to concede in practice what it had conceded in theory under the 'most favoured nation' clause. To no one's regret it was not so used. But another pebble had fallen into the international millpond and all too soon the spreading ripples were to lap against the dragon throne.

Once again circumstances uprooted Hudson Taylor and forced him to try another direction, bringing yet more experience to equip him for his unimaginable future in China.

PART 4

FROM PILLAR TO POST
1856–57

CHAPTER NINE

BURNS AND SWATOW
1855–1856

The man for the moment   *December 1855–July 1856*

Little realising that he was embarking on seven months of companionship with William Burns, on December 17 Hudson Taylor hired a boat to accompany him on a single 'excursion'. He found himself, like Timothy or Silas with the apostle Paul, in the company of a saint. As Thomas Carlyle in his definition of a good biography said, 'Few individuals, indeed, can deserve such a study . . . But Burns, if we mistake not, is one of those few individuals . . .',[1] so Burns and Hudson Taylor were to interact in such a way as to value each other's influence and fellowship.

William Chalmers Burns[2] was seventeen years older than Hudson Taylor and had behind him many years of experience as an evangelist. Ever since, in his twenties, he had abandoned his plans for a legal career and entered the ministry, he had wanted to be a missionary. But when a 'religious awakening' broke out through his preaching, he was led on from Scotland to Ireland and then Canada, the human catalyst in a chain reaction of spiritual transformation and revival. Only after eight years did he reach China as the pioneer of the English Presbyterian Mission and substitute a language he had to learn and people who were isolated from him by cultural barriers, for the great audiences and popularity he had known. By close contact with Chinese, however, he acquired 'an unusual command of the language of the common people', wrote popular hymns and was well fitted to translate *Pilgrim's Progress*.

Working closely with John and Alexander Stronach of the LMS at Amoy, he saw a congregation of new believers develop into a church standing firmly on its own feet before he returned briefly to the United Kingdom in 1854. At the Annual Meeting of the Chinese Evangelization Society in 1855, Captain Fishbourne, RN, paid a glowing tribute to William Burns. On the same occasion as Fishbourne had so dramatically rescued mutilated Chinese from the harbour when the imperialists wreaked vengeance after the Triad occupation of Amoy, Burns on land had rescued many more, he declared, 'and found himself looked upon almost as a father . . . He remained six months in the interior, habited as a European, an event . . . which was unparalleled in the history of China.'

Nevertheless, British supporters of the work in Amoy were finding it hard to understand why progress there seemed relatively slow, both in planting churches and distributing the Bible Society's million New Testaments. They needed to hear at first hand from someone they knew and could trust, that it had taken three years to print the Testaments and would take more than twice as long to scatter them in the accessible parts of China. It was after all only thirteen years since the end of the first opium war and the arrival of David Abeel and William Burns in Amoy. Yet there were already three churches in the city showing such 'harmony and love . . . as brethren in Christ' that one missionary said he had 'far less doubt of their genuineness than of the majority in church fellowship at home'. By 1857 there were a hundred and forty-eight members with the American Board, a hundred and sixty-one with the LMS and forty-seven with the English Presbyterians, attending each other's marriages and funerals without discrimination and developing their own united evangelistic outreach. By any reckoning of pioneer evangelism, Burns could point out, that was not slow but good progress.

When he returned to China, Burns brought back from Scotland with him an outstanding young man, Dr Carstairs Douglas, who became with Dr James Maxwell a pioneer of the Church in Taiwan and a leading missionary figure until his untimely death. William Burns set off to reach the Taipings at Nanking and, like several who made the attempt without success, was forced to fall back upon Shanghai. Living there in his houseboat as a base for itinerant evangelism, he was glad to join hands with Hudson Taylor to preach the gospel in cities where as far as they knew no evangelist had been before. Burns had had his full share of troubles. Both had been thwarted in doing what they had believed God had told them to attempt. Now as they travelled from place to place, he talked about the deep lessons he had learned from years of gruelling effort, opposition, persecution and disappointment, in Dublin, Canada and South China.

Three lessons in particular Hudson Taylor appropriated to himself and passed on to generation after generation of missionaries.[3] He called them 'seed thoughts . . . in the subsequent organization of the China Inland Mission'. The first was God's purposes in permitting his servants to undergo suffering and frustration. The second, the importance of evangelism as the great work of the Church. And the third, the place of lay evangelists as a 'lost order' in the Church 'that Scripture required to be restored'.

In his *Retrospect* thirty years later, Hudson Taylor passed over the Chongming adventure in a few lines, ending, 'I reluctantly returned to Shanghai, little dreaming of the blessing that God had in store for me there.' But he devoted ten pages to his association with Burns. In his home letter on their first journey together he wrote,

> He is one of those holy men one seldom meets with, who do possess a single eye to God's glory . . . The secret is easily learned and told – he is a man of prayer – added to which however, he possesses an iron frame, and a strong will, which would not be easily moved from its purpose. . . [And later] Those happy months were an unspeakable joy and privilege to me. His love for the Word was delightful, and his holy, reverential life and constant communings with God made fellowship with him satisfying to the deep cravings of my heart.

What William Burns quickly saw, as Hudson Taylor put it,

> (was that) while I was the younger and in every way less experienced, I [in Chinese clothes] had the quiet hearers, while he [in foreign garb] was followed by the rude boys, and by the curious but careless; that I was invited to the homes of the people, while he received an apology that the crowd that would follow precluded his being invited.

But there is no record of what Burns thought of his appreciative companion, except what he told his own mother, that seeing how well Hudson Taylor was received in comparison with himself, he concluded that it was his duty to live like a Chinese too.

Defying the consular ban[4]   *December 1855–January 1856*

If merchants, Frenchmen and the Hong Kong government regarded the old treaties to some extent as a dead letter, missionaries had all the more reason for treating a consular ban as mere formality. Their mandate was to 'preach the gospel to every creature' and that meant penetrating the interior of China. Neither Burns nor Hudson Taylor questioned the rightness of their action. If the consul demanded a fine, they would somehow pay it. Chongming was out of bounds for the sake of the Chinese accused with him, but there was plenty of virgin territory left to reach.

Eighty miles west of Shanghai a large lake, the Tai Hu, and smaller satellite lakes lay between the coastal regions and the northward stretch of the Yangzi from Jiujiang (Kiukiang) to Nanking (map, p 216). The Grand Canal passed to the east of the Tai Hu, through Jiaxing and Suzhou, linking its southern terminal Hangzhou with Zhenjiang (Chinkiang) on the Yangzi. So far, missionary travels had been concentrated on the fertile plains so freely intersected by canals east of the Grand Canal and north of the lakes. To the west and south lay most of Zhejiang province and big cities seldom if ever visited. Cobbold and Rankin were tackling southern Zhejiang from Ningbo. Huzhou (Wuxing), Wuzhen and Nanxun drew Burns and Hudson Taylor as they studied the maps. Wuzhen, Black Town, had the reputation of being a wild and lawless place, a refuge for salt smugglers, and therefore most needing the gospel. Like all provincial border regions, it drew the law-breakers.

They set off on December 17, a week before Christmas, their two boats travelling together, a teacher named Song going with them. When Tsien and Guihua returned from Dasha they were to join the others up-country. Hudson Taylor was better off than usual. He had

> a comfortable boat, that . . . gives me a nice little room for myself, one in front for my servant . . . and a berth behind for my teacher, as well as room for books, the boatmen, cooking, etc. My little room has an oyster-shell window that gives light, but prevents persons peeping in; a little table at which I write and take meals, a locker . . . over which my bed is placed at night, and a seat round the remaining parts, so that two friends can sit with me . . . How differently the Master was lodged! . . . God only knows what is to be my lot, whether I am to have a helpmeet and fellow-labourer, with me to serve and praise our dear Lord. *He* knows what is *best* . . .

The thought was never far from his mind. A wife could quite happily share such a cabin with him. For the present he was more than content with his circumstances. Chinese winter clothing is 'most admirable, unspeakably good and comfortable' in the cold weather, he claimed. And instead of blankets he was sleeping under two thick *pugai* (wadded Chinese quilts).

Heading south on the Huangpu and west past Songjiang, they went ashore to preach from time to time, each drawing his own audience. 'It was amusing to hear them discussing . . . whether I was a foreigner or not.'

IN A BUDDHIST TEMPLE YARD

William Burns' policy was to start quietly on the outskirts and work towards the main street of a town, and Hudson Taylor quickly saw the wisdom of this. Over a period of hours or days the people became gradually aware of their presence and the excited mobs of his earlier experience no longer thronged them when they came into a city. At a Buddhist temple he watched idol worship in progress and afterwards, feeling stirred by the sight, spoke to the worshippers. Some of them were well-dressed women; 'to my astonishment they stayed and listened for a considerable time. I never addressed a number of Chinese women before . . .'

At Nanxun the Presbyterian Burns introduced Hudson Taylor to a totally new approach. In the South Sea Islands John G Paton and James Chalmers did not hesitate to go in clerical habit between warring clans of cannibals and order them in the name of the Almighty to desist.[5] On this occasion Hudson Taylor had a sore throat and painful chest and only preached at two temples.[6] But Burns heard of an immoral play being held outside the city among the rice-fields, and 'determined to go and warn the people'. Unrestrained vice accompanied such plays. Together they found their way there. It was 'anything but inviting', patronised by 'men of the roughest description' and Hudson Taylor was alarmed when they came to a 'vast encampment, with some thousands of people, in sheds, gambling booths and brothels, a Vanity Fair surrounding the stage'. It was 'Satan's camp'. The din of a percussion and string band, hideous to their ears, showed that a play was in progress. William Burns at once mounted the stage, stopped the play and 'warned the players and people that this was very wrong, that they were on the way to hell, etc.' Then a great hubbub arose and Hudson Taylor could not hear his own voice.

Instead of roughly handling them the people simply took hold of them and led them away. But the next day they returned and preached from a ladder to the people who crowded round them. Each time they created a diversion they were escorted away and again at an army camp they were moved on, but at a temple were 'well heard by many for a long time and felt much encouraged'.

On Christmas Day Hudson Taylor yearned to be with his family, it was so long since he had seen them, but he and Burns spent the day preaching. That night he wrote, 'I feel a great love for these dear people – Oh! that the Lord would reveal Himself in them – I should be sorry to have to leave them for any reason.'

For the next two days they worked systematically through the streets of Nanxun. Respectable townsmen expressed approval and asked them to try again to stop proceedings at the encampment. It would be a miracle if that happened, but some individuals at least might mend their ways. They prayed together about it and decided that Hudson Taylor should make the second attempt. In his Chinese clothes he passed the gambling booths and wormed his way through the crowd, still unrecognised,

> and in a moment was on the stage. I ordered the players to stop, and the people to listen, and at once proceeded to address them, and hearing responses among the crowd, looked and found Mr. B. there in its midst.

When men came up to stop him he told them to sit down and wait until he had finished, but others joined them.

> I then turned to the players, entreated them to pity their own souls, and not be the bait to allure others also to endless perdition.

Dragged forcibly away, he went to a different part of the crowd and when a prostitute rose from the stool she was sitting on, he stood on it and preached to hundreds about the evil they were witnessing. Asking if it were not so, the people agreed with him. Then again he was led away. As they went Burns asked the bystanders if they would like their own daughters to reach such a state. It touched them on the raw and he heard his question being repeated in the crowd. Then why buy other people's daughters for immoral purposes, he asked? And as they passed groups of prostitutes in boats on the canal they preached to them. It was all they could do.

Amazed to reach their own boats unharmed, they thanked God for protection from injury during such 'perilous service' among such people. It had not been without effect. In addition to general approval in the town, one man followed them everywhere, came up and paid for their tea in a restaurant, and said he believed all they were preaching was the truth. Others came to talk with them in the boats. Some said they wished to be their disciples, but another, 'You are too sweeping in your condemnations; there are good as well as good-for-nothing idols'; in a nearby temple, for example, there were images of two men who during a famine gave away their master's rice and committed suicide. Another was prepared to talk about God but when Hudson Taylor suggested they pray to him he was aghast. To expose himself to the attention of the gods of any kind was too dangerous. Hudson Taylor overheard one ask his friend, 'Do you believe in this doctrine?' and the friend replied, 'Yes, I do.'

A young man from Peking said, 'I think we are very much alike': both were far from home, alone without friends among people of a strange language. He could not understand the Shanghai dialect.

> 'Don't you feel lonely?' he asked, 'or does God your Father prevent it?' I said to him, 'There are times when I feel this, particularly when unwell and often I long for my dear parents and relations, but (then) I kneel down and pray for them . . . and God puts a little heaven into my heart, and though the desire is not removed, I am enabled to wait . . .' He said 'Oh! that is good.'

By now Burns had learned his lesson. Hudson Taylor had the advantage over him. No noisy youths made facetious remarks about his clothes with useless buttons down the back, and his voice was not drowned by children's incessant chatter. If foreigners and even missionaries were so critical of Chinese clothes, he reasoned, no doubt the Chinese were as prejudiced against the English. But he found the change a difficult step to take. Three days after Christmas he put on a Chinese gown, over his foreign clothes, and cut the peak off his English cap. Half measures only drew comments. Someone in his audience the next day asked him why he did not have his head shaved and wear a cap and queue like Hudson Taylor's. That was enough. He held back no longer. In winter a skullcap was correct, and a *bianzi* could be attached to it.

So the year ended, 'a year of many eventful circumstances to China and to me'. They could not report 'a great awakening among the people', Hudson Taylor wrote, . . . 'it has not pleased the Lord to grant this'. But many had heard the gospel and some said they believed and knelt to pray with the missionaries. 'Straight is the gate and narrow is the way, and few there be who find it.' When he reckoned up the total of New Testaments, books and pamphlets he himself had handed out during 1855, mostly away from the treaty ports, it was twenty-nine thousand, one hundred and fifty.

For another week they 'worked hard' and systematically, completing eighteen days in the one town and on January 8 moved on to Wuzhen, the Black Town, larger and more important than Nanxun. From the great surprise shown, they judged that they must be the first missionaries to come there. No one they asked knew of a previous visit. They preached in the temple of the God of War, in an open space cleared by fire, at a tea-shop and from a humped bridge. Hudson 'never saw such attention or seriousness'.

So far so good. But the next day, after distributing books only to those who could read, Hudson Taylor was beginning his midday meal when –

> a battering began, and the roof was at once broken in. I went out . . . and found four or five men taking the large lumps of frozen earth turned up in a field close by – weighing . . . from seven to fourteen pounds each – and throwing them at the boat . . . a considerable part of the upper structure of the boat was broken to pieces . . .

Quickly Tsien got a passing boat to put him ashore a little way down the bank with some tracts and drew the attackers away. That was all they had wanted. Their violence was because being unable to read, 'their unreasonable demand for books was not complied with'. Two of the men were local inhabitants and the rest salt smugglers.

But the incident was not over. A crowd gathered and gave them a sympathetic hearing as Burns and Hudson Taylor preached to them, and on the next day too. When they spoke about the words, 'take joyfully the spoiling of your goods', 'it went *home*', the people saw it was so and said '*vu ts'ow*' (*bu cuo*), 'Quite right!' Two *yamen* officials came, no doubt to assess the situation, and stayed for a long conversation in mandarin. They were from near Peking. And after a peaceful evening of more preaching in a mulberry grove, the missionaries were visited at the boat by a Buddhist priest who agreed that in Buddhism there was no real hope after death.

On the evening of the 12th they decided to go to the far end of the town, about two miles distant. 'As Mr. Burns and I were accustomed to talk together in Chinese, this conclusion was known to those in the boats.' (To talk in English would have been a discourtesy to their companions.) But on the way they decided to go first to the tea-shop where interested people might be waiting to talk with them. After they had gone a man came to the boats demanding ten dollars and a pound of opium, saying that more than fifty salt smugglers were waiting for it. If it was not handed over, they would destroy the boats. He was told there was no opium and little money either, and left protesting he did not believe it. Song, the teacher, at once went to warn the missionaries, and the boatmen moved their boats in different directions, hoping one at least would escape.

Meanwhile night had fallen and Burns and Hudson Taylor were

on their way back again. They noticed that instead of being accompanied as was always the case, no one came with them. It was by then 'intensely dark' except for the light of the candle-lantern they were carrying. To their surprise one of the boatmen met them and his behaviour was very strange. He took the lantern and blew it out; and when they moved to relight it he threw the candle into the canal. Then going ahead in silence he led them to one of the boats in its new hiding place and explained what had happened. Song, unable to find the missionaries, returned past the place where the boats had previously been moored and, unrecognised, was asked by a dozen or twenty men where they had gone to.

To travel by night was as dangerous as to stay, and 'the morrow was the Lord's Day, when we should not wish to travel', so after rowing some distance they left it to the boatmen to decide where to stop, and at last, uncertain where they were, moored for the night.

Hudson Taylor woke at four am with a 'violent pain' in his knee and heard 'rain pouring down in torrents'. It continued, 'so heavy all day that no one could leave the boats . . . Had the day been fine we should most likely have been discovered.' Early on Monday they were told that in spite of the rain men had been searching all day for them. 'The boatmen were now so thoroughly alarmed that they would stay no longer . . .' Even then Hudson Taylor was so concerned for the people in Wuzhen who had responded to the gospel that he would have stayed to teach them, keeping only his bedding roll with him, had not inflammation in his knee become so severe as to demand an immediate return to Shanghai for treatment. So far they had been away for a full month.

Burns stayed on, and during the week that Hudson Taylor was recovering continued to preach the gospel as he moved towards Shanghai, to arrive on January 26. They spent the weekend restocking their boats and set out together again for two more weeks. Of that journey there is no record, beyond a remark in a home letter that Hudson Taylor was at Songjiang and sending it by the hand of John Burdon. Whether he had joined them for a few days or met them there is not mentioned. Out at Songjiang the ground was covered with snow and Hudson Taylor's Chinese face-cloth froze stiff while he was shaving, but his clothing was so 'wonderfully warm and comfortable' that he could say, 'I never spent such a pleasant winter before.'

But troubles were never far away. 'The Society have just placed me in a nice fix,' he told his parents.

They have withdrawn our credit, and decided on sending us out specie [in kind] or bills for our salaries . . . I came back with $20–$50 due for boats, wages, rents etc (to) find I have no money and can get none till their first remittance which is to arrive in April, *all being well*.

Fortunately he had more than a hundred dollars of his own in hand from Mr Berger and, by telling Tsien and Si that he could no longer employ them, he thought he might get by if he lived very frugally. To add to his quandary, however, Lobscheid was sending six boxes of printing blocks for Parker's use, the freight on them to be paid by Hudson Taylor. By selling his domestic stores of soap and candles he could raise some cash, but as a last resort he would ask the Shanghai agents to advance some money against a personal bill in defiance of the Society's resolution.

Before he had left England Hudson Taylor had been convinced that God would supply all his needs, and that confidence remained. But how God would probably do it remained in his understanding at this time a matter of salary or earnings. That he should have neither and yet be supplied with enough for his needs was still far from his thinking. William Berger's gifts had been generous, but he had given no hint of repeating them. When Hudson Taylor told Mr Pearse that the Bible Society had offered to pay the expense of his boat and carriers for the distribution of Scriptures, he saw it as a fortuitous deliverance from his own Society's mistakes, rather than as God's use of one means instead of another to supply him. In the slow Odyssey of faith he was still looking at circumstances and fears, but he was attempting to walk on the waves.

> I can trust myself between (the Society) and my own resources, but their instability makes me often doubt whether I could trust them with the support of a wife, because . . . if they failed me, it would be no joke to be left here, without (a) profession, 18,000 miles from home, and with a wife and perhaps children dependent on me for support. Sometimes I think I shall have to come home and qualify first – then I feel I cannot leave my work, and it may be that ere long the Soc⁷ will be in such a state that for me to leave them, or leave the work, would be to ruin them. All this comes from want of faith. The Good Lord has hitherto led me blindfold, as it were, – shown me step by step, and not one in advance. His way of getting me out of difficulties has ever been proved far better than any I could devise, and gradually I am enabled to throw my burden on the Lord and trust in Him, but unbelief will have its say sometimes.

A fortnight later he was even more candid, but another stride forward in spiritual maturity.

> I have been much tried for some days, and have had more fear of losing Miss Sissons than I have felt before, because I have felt I was making an idol of her, and my experience has been of too uniform a type to suffer me to think any idol will be allowed me. I think I can now say 'Thy will be done' but my deceitful heart often deceives me, . . . the Lord has been teaching me that I could not be happy without His favour . . .

Again he used Burns' simile of the dog following its master at a parting of the ways. If it came to a choice he must follow the Lord. But,

> My heart is full of evil . . . an abyss of iniquity, and of its blackness I see more and more. I can love anybody and anything else – but I love my Saviour so little.

Toward the end of February, in another letter soiled with ink, lamp oil and water for which he apologised by saying it was 'from the violence of the wind and waves,' he could say, 'I feel I have anew to dedicate myself, body, soul and spirit to His service, and place my *life* and *prospects* in His *hands*.' But he gave no indication of where he was, continuing,

> There has been some more trouble about the Tsungming affair, in the shape of a proclamation put out by the Mandarin against me . . . It frightened those who had let me a house and they came over and sought me out, but . . . no doubt their fears were groundless.

There is no other indication that he went across to Chongming again.

'Poor, miserable and vicious''   *February–March, 1856*

In mid-February 1856, two months after the end of his Chongming experiment, Hudson Taylor was looking for indications of where to go next. They had been very full months with the 'powerful but gentle' William Burns, and both hoped to continue working together. While Hudson Taylor's plan of action, a base in Shanghai and an out-post up-country (and for that matter even itinerant preaching) was for the present under Rutherford Alcock's prohibition, Burns' hope of working among the Taipings at Nanking had finally been dashed. Undoubtedly there was unlimited scope for evangelism from Shanghai, but several missions were engaged in it, overlap was inevitable until they learned to plan together, and some of the pioneers were as ceaselessly on the move as Burns and Hudson Taylor had been. At Shanghai itself a phenomenon was emerging which made Hudson Taylor's daily preaching at the South Gate house paltry by comparison. The born orators William Muirhead and Griffith John were developing the street chapel preaching for which they were to become famous. For five years they were at it for hours every day, never lacking audiences. As soon as Muirhead 'the most commanding figure in Shanghai' appeared, the chapel would begin to fill. 'I have seen him hold a congregation of three or four hundred Chinese spellbound for an hour and a half, and then move on to the next chapel and begin again,' a contemporary wrote. And not only in Shanghai. The two men went on preaching tours together to 'almost all the cities and towns in the whole region around Shanghai'. So was there an alternative?

In 1853 when Hudson Taylor was looking for a ship to bring him to China, he had visited the *Geelong* in the London docks, but all her accommodation had been taken. Now the *Geelong* was in port at Shanghai and Captain Bowers, a Christian, was putting before the missionary community the state of wickedness at Swatow (Shantou), eight hundred miles to the south and halfway between Hong Kong and Amoy, as a claim on their attention. Swatow was not a treaty port and therefore not legally open for trade, but foreign merchants of several nationalities were occupying Double Island at the entrance to its harbour, as a trading post unchallenged by the Chinese government or their own consuls. A Christian Frenchman, Doctor de la Porte,[8] who had come from Europe in the same ship as Burns, was practising among them, unable to do anything for the Chinese.

Moral standards among the merchants in Swatow were worse if anything than among the populace, as evil and degraded as could be found anywhere. And the reason was not far to seek. Apart from some trade in sugar-cane, the major commodities were opium and human bodies. A high proportion of Swatow women were bought and kept by their owners without hope of escape, and the 'coolie trade',[9] involving women and girls as well as men by the thousands, was little less than slave traffic. In three months of 1854 Chinese 'emigrants' to Australia totalled two thousand one hundred. In one month five thousand left Hong Kong and Canton for California and twelve thousand were waiting to go, in search of freedom from civil war and of gold which some succeeded in bringing back with them. But conditions of travel and the reception of most at the other end were another story. The *San Francisco Herald* on November 30, 1854, reported,

> The American clipper *Indiaman* is discharging and selling her cargo of Chinese slaves.

The *China Mail* of Hong Kong on January 24, 1855, commented that the *Indiaman*'s owners,

> who are merchants of high standing, and rather distinguished opponents of slavery in their own country (would be embarrassed to explain how the *Indiaman* loaded with) at least 565 Chinese coolies at Swatow on June last, disposed of them at Callao in October.

As Captain Bowers was pressing his point and Hudson Taylor was feeling strongly moved by his appeal, the *North China Herald* of February 23, 1856, reported on a shipment of girls from Ningbo by a Portuguese.

> . . . on account of the weather the vessel anchored in the harbour of Amoy. (Forty-four children) from five or six to thirteen years, all sallow and emaciated, unlike human beings (were brought ashore by the Chinese authorities). Many were dangerously ill . . . unable to walk . . . On shipboard they were crowded together and all shut up in one cabin, receiving daily but a single platter of cold rice, for which they were allowed to scramble . . . Some were starved to death . . . if two or three out of ten survived, (the trader's) profits would still be large . . . all said that they had been sold because of their parents' poverty. One of them was clad in silk, and demeaned herself unlike a child accustomed to want . . . she hung down her head, cried but did not speak . . . some of them were certainly kidnapped . . .

At Swatow men were being lured with the promise of a fortune or simply trapped and carried on board. Once there, or in detention centres waiting for a ship to come for them, they were prisoners, mercilessly beaten if caught trying to escape. Some ships carried three or four hundred, others as many as a thousand when they left China. As for the opium trade, thirty thousand pounds weight of opium was being imported each month and sent inland. Enough stayed in Swatow to reduce the people to misery and crime.

On purely rational grounds Swatow had its appeal to Hudson Taylor. Being outside the immediate jurisdiction of the consuls he might have greater liberty of movement. If the Hong Kong government were turning a blind eye to the activities of British merchants there, perhaps they would disregard the presence of missionaries. Swatow needed the gospel and had no one to preach it, while Shanghai and the other treaty ports each had some at least. The CES had pressed relentlessly for its 'agents', as it persisted in calling them, to leave the treaty ports. Swatow was not 'inland' but it was at least neglected. Rudolf Lechler of the Basel Mission had travelled extensively in this area preaching the gospel between 1848 and 1852, and 'driven about from place to place' had been forced to withdraw to Hong Kong.[10] Though he was not entirely forgotten, he had left no known believers. This could be the time to take up his work again. But reason alone could not satisfy Hudson Taylor. He must be assured that it was the will of God. And even that was not the whole answer, as he recalled in the *Retrospect*.

> The Spirit of God impressed me with the feeling that this was His call; but for days I felt that I could not obey it. I had never known such a spiritual father as Mr. Burns; I had never known such holy, happy fellowship; and I said to myself that it could not be God's will that we should separate.

One evening between mid-February and the 23rd when he wrote to his mother, he went with William Burns to tea with the Reuben Lowries. It was customary to gather round the piano or harmonium and sing together, and on this occasion Mrs Lowrie in all innocence sang a missionary song that was new to Hudson Taylor, with the refrain 'And I will go!' In the way it almost quoted his own thoughts, and phrases from his recent letters, it could have been written for him. When they left the Lowries, Hudson Taylor asked Burns to come home with him, and there –

> . . . told him how the Lord had been leading me, and how rebellious I had been and unwilling to leave him for this new sphere of labour. He listened with a strange look of surprise, and of pleasure rather than pain . . .

– and answered that he too was waiting to say that the Lord was calling him to Swatow. His only regret had been the severance of their partnership.

Captain Bowers was delighted. He offered them free passages on the *Geelong* and they prepared to sail in early March, not entirely sure of what they would find. Hudson Taylor wrote,

> If we go it will be on a Missionary *excursion*, to distribute the Word of God, and as the door is opened or otherwise, and as we are Providen-

tially led, we shall return sooner, later, or not at all . . . You must not
expect to hear often from me, nor regularly, and consequently must
not feel alarmed, or uneasy, when you have no letters . . . You will
need to pray much for me, and so will all our Christian friends, that we
may be delivered from the violence of unreasonable men . . . the
people in the South are not very lamb-like . . . Were not the Almighty
God . . . on our side . . . who dare go forth?

To George Pearse he said much the same. It was an 'excursion'
without any plan to stay long. To achieve anything, however, they
would need to learn the Tiechiu dialect of Swatow and he commented '(it) will be valuable' among the hundreds of Swatow sailors
frequenting Shanghai – 'will be', not 'could be'. All the same, he
gave up his South Gate house, storing his furniture and possessions
with the ever obliging Alexander Wylie. And Dr Lockhart undertook again to handle his mail and money matters for him. In this
note, written on the *Geelong* the evening before she sailed, an
interesting detail shows the kind of punctilio that made Hudson
Taylor's friends in England place confidence in him. Writing that
Mr Burns 'desires me to thank you' for a letter, he crossed it out and
reworded it accurately as 'to state that he has received it'.

On March 6, 1856, five days after the second anniversary of his
arrival in China, the *Geelong* was towed down the Huangpu and
Yangzi estuary 'by a steamer', to anchor off Gutzlaff Island and
make a fair start with daybreak. A six-day voyage took them down
the coast, off the Hangzhou Bay and Chusan (Zhoushan) islands,
between Fuzhou and Amoy on the mainland and Taiwan to the east,
to Double Island, seven miles from Swatow. There they saw enough
of the godless community of foreign traders to be wary of preju-
dicing their work by identification with them, and the next day went
on in the *Geelong* to Swatow at the river mouth.

The Cantonese supercargo, the agent handling the ship's freight,
put on a forty-course feast to welcome the captain and his friends,
with bird's nest and shark's fin, probably the first southern delicacies
Hudson Taylor had encountered. Burns speaking Cantonese and
Taylor mandarin, each explained why they had come to Swatow.
Then they returned to the ship for the night. That was the last they
were to see of luxury of any kind.

Hunt as they might, the following day, they could find no house or
room to rent. No one wanted or dared to take in barbarians, even in
Chinese clothes. Nor were their own first impressions reassuring.

The people are poor, miserable and vicious. They are wild, violent, and in a lower state of civilization than any Chinese I have yet seen.

Few could read. The aim of distributing Scripture would have to take a low priority. To achieve anything they would have to learn the dialect well enough to preach. At the moment Hudson Taylor could not understand a word they said.

Then Burns met a Cantonese who happened to be a relative of the highest official in the city. Delighted to be addressed in his own dialect, this man used his influence to find them a toe-hold – a room above an incense shop, entered by a ladder through a hole without a trap door and used as a passageway. It was little more than an attic, with bare tiles above their heads. There they could sleep, but some meals would have to be taken, for the present at least, at a food shop on the street. And the extortionate rent for this garret was more than eight times the rent of the South Gate house Hudson Taylor had left. Captain Bowers laughed at the cost. 'Mr. Burns', he exclaimed, 'that would not keep me in cigars!' But the squalor shocked him. At once they began to discover that Swatow was no better than they had been led to expect, but they were there, among the people, as Bowers and the *Geelong* sailed for Singapore.

Test of endurance   *March–July, 1856*

From Hong Kong to Amoy, a distance of four hundred miles, an imposing chain of mountains rises three hundred to three thousand feet and more above the ocean. Bays and river mouths break these ramparts. It was perfect pirate country. At the mid-point, equidistant from Amoy and Hong Kong lay Swatow, on a deep inlet. The Swatow region is exquisitely beautiful, with high ranges of hills and small fertile valleys cultivated in terraces. Tropical trees and shrubs, banyan, aloe, cactus, palms and banana plantations add to the impression of luxuriance. It ought always to have been a fat, flourishing community of contented people. Instead it had a history of internecine feuds, until powerful Cantonese merchants with armed retainers moved in and restored some law, order and trade. Under their influence the port was expanding rapidly, the shoreline was being reclaimed and at any time five or six hundred sea-going junks moored alongside represented trade with Thailand, Taiwan and North China.

The people however remained 'passionate and unruly' by nature. . . . the difficulties and dangers that encountered us here were so great and constant, that our former work in the North began to appear safe and easy in comparison. The hatred and contempt (by) the Cantonese was very painful, 'foreign devil', 'foreign dog', or 'foreign pig' being the commonest appellations; but all of this led us into deeper fellowship than I had ever known before with Him who was 'despised and rejected of men'. In our visits to the country we were liable to be seized at any time and held to ransom; and the people commonly declared that the whole district was 'without emperor, without ruler, and without law'.

A wealthy man was captured by another local clan and his ankles broken with a cudgel one after the other to extort a ransom.

There was nothing but God's protection to prevent our being treated in the same way. The towns were all walled, and one such place would contain ten or twenty thousand people of the same clan or surname, . . . frequently at war with . . . the next town. To be kindly received in one place was not uncommonly a source of danger in the next. Men here are sunk so low in sin as to have lost the sense of shame, . . . Their rulers and Mandarins are as bad as themselves . . . governed by money and opium. And if it be *possible* to be worse than the people, the sailors . . . and traders . . . on Double Island are so.

A fortnight after moving in, he heard for himself the sound that most missionaries heard sooner or later, not only in Swatow.

Only two nights ago, for nearly two hours my ear was racked by the most heart-rending screams from two female voices; on inquiring the cause I was told they were most likely two newly bought women, who, being unwilling to become prostitutes, would be beaten or otherwise tortured till they submitted . . . that is very common here.

At the time of writing he was alone. William Burns had gone to Double Island to draw money, having the Cantonese dialect at his command gave him liberty to move about, and his absences from Swatow increased as he took to preaching on the foreign ships. Seeing that only a knowledge of the Tiejiu dialect could give him any scope at all, Hudson Taylor was trying to learn it. He could find no one but an unintelligent farmer willing to teach him. But by listening and using Mandarin and the Shanghai patois, to his delight he began to discern linguistic rules that made the transition faster than he had dared to hope.

Using two sheets Burns and he divided their attic into three 'rooms', one cubicle each as a bedroom and the remaining space as a 'study' when it ceased to be used as a passage. Their beds were planks and their furniture one bamboo chair and two stools, with the lid of a box across bags of books as a table. This was where Hudson Taylor worked as the days grew hotter and hotter and the tiles over his head, near enough to touch towards the eaves, turned the place into an oven. He rigged up a *punkah*, a sheet suspended from the rafters, with which to fan himself by pulling a string. Revealingly his letters home became outpourings about the joys of heaven and of seeing his loved ones again.

On April 3 letters reached him from England. Useless and uncomfortable after being so busy and independent at Shanghai he was bleak and lonely, unready for what the letters said. One from his friend Benjamin told him what Hudson Taylor had been waiting for. He had asked if he might correspond with Amelia, and her parents had approved. It meant that his sister from now on could not divide her affection. So there in his garret he wrote to her, 'There is no one to whom I would so gladly see you united, . . . even during my voyage out, it was my prayer, that if (it) was His will he might be given you.' But it cost him deep pangs of heartache.

Worse still, Amelia's letter was critical of her brother's decision to go into 'barbarous' Chinese clothes. This was the Shanghai die-hards' criticism; surely not Amelia's. He was dejected, and replied,

> – if the Chinese costume seems so barbarous to you, the English dress must be no less so to them, and that it would not be a hindrance from going among them in the friendly way necessary to secure their love (the change was necessary). . . . Without it we could not be here for a single day. That Miss Sissons does not like it, I am very sorry to hear, but that does not make me sorry that I have adopted it. It is one of the matters for which I and my devoted companion Revd. Mr. Burns, thank God almost daily.

Elizabeth had also written, vaguely, in an attempt to be kind. Her mother still opposed her marriage to him, she said, but her father like her was in two minds. An outright rejection would have been too heavy a blow at that time, but Hudson Taylor could read the writing on the wall: 'each letter becomes less favourable', he lamented, and added, '. . . there is something in my nature that seems as if it must have love and sympathy.'

Time and again over the years after writing freely about his distresses, like David in his psalms, he came to the point where he said to himself, Enough! and changed his tune. So now, to Amelia.

> Pray for me – I have very little light on my future course – but 'I know that my Redeemer liveth' and if sorrow and trial are to be my portion here, I shall not miss that 'inheritance, incorruptible, undefiled, and that fadeth not away'.

To his mother he said more. The rebels, referring to the Triads in the Canton region, were extending their conquests and some people were expecting a rising in the Swatow area, as there had been in other coastal ports. This too was unsettling. As for the CES, they were doing well in exposing the opium and coolie traffic; but for two quarters now they had sent him no money at all, simply presuming upon the knowledge that Mr Berger was occasionally sending him personal gifts. They had none to send. After a boom period when the public subscribed well, the Society was in debt.

> If it were not for the desire to get settled . . . I should at once resign my connection with the Society, in a friendly way – indeed I have privately hinted the possibility of such a thing to Mr. Pearse . . .

But Mr Berger has 'very opportunely' sent another fifty pounds, so that –

> I have now got more than I shall need in hand for half a year to come, if no unexpected expense occurs. Thus the Lord cares for me.

It seems incredible that even so Hudson Taylor should be writing to Charles Bird to say that he had sent a box of curios but no carved pagoda yet. They were expensive, six to sixteen dollars for a two- to four-foot model, but one in ivory would cost a great deal. Photography, he told George Pearse, he had had to stop, for his supplies had been damaged in transit and the climate and conditions on a boat when travelling made the development of plates impossible. When coming to Swatow he had left everything in Shanghai. As for his financial needs, with the Berger's encouragement his own confidence was growing.

> If we are doing His work, there is no doubt He will provide what is needful. He can increase the means, or make what He supplies go further, by diminishing expenses . . .

In a letter dated January 31, Mrs Berger reminded him of what he had proved to his own satisfaction in London:

I told (a friend) of some of your difficulties when desiring to go to China, and of the confidence you had in God as to its being His good pleasure that you should go; and how this fixedness of purpose on your part acted on some of your fellow Christians in England; how God accomplished your desire, how He answered your prayers as to acquiring that difficult language in such a short period, and how you were occupied in that land of idols . . . She was so delighted with (your) suggestions (in the *Missionary Recorder*) as to missionary work being taken up *by the churches*, and altogether approved of *that way* of carrying on the work.

By the end of April he could say that he had made considerable progress in the dialect and they had met with no open opposition to their staying quietly as they were. 'What may take place when we get a place and begin preaching publicly, remains to be seen . . . They are indeed a wicked people, and are idolatrous with all their heart and soul – not like those in the north . . .' As for the British authorities, he was glad he had not brought Sir John Bowring into the Chongming affair. 'Now . . . I am where there is little to fear from consular interference.'

From time to time William Burns and he attempted short journeys together into the countryside as Burns was managing to make himself understood in the Amoy dialect and the country-folk showed them no dislike or disrespect.[11] But Burns was often away at Double Island among the sailors. And travelling could not be worse than staying in the city among unfriendly people where the heat was stifling and Hudson Taylor's appetite was failing, so he began to venture out alone into the villages. By mid-May he was able to hold a conversation and even to pray extempore in Tiejiu. To learn Chinese faster 'one must speak, read and write English the less', he explained, so he was rationing the letters he wrote and only reading an English Bible and hymnbook and Chinese books. In this letter to Charles Bird he also said that he was sorry to hear of attempts to print more and more Scriptures when there were so many in print already but not enough people to distribute them. The funds should be used to send and support missionaries, 'there is an immense field crying for them.'

Activity and growing ability to speak in Tiejiu gave him a new lease of life, his spirits picked up. He referred to his 'tolerably comfortable circumstances', and he made more lone day-trips to preach. It was impossibly dangerous to go far by boat or for long periods. 'You could not pass a single night in it without being robbed, probably of boat and all it contained . . .' With 'the small box of medicines Father gave me, which has proved about the most useful thing in its way that I got in England', and with his knowledge of Chinese materia medica, he began to treat patients. But without the great convenience of a boat as a home to withdraw to, travelling far from Swatow involved having no certain sleeping place and being exposed to all moods of the weather. So for the present he was limited to within walking distance of their attic, heat and rain permitting.

He was coming to appreciate the people of Swatow and to understand if not to approve of their viewpoint.

News of his Chongming misfortunes had at last reached home and brought replies, so he continued,

> If *that* caused the exclamation 'when and where will the dear lad find a resting place', what will you say when you hear of me in the province of Canton? (The people of Swatow were poor and illiterate) but there is great force of character and a good deal of push in them, so that they become sailors, immigrants largely, and become successful traders in other parts of the Chinese empire. (Falsehood instead of being considered wrong is) looked on as rather clever, and a person detected in it is laughed at and laughs, as one not skilful enough to carry it through.

Meeting some of the false members of Gutzlaff's Chinese Union had reminded him of this characteristic. These men still had a head knowledge of the gospel, but their lives were no better than those of the people around them.

On his twenty-fourth birthday, May 21, it was so hot and he was so weary and sunburnt that he did not begin to write until the room cooled down after midnight. Then he said he had been in the country for the last two days, being treated well, a change from the offensive name-calling of the townspeople, and instead hearing comments that he was pink and white like young ginger, like a white mouse, prettier than a BA bleached by confinement in a room with his books. The great news was that they had rented a two-room house in the village of Topu a few miles away; and that when the Swatow landlord staged a feast for a relative on becoming a mandarin, Burns and Hudson Taylor were invited with other guests – a move towards acceptance even in the city. Three years later Dr de la Porte addressed the Annual Meeting of the CES in London and his remarks were reported in *The Gleaner*.

He had the pleasure and the honour of being identified with one (Mr. Taylor) to whose zeal, devotion, and energy he could bear most cordial testimony. He had seen that young man come home after his day's toil, his face covered with blisters from the heat of the sun, footsore and weary, and throw himself down to rest in a perfectly exhausted state, only to rise again in the morning to another day's hardship and toil. He enjoyed the highest respect among the Chinese, and he was doing a great amount of good among them.[12]

Allowing for the euphoric climate of an annual meeting, his word picture could be true of the month between mid-May and mid-June.

Even then it was hard-won freedom to preach the gospel. When Hudson Taylor went out to Topu to occupy the newly rented house, the landlord begged him to go away. He was afraid of the consequences. Instead of retreating, Hudson Taylor went to the village temple and preached there until it was too late to get back to Swatow. Asked where he would sleep, he answered that he did not know but was not worried. God would provide for him. Sure enough, a Hakka barber invited him to sleep above his shop and gave him supper. He found it easy then to speak about the love of God to all who gathered round him, and heard someone remark, 'It is very strange, the way he speaks of God in connection with everything.'

William Burns arrived the next day, but during the night Hudson Taylor fell ill with dysentery and had to go back to the garret and the vermin that were home. It was a weird existence. There were three women in the household, and after three months he had yet to see any of them for the first time, so cloistered were they. As a missionary outlet he took to visiting the junks from other parts of China, to preach on them and distribute books. And later on, like Burns, he went to Double Island to talk with the officers and crews of British ships. To his joy he led a backsliding ship's captain back to God. But on May 30 he was lonely and depressed again, dreading the expected rejection by Elizabeth. 'I sometimes feel as if it would be *more* than I could bear and would quite break me down.' Then unexpectedly two Chinese Christians arrived from Hong Kong to visit relatives and help in the work. He took them out to Topu to join Burns, but Burns had gone and they went on to their homes.

[The next mail brought] letters from five of the Tottenham people – I cannot tell you what comfort I have in their prayers, and aid, and sympathy and love . . . I love them as if they were my own brothers and sisters, and if they were they could not remember me more kindly.

Not only that, but 'a letter from Father, did (you) ever know of such a thing?' – with one exception, he thought, it was the only letter he had ever received from him – and another from Amelia, talking of her hopes of coming to China. Now he became anxious lest she come for his sake. His hopes for her were higher than that, and he sensed that his rootless existence was in preparation for a future as yet unrevealed.

> If you come, do not do it to live with or near me . . . What and where he is training me for, I know not . . . What I want you to do is to give up *all* to the Lord, and the more fully you do that, the more *he* will give you back again, yea far more than you ever gave up for Him.

Some friends were urging him to return to England to finish his medical course and get diplomas, for the sake of the knowledge, the status and the capability of earning a livelihood when desirable. The idea attracted him. He might bring back a wife, and a change would be good for his health. But the advantages were outweighed by the contra-indications. The expense would be no trifle, but the idea of two years' removal from his proper sphere of work settled the matter. In a passing mood he complained,

> I have a very low opinion of the value of medicine, and believe it to be oftener a hindrance than a help to a missionary, from the time it takes up.

But a few days later he thought differently, for the local mandarin fell ill and nothing the Chinese doctors did for him was successful. He had heard from some people, however, of Hudson Taylor's skill and sent for him.

> God blessed the medicines given, and grateful for relief, he advised our renting a house for a hospital and dispensary. Having his permission, we were able to secure the entire premises, one room of which we had previously occupied.

Hudson Taylor had written to George Pearse on June 14 saying that the Swatow people were so suspicious by nature that medical work might be necessary, to create friendliness. He had avoided getting too involved because it consumed too much time and strength, but no one had been able to understand their wish to spend money on renting premises solely for the purpose of preaching their religion. Not even the two Swatow Christians from Hong Kong could persuade their own people to believe that. There must be a sinister motive. So no one would agree. But to run a medicine shop was quite another matter.

The rainy season in coastal China tended to begin in the south in April or even March, in mid-China in May or June and a month or two later still in the north. But tropical cyclones known as typhoons[13] swept in from the Pacific in summer and winter. Burns was out in the country when the sky darkened threateningly and the wind began to rise after an ominous stillness. At once he returned to the city, and only just in time. Rain such as Hudson Taylor had never before seen began to pour down on the land. The day after Burns left the little town of Anbu the water in the streets was breast-high within hours. Two hundred towns and villages were inundated by flood. Lives were lost, harvests of rice and sweet potato were swept away. Ships fifty miles out at sea after the storm saw coffins afloat in the flotsam. One town, deprived of all its food, picked a quarrel with another more fortunate one, attacked it and reaped its harvest.

The house in Swatow had not yet been vacated by the landlord, and with the return of Burns and the Hong Kong evangelists the occupants of the little garret were literally 'quite thick on the ground'. When the sun shone, the heat was intolerable. The tiles were too hot to touch. And Hudson Taylor could not cure his dysentery. Burns and he decided that while work in the countryside was impossible he should go to Shanghai for 'a temporary change', settle his affairs there, collect all his medical equipment, and on his return open the dispensary.

A Christian captain offered him a free passage, and on July 5 he sailed in the *Wild Flower* with two hundred and fourteen Chinese fellow-passengers. Half of them were on their way to join the army and fight the Taiping rebels who had daringly broken through the imperialist army cordon and bottled up forty Manchu warships in the Yangzi between Zhenjiang and Nanking.

CHAPTER TEN

MUST EVERYTHING GO WRONG?
1856–57

Taking stock   *July 1856*

By the time the *Wild Flower* reached Shanghai on July 14, Hudson Taylor was rid of his dysentery and the depression that had sapped his courage in Swatow. Ten days at sea had been the holiday he needed.

Going straight to the LMS he received his first shock. Fire had destroyed the warehouse and its contents, thirty thousand New Testaments, valuable Manchu types, and most of his own possessions. Only a few surgical instruments had escaped. If he was to return to Swatow with the medical supplies he had come for, only one course lay open. He must make his way to Ningbo to see what Dr Parker could do to help. If he could buy enough from him, pending the arrival of replacements from England, he would need more money.

He intercepted some letters before Dr Lockhart could forward them, but the one from his Society containing the quarter's remittance had gone already. The miscarriage of the Society's new system for sending funds was what he had foreseen; the previous remittance 'was sent to Fuchow by ship, to be forwarded *overland* to Amoy, thence by vessel to Double Island, in native boats to Swatow, and then has to be sent back to Shanghai ere I receive it. Think how many hands it has to pass through, how many chances of loss or forgetfulness, and *if* lost I have no means of obtaining money . . .' In the event that letter survived but reached him eight weeks later. Meanwhile his remittances for half a year were following him around and William Berger's gifts were still all he had to live on. He would not go into debt, so if medical supplies were to be bought he would have to wait.

Again he wrote to his Society, 'firmly but mildly' asking that letters of credit be used as before, but assured his mother, 'I do not intend there to be anything in my correspondence that could be viewed as objectionable if published.' That in itself was an advance in grace, for he had not minced matters in some earlier protests. His growing ability to profit from these frustrations, instead of nursing resentment, was fitting him to become the wise administrator of the future. Experience of suffering from such business inefficiency was to prove invaluable.

After three years' probation and with the sober age of twenty-five approaching, he believed he ought to be on a stable footing with some element of permanence. If he had known more of what lay behind the Society's shortcomings, he would have been even more disconcerted. The bank which the CES used had failed; although donations in the past financial year had actually improved, expenses had risen steeply; the cloud of depression cast over Britain by serious setbacks in the Crimea was affecting its income and the Society was deeply in debt; yet in spite of all this, new commitments had been undertaken. As George Pearse told Wilhelm Lobscheid in June, 'We are passing through a crisis – £600 in debt and need near £1000 within a few weeks and I cannot tell how we are to act.' W C Milne joined the CES as Travelling Secretary to give supporters a first-hand account of conditions in China and to raise funds. But by October Charles Bird, nearing his resignation, was writing of panic in the City of London and Paris since the retreat from the Crimea. 'You cannot conceive the anxiety I suffer.' By the following April inflation was at thirty per cent, and charities were suffering while speculators made fortunes. China was under severe criticism and 'people say they are *too* bad for any effort . . . on their behalf.' If these facts troubled the directors, however, they allowed them to make little difference to their policies. In September 1855 they had sent a new missionary, John Jones, to China with his wife and children, and others to Penang. The Jones family had already reached Ningbo.

The Chinese Evangelization Society's financial blunders were then matched by another serious indiscretion. In May 1856 at a breakfast meeting of the Society an 'Honourable and Reverend' member of the General Committee delivered a speech, the rhetoric of which in spite of its faults might have passed unnoticed had it not been published as a leaflet. In a florid introduction he claimed that 'Protestant missionaries (in China) go everywhere, 150 or 200 miles into the interior proclaiming the gospel, and are received with respect and attention.' They now numbered a hundred in eighteen societies, apart from wives and children, he said. He then claimed that his Society had 'adopted a principle which was in advance of every other society of the kind', no less than 'the combination of all denominations in the employment of pastors . . . or evangelists to form churches . . . While the London Missionary Society had adopted it as a principle, they never appeared able to carry it out . . .'[1]

When this indiscretion became common knowledge in Shanghai, Hudson Taylor was appalled and wrote rebuking the directors. Did they not know that their missionaries were irretrievably indebted to the LMS for rescuing them from repeated blunders by the CES? His confidence in his Board was at rock bottom. But in loyalty to numbers of his close friends who were implicated with it he said what he could in the Society's defence. His Shanghai friends were unconvinced, while their friendship with him personally was unspoilt.

Another shock he received on arrival at Shanghai was a firm rejection by Elizabeth of his proposal. In his new frame of mind he could accept this blow and comment on it calmly. 'Had this come a month ago', he told Amelia, 'I think it would have been more than I could have borne, but I have been prepared for it, and was not at all surprised . . .' But after her previous, encouraging letter how could he take it as final? Nearly two years had passed since he had first written to her, and this was the first definite refusal. Perhaps she would relent.

As he caught up on the news from Wylie and his Shanghai friends, he dropped straight back into his old routines. The day after his arrival he was in the city giving out tracts and drawing a crowd to preach to, only to find that Tiejiu expressions were now uppermost in his mind. As he was telling some Swatow sailors the gospel in Tiejiu, perhaps the first time it had been possible in Shanghai, some Shandong sailors came up and he switched over to mandarin. To his delight he realized that he now had a working knowledge of three dialects. And to add to his joy, he found Guihua standing firm in his faith, and that Joseph Edkins was in Chinese clothes, renting a house near Jiading and trying to establish himself there permanently. 'If so I am sure it will lead to other attempts,' he prophesied.

John and Mary Jones   June–July 1856

During Hudson Taylor's absence, John Jones and his family had passed through Shanghai and received the customary hospitality of this remarkable body of missionaries. Originally bound for Amoy, it had been decided that he should join the Parkers at Ningbo instead.

Little is known of John and Mary Jones,[2] apart from what Hudson Taylor wrote, but obscured by their inconspicuous names were two exceptional people. If William Burns' influence on Hudson Taylor was profound, the evidence is that the influence of John and Mary Jones was no less significant in shaping his spiritual personality. Whether they already had the measure of the CES is uncertain, but the financial arrangement under which they sailed was heroic. They had agreed to accept whatever the Society could send them, but to hold it under no obligation, trusting in God to supply their needs whether through or apart from the CES. In this they anticipated Hudson Taylor by two years and the China Inland Mission by ten. They stood in the spiritual succession of A H Francke, Anthony Norris Groves, George Müller and those from whom they had learned to have faith in God.

To Hudson Taylor this attitude was praiseworthy, but the focus of his own attention was still upon the Society.

> They are not guaranteeing his support, but only promising him aid, when the funds will allow it!!! [he exclaimed].

The Jones' voyage from Britain had been relatively uneventful. After two narrow escapes from being wrecked on the reefs off Papua New Guinea they arrived safely at Hong Kong, and for Mary Jones' sake stayed there. With them were a German lady missionary and a blind Chinese girl known as Agnes Gutzlaff.[3] Rescued from beggary by Mrs Gutzlaff, she had been educated in Europe and was returning to teach in Miss Aldersey's school at Ningbo. She could read 'by touch' and play the piano, but 'brought up in the drawing room' and ignorant of things Chinese she appeared to some as little more than a potential liability. Added to which, her only support was ten pounds per annum, conditional upon her not being given menial work to do.

The German missionaries at Hong Kong took them all in and on March 5 Mary Jones survived a difficult confinement. For weeks she was dangerously ill. Then one by one the family fell victim to dysentery. On April 12 John Jones wrote, 'My eldest child lies by me apparently dying,' and on May 1 reported his death and his own illness. Remarking on the high cost of shipping to Ningbo, he said, 'We shall proceed as soon as we can – if we can at all.'

Still unwell they boarded a steamer, at the cost of two hundred dollars, less expensive than a sailing ship, and reached Shanghai only to find to their alarm that the price of getting from there to Ningbo would be as much again and more than they could afford, if some was to be kept for living expenses. They had no need to be anxious. With characteristic sympathy and generosity the LMS missionaries received them. The Medhursts and Alexander Wylie made them at home and disarmingly planned an evangelistic journey to Ningbo and back on which two (unnamed) missionaries would escort them. The houseboat and even supplies for the journey would cost them nothing. There would be the usual risk of attack by pirates in Hangzhou Bay, but the same risk existed by the sea route, for a longer period. 'Most of the missionaries helped them more or less,' Hudson Taylor was to write after hearing all about it. 'As you may suppose this has caused no little sensation.' CES missionaries had a way of making news – and this was not the last time.

On the way overland to Ningbo, John and Mary Jones were delighted by the reception the Chinese also gave them, pressing them to bring the three remaining children into their homes and producing cakes and tea. The freedom given to the missionaries to preach in the temples impressed John Jones. They were allowed to sit and even to stand on tables with their backs to the idols while addressing the crowd.

By June 15 all were safely at Ningbo, and there the welcome by the community was as warm. The Parkers prepared rooms for them in their home among the rice-fields, and others offered to have them in their houses. However bizarre the circumstances of their arrival, the peaceful friendliness of John and Mary Jones themselves won its way and assured a welcome.

Progress   *September 1855–July 1856*

Dr and Mrs Parker were well-established at Ningbo. What had been intended as temporary accommodation was still all they could find, and in order to get them out of that malarious place Parker was looking for a site on which to build a missionary complex of hospital, chapel and home. All that the CES had said to help them was a lame comment that they were 'not indifferent to a hospital', but that was all he needed. He went ahead, saying, 'If you wish to do much in China you must build.' He told his directors finally that if they wished to finance it he would probably be willing to relinquish his arrangement with the Ningbo community, but if not he would proceed anyway. If he could be given no firm assurance about his own salary he would consult his Glasgow supporters and let the CES know his decision. Everything with him was cut and dried, and his letters were brief and energetic.

Within a few days of Parker's arrival at Ningbo, he had begun seeing patients before breakfast, and soon made a reputation in the city and countryside. All the time that he was doctoring, either a missionary or Chinese Christian preached and talked with the waiting patients, one thousand three hundred and sixty-five of them by Christmas. One, the victim of an attack by pirates, was living at Parker's home for treatment. Soon, however, the CMS provided facilities for a dispensary at their chapel in the city and the LMS a building at their printing press for use as a hospital with ten beds, almost constantly full. 'I am now looked upon as the friend of a very large number of the inhabitants of this city . . .' Parker wrote. 'At a house where I attended a young woman said to be dying . . . there is now a weekly meeting for females conducted by Miss Aldersey's young ladies' – the daughters of Samuel Dyer.

Shocked by the inability of so many to read, Parker advocated a literacy movement and the opening of schools simply to bring people to the point of being able to read Scripture and Christian books. He urged the Society to send out 'either a clergyman or a gentleman' to superintend them! Other missions were doing well in Ningbo and the CES could quickly do so too. There were thirty Chinese Christians in the CMS church, thirty-nine with the American Presbyterians, seventeen with the American Baptists, and no restrictions on travelling in the country. R Q Way and a fellow-missionary had walked four hundred miles from Fuzhou in foreign clothes without hindrance.

By comparison, in Fuzhou there were ten missionary families but not a single convert among the million inhabitants. Hatred and opposition, scorn and contempt were directed against foreigners and their religion. No lady missionary dared to appear in the streets, even in a sedan chair. Ningbo, Parker claimed, was 'one of the best fields for missionary effort in China' – not least because relatively free from foreign traders and their way of life. The Chinese were 'agreeable and friendly to foreigners', in part a legacy of Gutzlaff's brisk and impartial justice when, as chief magistrate, he was known to the people as 'Daddy Guo' (Appendix 8).

So the fourteen missionaries and their families, and Miss

Aldersey and her assistants, were strategically scattered through the city, with six preaching points and two more in the country (map, p 272). The American Baptists also went every month to the Chusan (Zhoushan) islands. They had three boarding schools and six day schools. Many of the Christians in fact were converted scholars. 'We ought to have at least three European missionaries here . . .', Parker concluded. In June he reported that he had bought with money obtained in Ningbo 'a plot of ground in an excellent situation . . . close by one of the city gates, on the river bank'. This then was the situation the Joneses found when they arrived on June 15, and that Hudson Taylor was soon to see for himself.

In the last week of August, 1855, before the Joneses had left England, an international conference had been held in Paris of eight missions and Chinese Associations to discuss the progress made in five years since their initiation and Charles Gutzlaff's inspiring tour.[4] Some societies had been finding it difficult to make ends meet and before long ceased to exist or amalgamated, as did the Berlin Society with the Rhenish Mission. Others were well-established. In South China they had a great deal to be satisfied with. In spite of the disturbed countryside and sickening bloodshed around Canton where three hundred thousand were said to have died, 'a new and large district' was opened up through a ranking mandarin offering to escort and introduce Lobscheid to influential Chinese and to secure a welcome for him in several places. At Pukak, Lechler and Winnes had their base and the mother church (map, p 191).

Lobscheid was preaching, doctoring and travelling almost continuously. For the first time in history, he claimed, Chinese had made war on Chinese to right the wrongs of a foreigner: without a shot or injury to anyone the gentry of Pukak had forced the men who robbed his messenger to repay all they had stolen. In February he reported twenty-five baptisms and twenty more applications. Four years of continuous residential work on the mainland was paying dividends. In March fourteen more were baptised. Now there were two hundred and twenty Christians in two congregations, and the need, he declared in a statement of strategic importance, was for a training school on the mainland such as the Basel Mission had in Hong Kong,

in order to get men of talent and education who are capable of bringing the truth of our Gospel into the inaccessible courts of the Mandarins. This *cannot* be achieved by sending the Chinese to Europe, for there they get estranged from their own people, and dislike them after their return . . . They must be educated *on the spot*, and not only versed in European sciences, but also in their own. I feel very uneasy about the prospect of not soon getting at least two men for this purpose . . . [Zealous Christians were preaching the gospel, he continued, and] . . . the difficulty does not consist in getting a footing in China, but in thoroughly cultivating the occupied ground . . . with the least expense.

The same could have been said in the treaty ports of Amoy or Ningbo, but that it was said of a congregation on the mainland of China fifty miles from Canton and Hong Kong marked a milestone in the progress of Protestant missions in China. It had taken almost fifty years from the arrival of Robert Morrison in 1807 to reach this point. The price had been much blood, sweat and tears, but the reward would never be snatched away. Tragically, in Hong Kong there were two other training schools theoretically of the kind Lobscheid had in mind but with a fatal difference.

James Legge of the LMS brought Morrison's Anglo-Chinese College from Malacca to Hong Kong in 1843, and had changed its nature to educate young Chinese specifically with the hope of their being converted and becoming ministers in the Church – a noble concept. After a decade he himself conceded failure. His basic policy was wrong. He had put the cart before the horse. But before Legge gave up hope, Bishop Smith opened an Anglican college on the same lines – and it failed for the same reason. In 1876 E J Eitel observed in the *Chinese Recorder* that few in either college became Christians and none preachers. The perspicacity to send them all home and start again with the products of the new churches did not come to either man. And missionary reinforcements for Lobscheid's purpose failed to come before he himself retired.

In Ningbo, meanwhile, as healthy a family of churches existed as could arise from the work of such diverse missions as the Anglicans with their quasi-gothic building, the Presbyterians and the Baptists of three separate missions. John Jones could not have come to a more promising place for the start of his missionary life.

Robbed[5]   *July–August 1856*

Hudson Taylor's few personal possessions of any value had been safely held by Alexander Wylie in Shanghai and were spared when the warehouse burned down. There was no point now in leaving them there and they could not be taken to Swatow; his own colleagues were in Ningbo, so he decided to take them with him. He packed them up in a box one man could carry, and hired the same boat as he had used on the Nanxun trip with Burns, to go by an inland route. The bulk of his baggage was his books, his dictionaries, English, Greek, Hebrew and Chinese, his journals and other papers. Otherwise he had his camera and photographs, his concertina, both his watches, the remaining surgical instruments and his insect collection. That was all, apart from a *pugai*, the Chinese bedding roll inseparable from any traveller.

On the eve of starting he wrote decisively if disjointedly to his mother,

> I believe I have been sent to China, and I dare not leave my post, and so, much as I love you all, much as I feel the advantage it would be to me, if I possessed a medical degree, much as I believe it would effect, where letters seem to be in vain, – with dear Miss Sissons. But till I am as plainly sent home, as I was sent here, I cannot come – if this be necessary for me, will increase my usefulness, or benefit in any way the cause of God it will be brought to pass in His own good time, by Him who will withhold no good thing from His children. If not He can make me both happy and useful without it . . .

The normal route taken by Chinese travelling between Shanghai and Ningbo was down the Grand Canal to Hangzhou. For safety, certainty and the comfort of facilities along the way it was unrivalled. Missionaries travelled by a variety of less frequented routes purely for the sake of taking the gospel to as many regions as possible. Hudson Taylor's travels had covered most routes, ending at different points on the north shore of the Hangzhou estuary, from Zhapu where it broadened into the wide bay, to Ganpu farther west. When he left Shanghai on July 22 it was to follow the main route, visiting the ancient capital, Hangzhou, for the first time. He planned to preach along the way until he entered the Ningbo dialect area. To help him he employed a one-time servant of other missionaries, but was alone apart from him and the boatmen.

As they sailed up the Huangpu towards Songjiang, the flat countryside was so familiar and uninteresting that he busied himself with letter-writing. There was so much to tell and to comment on in the letters he had received. For one thing Louisa, just sixteen, had confessed in her last letter to him that she wished she could talk with Amelia and their mother about her spiritual perplexities but did not know how to begin. Hudson had the answer. Amelia would know how to give her an opening. Then Amelia herself had said that she and Benjamin were considering coming to China. If they did, what would Hudson advise? Undoubtedly, he replied, Benjamin should get ordained or he would be handicapped among his fellow-missionaries. This big departure from the views Hudson Taylor used to hold needed explanation.

> I . . . look on it not in the light of man's appointment, as of man's recognition of God's appointment . . . The Church Missionary Society (the only one except ours, I would come out under) might not accept him . . . [for Benjamin was a Wesleyan]. The Chinese Evangelization Society is not in a position, I fear, to add to . . . its missionaries . . . The older Societies of course provide what is necessary. [Later he added] I am continually becoming more of the opinion that the *mode* of worship is of small importance, the *power* is the main thing. And I believe there is more real liberty in the Church than in most of (the) dissenting bodies.

But after thinking this over he wrote again. The LMS, an inter-denominational society, would suit Benjamin the bookworm better.

> Their missionaries are all superior men, with a good knowledge of Chinese, and to be connected with such men is in itself an advantage. Then they have valuable mission libraries of Chinese books . . . [He would not be] obliged to read prayers, or be annoyed by the whims of a Bishop . . ., advantages . . . over the Church Missionary Society . . . The English Presbyterians greatly want missionaries for China. They are excellent people, but Calvinistic in their views – not more so than Paul was . . . If our Society does not improve (I shall have to) come out again under some other society.

Unfortunately they all had both strong and weak points.

During the first night of his journey, while they were at Songjiang some of his things, unimportant in themselves, disappeared. It was strange, for he thought he was among 'friends' whom he could trust. In the morning he began preaching, lapsing to his surprise into Tiejiu by mistake. They followed the same waterways as Edkins and he had taken nineteen months before and he reflected on all that had happened to him in that time, especially when they moored on the second night alongside an old tribute junk as they had done on that occasion.

At Jiashan (map, p 216) where in December 1854 the chief magistrate had come 'in great alarm' and urged them to return to Shanghai, his arrival attracted no attention until he began preaching. Then as everywhere he drew crowds. 'The visits of foreigners to the country have been more frequent since then, so that now no notice is taken of them by the authorities.'

A drought was threatening the crops and on the temple large white characters read 'Pray for rain', a good text to start from. The people called out 'Come again!' when he finished, so he stayed over the weekend, working all day, having a refreshing bathe in the evening, and feeling the better for it. Groundlessly, he was feeling 'quite sure of ultimate success' with Elizabeth and was prepared to wait, because 'the more I see and learn before marriage the better.' By the time these letters reached England, he said, he expected to be back in Swatow.

Jiaxing city was more receptive too, so he stayed there for four more days. His three dialects were proving invaluable. Soldiers from the far north he spoke to in mandarin, others from Swatow in Tiejiu, and local people understood the Shanghai dialect. Always it was crowds, crowds, crowds. The idols had failed them and famine threatened. The mandarins were praying at the temples and the farmers were ceaselessly on their treadmill irrigators lifting water from the canals into the irrigation channels and fields. But the sky was cloudless and the baking sun evaporated the water almost as fast as they pumped. People were anxious and listened intently.

He continued his journey. His supply of books and tracts was soon exhausted – two hundred New Testaments, twelve hundred booklets and one thousand six hundred tracts. The canal was so shallow that at Shimenwan he was forced to leave his boat, cut across country on foot to Haining on the estuary, only eighteen miles away, and sail to Ningbo without more delay. If he knew of it he made no mention of the fact that Hangzhou had just fallen into the hands of the Taipings. That name, Shimenwan, was to be burned into his memory. There he paid off his boat, hired carriers at a coolie agent's for his belongings and before sunrise the next morning, Sunday August 3, set off to do ten miles before the day grew hot.

This episode has been colourfully told and retold. In the *Retrospect* Hudson Taylor quoted at length from his home letters and a century later it is still in print. So it need not be repeated here in detail. To show the tenacity and composure of the man, an outline of events will be enough. The experience of reduction to near helplessness stood him in good stead in after-life, and in a sequel lay a strong link in the chain from which he forged the China Inland Mission.

From the moment they started the coolies dragged slowly along with no strength to do better. They were opium derelicts. So Hudson Taylor left the missionary's servant with them and went ahead to get breakfast and wait for them at Shimenxian, the county town, six miles away. When the men arrived it was still only six-thirty am and he promised them that at Chang'an, four miles farther on, he would replace them for the last eight miles.

They all set off again through the narrow streets of the city, but before reaching the south gate the coolies gave up. Telling the servant to hire replacements and come on after him to Haining on the coast, Hudson Taylor strode on. At Chang'an he waited again, but they failed to appear. Hours passed and there was no sign of servant or carriers. Asking other travellers if they had seen them he could get no clue until in the evening one said he had seen a coolie with a box and bedding like those he described. The carrier had said he was hurrying to Haining with it.

By then it was late and Hudson Taylor himself was too footsore to go on, so he looked for lodgings for the night. He was short of cash. At a labourer's inn of the humblest kind he was shown into a room with eleven beds of planks across trestles and told to look after his money if he did not want to lose it. He lay down as he was, with his umbrella and a shoe for a pillow. Instead of his reaching Haining by noon and peacefully crossing the head of the bay, his Sunday had been frittered away.

Still hoping to find his servant and baggage at Haining he made an early start in the morning, short-changed by the innkeeper on the last dollar he had on him, and forced to carry 1,400 heavy brass cash instead of lighter coins. The eight-mile walk and a long search at Haining failed to reunite him with his men. He realised that if he did not succeed, his money would not be enough to get him either to Ningbo or Shanghai. So he ate only a little rice gruel in a foodshop and when a crowd collected preached to them. He was very tired and wanted to be sure of somewhere to sleep, but a *yamen* underling began trailing him everywhere, and seeing him, no one would let him stay. Then a young man offered to help, and took him to his home a mile away, but his family would not receive him. Still unsuspicious, Hudson Taylor concluded that the servant had been arrested for helping a foreigner, and continued to search for somewhere to sleep.

At last he was told at a lodging house that if he spent the rest of the evening in a tea-shop and came back at night they would take him in. They tried to make him leave his Chinese gown and bundle of cash but he would only part with the umbrella as a pledge. Yet when he returned after dark the place was locked up. He wandered about until between one and two am, dropping with weariness, and eventually lay down on some temple steps with the money under his head, cold, damp and too exhausted to sleep.

He dozed off and suddenly awoke. Somebody's hands were feeling over him. He asked him what he wanted and the man went away. Hudson Taylor distributed his cash around his clothing and

'THE MONEY UNDER HIS HEAD'

lay down again. Soon the man returned and tried again, and this time would not leave him. Hudson Taylor sat up, propped against a wall, trying not to fall asleep. The tension continued. Then two others joined the first, watching and waiting, while he wondered what would happen. But day dawned and he and his cash were intact.

Again he bought a little rice gruel, was cheated out of his umbrella and in spite of several blisters on his feet began walking – back towards Shimenwan and the faint hope of finding his things along the way. By the time he had gone eight miles and reached Chang'an he was ready to faint. So he bought two eggs and some tea and cakes, the best meal he had allowed himself since Sunday, for his stock of cash was dwindling. And at last he slept. After five pm when it was cooler, he set off again for Shimenxian where he had parted from the servant, stopping to rest every half mile,

> . . . and I enjoyed a happy time of communion with God. I thought of our Saviour, despised and rejected . . . at times without a place to lay his head. I thought of Him at Jacob's well, weary, hungry and thirsty, yet finding it His meat and drink to do His Father's will – contrasted it with my littleness of love and was melted to tears. I looked to Him for pardon for the past, and grace and strength to do His will for the future . . . I prayed for myself, and you in England, and for my brethren in the work; thus occupied the road was passed, and with a light heart I approached Shihmen.

At Shimenxian he met one of the original coolies and his hopes rose. He led him to a tailor's shop where he had left the servant and the load. At last he was hot on the trail. The tailor was telling him what happened next, when 'some of the villainous spies from the *yamen* came up and my informant's memory failed him at once . . .' These underlings would lose no chance of personal profit from a new criminal case. As for Hudson Taylor, once under surveillance it was useless to stay in the town, so he started walking again. Now it was Shanghai or destitution, he thought.

He spent that night in an open boat under a heavy dew and too cold, excited and plagued by mosquitoes to sleep. It was a relief to get up and start off again before dawn – on Wednesday, the 6th. He had just enough cash left for the boat fare from Shimenwan and food along the way. He covered the six miles and found that a passenger boat had just left. He chased after it along the canal bank as fast as he could walk, caught up with it and asked if it was going to Jiaxing. It was not.

Hope fled. I sank down on the grass, drooped my head and thought about nothing.

Then he heard a voice saying, 'He speaks pure Shanghai dialect!' Looking up he saw a big Shanghai boat on the far side of the channel, marooned by the shallowness of the water. They sent a small *sanpan* across for him and were very kind, giving him tea and hot water for a wash and to soak his blistered feet. After he had enjoyed a long rest and a full meal with them, they went ashore with him to inquire for a boat going the right way – and to hear him preach. He could not let the opportunities pass. They found a fast mail boat going to Shanghai, but Hudson Taylor by now could not afford the 'express' fare and was for letting the boat go without him. To his delight he heard his new friends arranging for the fare to be paid at Shanghai and standing surety for the sum. The bliss, as he lay down in the bottom of the boat – 'how soft the planks felt!'.

It was a long narrow boat with two men sculling with hands and feet in shifts day and night. At each city, while they delivered and collected the mail, Hudson Taylor drew his audiences and preached the gospel. On the third morning, Saturday August 9, he was back in Wylie's 'hospital home . . . in good health (save a slight cold)'. 'Never since I have been in China', he wrote, 'have I had such opportunities of preaching the Word, as this last excursion has afforded me . . .'

Waiting for him were more letters from home, including one from his mother, overflowing with love and sympathy. He told her,

. . . in the midst of trial the love of God has abundantly been revealed, supporting and – I do not say *comforting*, merely – but causing me to rejoice in His wisdom, grace, power and love, far, far more than your weak faith had led you to expect. Oh yes! only let the Lord reveal *His* love, and sorrowing we rejoice, tried we are comforted, perplexed we are not cast down, bereaved we do not despair – 'Tho' earthly streams of bliss be dried, the *Fountain* is the same.'

The sequel to the story, however, took shape and grew more wonderfully than he could have imagined. Decades later he was still reaping the benefits. This perhaps was why the experience featured so largely in his memory in old age. He sent a messenger from Shanghai to hunt for the missing servant and goods, but without success. At last he believed that he had been robbed. All his most treasured things were in the missing load. That day, August 14, he wrote contritely to Amelia, 'I have lost several idols by it – for I fear

they are lost – among them your photograph and my concertina.'
But his hymnbooks, again, and the Bible given him by his mother in
1846, all his maps and his precious hobbies had gone too. To the
Society he simply reported the loss of his journals and statistical
records and more than fifty pounds-worth of clothing and valuables.

The thief, the hired servant, cooked his own goose a few days
later. Three letters to different people in Shanghai with different
signatures but sent in one envelope to save postage, were intercepted. They gave differing stories of what happened. He blamed
the carriers but was plainly the culprit. Friends told Hudson Taylor
how he could get his possessions back or at least be compensated –
by paying a mandarin's officer to put such pressure on the man as to
make him pay up with interest.

> I prayed about it and felt this was not a Christian course, so I have
> written to him a plain, faithful letter, telling him we know well of his
> guilt, and what its first consequences were to me. That at first I felt
> disposed to put it into the hands of the *yamen* people, but remember-
> ing Christ's command to return good for evil, I had not done so, and
> would not injure a hair of his head. I told him he was the great loser,
> not me – that I freely forgave him and exhorted him to flee from the
> wrath to come.

He asked him to return the foreign books and papers, his
journals, that were of no use to him. 'If his conscience only might be
moved and his soul saved, how infinitely more valuable that would
be than the recovery of a few pounds worth of goods.'

Characteristically the Shanghai missionaries wanted to contribute enough to cover Hudson Taylor's losses. He would have none
of it, but was cheered by their kindness. Forty pounds had arrived
for him from Mr Berger and with what he had reserved in Shanghai
he had enough for another journey to Ningbo and back. He sold the
furniture they had been storing for him (a few more dollars in his
pocket) and set off again. When his letters reached England and
excerpts were published in *The Gleaner*, George Müller of Bristol,
the saintly supporter of missions, so approved of Hudson Taylor's
forgiving spirit and maturely spiritual attitude that he at once sent
forty pounds and a warm letter of appreciation, the first of many
over the next decades.

Strange to say, on August 5, the day Hudson Taylor had started
back from Haining, William Burns and his two Christian companions at a village near Swatow were robbed of everything but what

they stood up in.[6] They had been finding the people willing to accept Christian books as a gift but unwilling to buy any. Left without anything to live on, what was his surprise when people began asking if they might buy the books and continued to do so until one of the evangelists returned from Double Island with more money. He scribbled a note to Hudson Taylor, using a Chinese brush pen, to tell him this news and to ask when they could expect to see him. But on August 18, as Hudson Taylor started southwards again, this time taking his old eastern route through Zhapu to Ningbo because there was said to be more water in the canals, unknown to him Burns and both his friends were seized by *yamen* officials and thrown into jail.

Ningbo interlude *August–September 1856*

John Jones and family were meanwhile settling in with the Parkers. His warm, affectionate personality shines from his early letters. He could not hide it. Nothing in the records hints that he had ever met Hudson Taylor, but when he sat down to write to George Pearse on August 22 he said that a month ago Taylor had written to say he was coming but had not arrived. 'I am very anxious about him. The Rebels are in Hangchow and it was thought he would make his road somewhere near there.' If Hudson Taylor had discovered the fact from the imperial soldiers he talked with on his abortive journey, his other experiences had driven it from his letters. But late that day John Jones added, 'Mr Taylor has just arrived; we met him when walking to the city. Dr. Parker recognized him' as if to say 'I would never have thought that Chinese coming toward us could be he.' And he added a postscript, saying, '. . . our dear brother Mr. J. H. Taylor. The two days of his stay have been very refreshing.'

Certainly John Jones' friendliness was reciprocated. Hudson Taylor's sympathy over their sufferings and the death of their son in Hong Kong drew them together. 'Pray, dear brother, that . . . we may be "partakers of his holiness" – what fulness of blessing! . . . We have been much cheered . . . by the companionship of, and communion with, our dear brother, Mr J Taylor.' And when Hudson Taylor took John Jones out into the country with him, they quickly came to know each other well. They travelled by boat 'under a fine ridge of mountains all the way', climbed a hill to see out over the valley and saw 'multitudes of insects and plants quite new to me.' 'We experienced delight in referring these thousands of beautiful things to the abundant love and wisdom and power of *our Father*.'

They collected attractive stones, and coming to a village preached to the people at the waterside laundry place as well as they were able without the local dialect. In some ways John Jones was very like Hudson Taylor. 'It very much moves me at such times to long to speak of Jesus – although I could not hope to make myself understood, having been three months or so among the people, I was constrained to speak a word.' People were always ready to listen, he went on, some with 'interest', especially when the missionaries returned to the same place a second time.

Hudson Taylor had come only to buy medicines from Dr Parker, but it was the end of September before he could start back. After losing everything except the clothes he stood in, he had to pay his fares and buy bedding, a change of clothing and daily necessities of all kinds. He then had not enough to pay for the drugs and instruments, and would not go into debt even to a fellow-missionary of the same society. He waited for the missing mail to bring his remittance before he would accept them, and then delayed further to escort John Jones and an American family, the Ways, to Shanghai.

He joined in the work of Dr Parker's clinic and the life of the various missions. Morning and evening Parker held services for his household and sixteen or eighteen of his patients. Mrs Way's brother, John Quarterman, came regularly to preach to the patients, and one or other of the CMS missionaries at other times, so Hudson Taylor renewed his acquaintance with R H Cobbold, W A Russell and F F Gough. Russell had married Miss Aldersey's namesake and protégé, Mary Ann Leisk, and was almost a son-in-law to Miss Aldersey. As medical attendant to all the foreigners, Parker saw a good deal of them. The merchant community was some distance away down the river, but the missionary and consulate staff met frequently, and as Dr and Mrs Parker had a standing arrangement to dine with Miss Aldersey and the Dyer girls each week, they took Hudson Taylor with them.

He could do little work without the Ningbo dialect, however, so while he waited for funds he set himself to acquire it. His experience with Tiejiu at once came to his aid. As in Swatow he isolated certain principles governing a change of consonant, vowel and tone, and learned to apply them in speech. He explained to George Pearse that although Swatow was in Guangdong province, the Tiejiu dialect was derived from Fujian, and –

> here (in Ningpo) I have found a good number of Fukien, Kwangtung and Formosa men and a Siamese, with whom I have been able to communicate by means of that dialect . . . There is much that is alike in all the dialects – and having a foundation in the character, I do not think I need to be more than a month in any part of China unable to speak a little intelligibly, or to tell of Jesus' dying love . . . What is really important is to be guided by God . . .

–, to speak with the people from areas remote from any other contact with the gospel.

To his mother he elaborated on this. He was using –

> a patchwork of [Ningbo], Mandarin and Shanghai. This patchwork is well understood, and is the way in which very many of the [Chinese] get on who are away from home . . . the people generally listen attentively, and repeat to others a good deal of what you say in their pure dialect, and this habit often enables you to perceive their misconceptions and correct them.

In Parker's opinion Ningbo was as strategic to the whole of China as was Shanghai and 'one of the best fields for missionary effort in China'. Hudson Taylor's letter went on,

> The fields are all white – extensive, extensive, extensive – . . . I bless God that He has given me such a wide field for sowing the seed of the kingdom . . . I wish sometimes that I had twenty bodies, that at twenty places at once I might publish the saving name of Jesus . . . It seems very strange that more missionaries do not come to China. No country is so large, none so interesting . . . The London Missionary Society is wanting men – the money they have in hand, but men they cannot get; so it is with the Church Missionary Society; so it is with the English Presbyterian Missionary Society; and other (American) Societies.

He fully expected to be back in Swatow soon. He was only filling in time. 'It would be very pleasant . . . to remain here, or at Shanghai, and labour among these more friendly and civilized people, but my present position calls me to a more arduous post, to pioneer work, and in my dear devoted brother, Mr. Burns, I have an inestimable companion, with whom I shall rejoice to meet again.' He still did not know of Burns' arrest and was expecting to open the dispensary in Swatow as planned.

As to my going to Swatow, I think I was not misdirected in that step
. . . Where the merchant, the opium dealer, the coolie [slave] dealer
are found, is the missionary to be absent? In Kiangsu and Chekiang,
the mass of the poor are better off than in the manufacturing districts of
England. [But the thought of Swatow made him write on]. I sometimes
wonder if I shall ever be settled, and long for a fixed, permanent
position, and a partner to share in all my joys and sorrows, labors and
encouragements . . .

John and Mary Jones, and the Goughs too, were couples deeply
in love – the kind of relationship he could not stop pining for.
Swatow conjured up very different images in his mind.

At home you can never know what it is to be alone – absolutely alone,
amidst thousands, as you can in a Chinese city, without one friend, one
companion, everyone looking on you with curiosity, with contempt,
with suspicion or with dislike. Thus to learn what it is to be despised
and rejected of men – of those you wish to benefit, your motives not
understood . . . and then to have the love of Jesus applied to your
heart by the Holy Spirit . . . *this* is *worth* coming for. Oh! to know more
of Him, and the *power* of His *resurrection*, and the *fellowship* of His
sufferings . . .

In that age of chaperones and the modestly averted eye, no more
could he know that nineteen-year-old Maria Dyer had been so
attracted by him as to 'take the matter at once to' God, than she
could guess where his hopes still lay. To his parents he reminisced
about 'this eventful month' of September, the month he had left
Hull for London, and London for China, and the Settlement for the
dangerous North Gate suburb of Shanghai, and a year later moved
into the sad city itself. He only knew that now he was at peace,
waiting to return to grim Swatow. He went on preaching trips with
John Quarterman and John Jones, down to Zhenhai at the mouth of
the river, out among the hills, and to the farming villages on the
plain. On junks and *lorchas* in the river they found men from
Taiwan and distant provinces, and some who could read the Portuguese New Testament.

At last on September 15 the mail brought twenty pounds from
William Berger and he bought his drugs and instruments from
Parker. Three days later another forty pounds arrived from Mr
Berger. In gratitude to God, Hudson Taylor contributed fifty
dollars to Parker's hospital building fund. The summer had been
worse than usual and most foreigners in the port had been ill. Mrs
Parker had just given birth to a second son and her husband wrote,

'. . . our dear little boy James . . . has been reduced to a skeleton by
ague, diarrhoea, etc . . . We are all very well just now, but so
exhausted by the long continued heat as to be unfit for much mental
or physical effort.' He needed his new premises on the river bank.
To spare himself he closed the dispensary, but patients came to his
home instead. To everyone's relief the hot season was coming to an
end, for the toll it took was heavy.

Hudson Taylor was ready to leave for Shanghai on Monday,
22nd, with John Jones and his son Tom, still ill and needing a
complete change. But the Way family asked them to wait a few
days. They were glad to oblige, for the *Wild Flower* came into port
and when Hudson Taylor went aboard and conducted a service for
Captain Brown, every man in the crew attended. It is justifiable to
speculate that on the short voyage from Swatow he had enjoyed
himself in the rigging with them, as on the *Dumfries*. They brought
no news of William Burns.

On Saturday, September 27, he hired boats, one for the Ways and
their two girls and one for John Jones, his son Tom and himself, to
go part way to the Hangzhou Bay where they would transfer to a
public ferry. Then a mail came in at last bringing the missing April
remittance – with the cheque presenting itself at the opening of a
torn envelope. It was Parker who at once wrote to Charles Bird. If
he must use this unsatisfactory method, he said, it would be better to
fold the cheque and enclose it inside the letter! He could be scathing
when he chose, and from Bird he drew a querulous plea for 'no more
scolding letters'. Mary Jones and the smaller children moved in with
the Goughs and on Tuesday, September 30, the party set out from
Ningbo on what was to be yet another harrowing experience.

'Back to Swatow'   *October 1856*

It was a new departure for Hudson Taylor to escort children on
such an overland journey, though the problem of securing some
privacy for Mrs Way fell largely to her husband. The first difficulty
arose when they found the canals too shallow ten miles short of the
coast and had to make a porterage. But when they were safely on
the public passage boat, surrounded by Chinese fellow-travellers
for the estuary crossing, John Jones began an agonising attack of
renal colic. Apart from the excruciating nature of the pain, the
classic characteristic of it is the inability of the sufferer to keep still.

He lashes about in fruitless search for a position of some relief. Jones' attack continued for some hours.

Arriving at the north shore they made another porterage to the inland waterway and again found the water level so low that boats much smaller than they would have chosen were their only hope. They crouched beneath low mat coverings sweltering in oven-like heat with inadequate space to move about. Even at night it felt 'like a stove'. To add to the sufferings of the peasants, the parched land was covered with swarms of locusts, 'millions and millions' everywhere. In Peking at this time the emperor and court were also watching swarms of locusts over the capital, the imperial *Peking Gazette* declared. To Chinese readers this had only one meaning – 'a direful calamity' was imminent.

To the travellers' joy the boatmen were co-operative, pressing on day and night to reach Shanghai and receive their pay as soon as possible – for John Jones was tortured by two more attacks of colic and Tom went down with dysentery again, so that their misery was extreme and Hudson Taylor worked incessantly to help one or the other or both at once. There was nothing the Ways in their equally small boat could do for them. 'A very anxious time' was how he described it, for only a fortnight previously Tom had been near death's door with the same disease. It is difficult to see how Hudson Taylor managed to go ashore and preach the gospel but on the Sunday he did not fail to do so. Not one of them would have allowed the day to pass without it.

By the time they reached Shanghai on the fifth day, and were in the comfort of Wylie's hospitable bachelor house, John Jones was better. On October 7 he went out with Hudson Taylor as his interpreter to buy supplies for his own and other Ningbo families, and what should they find but the *Geelong* lying in the river and due to sail for Swatow on the 10th. Captain Bowers naturally welcomed Hudson Taylor to sail with him, and from the canal boat moored in the *Yangkingpang* they trans-shipped all the medical supplies he had collected for opening his dispensary. That evening John Jones had another fierce attack of renal colic.

A mail ship arrived the next day, again bringing thirty pounds from William Berger. In a year he had sent three hundred pounds while the CES had provided no more than a fraction of their promised sum. Where he had loyally clung on in hope of improvement, Hudson Taylor was fast losing faith in them. 'I should not wonder if the Ch. Ev. Socy. is found defunct some day' he had told

Amelia on September 18. 'I doubt whether it can exist another year. I am well supplied with funds, the goodness of God is very apparent in this respect. I have more than enough and am just now able to subscribe $50 towards Dr Parker's hospital and ere I left Swatow was enabled to send $50 to aid Revd M A Stronach's school in Amoy . . . The dissolution of the Society therefore may not necessarily result in my coming home.'

To his mother he wrote,

> I doubt whether the (CES) will continue in being much longer . . . though I am sure *I* shall be provided for, yet I am not in a position to marry, or feel settled . . . But God only knows – and He will not let me walk in the dark.

Faith to believe for his own provision seemed not to extend further than that, as yet.

Now as he waited to sail with Captain Bowers in forty-eight hours' time he had all he needed and looked forward to his medical work winning a response and friends in cantankerous Swatow where nothing else had succeeded. But on that same day a hot spark fell on the tinder of Canton resentments which was to touch off another war. And on the 9th a letter came to William Muirhead in Shanghai which instantly dashed all Hudson Taylor's hopes.

It was from William Burns, not in Swatow but Canton, to say that he and his two Chinese colleagues had been arrested and imprisoned on August 19, that he had been held in custody and six weeks later handed over to the consul in Canton, now Harry Parkes. What the situation in Swatow was he did not know, and could not give Hudson Taylor any guidance. Everything was uncertain. 'I do not say whether it is Mr Taylor's duty to return to Swatow or not; I do not think Swatow closed but rather the contrary.'

The attitude of the Chinese authorities had been such that while obeying their imperial instructions to hand him over for punishment by the consul, once he had been arrested, they were even friendly and might shut their eyes if he returned. The consul had released him immediately, but everything else must be conjecture until the smoke cleared.

Hudson Taylor was disappointed. And his quandary was considerable. The consular ban on his travelling or living beyond the treaty ports still held, though Rutherford Alcock was on the point of leaving for the United Kingdom. To go to Swatow at this moment would be in blatant defiance of Chinese and British rulings, at a time when both were sensitive to Burns' infringement. To go and be arrested only to be carried to Canton as well had little to commend it. It could lead to expulsion from China. To stay at Shanghai where his last roots had been severed by the disposal of all his goods, would throw him back in dependence on the LMS until he could start up again, alone, in rented premises, near to the flourishing work of several well-ordered missions, for peace restored to Shanghai had brought freedom to expand. Griffith John was as active as Hudson Taylor had been. That avenue was as firmly closed as Swatow now appeared to be.

He told his faithful architect friend, John Whitworth of Barnsley, that without positive spiritual light on his path he dared not proceed. Negative indications were strong. What he needed was positive leading in the right direction. A few such pointers existed. In Ningbo were his CES colleagues – Parker well-established and preparing to build, and Jones gradually becoming able to speak the Ningbo dialect and in need of an experienced companion evangelist. Ample scope remained for him to join hands with them and the other missions in preaching the gospel and training Chinese Christians.

The obvious course for the present at any rate was to remove the medical equipment from the *Geelong* and rejoin John Jones, who was about to start for home, his errands completed, alone but for Tom and 'Peter', Dr Parker's Chinese companion on the voyage from Britain.

The decision was taken, the freight shipped back to the little canal boat and they set off southwards again. No record conveys what must have been John Jones' relief to have his friend with him, when faced with the daunting possibility of more illness on the way, but in the event that would have been mild torment compared with what soon happened.

The events and influences shaping Hudson Taylor's life at this stage were outside his control. Wanting to get back to Swatow he could only mark time. He felt torn.

> I must still pray in faith for further guidance [he wrote after they reached Ningbo] as I am not so sure as I wish to be of His will – for myself, I do most earnestly long to go back.

Why 'for myself'? Is the implication that circumstances were thwarting his personal preference or that pressure from others to stay at Ningbo now tugged at his emotions? Was he torn between two attractive alternatives, the companionship of William Burns in a difficult pioneer task such as he loved, and the equally warm friendship of John and Mary Jones and the other good friends he had made in the Ningbo church? Did some hope of settling somewhere at last echo from the clang of Swatow's gates?

With hindsight it is possible to see that this was in fact a major turning point in the tides of Hudson Taylor's life. Strong influences which shaped his thoughts, his faith and his hopes for China were brought to bear upon him in Ningbo. They came as much as anything from John and Mary Jones. For the moment he was doing the right thing, and later he was to say that he was 'providentially prevented' from returning. As he learned eventually, on that same day, October 9, Sir John Bowring placed a prohibition upon William Burns, saying, to quote Burns, 'he should deem it imprudent and improper that I should return to the district from which I had been sent.' So Burns had little option but to stay at Hong Kong, 'at least until I hear from Mr Taylor about his plans and prospects, and until the native brethren are . . . released.'

Unfortunately Hudson Taylor's letters to William Burns have not been preserved, but Burns' story has. After Hudson Taylor had left him, Burns and the two Chinese colporteurs had continued their work among the outlying towns and villages, undeterred by robbery. In August they had hired a houseboat and ventured into the more law-abiding region of the prefecture of Chaozhou[7] and were well-received – until an alarming report of a foreign intrusion was given to the authorities.

On the evening of August 19 they were arrested and taken with all their books to the magistrate. For two days he examined them, courteously, to obtain information rather than to find fault, and was satisfied that they posed no threat. That they were then allowed good opportunities to distribute all their books, so that many days' work was done in a day or two, augured well for them and the future – so they fondly hoped. But during this time the possibility of being summarily punished was never far from their minds. The anxiety was well-founded, for in February that year a French Catholic priest had been taken prisoner in Guangxi province and done to death. Connivance with the Taipings may have been suspected.

Auguste Chapdelaine of the Société des Missions Étrangères (the Paris Mission), according to the *Annals of the Propagation of the Faith* in November 1856, was given one hundred lashes on the face,

CAGE AND CANGUE

each of the kind to draw blood and knock out teeth, and one hundred strokes with a rattan on the back while lying prone, all without uttering a sound. Weeks later he was tortured with an iron chain and suspended with a young Chinese widow by their hands in a cage,

> so constructed that the sufferer's feet scarcely touch the ground, whilst his head is suspended above the cage by two boards, hollowed out a little, and fitted to the neck, so as to cause all the sufferings of strangulation, and yet leaving sufficient freedom of respiration to allow the patient to live for some time – even as long as five or six days. The sufferer . . . is placed in front of the prison and exposed to the public gaze.[8]

Chapdelaine lived two days, until he was removed from the cage, beheaded with a cutlass, mutilated and thrown to the dogs. Prisoners were always at the mercy of capricious mandarins. Protestants bore vividly in mind the fate of the martyred preacher Che Jinguang (Ch'e Kin-kwang) who this same year had been suspended all night by his thumbs and big toes before being beheaded and thrown in the river.[9]

On August 21, therefore, when Burns and his companions were told they had been arrested on a false report and would be released if one or more Cantonese merchants would stand surety for them, the tide of their hopes turned. 'The Canton merchants came forward in the kindest manner with the document required,' Burns later wrote. And Hudson Taylor reported, 'Representatives of Canton merchants at Swatow and the exertions of the Foreigners there to prove that he was a good man succeeded.'

Meanwhile in Chaozhou the magistrates to their own regret realised that having arrested a foreigner outside a treaty port they were under statutory obligation to deliver him to his consul. A week later, after eleven days in prison, Burns joined a party of officials in four boats to travel to Canton, while his two Chinese friends were left in jail. He was provided with a servant and whatever food he wished for, at the Chinese government's expense. For a month they moved in leisurely fashion up one river, over the watershed by road and down another river to Canton, stopping for sociabilities with local magistrates all along the way. Burns' opportunities for telling and retelling his message of the gospel were innumerable.

On September 30, the day Hudson Taylor, John Jones and the Ways left Ningbo, the governor-general of Canton sent Consul

Parkes a mildly-worded memorandum and delivered Burns to him, 'wonderfully preserved from the infliction of any punishment or penalty', but suffering from 'ague' contracted on the way. The two Chinese, the governor-general informed Parkes, had been sent to their home districts to be freed on finding proper securities, but on October 2 Burns received a note from them saying they were still in prison together and suffering no special punishment.

The newspapers soon reported that they were wearing the cangue, that heavy portable pillory of wood round their necks, and being held as criminals for abetting Burns' breach of the treaty. The renowned Dr Peter Parker, currently American Commissioner in Shanghai, confirmed that they were condemned to the cangue for a month, and Burns wrote in November that they had been beaten on the mouth but were worshipping together in their cell and hopeful of the conversion of a fellow-prisoner. They had been unfortunate enough to be still in custody when the *Arrow* incident took place and hostilities between the powers began. But Burns went to Swatow and succeeded in securing their release on December 15, mercifully before the furies were unleashed at Canton.[10]

Man overboard![11]   *October 1856*

The young man Peter who was with Hudson Taylor and John Jones on their boat was the one whom William Parker had found in England and employed as a servant and teacher on his voyage to China. On his arrival Peter learned that his home had been destroyed in the Shanghai battles, his wife and child were dead and his brother had been decapitated by the rebels for refusing to give them money when he looked as if he had it. After earning enough money as servant to the surgeon on an American frigate to marry again, Peter wrote to Dr Parker asking if he could come and work for him. Parker was only too glad, for Peter was intelligent and would make a good nurse. So here he was on his way to Ningbo.

That first evening Hudson Taylor and Peter had a long talk together and Peter, who had heard the gospel from Parker too, was moved to tears. He knew that Hudson Taylor intended to go ashore at Songjiang when they reached there the next morning, and asked if he might come to hear him preach. They made an early start under sail with a strong wind and while Hudson Taylor was shaving inside, Peter was outside with the boatmen. Unaccustomed to these canal boats, he had been cautioned several times against clambering along the narrow ledge past the cabin in getting from one end to the other. This time he was coming to the front and to steady himself took hold of a spar used to support the mast when it was lowered to pass under bridges. It was loose and came away. Peter fell backwards into the canal and went under.

Hudson Taylor heard the splash and dashed out, 'saw his feet kicking for a few seconds' and leapt to let down the sail and put the boat about. The boatmen were staring, impotent to act. The water was low and near the bank was deep sludge. Peter had fallen into this head first and been held fast. The bank was featureless and the boat had moved some distance. No one knew exactly where Peter had gone in. Hudson Taylor jumped overboard and waded about frantically hoping to discover Peter's body, but without success. Then he saw a fishing boat with a dragnet which he knew was barbed with hooks. He called out to the fishermen to come at once. The details of the dialogue which followed stayed with him for years. They answered, 'It's not convenient!' 'Don't talk of *convenience*!' cried he in agony; 'a man is drowning, I tell you!'

He told the story again and again in after years, and published it in his books *China: Its Spiritual Need and Claims*, his magazine *China's Millions* and his *Retrospect*. He had to promise every dollar he had, about fourteen, before the fishermen would move. At last, after an hour, they paddled slowly over and in less than a minute brought up Peter's body. 'The fishermen were clamorous and indignant because their exorbitant demand was delayed while efforts at resuscitation were being made. But all was in vain – life was extinct.' This to Hudson Taylor was a picture of the godless mind, indifferent to the value of life, of a human soul, concerned only for personal profit; and of the apathy of Christians, enjoying their own security and faith in Christ while others died in sin and ignorance, unwilling to raise a hand.

Even then Hudson Taylor would not give up hope. Peter had been submerged for two hours before he began artificial respiration but he worked at it for a long time before giving up. So much was at stake. He was in the forbidden hinterland of Shanghai, with the dead body of a Chinese to dispose of. Owing to the prevailing attitude to death and fear of departed spirits, especially through violence of any kind, he could meet with obstruction from people at every turn.

They set off at once, back towards Shanghai. But the weather worsened and throughout Saturday they were immobilised, all

sitting out on deck with only matting to protect them from the wind
and rain while the corpse became more and more offensive. That
evening a larger passage-boat moored near them and was left
empty, so they moved on to it to sleep. And when the passage-
boatmen returned before dawn without either freight or passengers,
owing to the weather, they agreed to take both corpse and
foreigners to the Settlement.

Leaving their own boat and baggage where it was, Hudson
Taylor, John Jones and Tom completed the journey by nine am.
The Joneses moved on to another boat and a small one was found
for the corpse. Then Hudson Taylor went to look for Peter's
relatives. As soon as they knew of his death no one would lift a
finger. His widowed mother refused to receive her son's body but
tried to see how much money she could wrest from Hudson Taylor,
forcing all responsibility for the funeral on him. He withdrew and
brought the body to a jetty near the mother's home, but people
gathered round refusing to have it left on shore or to carry it to the
house. The mother left home, the boatmen refused to take the body
on board again, and the neighbours held the boat with six or eight
boathooks to prevent it leaving. All day long the haggling and
waiting went on.

As darkness approached without agreement being reached,
Hudson Taylor seized a boathook, knocked the other boathooks
away, and set his boat free, a considerable feat. Surprisingly, he was
not molested. He went to Dr Lockhart for a stretcher and carriers
and returned to find the place forsaken but the corpse still there. No
one would stay after dark for fear of the roving spirit. They then
carried the corpse to the mother's house, 'whereupon such a row
ensued as baffles description. His sister and neighbours yelled and
howled and begged us to take it away'.

Hudson Taylor was learning pagan attitudes the hard way. He
quieted them, said he had Peter's possessions in safe keeping, only
to be told greedily, 'Bring them here!'; he gave the sister three
dollars towards funeral expenses and went away. But the next day
the mother found him and for the sake of peace he gave her two
more dollars.

That at last ended the affair and at noon he and John Jones
returned to where their own boat and baggage lay. But their
troubles were not over. Their boatmen refused to sail and they had
to trans-ship. But the new men were in no mood to work and the
journey dragged on and on. John Jones had 'a severe attack' and

Tom was still ill. Both were feeling the strain. Even so Hudson Taylor preached at Pinghu and along the way.

On Wednesday, October 15, they at last reached Ganpu on the Hangzhou Bay and began bargaining for a junk to cross over, refusing to pay the exorbitant price demanded. By then they knew that Mary Jones would be anxious over the long-delayed return of her husband and son, thinking they had no companion, but they refused to be cheated and spent the night in a temple. The following day also the boatmen would not reduce their price enough, and Hudson Taylor held out.

> 'Well, that night a storm arose and . . . from what we afterwards learned, it is most likely we should all have been lost.'

On the third day they tried again, and finding a co-operative junk captain made a contract with him not only for the crossing but for all stages of the journey to Ningbo, the porterage and the river journey on the Ningbo side. He guaranteed the safe arrival of everything at the end. But the crossing was difficult. All night and all the next day they were on board, finally running aground on the bank of a creek on an ebbing tide. There they had to stay.

The Gleaner later carried the whole story.

> We retired early; but about 11 p.m. I was awakened by loud thundering noises, and could not think what the cause could be, till I noticed a crack in one of the planks . . . I went out on deck, saw . . . that the stem and stern of the junk were supported . . . while the middle was (not).

The boat was breaking in two. He woke the others. They rolled up their bedding and escaped with it from the cabin without delay. Pausing to pray together they then climbed down to the mud-bank. By moonlight and a lantern they were guided for half a mile over the squelching mud to the safety of another junk and for the rest of the night, while the boatmen rescued all their baggage – the Ningbo medical equipment, the Shanghai purchases and the new winter clothes bought in Songjiang. But for the contract they had made, an unusual arrangement, it would all have been neglected by the crew. By soon after midnight the junk was a wreck and their cabin full of water.

Another Sunday had come round and the Joneses were in poor condition, so they all set off overland to end the porterage as soon as possible, giving thanks when they could rest in a boat on the Ningbo river until they reached the city two days later. For three long weeks they had suffered the hardships of a journey to Shanghai and back which in good conditions could have been made in eight days. And much more than the journey. No wonder then that after John and his son had rejoined their family at the Goughs and Hudson Taylor was back with the Parkers, he unburdened his feelings in a letter to Amelia.

> It pleased God to make the Captain of our salvation perfect through suffering, and He will not spare His loved, tho' erring ones, the same discipline . . . And so you think dear Elizabeth has fully made up her mind to reject my offer . . . *if* it *is* as you all seem to think, may God spare her from . . . an empty heart. I suppose it is this I am to learn that there *is* no rest in this howling wilderness.

This time, while he seemed to accept Elizabeth's rejection as final, he mourned,

> She used to say she loved me when at Mrs. Hodson's I used to visit as Miss V's intended, and then I liked her very much. Then when Miss V. had broken her engagement, she gave me some drawings. When I left England and gave her a brooch, she wrote me, telling me she had wished for some memento, but had not liked to ask for one. Then . . . after my proposal, she encouraged me, – at my request she gave me a lock of her hair . . . It cannot be that it *all* means nothing, that I have been deceived and deluded all the time . . . 'Why art thou cast down, O my soul . . .? hope thou in God; for I shall yet praise Him'.

The letter is unended, as if a page is missing.

After expulsion from Chongming, Hudson Taylor had learned useful lessons from William Burns about recognising God's hand in reverses of all kinds. Looking back on nearly three years since his arrival in China he had plenty to explain and few bright interludes, but his attitude fortunately continued to be 'none of these things move me', for his troubles were far from over.

The 'Arrow' incident[12]   *October–December 1856*

The spark that touched off four long years of hostilities between China and the Western nations was in reality no spark at all. It became one through an error by the British and the way they and other nations seized on a pretext of putting pressure on Peking. With the burgeoning of Hong Kong as a port and city, Chinese wanting protection from their own government officials increa-

singly made the colony their haven. A system of registration of
Chinese ships came into being, whereby they could fly the British
flag and claim immunity from interference by the imperial customs
and anti-opium mandarins. They had the support of the British
authorities even when engaged in opium-running and, it was said,
piracy.

On October 8, 1856, the *Arrow*, a Chinese *lorcha*, the foreign-
hulled, junk-rigged craft popular with the Portuguese, was boarded
in Canton waters allegedly while flying 'the British flag', the ensign
and Blue Peter. The operation was carried out in a deliberate way
by four mandarins and sixty men, on a charge of piracy. Reports
differed in detail but not on any except the vital major issue. Two of
the crew, including an Englishman, were away visiting another
vessel. They said they saw the flags hauled down and all the
remaining twelve members of the *Arrow*'s crew bound and carried
off. When the Chinese owner of the *Arrow* claimed British protection his word was accepted that the *lorcha* was registered in Hong
Kong. It was in fact known to have been so. H B M Consul Harry
Parkes, the admiring follower of the forthright Rutherford Alcock
who had trained him, immediately demanded of the viceroy and
governor-general of Canton that the men be released, and restored
to the *Arrow*, and that the flag be rehoisted.

The escalation of an incident into a dangerous confrontation
followed its predictable course. It was not yet twenty years since the
confrontation with Commissioner Lin had led to the war of 1840.
The growing pressure of trade due to industrial expansion in
Europe, and the dissatisfaction of both the Chinese and the West
with the treaties of 1842–44 could not be resolved by diplomacy, as
the court at Peking still thought in terms of tributary barbarians
petitioning for clemency. The treaties had been conceded under
duress and opium importation was continuing in flagrant and growing defiance of the emperor's proscription of it. Therefore relations
soured and friction increased, especially at Canton.

Interpretations of what followed upon Parkes' demand colour
and becloud the truth. Instead of complying, Viceroy Ye sent the
prisoners to the consulate. Young and perhaps hot-headed, Parkes
refused to receive them and referred the matter to Sir John
Bowring, Governor of Hong Kong (the day after his prohibition on
Burns). He 'ordered the Chinese authorities' to surrender all the
men, to apologise for the action and to give an undertaking that it
would never be repeated. Failing compliance within forty-eight

hours, Canton would be bombarded. According to the American contemporary, W A P Martin in his memoirs, the 'proud and obstinate' viceroy who boasted of having ordered a thousand decapitations, had the crew beheaded when Parker refused to receive them. The *North China Herald* held that in reply to Bowring the viceroy surrendered the men and pledged that great care would be taken to see that in future no British ship should be visited improperly by Chinese officials, but he could not apologise in the case of the *Arrow* as they had not been in the wrong.

Instead of accepting these conciliatory moves, Bowring was unwilling or unable to appreciate Viceroy Ye's position. He at once put the matter into the hands of Admiral Sir Michael Seymour commanding the fleet in Chinese waters. His culpability in this context is recorded in Admiralty despatch Number 127, dated October 11, 1856.

> it appears in examination, that the *Arrow* had no right to hoist the British flag; the licence to do so expired on 27th September, from which period she has not been entitled to protection.[13]

So Viceroy Ye was in the right.

Later investigation also revealed that the government in Hong Kong had had no legal ground for granting a licence to the *Arrow*, as the ordinance on which licensing was based had not yet been ratified by the British government. Only in August 1856 did the Secretary of State for the Colonies authorise such licensing, so making it legal. The *lorcha* had been licensed from September 28, 1855, to September 27, 1856, and the owner neglected to renew it. Astute Chinese officials had acted properly when they struck, and Viceroy Ye's failure to apologise was justified. Not only so, *The Gleaner* stated, but worse still, the alleged striking of the flag was a lie. 'It is clearly proved . . . that at the time . . . no colours were flying.'

By then things had gone too far. The affair had become a matter of prestige and face, of Britain climbing down. But in fact to Britain a provocation was most welcome. Public opinion was demanding not only a voice but the residence of a British ambassador in Peking and the opening up of China to foreigners. With the outcry over the *Arrow* proved hollow, 'The political and naval authorities were compelled to shift the ground to former causes of complaint.'

Preparations were made, and proceeding to Canton the admiral sent an invitation to Viceroy Ye to meet him outside the city gates. When it was spurned he announced his intention of calling at the palace. The gates were closed against him. From October 23 to 29 the naval force then attacked the defences of Canton. First the Red Fort opposite and commanding the foreign 'factories' was taken, followed by the Shamian Fort on an island in the river and the Bird's Nest Fort. The so-called Dutch Fort was occupied and manned with heavy guns from which the city walls were breached and the palace shelled. Storming parties blew up the city gate and drove the defenders from the battlements. Admiral Seymour and his entourage then entered as conquerors and marched to the vice-regal *yamen*. Governor Ye had gone, so Seymour took possession, surrounded by lacquered pillars, lattice work and porcelains.

What then? Bowring and Seymour were banking on the viceroy being brought to terms. The desecration of his city by the tramp of barbarian troops in its streets and the penetration of red-haired barbarians to the heart of his sacrosanct palace, the devastation by great guns and the death of hundreds of inhabitants all stiffened the viceroy's resolve. He maintained a masterly silence. For two weeks Seymour waited and then moved fifty miles downriver, capturing the extensive Bogue Forts on November 13, commanding the entrance to the Pearl River. He had temporarily stripped China of every fortification worth taking in the Canton area. But it was the old blunder all over again, the mistake Captain Elliott had made. To the Chinese withdrawal betokened weakness. Better never to have gone ashore, let alone to occupy Canton, unless it was to be held and the advantage pressed home.

If Bowring or the admiral thought the celestials would be cowed they were very wrong. *The North China Herald* of Shanghai commented that their action had been 'more patriotic than prudent'. It could have been their downfall. Fortunately for them, 'when it became known in England, it met with warm and hearty approval'. The axe could well have fallen if fire-eating Palmerston had not been the Prime Minister.

Not so among the missionaries, who protested strongly when the news became known. In China, it was far from the end of the story. All foreigners at Canton took refuge on ships when Seymour withdrew, and had no choice but to flee to Hong Kong and Macao. The viceroy, furious, put a price of thirty dollars on every British head and sullen Chinese plotted retaliation. Even in Hong Kong the foreigners were in peril from a Chinese uprising. And this was when Burns' Chinese colleagues were beaten on the face.

Retaliation *November 1856–March 1857*

What began as friction between Britain and China soon became an international imbroglio. On November 20 the re-occupied Barrier Forts four miles below Canton fired on the American flag and were silenced by the guns of the American squadron. American merchants in the China field demanded vigorous action but, while Washington pursued a resolutely pacific policy to gain concessions, Napoleon III saw his opportunity to enhance France's prestige and to win favour with the Pope. An ally of Britain in the Crimean War, though rid of hostilities since the Treaty of Peace signed on March 30, 1856, France was still belligerent. She had her *casus belli* in the judicial murder of Auguste Chapdelaine.

In solemn fact Paris and London were already contemplating joint action when the *Arrow* incident occurred.[14] National pride in both countries needed a success to mollify its Crimean wounds. Seymour's action was just the thing, a fitting preliminary. In addition to gains in China, this collaboration led on to France's annexation of Indo-China. Russia lay low, scheming for advantage. She was after all the worsted enemy of Britain and France in the Crimea and exerting all her injured influence against them.

Viceroy Ye's incitement in retaliation immediately placed the lives of all barbarians in jeopardy, but on December 14 a concerted attack was made on the 'factories' at Canton. For a second time they and three European banks were burned to the ground. In the city, premises used by foreigners were destroyed. No greater loss was sustained in this vandalism, by China as much as anyone, than the complete fount of Robert Morrison's exhaustive dictionary of about forty thousand different Chinese ideograms. They were beyond price. All back numbers of the *Chinese Repository* and a thousand other books from Wells Williams' press also went up in flames.

The viceroy now had no illusions about what would happen. The foreign devils would take time to gather reinforcements, but come they would. He urged Peking to prepare for war. Incredibly the *Peking Gazette* remained silent about developments in the south, as if what was happening was only local unrest. Could it be, the foreigners wondered, that Ye was keeping his masters in the dark? But early in the new year he was appointed Imperial Commissioner with funds and powers to mobilise defence. Peking had been too busy with the Taipings, Muslims and other rebels.

News was travelling faster to Europe since the electric telegraph was being widely extended. On January 23, 1857, after only five weeks by sea and land from Hong Kong, a telegram from Constantinople brought the first report. The 'factories' were ablaze, all business premises were destroyed, shelling was in progress. Five days later a garbled despatch from Alexandria startled Britain. The Chinese, it said, had destroyed English factories and a bank in Hong Kong. This was false, but Hong Kong was not immune.

The influence of the great merchant houses on the China coast was no less now than at the time of the first opium war.[15] On January 5, 1857, a letter from Jardine, Matheson and Company to Sir John Bowring complained that the naval commander-in-chief's energetic action had only made matters worse, and everything subsequent to it was intensifying the rupture. Trade was suffering disastrously. But in a memorandum to the Foreign Minister, Lord Clarendon, who knew that Bowring was unpopular, they laid the blame on weak application by successive consuls at Canton of the Treaty of Nanking. At the request of the Chinese, they said, its terms had not been properly implemented;

> this indulgence, instead of conciliating, has only encouraged the obstinacy and hostility of the provincial government and populace. If free intercourse were insisted upon and established at Canton, we have no doubt that animosity would gradually subside

and trade would increase beyond all expectation, as in the northern ports. They pressed him to appoint –

> a first class representative and plenipotentiary . . . to negotiate a new treaty, and to be permanently accredited to the Court of Pekin . . .

The treaty should secure permission to trade at any port, freedom for British subjects to travel in the interior, and the right to navigate the large rivers.

Trade was considerable, they pointed out, and ought to be placed permanently on a basis of 'peace, amity, and protection of persons and property'. The export of tea, for example, had risen between 1842 and 1856 from 42 million pounds to 87 million, and silk from 3,000 bales to 56,000 bales. The leopard's spots were unchanged; they did not mention that 81,000 chests of opium, 11,340,000 pounds net weight, were being delivered annually by British merchants, that China now suffered with 8 million opium smokers, that 32,000 chests of opium were offloaded at Shanghai alone, or that since a local agreement without Peking's approval, reported by the

North China Herald on October 25, 1856, opium was being openly handled with a duty of twenty dollars per chest, soon to be increased. No longer were semi-clandestine opium depot-barges skulking in the Huangpu river at Wusong. They were moored at the Shanghai Bund.[16] This was the trade they demanded greater freedom to conduct.

In London events in a sense no less dramatic were following fast upon each other's heels. Their outcome decided the policy and action in China for the next four years. At the opening of Parliament on February 3, 1857, the Queen's Speech contained protests against 'insults to the British flag and infraction of treaty rights'. Lord Palmerston, it continued, intended to take strong measures to bring China to her knees. In the Upper House Lord Derby was defeated when he moved a vote of censure with support from Lord Grey, Lord Robert Cecil and others. Lord Shaftesbury, Lady Palmerston's son-in-law, who had twice declined cabinet posts in order to continue his philanthropic work, brought forward a motion against the opium traffic.[17] Drawing upon the Parliamentary Blue Books, Joseph Ridgeway, editor of the *Church Missionary Intelligencer* echoed his protests:

> We first wrong them, contravene their fiscal regulations, grow opium for contraband purposes, and smuggle a large revenue out of China. They grow savage and retaliate and then we flog them. . . . The whole thing is vile and pernicious from beginning to end.[18]

In the Commons men of all parties united to denounce an unjustifiable resort to war. The Tories under Disraeli, the Peelites under Gladstone and the Radicals under Cobden and Bright carried Richard Cobden's motion of censure and the government fell. Cobden was an old friend of Bowring and his exposure of the illegality of Sir John's action was costly to him.

Undismayed, Palmerston appealed to the country, conducted a chauvinistic campaign and was returned with a large majority. Britain as a whole wanted action, success. Preparations for war proceeded. With the re-opening of Parliament the speech from the throne announced the appointment of James Bruce, Lord Elgin, until recently Governor-General of Canada, as plenipotentiary, and his imminent departure to China with a naval and military force.

Well might Britain and France look for an easy victory. China was bleeding already from years of civil war, and impotent against modern armaments and military discipline. Early hopes of the Taipings as a Christian force were dying fast. In place of delight over new discoveries – such as Dr Macgowan's report that while the rebel soldiers fought, their reserves sàng hymns and prayed for them – more references were being made to 'horrid massacres and revolting cruelties'. The rebellion had so far resulted in an estimated two million deaths and was expected to go on for years. The fact that in eight of the eighteen provinces the annual literary examinations had had to be suspended, measured the disruption of the empire.

Following a slow retreat from the environs of Tianjin during which they had occupied city after city in the province of Shandong, Shanxi and Henan, the Taipings had for a time been reduced to encirclement at Nanking. Thirty thousand were said to have died in that city alone. Yet their resilience seemed irrepressible. They kept hitting back and reoccupying cities in the Yangzi valley. Internal feuds threatened their existence and the Eastern King of the Taipings was killed, but with renewed vigour the movement tied down hordes of imperial troops. Hudson Taylor wrote on November 26, 1856,

> The movement is gaining strength if not ground. The whole of the province of Kiangsi is in the hands of the insurgents and most of it is *organized* into a kingdom.

He added that another imperial general was reported to have died at Nanking, a euphemism for suicide instead of public disgrace or decapitation for military failure. To die before denunciation and to be posthumously honoured was preferable. But popular report had it that another body was buried while the hero enjoyed the rewards in retirement with his family. A Gilbertian Manchu government and army stood no chance against the Western powers – except that while Lord Elgin was at sea the Indian mutiny broke out.

Caught in the storm   *1856–1857*

Church and missionaries were inevitably tarred with the same brush as merchants and military men. Denounce 'British guilt' as they might, they were barbarians and unwanted in the trouble zones.

> May God in mercy avert his righteous judgment from our guilty heads [the Secretary of the CES said to Hudson Taylor's mother, in writing to allay her apprehension over developments].

I dare not look upon our conduct in China but as of the worst character. Although we succeed in opening the country it will be with *wicked* hands, – the Lord of Glory was crucified with *wicked* hands, yet it *accomplished* God's will and counsel. I am so strongly impressed with the injustice of our cause that I will never support any Candidate who defends Sir J Bowring . . . we have dishonoured God before the heathen.

Many shared his indignation.

With George Pearse and Charles Bird under excessive pressure, G F Maberly, a member of the CES Committee, began corresponding with the missionaries. On January 8, 1857, he referred to the hostilities at Canton as having 'scarcely the shadow of a pretext'. The newspapers were treating it as a commercial question. 'They want Chusan and an Ambassador at Peking.' And in February in reference to the Society for Suppressing the Opium Trade, 'I trust a movement has begun which will not cease till the British Flag shall have ceased to protect the opium vessel.'[19]

Since 1844 the Roman Catholics had enjoyed greater peace and immunity than for several generations. Ironically, when France came to champion the church and began by open war the era of a French protectorate in China, anti-Catholic persecution increased. The inference was that the Catholics and Taipings were alike. Freedom to live and travel in China had always depended upon evasion of the authorities or their tacit toleration, an insecure, perilous position. Imperial edicts were always liable to reversal. But the hostilities of 1856–60 increased this insecurity. After the second opium war the situation changed. Because of people's contact with the Taipings, the Catholic priests in Henan were busy answering enquiries about Christianity.

In Siam relations with King Mongkut were so amicable that a treaty in 1856 guaranteed the right of Christians to preach, build churches, schools and hospitals, and to travel without restriction. But in Indo-China, vassal of Peking, anti-Christian laws were enforced and a storm broke out which drew France and Spain to intervene. Persecution was intensified. Between 1857 and 1862 five thousand Christians were killed and forty thousand beggared. To Professor Latourette, however, the beginning of the forty-year 'period of missionary penetration' began with France's armed intervention in China. The Catholic Church had a start of centuries over the Protestants, who were hardly past the starting line after fifty years of struggle.

In 1856 there were about ninety-five Protestant missionaries in the whole of China, including Hong Kong and those absent on leave. They still had barely a foothold even if making the most of it in four coastal provinces. When the *North China Herald* asked the veteran Elijah Bridgman in 1857 for an article to mark the half century of Protestant missions in China (after W H Medhurst had gone home, to die on January 24, 1857, three days after arrival in London), he showed that a current total of only two hundred and thirty-seven missionary men, women and children could be counted. Since the beginning only four hundred men and women had come to China of whom about two hundred were ordained ministers. In the first decade four missionaries arrived, fifteen in the second, thirty-nine in the third, one hundred and five in the fourth and double that number in the fifth. Among 'four hundred million' Chinese they were so few. Roughly thirty in Shanghai and Hong Kong, twenty in Ningbo, and ten in Fuzhou and Amoy, numerically counted for so little, after Canton had been evacuated.[20]

In Amoy the LMS and American Board had each baptised about a hundred and eighty believers in the last ten years, but many fewer in other places. Progress was disappointingly slow, but in view of the international tensions an increase of more new converts in the last year and a half than in all previous years had to be regarded with hope. The presence of women and children, even unmarried women, in these mission centres signalled great advances over 'those palmy days of monopolies and Cohongs'. Then, for 'such a monstrous act' as bringing foreign women to Canton, all commerce was stopped and 'the whole imperial Cabinet and Dragon Throne together were moved, for the immediate expulsion of two or three fair intruders.' Faith at that time had been rewarded, and the faith of those battling on after half a century was to reap even greater rewards.

By 1856 Christian associations were springing up in the universities and colleges of Britain and the United States. The YMCA, then wholly evangelical, played a big part in this. Evangelical Christians were giving rise to one new movement after another. When Sunday evening evangelistic services were held in the great Exeter Hall, off the Strand in London, the unheard-of innovation was strongly resisted as 'subversive of the ancient order'. Although Lord Shaftesbury led the movement, the Bishop of London withdrew the use of the hall. In 1856 the Rev William Pennefather, author of the hymn 'Jesus, stand among us in Thy risen power', began conferences at

Christ Church, Barnet, which soon developed into the Mildmay Conference, a forerunner of the Keswick Convention. Its evening meetings were always missionary in emphasis – in later years the forum of Hudson Taylor's strong spiritual influence.

To these and similar movements, as well as to the denominational churches, the missionaries increasingly addressed appeals for reinforcement. Dr Macgowan of Ningbo appealed for two missionaries to be sent to neglected Indo-China, and the CES *Gleaner* publicised it for the sake of 'those members of the great Chinese family who have none to care for their souls'. Roman Catholicism they discounted as turning the truth of the gospel into falsehood.

A missionary of the American Board wrote in the *American Journal of Missions*, of China, 'I firmly believe, that were the churches to send one hundred able men to this field, they would all find ample room for their labours long before they could (speak the language accurately).' For five years they waited, but then the men and women began to come.

Meanwhile the Bible Societies voted large sums for the support of Chinese Christians as colporteurs, if worthy men could be appointed. That was the problem. With so few Christians, potential workers were fewer still. In South China the German missionaries supervised a handful. In Hong Kong, Shanghai and Amoy there were some five men, as well as the two with William Burns. The heavy end of the load must still be borne by itinerant foreign missionaries of whom there were all too few.

The difficulty of the work came as close to disheartening Griffith John as ever it would. In June 1856 he wrote that he had been on several journeys with others,

> But the Chinese seem to me to be the most indifferent, cold, callous, irreligious people that I have ever seen or read of. [They were glad to listen to the gospel and accept books, but] it does not seem to reach their hearts.

In September the outlook seemed brighter. But was it?

> The good work in China is moving, but very slowly. The people are as hard as steel. They are eaten up, both soul and body, by the world [materialism] . . . Sometimes I am ready to give up in despair and think that China is doomed to destruction . . .

At the end of October, however, he went out on his first short evangelistic journey with a colporteur but no other missionary. At

Songjiang a most unusual thing happened. He had seen thousands of books and tracts distributed without ever witnessing the desecration or destruction of one. Confucian respect for the written characters prevented it. But this time a man took the book he proffered and tore it up – he was a Roman Catholic.[21]

When Admiral Seymour bombarded Canton, Peter Parker's and Benjamin Hobson's hospitals, where Liang A-fa had worked, Dr A P Happer's boarding school and the work of Methodists George Piercy and Josiah Cox, all in the Chinese city, had to close down and the missionaries to withdraw to Macao and Hong Kong. For a time Josiah Cox held on at the LMS hospital and then at the Shamian 'factories' to protect all mission interests as well as he was able, until it was foolhardy to stay longer. The hospital was occupied by Chinese troops and shelled by the British warships. When Admiral Seymour bombarded the viceroy's palace, the people vented their anger on mission property, although much of it belonged to Americans. With no hospital and no prospect of an early return to Canton, Dr Hobson moved up to Shanghai to join William Lockhart, until Lockhart went home on leave to Britain in 1857 and Hobson took over his work.

All these missionaries worked in treaty ports or itinerated from them. William Burns at Swatow and the Continental missions in Guangdong remained the exception, still living quietly among the mainlanders and under their protection in an atmosphere of great danger and alarm, robbery and ransom demands. Since his wife and Theodore Hamberg had died in 1854, Rudolf Lechler had been carrying on alone or with Winnes at Pukak, half-way between Hong Kong and Canton. The Rhenish missionaries Genähr and Krone worked at Saiheng near the coast and Ho'an farther away. Lobscheid was developing new work at Palowai to which he had been invited (map, p 191).

In the previous year, 1855, Rudolf Lechler had set out in a letter to George Pearse the policy which brought such good results and foreshadowed Hudson Taylor's action. He admired

> the zeal and devotion of the Catholic missionaries – their perseverance, and readiness to undergo sufferings, which nobody ever disputed (but) . . . What they are most anxious for is perfect concealment . . . most successfully assisted by their converts (both when travelling and at their destination). . . . Now concealment has never been a matter of purpose with me; wherever I went I was recognized as a foreigner, though I have adopted the Chinese costume, and I never wished to

proclaim the gospel . . . but openly as a message . . . which everyone
must accept and . . . also confess publicly . . . I was frequently öbliged
to change my place.

Bowring to the rescue   *November 1856*

When Theodore Hamberg had rented a house at Pukak in 1851
the contract drawn up by local believers had stated clearly that it was
for the purpose of 'living there and teaching the doctrine of God'. In
the four years following, two hundred and five believers had been
baptised and between thirty and forty local people had also discarded their idols and were asking for baptism.

News of the British squadron's attack on Canton, October 23–29,
1856, and occupation of the palace spread quickly. On November 7
Wilhelm Lobscheid, in Ho'an at the time, was advised by Chinese
friends to leave. Without sleep he went at once to Pukak, joining
Winnes. (It appears that Winnes' and Genähr's families were
already safely at Hong Kong.) From that moment an adventure true
to the missionary tradition – except in one feature – began. Lobscheid's account was published in *The Gleaner*, too fully to be
given verbatim.[22]

They were told that they were prisoners held to ransom, with a
price of a hundred and twenty dollars on each one's head. Winnes'
excellent relations with the leading gentry of the area led him to
believe that explanations would solve this problem. After all,
neither of them was British. They invited the Pukak literati to a
meal and they came. But their attitude had become unfriendly.
While they were still there Lobscheid wrote an urgent message to
I Irvin, British chaplain at Hong Kong. Would he see what the
British, American and French authorities could do to help them? A
Christian runner left with the note and they waited with the gentry
still in the house, but not for long.

Soon a mob forced its way in and the guests seemed indifferent,
except that when the missionaries retreated upstairs they went with
them. The mob followed. Here the bizarre note enters the story.
Winnes and Lobscheid 'took up their guns' – shotguns kept for
sport and for stocking the larder. Whether they meant business or
not is open to conjecture. The gentry at once ordered the mob
downstairs and the door was bolted. But the noise became louder
and louder as the mob grew and became inflamed with wine.

Winnes then told the gentry that he and Lobscheid would pay a ransom if they would negotiate with the rabble. Lobscheid was for attempting to escape, but Winnes was in bad health and afraid he could not survive it.

Two hours passed, and an ominous silence fell. By then it was dark. Suddenly with roars and yells the mob attacked the upstairs door with hatchets. It began to give way. Lobscheid ran on to a 'terrace' (perhaps a verandah) at the back and found his way blocked by men. He clambered quickly over the roofs of five adjacent houses, jumped eighteen feet to the ground and ran across a rice-field. There was enough moonlight to see his way, but the mob had also seen him and gave chase. Desperate, he jumped into the river and hid among wild pineapple plants near the bank, standing in the water up to his neck.

Fifty men lined the bank, showering stones and clods of earth around him. Others going down to the water's edge stabbed into the vegetation with spears and pikes. Two waded in, searching for him. They came within two feet. He could see their faces but they apparently failed to see him. He was so cold that he had to put his fingers between his teeth lest the chattering give him away. Even when it sounded as if all the men had gone he dared not move. He could feel the leeches crawling up and fastening on to him.

After two more hours a night bird fluttered in the bushes and he judged that no one was near. But the moon was now so bright and houses so near that he decided to wait until it set, then to roll across the path into the field and make his way to the corner of a wood. Before he could do this two men came up and began calling him softly. He recognised one as a person he knew well. Lobscheid guessed that Winnes had settled a ransom price, so he also gave himself up. They led him into the wood and there tried to extort money from him, in exchange for their help; but when he insisted on walking to Saiheng, twenty miles away, instead of following their plan, they let him go.

He travelled over rough country avoiding houses. It cost him falls into 'deep ravines' and once he thought he had broken his thigh. But he reached Ferdinand Genähr's house at seven am. Forty or fifty men had plotted to ambush Genähr but his servant had heard of it. Together Lobscheid and Genähr put off from shore in a junk, loaded the 'cannons' – whatever he meant by that, perhaps standard equipment against pirates – had 'everything ready for defence', and at last fell asleep, after two nights awake. They reached

Hong Kong at four am the next day. Genähr's home was plundered after they left.

Meanwhile Rudolf Lechler was in Hong Kong when Sir Michael Seymour bombarded Canton. As soon as he knew of it he realised the great danger the missionaries on the mainland would be in. The price set on every foreign head increased the urgency. He sent a warning to each of them, but then heard that two had already been captured and a thousand dollars must be paid for each if their lives were to be spared. On November 8 the Pukak Christian arrived with Lobscheid's note and Chaplain Irvin 'took up the matter with all the warmth and kindness which characterised all his actions'. He appealed to the governor, Bowring, for help. No steam warship was available. Admiral Seymour was enjoying the unusual luxury of the vice-regal palace in Canton, and all such ships were on active duty. Bowring turned to the P & O.[23] They gallantly put a steamship at his disposal. With a company of British soldiers Lechler proceeded via Deep Bay to Pukak, marching twelve miles inland from the coast. 'The appearance of soldiers had a most wholesome effect upon the treacherous gentry and mob of Pukak, and will, I trust, prevent them from repeating the experiment again,' was Lobscheid's comment.

When Winnes' door had given way before the mob onslaught, he had been seized and held for three hours with knives at his throat and threats to use them. He would not, or could not, yield to their demands for the ransom. Other men had taken over, continuing the threats all day until in the evening he had seen reason and promised the payment for his release. When rescued by the British troops Winnes was true to his word. He paid the ransom and all withdrew.[24]

An unanswered question remains: were the literati of Pukak grievously misjudged by Lobscheid and his friends? European inflexibility saw their part as implication in the crime. But, to speculate, if they knew the ugly mood of men intending mischief and could not safely intervene to protect their foreign friends, oriental wisdom might well have led them in the course they took. Appearing to side with the mob they stood between them and their victims. They defused an ugly moment when the missionaries took up firearms. Possibly they saved their lives by making the ransom figure of two hundred and forty dollars more attractive than the sixty dollars offered by the viceroy for two heads. That the sum was paid to keep a promise made under such duress no doubt surprised them all, and commended the gospel in the whole area after they returned.[25]

The sequel was satisfying. A month later Lechler wrote rejoicing that the missionaries had been 'kept from unbroken residence' in the area, because their removal had allowed the Christians to live in dependence on God alone. 'He can never be taken from them.' This fundamental insight showed his wisdom and was read by all who took *The Gleaner*. When peace returned they resumed their work and the churches flourished. But that was not until months later. In May 1857 Lobscheid wrote of fifty-four converts at Ho-an and Palowai.

Long before then Hong Kong itself was in danger. Only in the settlement of Victoria was any safety to be found for foreigners, and even there assassination and kidnap attempts were made. And this time Ningbo, the City of Peace on the Waves, was to share in the excitement.

After the drowning of 'Peter', Hudson Taylor and John Jones had arrived back from Shanghai (on October 20), three days before the bombardment of Canton began. But news from the south took two full weeks to reach Ningbo, and when it came it was for Hudson Taylor another 'sufficient reason' for delaying his return to Swatow. If in the absence of provocation the people of Swatow had been antagonistic, this turn in events would make it folly to go among them. Burns would be unable to leave Hong Kong until the emergency was over. So nothing remained for Hudson Taylor to do but to drop back into the daily round at Ningbo and await developments.

Christmas and the New Year came and went. On January 14, 1857, an attempt was made to poison every 'barbarian' in Hong Kong; and suddenly, on the 18th, a plot to massacre every 'foreign devil' in Ningbo, with the connivance of the highest mandarin, was unmasked.

Immediately, Hudson Taylor was thrust involuntarily into the situation which led directly to his life-work.

POSTSCRIPT

Only the sheer length of this biography demands a break at this point. The story goes on without interruption in the next volume.

As the prospects for the imperial government of China deteriorated, through the successes of the Taiping insurrection and the growing demands of the West, Hudson Taylor's apprenticeship had been running its course. By the end of 1856, three years of preparation in England and three in China had made a man of the young student of 1850. The realities of life in China and his own emotional turmoils had confronted him with choices which could have wrecked his hopes of future effectiveness. Now nearing twenty-five, and as experienced a trail-maker as any of his missionary contemporaries, he found the way barred against him once more. Uprooted from Swatow and Ningbo he was reduced to doing whatever came to hand at Shanghai while rethinking his whole position, and asking God to open up the way ahead of him unmistakably.

In those few years of initiation Hudson Taylor had survived dissection fever, near-shipwreck, mob violence, war, loneliness and temptation to the verge of defeat, enough experiences for a lifetime – but they were only a beginning. *If I had a Thousand Lives* continues the epic through the second opium war, the last years of the Taiping rebellion and the expansion of missions in China. From Hudson Taylor striking out with John Jones on a venture of their own and before long despairing of life itself, it builds up to its climax in his bid to take the gospel far from the coastal areas, into every remote province of the Chinese empire.

RÉSUMÉ
of BOOK ONE: BARBARIANS AT THE GATES

James Hudson Taylor was one of a long line of Christian missionaries to China stretching through the centuries from Alopen the Nestorian in the sixth century to the present day. Intolerable suppression and fatal compromise wiped out the Nestorian Church, but after a long interval the Roman Church succeeded in obtaining a new foothold in Peking, the heart of the empire. Periods of persecution with total bans on foreigners and Christianity failed to eliminate the brave men who for decades lived in hiding, working through their loyal Chinese followers. Purposeful Protestant Christianity first came to China in 1807 in the person of Robert Morrison of the London Missionary Society (LMS), who lived and died with few companions. By translating the Bible, the key to China's awakening, in the view of Sun Yat-sen, and by a massive dictionary, a Chinese Grammar and other works of scholarship, he laid the foundations for those who succeeded him.

With the eruption of the Industrial Revolution in Europe, Western commerce backed by Western arms pressed relentlessly upon China, demanding better facilities for trade. Britain's control of India gave her the twin factors of a great nation and territory to govern, and a source of government revenue in the opium being grown. Exploiting the opium, she made China the chief consumer. Alert to the danger but averse to 'barbarian' foreigners anyway, the emperor resolutely attempted to restrict trade to Canton. But smuggling and aggression by the ships of many nations among whom the British excelled, led inexorably to war. By the Treaty of Nanking in 1842 five ports were opened and foreign settlements established there and at Hong Kong.

From 1827 until 1851 a colourful figure on the Asian scene named Charles Gutzlaff made a great reputation as a missionary-explorer and interpreter-negotiator. While serving for a decade as Chinese Secretary to the Governor of Hong Kong, the British Plenipotentiary, he strenuously promoted the cause of Christian missions to

China, and in the two years before his death inspired the formation of several new missions on the continent of Europe and in Britain to promote the work in China. With the development of international settlements at the treaty ports, missionaries of all societies congregated in them, working however they could while waiting for barriers to travel and to residence in the interior to be lifted. Gutzlaff could not be fettered like that. Appealing for missionaries to move inland, disregarding the limitations at the treaty ports, he was successful in placing some in friendly parts of Guangdong (Kwangtung) province.

But an obscure sect in the hinterland of Canton, known as the Worshippers of Shangdi, with pseudo-Christian tenets, linked up with anti-Manchu factions and began to resist the imperial government. The seeds of the devastating Taiping Rebellion had been sown, a movement which was almost to topple the dynasty.

Back in the days of John Wesley a family of fearless Methodists in Yorkshire had endured stoning and abuse for two generations to preach the gospel and build up a church of new believers. James Taylor's equally brave son John became the grandfather of James Hudson Taylor, a worthy product of such stock. Before Hudson Taylor was born in 1832 his father, another James, took China to his heart and dedicated his unborn son to God to be a missionary. He and his wife kept the fact a secret until nearly thirty years later, but through his parents' continuing concern and the books they read, Hudson Taylor grew up knowing of Morrison, his colleague Medhurst, Gutzlaff and the cause they served. In 1849 he committed his life to God, to go himself to China in due time. When Gutzlaff announced his return to Europe and a Chinese Society was formed, with a monthly periodical reporting Gutzlaff's plans for the evangelisation of China, the Taylor family subscribed.

In China all was not well. The emperor died, unrest increased and in Hong Kong Gutzlaff's Chinese Union of colporteurs, organised to carry the gospel to the remotest provinces, was exploited by unscrupulous men. Most of the members were found to be frauds, drawing funds but never leaving Hong Kong. So in Europe Gutzlaff was discredited, but the Chinese Society in Britain and the new missions he initiated on the Continent believed in the soundness of his policies, and some of them loyally continued to support him. Hudson Taylor himself was unshaken. *Over the Treaty Wall* takes up the history at this point.

THE FOREBEARS OF JAMES HUDSON TAYLOR

JAMES TAYLOR, mason, Barnsley, Yorkshire; host to John
Wesley
    b. 1749   d. 1795
    m. 1776 Elizabeth Johnson
    2 sons, 3 daughters

JOHN TAYLOR, linen reed maker, Barnsley
    b. 1778   d. 6 Oct. 1834
    m. 1799 Mary Shepherd b. 1776   d. 1850
    4 sons, 4 daughters

JAMES TAYLOR, second son, chemist, Barnsley
    b. 1807   d. 1 Nov. 1881
    m. 5 April 1831 *Amelia Hudson* b. 27 Jan. 1808   d. Nov. 1881
    3 sons, 2 daughters   *James Hudson*, William Shepherd, *Amelia*
      Hudson, Theodore, Louisa Shepherd

BENJAMIN BROOK HUDSON, Wesleyan Methodist minister,
    artist
    b. *circa* 1785   d. *circa* 1865
    3 sons, 4 daughters
    Amelia, b. 27 Jan. 1808   d. Nov. 1881 m. James Taylor
    Mary, m. Hodson, scholar, Barton-on-Humber
    Joseph, Vicar of Dodworth, Barnsley
    Hannah Maria, portrait artist m. Richard Hardey, photo-
      grapher, brother of Robert Hardey, surgeon, Hull
    James, artist, died aged 21
    Sarah Ann, m. Rev Edward King, C I M Australian Council
    Benjamin, portrait artist, Soho and India

QING (CH'ING) DYNASTY DEGREES OF RANK, civil and military

Office	Style	Cap Buttons
1 Ministers of State and Presidents of Tribunals	Da Ren (Ta Jen) (Grandee)	Plain red gem or precious stone
2 Viceroys and Governors of Provinces	do.	Carved red inferior gem, stone or coral
3 Judges and Treasurers	do.	Dark blue gem, stone
4 Lieutenant Governors of Counties and Superintendents of Circuits	Da Lao Ye (Ta Lao Yeh) (Great Father)	Light blue gem or stone
5 Rulers of Departments	do.	Crystal globe
6 Magistrates of Districts	do.	Milk white opaque stone
7 do. inferior	do.	do.
8 Assistant Magistrates	Lao Ye (Father)	Patterned gilt
9 Village and inferior officers	do.	Plain gilt
Lower ranks, government underlings	—	entitled to silver buttons, never worn

Sources: W H Medhurst: CHINA
W A P Martin: A CYCLE OF CATHAY
R Morrison: MEMOIRS

THE DELEGATES' BIBLE[1]
(*see also* Book One, Index)

The publication of this translation of the whole Bible into Chinese was one of the great achievements of the first decade after the opening of the 'treaty ports'. The 'Delegates' began work soon after the conference of missionaries at Hong Kong in 1843 appointed them. The various books of the Bible were apportioned between Walter Medhurst of LMS, William Boone, the American Episcopal surgeon and later bishop, W M Lowrie of the American Presbyterian Mission (son of the senator), John Stronach of LMS and Elijah Bridgman of the American Board. All were competent scholars and men of God; but problems arose almost at once. The 'term question' (*see* Appendix 5) of what Chinese words to use for 'God' reared its ugly head and Boone withdrew, Lowrie was caught by pirates not far from Shanghai, on his way home to Ningbo, and thrown into the sea. W C Milne, son of Morrison's friend, took his place on the Committee. Working from Robert Morrison's and Medhurst's versions, and Gutzlaff's revision of Medhurst's, the Committee published the New Testament in 1852 and the whole Bible in 1855. They decided to use neither the high *wenli* of the literati nor a colloquial variant, but an approved form between the two, suitable for educated Chinese.

The Delegates' Version was well received. Elijah Bridgman heard of a man from south-west of Nanking who took home with him a New Testament and showed it to friends. Full of admiration they regarded it as the source from which Confucius must have drawn his wisdom, and laboriously made seven copies by hand. One secret of its success lay in Dr Medhurst's employment of a Chinese scholar as his pundit. When the right phrase was wanted Medhurst would go to great pains to convey its sense in a variety of ways to the scholar. The old man had a well-catalogued mind. He would go away, think, and return with a pile of books from his library from which he would provide examples, classic expressions from prose and poetry with differing nuances. From these Medhurst would pick the most appropriate. William Lockhart wrote,

The excellence of the present version . . . is mainly attributable to the wonderful knowledge of the language possessed by . . . Rev. Dr. Medhurst, and to the scholarlike ability and critical exactitude of the Rev. J. Stronach.[2]

When the progress of the Taiping rebellion was thought to herald an early opening of the whole of China to the gospel, the British and Foreign Bible Society marked its jubilee by passing a resolution, dated September 19, 1853,

That the Committee . . . are prepared to take upon themselves all the measures necessary for printing, with the least practicable delay, ONE MILLION copies of the Chinese New Testament.[3]

Britain alone raised thirty-seven thousand pounds for this purpose in the first two years and increased the sum to fifty thousand. In Shanghai several hundred thousand Testaments were printed 'by the metallic process' using movable founts, on the LMS's huge presses powered by bullocks and buffaloes.

But the CES *Gleaner*'s perspicacious comment on the resolution was 'This subject involves the important question of their distribution'[4] – there were too few missionaries and even fewer Chinese colporteurs. Both must be increased, and CES missionaries must give first priority to this work, as the LMS and European societies were doing. In 1854–55, however, Alexander Wylie was using all available time distributing Scripture himself, with Hudson Taylor as his zealous apprentice.

To anticipate by a decade, when Alexander Wylie saw his warehouse stacked with 40,000 Scriptures in danger from rats and termites, he forsook printing and in 1863 was seconded for some years to the Bible Society to promote a comprehensive system of distribution. In his travels, after China was widely opened to foreigners, Wylie secured a passage on one of Lord Elgin's ships up the Yangzi, and in 1868 was one of the first to penetrate to Sichuan province in the deep west. Travellers from other provinces carried his books with them, and the crews of long distance junks were made a special object of attention – in the tradition of Charles Gutzlaff in Siam twenty-six years before. With the lesson of Gutzlaff's victimisation by frauds to help them, and acknowledging that his principle was right, the missionaries chose reliable Chinese Christians as colporteurs. They took five thousand New Testaments at a time and travelled often by boat from town to town selling to all who would buy. Some suffered torture and lost their lives as true martyrs to the faith.

Hudson Taylor, as soon as he was in a position to judge the merits of different versions, saw the Delegates' version in another light. It was not as gratifying to him as some suggested, that two million Delegates' New Testaments, instead of one million, should be printed. It was a scholars' version. There were too few Chinese who could read and understand its literary style. Some missionaries said one half but some only one tenth of *literate* people could read it intelligibly.

> I hope they will undertake the colloquial Mandarin version [Hudson Taylor wrote]. The present (Delegates') version is *not* the bible for the people . . . *no one*, be they ever so learned, could understand it when read to them (by ear alone) . . .

– for comprehension depended on seeing the particular characters used.

> Room therefore does and must exist for patois versions in several dialects, if we would give the word to every class.

Hudson Taylor pioneered a vernacular version for Ningbo, and a score of other vernacular versions followed, for in after years this became the accepted view and the literary style known as *wenli* fell largely into disuse.

THE 'TERM QUESTION'

The question of what Chinese words to use for 'God', had split the Roman Church in China until eventually determined by papal fiat. It was to divide Protestants for a century.[5] James Legge, the profound scholar of Chinese classics, was convinced, like the Jesuits, that *Shangdi* (*Shang-ti*) was the right term to use, quoting 'All spirits (*shen*) and men are made by *Ti* as their Potter.' The 'term' dispute was 'a long enduring nightmare' to him, but he felt duty-bound to contribute his extensive knowledge and opinion. Other equally erudite scholars preferred *Shen* as the Dominicans had done, or *Zhen* (*Chen*) *Shen* (True God). Rome avoided both terms in favour of *Tian Zhu* (*T'ien Chu*) (Lord of Heaven) 'a name found in ancient history as one of the eight minor divinities worshipped by the wall-builder [of the Great Wall, 240 BC] but so little known that it was regarded as practically fresh coinage'. When John Shaw Burdon was bishop of Victoria, Hong Kong, he with other Protestants strongly advocated the use of *Tian Zhu*. W A P Martin, Hudson Taylor's contemporary, commented in later years 'the Spirit of God appears to have shown no marked preference for any, converts being as readily gathered by the use of one term as by another'. In practice the rank and file missionary and Chinese Christian tended to use both, separately or together, as *Shangdi Zhen Shen* in the sense of 'God the True Spirit'.

GUTZLAFF'S VERSION OF THE BIBLE IN CHINESE

Charles Gutzlaff amended Medhurst's version with the Cantonese southerners primarily in mind and in a more colloquial form, and, because the Bible Society was waiting for the Delegates' Version to be completed the Chinese Evangelization Society took up his 1849 proposal that thirty to forty sets of printing blocks should be prepared and 'at least 20,000 copies per annum' be printed.[6] In this they had the strong support of George Smith, first Bishop of Victoria, Hong Kong, who, seeing a place for both, even in April 1854, wrote to George Pearse:

> The (Delegates') Version of the Old Testament might be for the more educated scholars, Dr. Gutzlaff's for the more plain and less educated reader . . . I could encourage a Society such as yours to print Dr. Gutzlaff's. This version has a *prestige* and must command an influence from the fact that it is now being reprinted by the Tai-ping-wang, at Nanking.[7]

Lobscheid wrote that the bishop offered to bear the whole cost if the CES did not have the funds, and had made a generous donation to avoid delay. A Dr Charles Taylor also wrote that although using colloquial Chinese in print was a departure from Chinese custom, its acceptability was demonstrated by the Taipings' use of it. So here again Charles Gutzlaff was shown to be ahead of his time.

In April 1853, after the publication of the Delegates' New Testament, George Pearse asked William Burns in Amoy, a different dialect area, for his opinion. He received a characteristic reply, considerate but strong:

> . . . the version of the New Testament commonly called Medhurst's and sometimes Medhurst and Gutzlaff's, was in general use here until the issue of the new version. Since that time it has not been used . . . publickly . . . When I came here I brought with me about 20 copies of Dr. Gutzlaff's last edition . . . but as soon as the New Version came to hand the (Chinese) teacher . . . of his own accord adopted it and laid aside the other, which has never been used since . . . Might it not

be best to leave the responsibility of choosing what version shall be used to your missionaries themselves instead of deciding for them beforehand and in ignorance as you must necessarily be in great measure? . . .

This percipient advice was not taken, nor its implications heeded. Instructions were sent to Lobscheid, and he proceeded to employ thirty men to engrave Old Testament page blocks in wood, while the CES appealed for twelve hundred pounds to print the first ten thousand copies. Printing proceeded as long as Lobscheid controlled it.

LIANG A-FA
1835–55

The part played by this leading Chinese apostle has necessarily been told phase by phase as the history of his times have unfolded (*see* Book One, Index, Personalia and Bibliography), and a summary of his last twenty years is needed to fill in some gaps. While Liang A-fa was working in exile with Samuel Dyer, Medhurst's success in distributing Scripture and tracts up and down the entire coast of China from D W C Olyphant's ship *Huron* in 1835 quickly had its repercussions at Canton. A search was mounted for the printers of the foreign poison and both Qiu A-gong and Liang A-de (A-fa's son) had to be spirited away to Singapore once more.

Liang A-fa paid a secret visit to his family in 1836, and in 1839 was able to return to Canton, just before the outbreak of the opium war. The prospect of war between his beloved China and Britain distressed him acutely, and drove him to a desperate act. He called on John R Morrison, whom he had known from childhood but who now represented the enemy government at Canton, and entreated him to use his influence to preserve peace. 'He said he feared if the British came to fight with the Chinese, his countrymen would never afterwards receive the Scripture nor listen to the preaching of the gospel by British missionaries.' But it was too late, beyond John Morrison's power to influence events.

Then an extraordinary thing happened. The great Commissioner Lin heard of Liang A-de, now twenty, with eight years of personal tuition by Bridgman to his credit. Lin, the strong man who was taking opium traders and British lion to task, needed a translator. A-de joined his staff – and in beautifully oriental sequence, his father A-fa was allowed to preach openly at Canton, while Commissioner Lin turned a blind eye to his activities. A-de's work was mainly to translate foreign newspaper articles into Chinese for the emperor and Lin and their advisers' use. He brought the foreign viewpoint to the attention of the Court and was believed to have influenced Lin's attitude at Canton.

When Qi Shan succeeded Lin in 1840, A-de left government employ and joined a Chinese merchant firm, never doing the Bible translating for which Elijah Bridgman had so hopefully trained him. He accompanied the British envoy Pottinger to negotiate the Treaty of Nanking, and the American envoy to negotiate the American treaty with China in 1844. The 'diplomatic honeymoon' followed, with Qi Ying, the Viceroy and High Commissioner, calling upon A-de for help when reporting to Peking on foreign attitudes, customs and history. A-de found himself often in demand by one side or the other and in later life served in the Imperial Maritime Customs under Sir Robert Hart. Qi Ying was between sixty and seventy years of age and glad of Dr Peter Parker's medical attention. He wrote in 1845,

> Last year I received the Emperor's command to tranquillize the affairs of the foreigners. I therefore made direct inquiry concerning the religion practised by Western men in order to ascertain whether it was corrupt or pure. Having carefully examined (it) all the time I was there, I came to know that what they taught had really nothing in it which was not good. I felt therefore that I ought to memorialize the Emperor, and request that, showing kindness to men from afar, he would not persecute or prohibit it.

When John R Morrison and Samuel Dyer died so tragically in 1843, just as the treaty ports stood open at last, Liang A-fa was very moved. He loved these Westerners who had introduced him to Jesus Christ, and their children. When the young W C Milne first arrived back in China, with Dr Benjamin Hobson, and sent word to A-fa of his coming, A-fa was filled with joy and gratitude to God. He reminisced about his journey in April 1815, fleeing to Singapore with the sparkling Rachel Milne, when William C Milne was one of the twins born to her on board ship. And about her tragic death at Malacca in 1819 and the sad parting from her four children when they were being sent to England – how little William refused to go and, weeping, tried to return home to the Anglo-Chinese College. And how A-fa had to hide his own tears in the privacy of his bedroom. Often through the eventful years he had prayed for those children.

After the opium war (1840–42) Liang A-fa was pastor of the little Church in Canton, only twelve strong. When Hong Kong was developing fast and Chinese from the mainland flooded in, the LMS asked A-fa to go there for a time. He was reluctant. He had

memories of foreign arrogance, of an Englishman trying to ride him
down, on a previous visit. But he went, working with the son of one
of his former printers, Ho Cun-xin. Ho was a graduate of the
Anglo-Chinese College and read the Old and New Testaments in
the original Hebrew and Greek. He was also a most eloquent
preacher. James Legge described how he was listening to Ho one
evening in a crowded church with many standing. As Ho made his
audience live with Job through his sufferings, he stooped as if to pick
up a potsherd to scrape his sores. To Legge's embarrassment he
found himself with his own hand on the floor, until he looked
around and saw scores bent double doing the same. Time and again
Ho, when he became first pastor of the first Chinese church in Hong
Kong, was offered by merchant firms and the government five times
the stipend he received as pastor. He never wavered. As Liang
A-fa looked back and around at progress like this, he was encouraged.

In 1845 A-fa barely escaped with his life when a mob smashed his
rented house and possessions in a Canton suburb. After that he
joined Dr Peter Parker as evangelist at his hospital. By then his
reputation was extensive. Parker, himself famous as medical missionary and periodically as American chargé d'affaires in China,
was invited to address the Senate and House of Representatives. He
chose to speak about Liang A-fa. A commission of the British
House of Commons cited A-fa in 1847. But to A-fa himself it was
enough to preach 'Jesus Christ and him crucified'. The first time he
preached at Parker's hospital, eighty attended. The next time one
hundred and eighty came. And the third time, two hundred. Parker
reckoned that in the first three and a half years over fifteen thousand
heard the gospel in A-fa's meetings.

In the Gordon Museum of Guy's Hospital, London, today there
hangs a set of medical portraits of Parker's Canton patients, painted
by a Chinese pupil of the famous George Chinnery. Those paintings
hung originally in Peter Parker's hospital waiting hall. Liang A-fa
would point to them and preach on the goodness of God who gave
the healing. In 1848 Dr Benjamin Hobson opened the new LMS
Hospital of Merciful Love in Canton. A-fa was an LMS worker, but
perhaps partly because Hobson's wife was Robert Morrison's eldest
daughter, A-fa joined them, preaching to two hundred and fifty
people daily. 'Dear old Liang A-fa', Hobson wrote, 'is listened to
with great attention. (But) he has converted few, very few, and
several whom he baptized many years ago he has seen lapse again

into idolatry and sin.' The servant was not greater than his Lord, nor the native Christian immune from the griefs of the alien missionary. [For Liang A-fa's closing days and final hours, *see* p 168].

'DADDY KUO'
A CHINESE POEM ABOUT CHARLES GUTZLAFF
(Guo Shi-li)[8]

translated by Arthur Waley: *The Opium War through Chinese Eyes:*
George Allen & Unwin (*Appendix, pp 117–8*)

Up to his high dais Daddy Kuo comes.
If you are in trouble he'll get things straight,
If you have been wronged he'll come to the rescue,
If you have got into difficulties he'll arrange things for you.
He's a master at speaking the Chinese language,
There is not an ideogram he cannot read.
Daddy Kuo is nothing short of a genius!

Big trouble about a bull,
Small trouble about a chicken –
He'll settle the case with a pen
    that seems to have wings!
And sooner will the Southern Hills move
    than this decision be altered.

On his dais he sits passive and majestic,
While the mob throngs below.
He has no scribes to assist him,
There are no papers on his desk;
Yet never has the business of the court been handled
    so swiftly as by Daddy Kuo.

From down at the side of the dais
Someone cried out that he has been wronged;
A fellow from who knows where came to his house
    and extorted money from him.
Directly he hears it, Daddy Kuo, without another word,
Picks up his stick, climbs down from the dais, and
    waddles off into the town.

APPENDICES

A moment later he reappears, dragging the culprit along,
Ties him up, bears his back and gives him
      fifty with the lash.
The man who made the complaint,
Goes home delighted, trusses a pair of fowls
And sacrifices them to heaven. ....*

Daddy Kuo has come,
He is going up on to his dais.
Trouble or no trouble, day after day the people
      press and throng.
Yesterday an old peasant passed down the street
On which his office stands.
When he got home he heaved a sigh; his heart was very sad.
'We once had magistrates of our own; where are they now?'

abridged

HUDSON TAYLOR'S 1854–57 ITINERARIES

– excluding brief local 'excursions'

1	1854 Dec. 16–23 (8 days)	SOUTH: Songjiang & Jiaxing	J Edkins & J H T
2	1855 Jan. 25– Feb. 1 (7 days)	EAST & SOUTH: Chuansha, Nanhui & Zhapu, Hangzhou Bay	J H T & Chinese
3	1855 Feb. 16–22 (7 days)	WEST & SOUTH-WEST: Qingpu, Songjiang	A Wylie, J S Burdon & J H T
4	1855 March 19– 26 (8 days)	NORTH-WEST & SOUTH: Jiading, Qingpu, Changzhong (Songjiang)	J H T & W. Parker
5	1855 April 17–28 (12 days)	NORTH: Yangzi estuary, Chongming Is., Dushan Is., Haimen, Lang Shan, Nantong (Tongzhou)	J S Burdon & J H T
6	1855 May 8– June 1 (24 days)	NORTH-WEST: Yangzi reconnaissance; Wusong, Qianjing, Liuhe, Huangjing Fushan, Changshu, Qingdaosha Is., Jiangyin, Jingjiang	J H T & Chinese
7	1855 June 11–25 (15 days)	SOUTH-WEST & SOUTH: Jinshan, Zhapu, Hangzhou Bay, Ningbo (1)	J S Burdon, W Parker & J H T
8	1855 August 24–31 (8 Days)	SOUTH: Hangzhou Bay, Ganpu, Haiyan	W Parker & J H T
9	1855 Oct. 18– Dec. 6 (7 weeks)	NORTH: Chongming; four Yangzi crossings, Xinkaihe, Chongming	J H T & Chinese

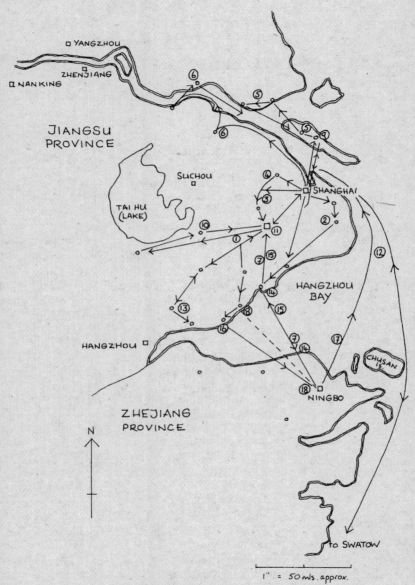

1" = 50 mls. approx.

HUDSON TAYLOR'S TRAVELS IN 1854–57

(See map p 216)

10	1855–56 Dec. 18–Jan. 17 (1 month)	SOUTH-WEST: Tai Hu, Nanxun, Wuzhen	W C Burns, J H T & Chinese
11	1856 Jan. 29– Feb. 12 (?) (2 weeks)	SOUTH-WEST: Songjiang	W C Burns & J H T (? Burdon)
12	1856 March 6– July 14 (4 months)	SOUTH: Shantou (Swatow)	W C Burns & J H T
13	1856 July 22– Aug. 9 (3 weeks)	SOUTH-WEST: Jiashan, Jiaxing, Shimen, Chang'an, Haining and back	J H T alone
14	1856 Aug. 18– Sept. 30 (7 weeks)	SOUTH: Ningbo (2)	J H T alone
15	1856 Sept. 30– Oct. 4 (5 days)	NORTH: Ningbo- Shanghai (overland)	J Jones & son, R Q Way family & J H T
16	1856 October 9–20 (12 days)	SOUTH: Ganpu, Ningbo (3)	J Jones & son, J H T & 'Peter'
17	1857 January 25–30 (6 days)	(NORTH): Ningbo- Shanghai (by sea)	J H T, Jones & Gough families
18	1857 June 16–20 (5 days)	SOUTH: Ningbo (4) (overland)	Jones & Hall families, Miss Magrath & J H T

NOTES

As *The Gleaner*, magazine of the Chinese Evangelization Society, is more accessible than the original manuscripts from which it quotes, references below to CES *Gleaner* are given rather than to OMF Archives. The latter are the source of most of the Hudson Taylor narrative. The CES *Gleaner* appeared under three successive titles, the third being *The Chinese Missionary Gleaner*; but William Milne's magazine, Malacca 1820, was also *The Gleaner*, and the CMS published a *Church Missionary Gleaner*. For clarity we use 'CMS *Gleaner*" and 'CMS *Intelligencer*'.

Page Note

Prologue
19   1   The modern *pinyin* romanisation of Chinese words is normally used, with the Wade-Giles or early postal form in brackets. But a few more familiar names, eg Peking, Nanking, Canton, Hong Kong, Swatow, Amoy, are retained, with the *pinyin* in parenthesis.
20   2   Liang A-fa: colleague of Robert Morrison (*see* Book One, Personalia, Index)
21   3   Stock, E: *The History of the Church Missionary Society*, Vol II, p. 7
21   4   ibid, II. 4–6, 9
21   5   Canton (Guangzhou), Amoy (Xiamen), Nanking (Nanjing)
22   6   CES *Gleaner*, Sept. 1850, p 55
22   7   Dr Mullens, LMS, first *Decennial Statistical Tables*, publ. 1853, showed: 1851 – 91,000 Protestant Christians in India, of whom 15,000 were communicants.
22   8   CES *Gleaner*, March 1850

Chapter 1
24   1   Taylor, J Hudson: *A Retrospect*, pp 15–16
24   2   *Hudson Taylor & China's Open Century*, Book One, pp 352–6
26   3   Quoted in CES *Gleaner*, Dec. 1850
27   4   ibid. Jan. 1851; 'PRESS' meaning the printing press, not the 'media'
29   5   Latourette, K S: Tipple Lectures, 1950, Drew Univ., *These Sought a Country,* Harper & Bros.

·32   6   Oxford Dicty. since 1546; cf Chambers, etc
33   7   Geo. Müller: *see* Book One, Personalia, Bibliography; contrary
          to the popular misconception, Hudson Taylor's principles and
          practice of 'faith' took years to develop.
34   8   Bentley-Taylor, David: *My Love must Wait*, Hodder &
          Stoughton
34   9   Wilhelm Lobscheid: *see* Personalia; CES *Gleaner* 1859–60
          and OMF Archives contain much from Lobscheid's pen
35   10   CES *Gleaner*, 1851, pp 3, 6
38   11   James Taylor, Hudson's father, was always conscious of humble
          origins but, like his mother – from a family of professionals with
          whom he had much to do – Hudson Taylor grew up speaking
          'Southern English', with minor variations the form common to
          professional people throughout the British Isles, and was at
          home in that circle.
38   12   Wooden cages 3' high × 2'6″ × 2' wide, in which the victim was
          cramped and chained for days in a crouching position, while
          carried on a pole through the centre by two men; full details,
          Bridgman, E J G: *Life and Labors of Elijah Coleman Bridgman*,
          pp 114–15
43   13   *Retrospect*, pp 19–21
44   14   CES *Gleaner*, Nov. 1852

Chapter 2
49   1   *Retrospect*, pp 20–1ff; although referring to 1852, Hudson
          Taylor used these words in 1890, retrospectively.
00   2   Hannah Hardey, née Hudson, painted at least two portraits of
          Hudson Taylor. In the best known, property of OMF/UK, he
          looks about seventeen; in another he is wearing spectacles and
          could be twenty, though FHT dated them 1852 and 1850.
56   3   G Müller autobiography; 1905 edn. p 143: May 10–11, 1842
57   4   Manuscript material is being used more freely at this period
          because it demonstrates the principles Hudson Taylor had
          already accepted (while still unsettled about others) and by
          which he was guided throughout life. This period of his
          apprenticeship of faith is important to the story.
59   5   Hudson Taylor is known as much for his enunciation and
          application of these truths as for the work he did and the mission
          he founded. The phrase 'effortless confidence, never betrayed' is
          not quoted from Hudson Taylor but originated in a document
          presented to the OMF Overseas Council, Singapore, *circa* 1960.
59   6   *Retrospect*, p 28
62   7   CES General Committee of sixty members and Board of
          Management of fifteen, included thirty-three ordained
          clergymen (Robert Bickersteth, future Bishop of Ripon and Dr

Arthur Tidman, LMS, among them), four members of the armed forces, four physicians, three Members of Parliament including Hon. A Kinnaird and the Earl of Cavan.

64 8 *Retrospect*, p 30
64 9 Collier, Richard: *The General next to God*, Collins, 1965, pp 22–4
65 10 London Hospital By-laws and Standing Orders, 1856; Morris, E W: *The London Hospital*, Edward Arnold, 1910; Clark-Kennedy, A E: *The London*, Vol II; Lenton, E L: *At Night in a Hospital*, article in *Belgravia*, July, 1879.
68 1I *Retrospect*, p 30ff
69 12 Liang A-fa: *see* p 231 and Appendix 7
69 13 George Piercy: CES *Gleaner*, Nov. 1852, p 52
69 14 Perry, Commodore Matthew Calbraith (1794–1858); treaty of 1854 opened Japan to Western trade.
69 15 Issacher Jacocks Roberts: *see* Book One, Personalia; note his own spelling of Issacher (Neill, S C: *A History of Christian Missions*; Latourette, K S: etc.)
71 16 *Retrospect*, p 31ff
74 17 Also recalled by one of the Howard children years later.
78 18 CES *Gleaner*, Jan.–Feb. 1853
78 19 Hong Xiu-quan saw himself as Heavenly Emperor (*Tian Wang*), and King of Tranquility and Peace (*Tai Ping Wang*), taking the reign title of Heavenly Virtue (*Tian De*) of the Heavenly Kingdom of Tranquility (*Tai Ping Tian Guo*).
79 20 Wuhan today is the metropolis of Hanyang, Wuchang and Hankou combined. The term now used for the Yangzi is Chang Jiang.
82 21 Latourette, K S: *A History of Christian Missions in China*, p 243
82 22 *see* Book One, Appendices 3, 4
82 23 F. O. Records Library: Parliamentary Blue Books, Sir G Bonham to Lord John Russell, Shanghai, March 28, 1853 *et seq*.
84 24 Chinese secret societies: the Triad Society, so-called from their oath which appealed to Heaven, Earth and Man, the trinity of powers in the Chinese universe, began as one of many branches of the earliest, mid-seventeenth-century secret society the *Hong Men*, sworn to the overthrow of the Manchu Qing dynasty. It contained several factions, of which the *San Ho Hui*, the *Xiao Dao* (*Hsiao Tao*) *Hui* or Small (Short) Swords, the name commonly used by Westerners, were most aggressive. The *Ko Lao Hui*, Society of Elders, strongest in central and west China, has been the most influential in recent years. The Triads' undercover ramifications were all along the coasts of East Asia, in Siam and Singapore. They took an active part in the Revolution of 1911 and against the Japanese invaders of the

second World War. Today they are throughout the world, not
least in London.

84 25 *ketou*: *see* Book One, pp 91–2

Chapter 3

85 1 Latourette, K S: *A History of Christian Missions in China*, p 382,
cf. 259

87 2 MRCS: Member of the Royal College of Surgeons of England;
MD: Doctor of Medicine.

92 3 Latourette, K S: Tipple Lectures, 1950

94 4 Gilfillan: CES *Gleaner*, Aug. 1853, p 19

97 5 'accommodations': a form current in USA though lapsed in UK,
as with many forms of speech; cf. Hudson Taylor's use of
'honor', etc.

98 6 Hudson Taylor recalled in China: 'the engine dragged the train
out of sight. How all the circumstances crowd into my memory.'

101 7 BFBS: *see* Appendix 4, note 3

108 8 OMFA-2221: 32°27′S, 104°28′E by JHT's log, used on the back
for a letter home, Shanghai, 24 June 1854.

109 9 No isolated case; a belief common among seamen.

Chapter 4

123 1 Michie, A: *An Englishman in China – as illustrated in the career
of Sir Rutherford Alcock*, Wm. Blackwood & Sons, 1900

123 2 Shanghai: Pott, Hawks, F L: *A Short History of Shanghai*;
Woodcock, G: *The British in the Far East*, *passim*; Fairbank, J K:
Trade and Diplomacy on the China Coast, 1953, 2 vols., *passim*;
Chinese Recorder, *passim*; Lockhart, W: *The Medical
Missionary in China*, *passim*; OMF Archives, etc.

124 3 Fairbank, J K: op. cit. p 159f

124 4 ibid. ff; Woodcock, G: op. cit. p 178

125 5 Fairbank, J K: ibid.

125 6 Robert Fortune: *Journal of the Royal Horticultural Society*, Vol
105, May 1980, pp 219–20

125 7 Tea districts, 'Bohea' mountain region: Xianxia Ling and upper
Qu Jiang area, near borders of Zhejiang, Anhui, Jiangxi and
Fujian.

127 8 Triads: *see* note *re* p 112 no. 24, above

131 9 *see* note, p 112 no. 24

134 10 Boone, M: *The Seed of the Church in China*, St. Andrew Press,
Edinburgh, 1973, p 187

140 11 Stock, E: *The History of CMS*, II. 307; John Hobson 'who had
gone out as a CMS missionary but with the Society's cordial
goodwill had become chaplain to the English community . . .
died at his post . . . 1862.'

145   12   Korea: summarised in Latourette, K S: *A History of the
             Expansion of Christianity*, Vol VI, pp 425–6; Nevius, Helen S C:
             Life of John Livingston Nevius, Revell, 1895 (*see* Books Five and
             Six in the present series).
150   13   *see* Book One, Appendix 7
150   14   Muddy Flat, main sources: Morse, H B: *The International
             Relations of the Chinese Empire*; Fairbank, J K: op. cit.; Pott,
             Hawks: op. cit.; Woodcock, G: op. cit.; Lockhart, W: op. cit.;
             Michie, A: op. cit.; CES *Gleaner*, July 1854, pp 112–13;
             OMFA–221, 222
153   15   The Shanghai Volunteer Corps continued, with a brief
             intermission in 1869, until the second World War. After the
             battle of Muddy Flat a full-time commanding officer was
             seconded from the Bengal Fusiliers in Hong Kong. By 1920 the
             Corps was a citizen army with artillery, armoured car company
             and engineers, and in 1930 numbered 2500 volunteers
             (Woodcock, G: op. cit. pp 46–7).
157   16   Martin, W A P: *A Cycle of Cathay*, p 29; CES *Gleaner*, Sept.
             1853, p 32
157   17   Boone, M: op. cit. p 184

Chapter 5

159   1   Ship *Morrison*: *see* Book One, pp 235–7; *Chinese Repository*,
             Vol VI, 1837, S Wells Williams; *Chinese Recorder*, Vol 7,
             Nov.–Dec. 1876.
160   2   Jonathan Goble in 1870 improvised an armchair on wheels
             drawn by a servant for his invalid wife, and the 'jinricksha'
             (*jen-la-ch'e*, *renlache*, in Chinese) had made its debut
             (Woodcock, G: *The British in the Far East*, p 183).
161   3   Boone, M: *The Seed of the Church in China*, pp 113–14
161   4   Latourette, K S: *A History of Christian Missions in China*, p 479;
             A History of the Expansion of Christianity, VI, p 337
163   5   Boone, M: op. cit. p 110
163   6   Latourette, K S: *Expansion of Christianity*, p 300
164   7   Ph. Winnes: sources thus.
165   8   Liang, A-fa: *see* Appendix; Book One, Index.
167   9   Morrison: *Memoirs*, II. p 494
167   10   Huangbo: 'Whampoa' of C18–19, meaning Yellow Anchorage;
             the town is Huangpu, but to avoid confusion with the river at
             Shanghai, Huangbo is retained here.
169   11   In the autumn the gravemounds between the LMS and 'the
             ramparts of Shanghai' were decked 'luxuriantly' with carpets of
             Anemone japonica. Robert Fortune had described and
             introduced them and many other beautiful plants to Britain only
             eight years previously (1846). Many came from Chusan

(Zhoushan) Island, in his words 'one of the most beautiful islands in the world' (*Journal of Royal Hort. Soc.* Vol 105, May 1980, pp 219–20).

170 12 Exchange: *see* p 270: $1 = 5s6d to 8s6d daily fluctuations in 1854; p 277: £1 = $3 to $8; *see* Book One, Appendix 7, p 373; cf. Phelps Brown & Hopkins: *Seven Centuries of the Prices of Consumables*, Publ. Economica.

173 13 Lockhart, W: *The Medical Missionary in China*, preface; OMFA–1/2 (CES letters L–68/84)

175 14 Taels: the Chinese silver ounce; *see* Book One, Appendix 7, p 373

177 15 CES *Gleaner*, Nov. 1854, p 142, quoting *Hong Kong Gazette*.

178 16 Dyson, Verne: *A Hong Kong Governor*, Macao 1930; CES *Gleaner*, 1854, pp 145–6; 1855, pp 165, 194; Fairbank, J K: *Trade and Diplomacy on the China Coast*, pp 278, 447; Woodcock, G: op. cit. *passim*; *see* Book One, Personalia.

179 17 CES *Gleaner*, Sept. 1854, p 126, quoting CMS Report.

Chapter 6

190 1 'To direct us as to the day on which we are to draw [quarterly], and yet to limit the amount by £s instead of $s is, I am persuaded, the result of your forgetting the fluctuations of the exchange. It may be 5s6d on that day, but it may also be 8s6d and to direct us to draw at that rate renders the amount drawable too small to be sufficient for a quarter.' JHT.

191 2 To suppress all such material from the correspondence would give a false impression of the times and mask the atmosphere of strain and fear in which missionaries constantly lived.

207 3 'Tiffin': from tiff (Engl.), to sip, was still in use to mean a light lunch in mid-twentieth century Shanghai.

210 4 Lockhart, W: *The Medical Missionary in China*; Morse, H B: *International Relations of the Chinese Empire*.

227 5 In Lockhart, op. cit., he gives this event as occurring in 1854, but in fact it was 1855, while Hudson Taylor and the Parkers were living next door (*see* journals of both).

Chapter 7

232 1 CES *Gleaner*, 1855, p 168

232 2 'tradition': cf. Latin, to give up, hand over; op. cit. p 233

233 3 op. cit. Dec. 1854, p 147–51, a full account of the CES case, and of Lagrené's honourable part.

233 4 ibid: dated 28 Dec. 1844

234 5 op. cit. Feb. 1855, pp 163–5

235 6 op. cit. May 1855, p 192

237 7 Michie, A: *An Englishman in China* (Rutherford Alcock)

237 8 Welton, W: CES *Gleaner*, Feb. 1855, p 168, quoting *Church Missionary Record* at length.

237 9 Chinese classic: 'Above, Heaven; below, Hangzhou and Suzhou'.

242 10 Apart from OMF Archives, Lockhart, W: *The Medical Missionary in China*; Morse, H B: *International Relations of the Chinese Empire*.

246 11 'I showed Messrs Gibb, Livingstone & Co. the part of your letter about my credit, whereupon the partner here, Mr. Skinner, said that . . . it was evident our board were not men of business . . .'
'. . . as dollars are the standard we have to go by, you should make this question of exchange a matter of deliberation and let it enter into your arrangements and calculations of expenditure.'
'You will see that the interest of a thousand pounds, fifty pounds, would be much less than our present rent, £120; and that £1000 would cover hospital, chapel and school rents as well in all probability.' At ten pounds a month for rent, fifty pounds were being lost in five months, and a thousand pounds, a very large sum at that time, in only a few years.

252 12 Medhurst, W H: *China: Its State and Prospects*, 1838, p 430f

252 13 Chongming Is:, main sources: Hudson Taylor journal, OMFA–2312 (cf. C413); CES *Gleaner*, August 1855, pp 213–25; CMS *Intelligencer*, 1855, VI. 258ff, J S Burdon journal.

256 14 Tongzhou, now Nantong

257 15 CMS *Intelligencer*, loc. cit.

258 16 ibid.

263 17 List not preserved; Royal Hort. Soc. personal communication, OMFA–231: 'The great majority of climbers climb anti-clockwise (when viewed from above), and with very few exceptions the direction of growth in any particular species is invariable.' Nine species then listed which climb clockwise: Darwin, C: *The Movements and Habits of Climbing Plants*, 1891; Herklots, G A C: *Flowering Tropical Climbers*. The Royal Botanic Garden, Edinburgh ('long a centre of work on Chinese plants') mention the genus *Dioscorea* as also having species twining clockwise, and others anti-clockwise. The old mandarin's observation was not superficial.

Chapter 8

267 1 Bed: planks, bamboos or coconut fibre rope across a wooden frame, covered by a mat and perhaps draped with heavy mosquito curtains, not the airy nets of today.

269 2 Grand Canal: the first, oldest and longest canal in the world, 1290 miles; begun 7th century, Tang dynasty, finished 13th century.

269 3   Ningpo: Martin, W A P: *A Cycle of Cathay*, *passim*; Moule, A E: *The Story of the Cheh-Kiang Mission*, *passim*; *Recollections of the Taiping Rebellion* (OMFA); Nevius, H S C: *Life of J. L. Nevius*; CES *Gleaner*, *passim*; OMF Archives, etc.

274 4   Martin, W A P: op. cit.; Covell, Ralph: *W A P Martin: Pioneer of Progress in China*; 1978, Wm B Eerdmans Publ. Co., the definitive biography.

278 5   Chinese clothes: *see* Index; Medhurst, W H: *A Glance at the Interior of China in 1845*; *China: Its State and Prospects*; Woodcock, G: *The British in the Far East*, p 87; Fairbank, J K: *Trade and Diplomacy on the China Coast*, p 300f, *re* R Fortune.

284 6   CES *Gleaner*, Dec. 1855, p 249

286 7   J H T in Chinese clothes, following Medhurst, W H: op. cit.

291 8   A Williamson: Thompson, R Wardlaw: *Griffith John*, 1907 RTS, *passim*

291 9   G John: ibid.

291 10 ibid. p 22

293 11 29 April 1905, at Hankou

293 12 Fortune: Fairbank, J K: op. cit., p 300f

293 13 Woodcock, G: op. cit., p 99

294 14 Chinese clothes: *see* Book One, Claudio Aquaviva, p 64; Robert Morrison, p 123; cf. Abbé Huc and J Gabet, p 296; Robert Fortune, p 296.

296 15 C Bird: the failure of the Chinese Evangelization Society is common knowledge; the significance of this major factor, Bird's mental health, may not have been adequately recognised by historians; George Pearse attributed the failure primarily to this salaried secretary; lack of space forbids quoting specific peculiarities. (OMFA)

301 16 Illustrations reproduced in *China's Millions*, 1880 *passim* (OMFA)

305 17 Summons: OMFA–2313; CES *Gleaner*, April 1856, p 47

306 18 French: op. cit. p 45

306 19 French flag; *see* also note 26 below.

310 20 Consul: op. cit. pp 37, 44–7; May 1856, p 53

312 21 Committee: and Board, named for first time, CES *Gleaner*, May 1856, p 59, Sixth Annual Report.

312 22 Burns and JHT: Latourette, K S: *The Expansion of Christianity*, VI. 327: 'each found in the other a kindred spirit'.

312 23 Proclamation: CES *Gleaner*, July 1856, pp 84–6, verbatim.

313 24 Mouly: op. cit. July 1856, pp 81–4

314 25 Bowring: op. cit., June 1856, pp 74–5

134 26 French flag: CES *Gleaner*, April 1856, pp 45–6; May, p 53; July, p 84; OMFA–1/3–46/232, 25 August 1856

Chapter 9

319 1 Carlyle: *Scottish and Other Miscellanies*, pp 3–4
319 2 Burns: Burns, Islay: *Memoir of the Rev. William Chalmers Burns*, London, 1885; Latourette, K S: *A History of Christian Missions in China*, pp 257–9, 264, 383, 396; Broomhall, M: *The Chinese Empire*, pp 17, 24, 111, 311; CES *Gleaner*, 1855, p 192; Jan 1856, pp 20–1; April 1858, p 43; Clarke, Agnes L: *China's Man of the Book*, OMF Books (68pp).
320 3 Burns and JHT: OMF Archives: 2321–2; D211, D21–10–12, D22–1–9
321 4 Consul: OMFA–2314
324 5 Paton: Neill, S C: *A History of Christian Missions*, p 354 footnote: Chalmers was one of the first to discard Victorian garb in the field.
324 6 Hudson Taylor habitually named the temples he visited.
330 7 Swatow: OMFA–2314–5
331 8 de la Porte, De la Porte, Delaporte – variously in correspondence and *Gleaner*.
331 9 Coolie trade: Martin, W A P: *A Cycle of Cathay*, p 29f; CES *Gleaner*, June 1856, pp 80–1; July 1857, pp 111–3; Aug. 1857, p 125; June 1858, pp 78–9; Covell, R: *W.A.P. Martin*, pp 97, 214, 227–8
333 10 Lechler: Taylor, Dr & Mrs Howard: *Hudson Taylor* (biography), I. 365 footnote
339 11 The people of Swatow came originally from Fujian province, and 'Tiejiu' dialect is related to Hokkien, the Amoy dialect with its sing-song multiplicity of tones.
341 12 de la Porte *re* JHT: CES *Gleaner*, July 1859, p 86
343 13 Typhoon: from Chinese *tai feng*, *da feng*, great wind; in India from Urdu, *tufan* and Arabic *tafa*, possibly from Greek τυφῶτ (Oxf. Dicty.)

Chapter 10

346 1 The Hon. and Rev Baptist Noel, an Anglican turned independent, orator-evangelist, drew thousands in the Evangelical Revival, Bristol and N. Ireland: OMFA–2316; Orr, J Edwin: *The Second Evangelical Awakening in Britain*, 1949.
347 2 What little is known of John Jones is from CES *Gleaner*, 1856–60; OMFA–1/3 letters to CES; 12/B; 3122; and Hudson Taylor papers, 1856–60, *passim*.
347 3 Agnes Gutzlaff: OMFA–2314, 2411; Charles Gutzlaff rescued six blind girls in Canton, sent two to USA, four to UK (*Encycl. Sinica*, p 51) cited by Latourette, K S: *A History of Christian Missions in China*, p 461

350 4   Paris Conference: CES *Gleaner*, Oct. 1855, p 227, lists 'Continental Associations on behalf of China'.

351 5   Robbed: *Retrospect*, pp 77–90; *China: Its Spiritual Need & Claims:* p 96ff; OMFA–231; CES *Gleaner*, Dec. 1856, pp 143–9

360 6   Burns: OMFA–2321

368 7   Chaozhou, locally called Tiejiu, now Chao'an.

370 8   Chapdelaine: CES *Gleaner*, 1857, p 109

370 9   Che Jin-guang: Legge, H E: *James Legge, Missionary and Scholar*, RTS, 1905.

371 10   Burns: Latourette, K S: op. cit. p 258

371 11   'Peter': *Retrospect*, p 91–3; *China: Its Spiritual Need and Claims*; OMFA, etc.

375 12   *Arrow*: Parliamentary Papers: *A Century of Diplomatic Blue Books*, 152/526; Morse, H B: *International Relations of the Chinese Empire*; Martin, W A P: *A Cycle of Cathay*, p 143ff; Latourette, K S: *A History of Christian Missions in China*, pp 272–3; MacNair, H F: *Modern Chinese History*; CES *Gleaner*, Feb. 1857, pp 25ff

377 13   CES *Gleaner*, loc. cit.

379 14   *casus belli*: summaries, Stock, E: *A History of the CMS*, II. 300–6; Latourette, K S: op. cit. p 273; CES *Gleaner*, 1857, Feb. p 25, July p 110, Dec. pp 174–5

380 15   Merchants: op. cit. April 1857, p 51

381 16   Shanghai: Pott, Hawks: *A Short History of Shanghai*, pp 46–7

381 17   Shaftesbury: *Life of Lord Shaftesbury*, III. 38–46, cited by Stock, E: II. 301

381 18   Ridgeway: CMS *Intelligencer*, 1857, cited loc. cit.

383 19   Society for Suppressing the Opium Trade, 13 Bedford Row, Holborn (CES, 15 Bedford Row): President, the Earl of Shaftesbury; Committee: Henry Venn and Joseph Ridgeway, CMS; Dr Arthur Tidman, LMS; F Trestrail, BMS; S B Bergne, BFBS; Capt. Fishbourne, RN; John Eliot Howard and G F Maberley, CES; etc. listed in CES *Gleaner*, Aug. 1856, p 105; founded January 1856. (Also used: 'Society for the Suppression of the Opium Trade')

384 20   CES *Gleaner*, Dec. 1857, p 167

386 21   RC: not to denigrate (*see* commendation below and elsewhere) but to give facts.

387 22   Pukak: *Chinese Recorder*, 1877, 8. 49–50; CES *Gleaner*, Feb. 1857, pp 27–9

389 23   P & O: Peninsular & Oriental Steam Navigation Company.

389 24   Pukak: British troops rescued German and Swiss missionaries. During World War II German missionaries in Shanghai cared for the needs of British and Americans in Japanese internment

camps, and the needs of Germans in Free China were met by British and American missionaries.

390 25 Pukak: the latter explanation appeals to me as most likely, from personal experience in China and South-East Asia during much of my life. (AJB)

Appendices

397 1 Delegates, sources: Latourette, K S: *A History of Christian Missions in China*, pp 261–3, 266; Boone, M: *The Seed of the Church in China*, pp 130–1; Broomhall, M: *The Chinese Empire*, pp 381–2; *The Bible in China*; CES *Gleaner*, Nov. 1853, p 41

398 2 Lockhart, W: *The Medical Missionary in China*

398 3 CES *Gleaner*, Nov. 1853, p 4, quoting BFBS report.

398 4 CES *Gleaner*, loc. cit.

400 5 Term Question: Martin, W A P: *A Cycle of Cathay*, pp 34–5; *Chinese Recorder*, successive vols., *passim* (decades from 1843).

401 6 Gutzlaff's version: CES *Gleaner*, Nov. 1853, p 42; Jan. 1854, pp 57–9; May 1854, p 91; etc; Broomhall, M: op. cit. pp 380–1

401 7 CES *Gleaner*, Sept. 1853, p 123; the Taiping edition (1853) had the imperial Taiping arms emblazoned on each volume.

407 8 Gutzlaff, as governor for the occupying power in Zhenjiang, Chusan, twice, and Ningbo, naturally made use of Chinese informers and employees – quislings to their own people. Arthur Waley translates denunciations of these men and of the inevitable accusations against Gutzlaff, including slanders inconsistent with attested history and his character.

PERSONALIA: to 1865

ABEEL, David, American Seaman's Friend Society, chaplain; 1830–33 Canton (Guangzhou), Bangkok; 1839–45 Am. Board (ABCFM); 1842 Gulangsu Is., Amoy; initiated women's missionary socs. in UK, USA.

AITCHISON, William, Am. Board; 1854 Shanghai, Pinghu.

ALCOCK, Sir John Rutherford (1809–97); MRCS at 21; 1832–37 Peninsular Wars, Dep.-Director of Hospitals; 1835 partially paralysed; 1843 Diplomatic Service; 1846 HBM consul Fuzhou (Foochow), Amoy, Shanghai; 1861 knighted, HBM minister, Peking.

ALDERSEY, Miss Mary Ann (c 1800–64); 1824–5 learned Chinese from R. Morrison; 1832 Malacca (Melaka); Batavia (Jakarta); 1842 Hong Kong; 1843–59 Nongbo (Ningpo).

ALOPEN, Syrian Nestorian named in Nestorian monument, Xi'an (Sian); AD 635 arr. China.

AMHERST, William Pitt, Lord Amherst; 1816 Peking embassy; 1823 Gov.-Gen. of India; first Burma war; 1826 earldom; d. 1857.

BALFOUR, Capt. George, officer 1840 opium war; 1843–46 first consul Shanghai; Major-Gen., CB, nominated J.H.T. (Hudson Taylor) for FRGS.

BALL, Richard, businessman, Taunton, Somerset; moving spirit in Chinese Association and Chinese Evangelization Society (CES); editor, *Chinese Missionary Gleaner*; author, *Handbook of China*, 1854.

BARCHET, Stephan Paul, German; 1865 Ningbo (Ningpo), sent by J.H.T.; later doctor of medicine.

BAUSUM, J. G., independent, Penang; m. Maria Tarn Dyer, mother of Maria Jane.

BAUSUM, Mrs., 2nd wife of J. G. Bausum; mother of Mary; later m. E. C. Lord (qv).

BAUSUM, Mary, daughter, m. Dr. S. P. Barchet.

BERGER, William Thomas (c 1812–99); London starch manufacturer; J.H.T.'s friend, supporter, co-founder of China Inland Mission (CIM); first Home Sec., benefactor.

BERGNE, S. B., co-Sec. British & Foreign Bible Society.

BIRD, Charles, Gen. Sec. Chinese Evangelization Society (CES).

BLODGET, Henry, DD (1825–1903); Am. Board; 1854 Shanghai; first to preach at Tientsin (Tianjin); translator, Peking.

BOGUE, Dr., principal, Missionary Academy, Gosport, c 1805–20; friend of Dr. Wm. Moseley (qv); nominated R. Morrison, S. Dyer to LMS for China.

BONHAM, Sir George, c 1856 HBM plenipotentiary, Hong Kong, after Bowring (qv).

426   PERSONALIA

BOONE, William Jones, Sr., MD, DD; Am. Prot. Episcopal Church; 1837 Batavia; 1840 Macao; 1842 Gulangsu Is., Amoy, with Abeel; 1844 bishop, Shanghai; d. 1864.

BOWRING, Sir John (1792–1872); HBM consul, Siam, Canton; 1854 plenipotentiary, last Supt. of Trade; Sinologue.

BRADLEY, Daniel Beach, MD, Am. Board (ABCFM); 1840–49 Bangkok, physician to Thai royal family.

BRIDGMAN, Elijah Coleman, DD (1801–61); Am. Board (ABCFM); 1830 Canton; 1832 first editor *Chinese Repository* with R. Morrison; 1843–44 US interpreter-negotiator; 1845–52 translator, Chinese Bible, Delegates' Committee, Shanghai.

BRIDGMAN, Mrs., 1845 Canton; 1847 Shanghai; 1864 Peking.

BROOMHALL, Benjamin (1829–1911); m. Amelia Hudson Taylor; 1878–95 Gen. Sec. China Inland Mission (CIM); editor, *National Righteousness*, organ of anti-opium trade campaign, to 1911 (*see* Maxwell).

BRUCE, Sir Frederick, brother of Lord Elgin (qv); 1858 envoy, rebuffed by emperor; 1859 repulsed at Dagu (Taku), Tianjin.

BURDON, John Shaw (1829–1907); CMS; 1853 arr. Shanghai; pioneer evangelist; m. Burella Dyer (qv); 1862 Peking; 1874 3rd bishop, Hong Kong; Bible translator.

BURGEVINE, H. A., Am. soldier of fortune; after F. T. Ward, commanded Ever-Victorious Army; later joined Taipings.

BURLINGAME, Anson (1820–70); barrister, Congressman, Methodist; 1861–67 US minister, Peking, appointed by Abraham Lincoln; ambassador-at-large for China.

BURNS, William Chalmers (1815–68); first English Presby. to China; 1847 Hong Kong; Amoy; 1855 Shanghai; 1856 Swatow; 1863 Peking; d. Niuchuang; translator of *Pilgrim's Progress*; close friend of J.H.T.

CAREY, William (1761–1834); Baptist Miss. Soc., founder; 1793 India; 1800–30 Prof. of Oriental Languages, Calcutta.

CARLYLE, Thomas (1795–1881); historian, biographer.

CASWELL, Jessie, Am. Board (ABCFM) Bangkok, tutor to Prince Mongkut.

CHALLICE, John, deacon, Bryanston Hall, Portman Square; member, first CIM council.

CHAPDELAINE, Auguste, Paris Mission (Société des Missions Étrangères de Paris); 1856 executed.

CHAPMAN, Robert (1802–1902); High Court attorney; 1832 Strict Baptist minister; 2nd Evang. Awakening evangelist; J.H.T.'s friend.

CHATER, Baptist, with Felix Carey, first Prot. missionary to Burma.

CH'I SHAN, *see* Qi Shan; CH'I YING, *see* Qi Ying; CHIA CH'ING, *see* Jia Qing; CH'IEN LUNG, *see* Qian Long; CHU CHIU-TAO, *see* Zhu Jiu-Dao; CHUNG WANG, *see* Zhong Wang.

CI XI, (Tz'u Hsi) (1835–1908); Empress Dowager; Yehonala, the Concubine Yi; empress regent to Tong Zhi (Chih); 1860–1908 supreme power in China.

CLARENDON, Earl of (1800–70); Foreign Sec. to Lord Aberdeen 1853, Lord Palmerston 1855, Lord Russell 1865, Gladstone 1868.

CLELAND, J. F., LMS, 1850 Hong Kong.

COBBOLD, R. H., CMS, 1848–62, Ningbo (Ningpo); translator, Ningbo romanised vernacular NT.

CONFUCIUS, c 551–479 BC; Chinese philosopher-sage.

COKE, Thomas, Oxford Univ.; Anglican clergyman; 1776–1813, Wesley's colleague; 1786 appealed for missions to New World; first bishop, Am. Methodist Episc. Church; d. 1813 on way to India.

COX, Josiah (d. 1906); Wesleyan Meth. Miss. Soc.; 1852 Canton; 1862 Hankow; 1865 Jiujiang (Kiukiang).

CROMBIE, George, Aberdeen farmer; 1865 J.H.T.'s second recruit, to Ningbo.

DAO GUANG (Tao Kuang); 6th Qing (Ch'ing) emperor, 1820–51; China torn by rebellions.

DAVIES, Evan, LMS Malaya; author, 1845, *China and her Spiritual Claims*; 1846 *Memoir of the Reverend Samuel Dyer*.

DAVIS, Sir John Francis, Bart., Chief, Hon. East India Co., Canton; friend of R. Morrison; 1844 HBM plenipotentiary, after Pottinger (qv); Supt. of Trade, Hong Kong.

DEAN, William (1806–77); Am. Baptist; 1834 & 1864 Bangkok; 1842 Hong Kong.

DELAMARRE, Abbé, Paris Mission; 1858–60 interpreter, French treaty; falsified Chinese version.

DE LA PORTE, Dr., French Prot. medical; 1847–57 Swatow, Double Island.

DENNISTON, J. M., Presby. minister, London, Torquay; associated with W. C. Burns revivals and J.H.T. founding CIM; co-founder Foreign Evangelist Soc.

DENT, Thomas and Launcelot, high-living merchant ship-owners; chief rivals of Jardine, Matheson.

DE TOURNON, Charles Maillard (1668–1710); papal legate to China 1705; antagonised Kang Xi (K'ang Hsi) over Confucian rites.

DEW, Capt. Roderick, RN; 1862 commander, Ningbo front, against Taipings.

DOUGLAS, Carstairs, LL. D (1830–77); English Presby. Mission; 1855 Amoy; introduced J. L. Maxwell (qv) to Formosa (Taiwan); knew J.H.T. Shanghai, London.

DYER, John, Sec., Royal Hosp. for Seamen, Greenwich; 1820 Chief Clerk to Admiralty.

DYER, Samuel (1804–43); son of John Dyer; Cambridge law student; LMS; m. Maria Tarn, daughter of LMS director; 1827 Penang; 1829–35 Malacca; 1835–43 Singapore; d. Macao.

DYER, Samuel, Jr., Burella and Maria Jane, children of Samuel and Maria Tarn Dyer; Burella m. J. S. Burdon (qv); Maria m. J.H.T.

EDKINS, Joseph (1823–1905); LMS evangelist, translator, philologist, expert in Chinese religions, author, well-known to Taiping rulers; 1848–60 Shanghai; 1860–61 Shandong, Yantai and Tianjin; 1861 Peking.

EITEL, E. J., PhD; Basel Mission, S. China, 1862–65; 1865–78 LMS Peking; Sinologue; Dec. 1862 baptised first Peking Prot. Christian; 1878 *et seq* adviser to Hong Kong govt.

ELGIN, Earl of, son of Thomas Bruce, 7th earl (Elgin marbles); 1857 Indian mutiny; 1858 envoy, Treaty of Tientsin; treaty with Japan; 1860 second opium war, captured Peking, burned Summer Palace, negotiated Peking Convention.

ELLIOT, Capt. Charles, RN; 1835 third Supt. of Trade, Canton; 1836 Chief Supt.; confronted Commissioner Lin (qv); 1840–41 political chief in first phase of first opium war; HBM plenipotentiary, negotiated Convention of Chuanbi.

ELPHINSTONE, J. T., president, Select Committee, East India Co., Canton; friend of R. Morrison; later Member of Parliament.

FAULDING, Jane E. (1843–1904); m. J.H.T. 28 Nov. 1871; 1877–78 led CIM team, Shanxi famine relief; first Western women inland.

FISHBOURNE, Capt. RN, rescued Amoy victims; strong supporter of missions and anti-opium soc.; later, evangelist.

FLINT, James, East India Co. official; petitioned Qian Long (Ch'ien Lung) emperor for trading rights; imprisoned.

FORTUNE, Robert, Royal Hort. Soc. botanist; 1843 arr. China; explorations 1843–46, 1848–51, 1853–56, 1861–62, disguised as a Tartar; supplied India with tea-plants.

FRANCKE, August Hermann, pietist; 1696 founded Orphan Houses, extensive by C 19; prof. divinity, Halle Univ. Germany; d. 1727.

FULLER, W. R., first United Meth. Free Ch. missionary to China; 1864 Ningbo; trained by J.H.T.

GAMBLE, William, Am. Presby. Mission Press; 1858 Ningbo; 1860 Shanghai; friend of J.H.T., CIM, received Lammermuir party.

GENÄHR, Ferdinand, Rhenish (Barmen) Mission; 1847 Hong Kong, Guangdong (Kwangtung) under C. Gutzlaff; m. R. Lechler's sister; one of the first Prot. missionaries to reside outside treaty ports; d. 1864.

GENGHIS KHAN (1162–1227); Mongol conqueror of N. China, W. Russia, Central Asia, N.W. India to Adriatic; military genius.

GLADSTONE, William Ewart (1809–98); three times prime minister, 1868–97.

GOBLE, Jonathan, Am. marine under Commodore Perry, to Japan as missionary; 1870 invented rickshaw.

GODDARD, Josiah, Am. Baptist, Bangkok; 1848 Ningbo.

GORDON, Col. Charles George (1833–85); 1860 Tianjin, Peking campaign; 1862 Shanghai, commanding Ever-Victorious Army; 1864

Taiping Rebellion ended; honoured by emperor and Queen Victoria (CB); 1865–71 London; donor to J.H.T.; 1880 adviser to Chinese govt.; 1883–5 Major-Gen., Sudan.

GOUGH, Frederick F. DD; CMS 1849–62 Ningbo; 1862–69 London, Ningbo vernacular NT romanised edition, with J.H.T.; 1869 Ningbo; m. Mary Jones (qv).

GRANT, General Sir Hope, 1860 commander, land forces, under Lord Elgin.

GROS, Baron, 1860 French plenipotentiary, second opium war, Peking treaty.

GROVES, Anthony Norris (1795–1853); early exponent of 'faith principle'; brother-in-law of G. Müller; missionary to Baghdad; initiator of Brethren movement.

GUINNESS, M. Geraldine (1862–1949); daughter of H. Grattan Guinness (qv); m. F. Howard Taylor (qv); author, biography of J.H.T.

GUINNESS, H. Grattan. DD; gentleman-evangelist, 1859 Ulster revival; J.H.T.'s friend; founded East London Institute, trained 1,330 for 40 societies of 30 denominations.

GUTZLAFF, Charles (Karl Frederich August) (1803–51); 1826–28 Netherlands Miss. Soc., Batavia (Jakarta), Java; 1828 independent, Bangkok; m. Miss Newell, Malacca, first single Prot. woman missionary to E. Asia; 1831–35 voyages up China coast; 1839 interpreter to British; 1840 & '42 governor of Chusan Is.; 1842 interpreter-negotiator, Nanking Treaty; 1843–51 Chinese Sec. to British govt. Hong Kong; initiated Chinese Union, Chinese Associations and missions.

HALL, Capt. Basil, RN; 1816 voyage up China coast, Korea, Ryukyu Is.; author, *Narrative of a Voyage* . . .

HALL, Charles J.; 1857 CES missionary Ningbo; 1860 Shandong; d. 1861.

HALL, William, deacon, Bryanston Hall, Portman Square; member of first CIM council.

HALL, William Nelthorpe, Methodist New Connexion; 1860 Tianjin; d. 1878.

HAMBERG, Theodore, Basel Mission; 1847 Hong Kong, under Gutzlaff (qv); with R. Lechler to Guangdong (Kwangtung) Hakkas; first Prot. missionaries to reside outside treaty ports; d. 1854.

HANSPACH, August, Chinese Evangelization Soc. of Berlin (Berlin Missionary Soc. for China); 1855 Hong Kong; 11 years extensive inland travel.

HAPPER, Andrew P., DD; Am. Presby. 1844 Macao; 1847 Canton.

HARDEY, Richard, early photographer, Hull; m. Hannah Hudson, portraitist.

HARDEY, Robert, surgeon, Hull Infirmary & medical college; J.H.T. his assistant.

HART, Sir Robert (b. 1835); 1854 Ningbo, consular interpreter; 1857 Canton; 1863 Inspector-General, Chinese Imperial Maritime Customs.

HOBSON, Dr. Benjamin, LMS; 1841 Macao; 1843 Hong Kong; 1846 Canton; 1856 Shanghai.

HOBSON, J., CMS, chaplain to Br. community, Shanghai; J.H.T.'s friend.

HODSON, Thomas & John, sons of Mary, née Hudson; J.H.T.'s cousins.

HOLMES, J. L., Am. Southern Baptist; 1860 pioneer of Shandong Yantai (Chefoo); killed.

HONG XIU-QUAN (Hung Hsiu-ch'üan) (1813–64); Taiping Wang, leader of Taiping rebellion; 1837 visions and fantasies; 1844 began preaching; 1846 with Hong Ren (Hung Jen) (qv) taught by I. J. Roberts (qv); 1849 led Worshippers of Shangdi; 1851 began hostilities; 1852 assumed imperial title; 1853–64 Nanking; 1853 advance to Tianjin halted; 1864 suicide.

HONG REN, cousin of Hong Xiu-quan; known as Gan Wang, Shield King; ex-evangelist.

HOPE, Vice-Admiral Sir James; 1860–62 naval commander-in-chief, China; 1861 negotiated 'year of truce' with Taipings; 'opened' Yangzi River to foreign shipping.

HOWARD, John Eliot, FRS; Fellow of Linnaean Soc.; manufacturing chemist; early leader of Brethren, Tottenham; J.H.T.'s close friend.

HOWARD, Robert, brother of J.E.; also chemist, leader of Brethren.

HOWARD, Luke, meteorologist, father of J.E. and R.

HSI SHENG-MO, see Xi; HSÜ KUANG-CH'I see Xu; HSIEN FENG see Xian.

HUC, Abbé Evariste Régis, travelled with Gabet 1844–46, Mongolia, Tibet; 1846 in Lhasa, deported; 1857 author, *Christianity in China, Tartary and Thibet*; d. 1860.

HUDSON, Benjamin Brook (c 1785–1865); Wesleyan Methodist minister; portraitist; grandfather of J.H.T.

HUDSON, Amelia (1808–81); m. James Taylor; mother of J.H.T.

HUNG HSIU-CH'UAN, see Hong Xiu-quan; HUNG JEN see Hong Ren.

INNES, James, obstreperous ship's captain, Jardine, Matheson.

JARDINE, William, surgeon, merchant ship-owner; 1841 Member of Parliament; d. 1843.

JIA QING (Chia Ch'ing); (1796–1820); mediocre 5th emperor of Qing (Ch'ing) dynasty.

JOHN, Griffith (1831–1912); LMS; 1855 Shanghai; pioneer evangelist; 1861 Hankow; 1863 Wuchang; 1867 Hanyang.

JOHNSON, Stevens, Am. Board, Bangkok; 1847 Fuzhou (Foochow)

JONES, John; CES 1856–57 Ningbo; independent, 1857–63; early exponent of 'faith principle', influenced J.H.T.; d. 1863.

JONES, Mary, wife of John; 1863–66 with Hudson Taylors, London; 1866 m. F. F. Gough.

JUDSON, Adoniram (1788–1850); Am. Board, became Baptist; 1813 pioneer with wife in Burma.

JUKES, Andrew, East India Co. officer; deacon, Anglican Church; c 1842 independent minister, Brethren congregation; 1866 built Church of St. John the Evangelist, Hull.

KANG XI (K'ang Hsi); (1622–1722); 2nd Qing (Ch'ing) dynasty emperor, for 60 years; aged 7 dismissed his regents; one of China's strongest rulers; pro-Christian; 1692 Edict of Toleration; 1700 pro-Jesuit, anti-Rome.

KEW A-KANG (Chiu A-Kung), see Qiu A-gong.

KIDD, Samuel (1799–1848) LMS; 1824–32 Malacca; third after Morrison and Milne, before Dyer, Tomlin; Prof. of Chinese Language and Literature, University College, London.

KING, Charles W., Am. merchant ship-owner, partner of D. W. C. Olyphant (qv).

KINGDON, Edwin F., BMS recruit trained by J.H.T.; 1864 Shandong, Yantai.

KLOEKERS, Hendrick Z., Netherlands Chinese Evangelization Soc.; 1855–58 Shanghai; 1862 BMS; 1862–65 Shandong, Yantai.

KNOWLTON, Miles J. (1825–74); Am. Baptist; 1854 Ningbo; friend of J.H.T.

KONG, Prince (Prince Kung); (1833–98); brother of Xian Feng (Hsien Feng) emperor; 1860 et seq, leading statesman.

KREYER, Carl T., Am. Baptist Missionary Union; 1866 Hangzhou (Hangchow); lent his home to Lammermuir party.

KUBLAI KHAN, Mongol ruler, 1216–94; conquered Song (Sung) dynasty, founded Yuan (Yüan) dynasty; ruled all China, Central Asia, Persia, E. Europe.

LAGRENÉ, M., French envoy, 1843 treaty; negotiated edicts of toleration by Qi Ying (Ch'i Ying), for Prots. as well as RCs.

LAOZI (Laotze), 'the Old One'; alleged, possibly mythical, originator of Taoism, fifty years before Confucius.

LATOURETTE, Kenneth Scott, late Willis James and Sterling Prof. of Missions and Oriental History, Yale Univ.; author, see bibliography.

LAUGHTON, R. F., BMS; 1863 Shandong, Yantai.

LAY, George Tradescant, naturalist; 1836–39 agent for Bible Soc. (BFBS); 1840–42 interpreter, opium war; HBM consul, Canton, Fuzhou (Foochow), Amoy; co-founder of 'Medical Missionary Soc. in China'; d. 1845, Amoy.

LECHLER, Rudolf (1824–1928); Basel Mission pioneer; 1847 Hong Kong, Guangdong (Kwangtung) Hakkas, under Gutzlaff, with Hamberg (qv); 52 years in China, to 1899.

LEGGE, James, DD, LL D (1815–97); LMS; 1839–43 Anglo-Chinese College, Malacca; 1843–70 Anglo-Chinese College, Hong Kong; translator, Chinese classics; 1877–97, Prof. of Chinese, Oxford Univ.

LEWIS, W. G., Baptist minister, Westbourne Grove Ch., London; urged J.H.T. to publish *China's Spiritual Need and Claims*.

LI HONG-ZHANG (Li Hung-chang) (1823–1901); holder of the highest academic degrees, highest honours after defeat of Taiping rebels; the Grand Old Man of China, leading statesman until death.

LIANG A-FA (1789–1855); Canton engraver-printer; 1815 to Malacca with W. Milne; 1819 Canton, colporteur; arrested, flogged; 1821 Malacca; 1828 Canton; 1834 arrested, escaped, betrayed, escaped; 1839 returned, tolerated by Lin Ze-xu (qv); first Prot. pastor; 1845 mobbed; d. 1855.

LIANG A-DE (Liang A-teh); son of A-fa; translator to Lin Ze-xu (qv); interpreter for British, Nanking Treaty; Chinese Imperial Maritime Customs.

LIGHT, Francis, captain of merchantman; 1786 occupied Penang Is., founded Georgetown.

LIN ZE-XU (Lin Tze-hsü), gov. gen. of Hubei-Hunan; viceroy-commissioner, Canton, to control opium traffic; 1839 strong-arm methods contributed to war, 1840–41; disgraced, exiled.

LINDSAY, Capt. Hugh Hamilton, RN; 1832 commanded ship *Lord Amherst*, on survey of China coast, Korea, with Gutzlaff (qv).

LOBSCHEID, Wilhelm, Rhenish (Barmen) Mission to China; 1852, first medical 'agent' of Chinese Evang. Soc., Hong Kong; Guangdong (Kwangtung); 1855 interpreter, *Powhattan* voyage to Japan.

LOCKHART, William (1811–96); surgeon, FRCS; LMS; 1839 Macao; 1840 and 1843 Shanghai; 1840–41 Chusan with Gutzlaff; first British missionary Hong Kong, 1848 mobbed in 'Qingpu (Tsingpu) Outrage', Shanghai; 1861 first Prot. missionary in Peking.

LORD, Edward C.; 1847 first Am. Baptist, Ningbo; 1863 independent Am. Bapt. Mission, Ningbo; 1877 still there; J.H.T.'s friend.

LOWRIE, Walter, US senator, resigned to become Sec. of Am. Presby. Mission.

LOWRIE, William (Walter, in some sources), son of senator; 1845 Am. Presby. Mission, Ningbo; 1847 drowned by pirates.

LOWRIE, Reuben (Robert, in some sources), took brother's place; 1854 Shanghai.

MACARTNEY, Lord, 1793 embassy to Peking, failed.

MACGOWAN, Dr. D. J., Am. Baptist physician; 1843 Ningbo.

MAGELLAN, Ferdinand (*c* 1480–1521); Portuguese explorer; served Spain; via Cape Horn to Leyte, Philippines; killed, but expedition completed first voyage round world.

MARJORIBANKS, Charles, ex-Chief, East India Co., Canton; 1843 Member of Parliament; friend of R. Morrison.

MARA, John, United Meth. Free Ch., trained by J.H.T.; 1865 Ningbo.

MARSHALL, Thomas D., minister, Bryanston Hall, Portman Square.

MARSHMAN, Joshua (1768–1837); 1799 with Carey, Serampore; 1811 completed Chinese NT; 1822–23 OT.

MARTIN, William Alexander Parsons, DD, LL D; (1827–1916); Am.

Presby. Mission; educationalist; 1850–60 Ningbo; 1862 Peking; 1869 president, Tungwen Imperial College; 57 years in China; book on Christian evidence had huge circulation, China, Japan.

MARTYN, Henry (1781–1812); 1801 Senior Wrangler, Fellow of St John's, Camb.; 1806 Calcutta; 1810 completed Hindustani (Urdu) NT; 1811 Shiraz, Persia; 1815–16 Martyn's Persian NT published.

MATHESON, Donald, merchant partner, Jardine, Matheson; 1837 Hong Kong; converted, resigned 1849 over opium traffic; active in Presby. Missions; 1892 chairman, Soc. for the Suppression of the Opium Trade.

MATHESON, James, heir to baronetcy; merchant ship-owner, partner of Jardine (qv); Member of Parliament.

MATHIESON, James L., gentleman-evangelist in C 19 revivals; active in anti-opium campaign (*see* Maxwell).

MAXWELL, James L., MD; (1836–1921); English Presby. Mission; 1863 Amoy; 1865 pioneer, Taiwan; 1885 founder, Medical Missionary Association (London); 1888 co-founder with B. Broomhall (qv), 'Christian Union for the Severance of the Connection of the British Empire with the Opium Traffic'.

McCARTEE, Dr. D. B., MD; Am. Presby; 1844 Ningbo; adopted orphan became first Chinese woman doctor educated in USA.

McCLATCHIE, Thomas, CMS; 1845 Shanghai with George Smith (qv).

MEADOWS, James, J. (1835–1914); J.H.T.'s first recruit to Ningbo Mission, 1862, and CIM; wife Martha d. 1863.

MEADOWS, Thomas Taylor, heroic interpreter; HBM vice-consul, Ningbo; certified J.H.T.'s marriage.

MEDHURST, Walter Henry, DD; (1796–1857); LMS printer; 1817–20 Malacca; 1820–21 Penang; 1822–43 Batavia, Java; 1826 toured Chinese settlements on Java coast; 1835 voyage of *Huron* up China coast; 1843 Shanghai, interpreter-adviser to Br. consul G. Balfour (qv); 1845 inland journey in disguise; 1848 victim of 'Qingpu (Tsingpu) Outrage', Shanghai; translator, Delegates' Committee, 1852 Chinese Bible; doyen of Br. community.

MEDHURST, Sir Walter Henry, son of W. H. Medhurst DD; HBM consul, and ambassador, Peking.

MELBOURNE, Viscount, Prime Minister, 1835–41; chief adviser to Queen Victoria.

MENGKU KHAN, Mongol ruler, grandson of Genghis Khan; tolerant of all religions, attended Nestorian worship.

MÉRITENS, Baron de, with Abbé Delamarre (qv) interpreter to Baron Gros (qv) 1860.

MEZZABARBA, 1720 papal legate after Mgr de Tournon; concessions on Chinese rites repudiated by Rome.

MILNE, William, DD; (1785–1822); 1813 Macao; 1815–22 Malacca; 1818 Anglo-Chinese College, Malacca; Hon. DD Glasgow; 1819 baptised

Liang A-fa (qv); 1822 completed OT translation with R. Morrison.

MILNE, William C., son of William and Rachel Milne; 1842 Chusan Is.; 1842–43 Ningbo; 1846 Shanghai; 1857 travelling sec., Chinese Evang. Soc.

MONTE CORVINO, John of, first RC priest to China; dep. 1289, arr. 1294; 1307 archbishop of Cambalac (Peking); d. c 1328–33.

MORGAN, R. C., editor, *The Revival (The Christian)*; director, Marshall, Morgan & Scott; co-founder, Foreign Evangelist Soc.

MORRISON, Robert, DD, FRS; (1782–1834); LMS; 1807 Macao, Canton; 1813 completed Chinese NT; 1814 first convert; 1816 interpreter-negotiator to Lord Amherst embassy; 1817 Hon. DD Glas.; 1819 completed OT with Milne (qv); 1822 completed Chinese dictionary; 1824 FRS etc.; 1834 interpreter to Lord Napier; d. Aug. 1.

MORRISON, John Robert (1814–43); son of R. Morrison; aged 16 official translator, East India Co.; Canton; 1842 interpreter-negotiator to Sir H. Pottinger, Treaty of Nanking; 1843 Chinese Sec. to Gov. of Hong Kong; chairman, first LMS and General Missions Conferences, Hong Kong.

MOSELEY, William, LL D; Congregational Minister; 1798 found in British Museum MS of RC Chinese translation of NT books; urged translation of whole NT; introduced R. Morrison to LMS and to Dr. Bogue (qv).

MOULE, Arthur Evans, CMS; 1861 Ningbo; 1876 Hangzhou (Hang-chow); archdeacon.

MOULE, George Evans, CMS; 1858 Ningbo; 1864 Hangzhou (Hang-chow); 1880 bishop in Mid-China.

MOULY, Mgr. Joseph Martial, Lazarist; 1841 vicar-apostolic, Mongolia &c; sent Abbé Huc and Gabet on Tibet journey; 1853 deported; 1856 vicar-apostolic N. Zhili (Chihli) (Peking); 1861 obtained territorial concessions for RC church.

MUIRHEAD, William, DD; (1822–1900); LMS; evangelist, renowned preacher, translator; 1846–90 (53 years) at Shanghai; 1848 victim of 'Qingpu (Tsingpu) Outrage', Shanghai.

MÜLLER, George (1805–98); German-born; married sister of A. N. Groves (qv); 1832 read biography of A. H. Francke; 1835 founded Orphan Homes, Bristol, 2,000 children, financed 'by faith in God'.

NAPIER, Lord; 1834, William IV's envoy to China; Chief Supt. of Br. Trade; d. 1834.

NEATBY, Thomas, FRCS; boyhood friend of J.H.T.; assistant to James Taylor and Robert Hardey (qv); surgeon, St Bartholomew's hospital; biblical expositor.

NESTORIUS, bishop of Constantinople until Council of Ephesus, AD 431; d. 451; Nestorianism extended to Syria, Persia, India; AD 635 to China (*see* A-lo-pen); Nestorian monument erected 781, discovered 1625 near Xi'an (Sian).

NEUMANN, Robert, Berlin Miss. Soc. for China; colleague of Gutzlaff; 1850–54 Hong Kong, Guangdong (Kwangtung).

NEVIUS, John Livingston (1832–93); Am. Presby. Mission; 1854 Ningbo; 1859 Hangzhou (Hangchow); 1860 Japan; 1861 Shandong (Shantung); Bible translator, author; 1890 Korea, exponent of 'indigenous church' policy.

NOMMENSEN, Ludwig Ingwer, Rhenish (Barmen) Mission; 1862 pioneer of Bataks, Sumatra.

NORRIS, Sir William, Chief Justice, High Court, Straits Settlements; friend of Dyers (qv).

NOTMAN, Jean, recruit sent by J.H.T. to Ningbo, 1864; assistant to Mrs Bausum (qv).

OLYPHANT, D. W. C., Am. Presby. merchant ship-owner, partner of C. W. King (qv); 1826 Canton, donated press and office for *Chinese Repository*; donated 51 trans-Pacific passages for missionaries; d. 1851.

PALMERSTON, Viscount (1784–1865); Tory, Whig statesman, 1808 –65; 1830–51 periodically Foreign Sec.; 1855, 1859–65 Prime Minister.

PARKER, H. M., Am. Episc.; Shangdong (Shantung); 1861 martyred Yantai (Chefoo).

PARKER, Dr. John, brother of Dr. Wm. Parker; 1863 Ningbo, independent; 1865 United Presby. Ch. of Scotland, Ningbo.

PARKER, Dr. Peter, MD; (1804–88); Am. Board (ABCFM); 1834 Canton; first medical missionary in China (not first western physician); 1835 Ophthalmic Hospital; 1838 formed 'Medical Missionary Soc. in China'; 1843–44, semi-skilled interpreter-negotiator for US treaty; 1850 General Hosp., Canton; several times US chargé d'affaires and minister.

PARKER, Dr. William, CES 1854–63; Shanghai, Ningbo.

PARKES, Sir Henry (Harry) S.; *c* 1850 HBM interpreter (consular cadet); 1860, hero of Tientsin-Peking campaign; 1856 vice-consul, Canton; knighthood; HBM minister, Peking.

PEARCY, George, Am. Southern Bapt., Shanghai; cholera at Shanghai, nursed by J.H.T.

PEARSE, George, London stockbroker; CES foreign sec.; co-founder Foreign Evangelist Soc.; friend and adviser of J.H.T.; later missionary to N. Africa, initiated N. Africa Mission.

PENNEFATHER, William, vicar, Christ Church, Barnet; later Mildmay, N. London; convener, Barnet and Mildmay conferences; hymn-writer, friend of J.H.T.

PERRY, Commodore Matthew C., 1853–54 Am. treaty with Japan.

PIERCY, George; 1850 to China at own expense; 1851 Canton; 1853 adopted by Wesleyan Meth. Miss. Soc.; joined by Josiah Cox (qv).

POLO, Nicolo and Matteo; 1260 to China; 1267 welcomed by Kublai Khan; 1269 arr. Venice with Khan's request to Pope for 100 wise men; 1271 to China with Marco (qv).

POLO, Marco (1245–1324); son of Nicolo; 1275 Peking, served Kublai

Khan; 1275 (aged 30) gov. of Yangzhou (Yangchow); official journeys to S.W. China, Burma, Indo-China, India; 1292 with Nicolo and Matteo escorted royal princess by sea to Persian Gulf and N. Persia; to Venice via Black Sea; 1298 commanded ship in war with Genoa, imprisoned with a writer, dictated travels.

POTT, F. L. Hawks, DD; Am. Prot. Episc.; president, St John's Univ., Shanghai; historian of Shanghai.

POTTIER, François, founder 1756, West China mission of Soc. des Missions Étrangéres de Paris.

POTTINGER, Sir Henry; 1841 HBM plenipotentiary, Supt. of Trade, succeeded Capt. Charles Elliot; concluded first opium war; 1842 'diplomatic honeymoon' with Qi Ying (qv), negotiated Nanking Treaty.

QIAN LONG (Ch'ien Lung) (1736–96); 4th emperor, Qing (Ch'ing) dynasty.

QI SHAN (Ch'i Shan); 1840 gov. of Zhili (Chihli); viceroy of Canton after Lin Ze-xu (qv); cashiered, exiled, after Convention of Chuanbi (Ch'üanpi).

QIU A-GONG (Ch'iu A-kung; Kew A-gang); Christian printer, Malacca, with Liang A-fa (qv).

QI YING, 1842 succeeded Qi Shan; initiated 'diplomatic honeymoon', negotiated Nanking Treaty; gov. of Canton; issued edict of toleration.

QUARTERMAN, J. W., Am. Presby.; 1847–57 Ningbo; smallpox, nursed by J.H.T.; d. 1857.

RADCLIFFE, Reginald, solicitor, gentleman-evangelist of second evangelical awakening; friend of J.H.T.

RADSTOCK, Lord, evangelical Anglican evangelist in aristocratic Russian, E. European society; closely associated with Brethren; friend of J.H.T.

RAFFLES, Sir Thomas Stamford (1781–1826); 1805 Penang; 1811–16 lieut-gov., Java; 1817 knighted; 1817 et seq gov. of Sumatra; 1819 founded Singapore; 1820–24 gov. Singapore and Bencoolen, Sumatra.

RANKIN, Henry V., Am. Presby.; 1847 Ningbo; co-translator of Ningbo vernacular NT.

REED, Hon. W. B., US ambassador, Peking, 1858–60.

RICCI, Matteo/Matthew (1552–1610); Soc. of Jesus; 1582 Macao; 1585 –89 Zhaoqing, Zhaozhou (Chaoch'ing, Chaochow); 1601 Peking; by 1605 had converts at Court and Hanlin Academy, 200 neophytes; enjoyed confidence of Kang Xi (K'ang Hsi); policies repudiated by papacy.

ROBERTS, Issacher Jacocks (not R.J.R. as in some sources); Am. Bapt.; 1833–67 Canton, Shanghai; 1837 Canton, taught Hong Xiu-quan (qv), Taiping leader; 1842 first missionary in Hong Kong, with J. L. Shuck.

RUSSELL, William Armstrong, CMS; 1847 Ningbo; 1872–79 first bishop of N. China; d. 1879.

SCHALL von BELL, Johann Adam (1591–1666); Soc. of Jesus; astronomer; 1622 Peking; 1645 president, Imperial Board of Astronomers; chaplain to imperial palace.

SCHERESCHEWSKY, Samuel Isaac Joseph (1831–1906); converted rabbi; Am. Prot. Episc.; 1839 Shanghai; 1862 Peking; 1877 bishop; 1881 paralysed; for next 25 years China's greatest Bible translator.

SCHMIDT, Charles; 1864 officer of Ever-Victorious Army, converted through James Meadows; became missionary in Suzhou (Soochow); friend of J.H.T.

SEYMOUR, Admiral Sir Michael, commander-in-chief, East Asia; 1856 blockaded, bombarded, occupied Canton; deported viceroy, Ye Ming-sheng (qv).

SHEPHERD, William, one of Wesley's first seven travelling preachers; daughter (? grand-daughter) m. John Taylor, J.H.T.'s grandfather.

SHUCK, J. Lewis, first Am. Baptist in China proper; 1836 Macao; with I. J. Roberts (qv), first missionary in Hong Kong; member of Delegates' Committee, 1852 Bible.

SHUN ZHI (Shun Chih) first Qing (Ch'ing) dynasty emperor, 1644–61.

SISSONS, Elizabeth, rejected J.H.T.'s proposals.

SKINNER, Anne, fiancée of George Crombie (qv); 1865 Ningbo.

SMITH, George, CMS; China survey, 1844; 1846 returned with T. McClatchie (qv); 1849–64 first bishop of Victoria, Hong Kong.

SOONG (conventional, for Song), Methodist minister, m. descendant of Paul Xu (Hsü) daughters m. Sun Yat-sen, Chiang Kai-shek, H. H. Kung.

SOOTHILL, W. E., United Methodist Free Church, Ningbo, Wenzhou (Wenchow); educationalist, author, translator; 1920–35 Prof. of Chinese, Oxford.

STACEY, Miss, one-time Quaker, member of Brook Street chapel, Tottenham; long a friend of J.H.T.

STALLYBRASS, Thomas, Mongolian-speaking son of Edward Stallybrass, LMS missionary to Buriat Mongols, 1817–44; offered to CES.

STAUNTON, Sir George Thomas, Bart., aged 15 to China; 1793 interpreter, East India Co. and Lord Macartney's embassy; Chief of East India Co., Canton; 1816 First Commissioner on Lord Amherst's embassy.

STAVELEY, Sir Charles, 1862 commander, British land forces, China.

STEVENS, Edwin, Am. Seamen's Friend Soc. and Am. Board (ABCFM); 1832–36 Canton; d. 1836.

STEVENSON, John Whiteford (1844–1918); grandson of laird of Thriepwood, Renfrewshire; with G. Stott (qv) first of CIM after Crombie (qv); Oct. 1865 dep. UK; 1866–74 Ningbo, Shaoxing (Shaohsing); 1875–80 Burma; 1880 crossed China W. to E. 1,900 miles; 1885–1916 deputy-director, CIM.

STOCK, Eugene, CMS Gen. Sec. after H. Venn; historian.

STOTT, George, Aberdeenshire schoolmaster, one-legged; Oct. 1865 dep. UK; 1866 Ningbo; 1869–89 Wenzhou (Wenchow); d. 1889.

438   PERSONALIA

STRONACH, John, LMS (1838–76), 30 years without furlough; 1838–44
Singapore; 1846 Amoy; Bible translator, Delegates' Committee, 1852;
S. Dyer's friend.
STRONACH, Alexander, LMS; 1838–39 Singapore; 1839–44 Penang;
1844–46 Singapore; 1846 Amoy.
SUN YAT-SEN (1866–1925); 1891 first medical graduate, Hong Kong;
1905 founded China Revolutionary League, in Europe, Japan; 1911–12
founder and first president Republic of China; m. descendant of Paul Xu
(*see* Soong).
TAMERLANE (Timur-i-leng) (1335–1405); descendant of founder of
Mogul dynasty, India; conquered Turkestan, Persia, Syria; a scourge;
died preparing to invade China.
TAO KUANG (*see* Dao Guang).
TARN, William, brother of Samuel Dyer's wife; director, Religious Tract
Soc.; guardian of Burella and Maria Dyer.
TAYLOR, Amelia (1808–81); first daughter of Benjamin Brook Hudson;
J.H.T.'s mother.
TAYLOR, Amelia Hudson (1835–1918); J.H.T.'s sister.
TAYLOR, Arthur, CES missionary, Hong Kong; 1853–55.
TAYLOR, James, Sr. (1749–95); host to J. Wesley.
TAYLOR, John (1778–1834); 1799 m. Mary Shepherd (*see* Wm.
Shepherd).
TAYLOR, James, Jr. (1807–81); J.H.T.'s father.
TAYLOR, James Hudson (21 May 1832–3 June 1905); 1853 dep. UK;
1 Mar. 1854 arr. Shanghai; 20 Jan. 1858 m. Maria Jane Dyer; 1857
with J. Jones (qv) began Ningbo Mission; 1865 founded China Inland
Mission; 28 Nov. 1871 m. Jane E. Faulding; 3 June 1905 d. Changsha,
Hunan.
TAYLOR, Maria Jane, née Dyer (1837–70), daughter of Samuel Dyer
(qv); wife of J.H.T.; mother of Grace, Herbert Hudson, Frederick
Howard, Samuel, Jane, Maria, Charles, Noel.
TIDMAN, Dr. Arthur, Foreign Sec., LMS; member CES Gen. Commit-
tee.
TOMLIN, Jacob, LMS; 1827 Malaya; 1828 Bangkok with Gutzlaff.
TOURNON (*see* de Tournon).
TRUELOVE, Richard, 1865 recruit for Ningbo; failed to go.
TSENG KUO-FAN (*see* Zeng); TZ'U HSI (*see* Ci Xi).
UNDERHILL, C. B., Sec. BMS; friend of J.H.T., nominated him for
FRGS.
VALENTINE, Jarvis D., CMS recruit taught by J.H.T.; 1864 Ningbo.
VALIGNANO, Allesandri (1537–1606); 1579 Jesuit Visitor to Japan.
van SOMMER, J., member, Hackney Brethren circle with W. T. Berger
(brother-in-law) and Philip H. Gosse; editor, *The Missionary Reporter*.
VAUGHAN, Marianne, first fiancée of J.H.T.
VENIAMINOV, John (Innokenty); (1797–1879); Russian Orthodox

pioneer, Aleutians, Kuriles, N. Siberia, Manchuria, Japan; Metropolitan of Moscow; founded Orthodox Missionary Soc.

VENN, Henry, Sr. and Jr., secretaries of CMS.

VENN, John, member of Eclectic Society (Clapham Sect); father of Henry, Sr.

VERBIEST, Ferdinand (1617–88), Jesuit astronomer, Peking.

VIGEON, Mr. and Mrs., 1865 recruits for Ningbo, prevented from going.

VOGEL, Karl, Kassel Miss. Assoc.; 1847 Hong Kong, Guangdong (Kwangtung); Gutzlaff's recruit.

WADE, Lieut. Thomas Francis; British forces, Ningbo, 1841; vice-consul Shanghai under Alcock; Battle of Muddy Flat; became Sinologue, HBM minister, Peking.

WANG LAE-DJUN (Wang Li-jun); Ningbo Mission convert; with J.H.T. London, 1860–64; pastor, Hangzhou (Hangchow).

WARD, Col. Frederick Townsend, Am. commander, Ever-Victorious Army; 1862 mortally wounded at Cixi (Tzeki), Ningbo.

WARD, Hon. John E.; 1859 US plenipotentiary; 1860 at capture and Convention of Peking.

WAY, R. Q., Am. Presby.; 1844 Ningbo; brother-in-law of J. W. Quarterman (qv).

WELLS WILLIAMS, Samuel, DD; (1812–84); Am. Board, printer, scholar; 1833 Canton; 1847 author *The Middle Kingdom*; 1851 succeeded E. C. Bridgman (qv) editor, *Chinese Repository*; interpreter to US legation, Peking; chargé d'affaires to 1876; Prof. of Chinese, Yale Univ.

WELTON, Dr., CMS; first medical, Fuzhou (Foochow).

WHITEFIELD, George (1714–70); at Oxford with J. and C. Wesley; Methodist until 1741, then independent; d. in America.

WILLIAMSON, Alexander, LL D; (1829–90); 1855 LMS Shanghai; 1863 National Bible Soc. of Scotland, Shandong, Yantai; 1865 Peking, Mongolia, Manchuria; 1887 founded Christian Literature Soc.

WINNES, Ph., Basel Mission; 1852 joined Theodore Hamberg (qv), Guangdong (Kwangtung) after R. Lechler died.

WYLIE, Alexander (1815–87); LMS; 1847 Shanghai, printer, Delegates' version of Bible; 1863 Bible Soc. (BFBS); one of the greatest Sinologues.

XAVIER, Francis (1506–52); Basque co-founder with Ignatius Loyola of Jesuit order; 1542 India; 1549 Japan; 1552 d. Shangchuan (Shangch'üan) Is., near Macao.

XI LIAO-ZHU (Hsi Liao-chu, Hsi Sheng-mo), (1835–96); graduate (Xiucai) of Shanxi (Shansi); 1879 converted through David Hill; hymnwriter, well-known as 'Pastor Hsi'.

XIAN FENG (Hsien Feng), (1851–61); 7th Qing (Ch'ing) dynasty emperor.

XU GUANG-QI (Hsü Kuang-ch'i, Paul Hsü); Ming dynasty official; convert of Matthew Ricci before 1610; 1850 his family home Xu Jia Wei (Siccawei) became Jesuit headquarters, near Shanghai.

YE MING-SHENG (Yeh Ming-shen), imperial commissioner and viceroy, Canton; 1856–57 'Arrow' incident and Br. attack on Canton, captured, d. Calcutta.

YEHONALA, *see* Ci·Xi.

YONG LU (Jung Lu); imperial bannerman (equiv. Brigade of Guards); perhaps father of Yehonala's son, Tong Zhi (Tung Chih) emperor; long-time adviser to Ci Xi, Empress Dowager.

YONG SAM-TEK, Chinese mandarin in London, 1805; taught Chinese to Morrison; later helped him in Canton.

ZENG GUO-FAN (Tseng Kuo-fan), (1811–72): scholar, provincial governor; 1854 defeated Taipings; viceroy of the 'Two Jiangs' (Jiangxi, Jiangsu), Zhili.

ZHONG WANG (Chung Wang), Taiping 'Loyal Prince'; military strategist, commander in final successes, 1863–64, before defeat ending rebellion.

ZHU JIU-DAO (Chu Chiu-tao), Taiping rebel leader; planned anti-Manchu, pro-Ming revolt; joined Hong Xiu-quan (qv) to wage Taiping rebellion.

BIBLIOGRAPHY
(for Books One to Three)

British
Library ref.

BALL, Richard, *Handbook of China*, 1854, OMFA 11

B & FB Society, *Monthly Reporter,* Vols 1 & 2,   London III,
1858–88   pp. 926.f

BENTLEY-TAYLOR, David, *Java Saga:*
Christian Progress in Muslim Java (The Weathercock's
Reward), CIM/OMF Books 1967/1975; *My Love*
must Wait, Hodder & Stoughton

BERESFORD, C. W. D., *The Break-up of China, 1899*   8022.dd.32

BOONE, M. Muriel, *The Seed of the Church in China*,
St Andrew Press, Edinburgh

BREDON, Juliet, *Sir Robert Hart*, Hutchinson &   010817.de.10
Co 1909

BRIDGMAN, Mrs. E. J. G., *The Life and Labors of Elijah*
Coleman Bridgman, 1864

BRIDGMAN, Elijah C. & Eliza J. G., *The Pioneer of*   4985.aaa.27
American Missions in China, 1864

BRINE, Lindesay, *The Taeping Rebellion*, 1862   9056.b.10

BROOMHALL, Marshall, *Heirs Together: A Memoir of*   4908.e.6
Benjamin & Amelia Broomhall
Morgan & Scott/CIM 1918
   John W. Stevenson: One of Christ's Stalwarts   4956.aa.33
Morgan & Scott/CIM 1919
   Hudson Taylor: The Man who Dared   4907.aa.34
Religious Tract Society/CIM
   Hudson Taylor: The Man who Believed God   4907.dd.21
Hodder & Stoughton 1929
   Robert Morrison: A Master-builder CIM 1924   4908.ee.24
   The Jubilee Story of the China Inland Mission   4763.g.4
Morgan & Scott/CIM 1915
   Hudson Taylor's Legacy Hodder & Stoughton 1931   10823.a.16
   By Love Compelled: The Call of the China Inland Mission   4768.a.34
CIM 1947 (H & S 1936)
   The Chinese Empire: A General & Missionary   4767.eeee.4
Survey Morgan & Scott/CIM 1907

BRYANT, Sir Arthur, *A Thousand Years of the British Monarchy*, Collins

BURNS, Islay, *Memoir of the Rev. William Chalmers Burns*, London 1885

CARY-ELWES, Columba, *China and the Cross*, Longmans,   4768.ccc.21
Green & Co 1957

CHINA MAIL (Hong Kong)   British Library

CHINA'S MILLIONS, Magazine of the China Inland Mission
1875–1951

Chinese Evangelization Society REPORT 1853 OMFA
(Archives of OMF)

CHINESE RECORDER AND MISSIONARY JOURNAL:
Vol 1 1868 et seq

CHINESE REPOSITORY, The, Canton 1832–42

CLARK-KENNEDY, A. E., *'The London' (Hospital)*,   9059.df.15
2 vols

CMS *Gleaner, Intelligencer, Register, Reports*, Church
Missionary Society

COAD, F. Roy, *A History of the Brethren Movement*, The
Paternoster Press 1968

COLE, R. A., *The Gospel according to St Mark:* Tyndale
Commentary, The Tyndale Press 1961

COLLIER, Richard,*William Booth: The General Next to God*, X.100.1629
Collins 1965

COLLIS, Maurice Stewart, *Foreign Mud*, 1946

CORDIER, Henri, *The Life of Alexander Wylie*, 1887   10803.cc.4/6

COVELL, Ralph, *W A P Martin, Pioneer of Progress in
China*, Wm. B. Eerdmans Publishing Company 1978

DAVIES, Evan, *China and her Spiritual Claims*, John Snow   1369.b.24
1845

    Memoir of the Reverend Samuel Dyer, John Snow 1846   1372.6.20

DU BUSE, H. C., *The Dragon Image and Demon: The Three
Religions of China*, A. C. Armstrong (USA) 1887

DYSON, Verne, *A Hong Kong Governor: Sir John*   010822.df.39
Bowring, Marcao 1930

EAMES, James Bromby, *The English in China*, 1909   09008.f.19

FAIRBANK, John King, *Trade and Diplomacy on the*   Ac.2692.10
China Coast, 2 vols. 1953 Edn. Cambridge,
Massachusetts

FORBES, Archibald, *Chinese Gordon*, George Routledge &
Sons 1884

FOREIGN OFFICE LIBRARY China FO/17 Public Records
Office

FOSTER, John, *The Nestorian Tablet and Hymns*, SPCK

GLEANER, CES, *The Gleaner in the Missionary Field*,

The Chinese & General Missionary Gleaner,
The Chinese Missionary Gleaner, Chinese Evangelization
Society 1850–60 OMFA

GROVES, Mrs., Memoir of the late Anthony Norris
Groves, 2nd Edn. 1857

GUTZLAFF, Charles, A Journal of Three Voyages along   1046.c.16
the Coast of China in 1831, 1832 & 1833 with notices of Siam,
Corea and the Loochoo Islands, 1833
    Report of Proceedings on a Voyage to the Northern Ports   1046.c.15
of China (see LINDSAY, H. H.), 1833

HACKNEY GAZETTE, North London: Historical Associations,
1928

HALDANE, Charlotte, The Last Great Empress of China, Constable
1965

HALL, Capt. Basil, RN, Narrative of a Voyage to Java, China   982.i.16
and the Great Loochoo Island, Edward Moxen 1818
    1840 edn.   G.15729

HART, Sir Robert, These from the Land of Sinim   8022.cc.48/
     010817.d.10

HOLT, Edgar C., The Opium Wars in China, 1964 edn.   X.709-581

HOOK, Brian, China's Three Thousand Years: The Modern
History of China, THE TIMES Newspaper (publishers)

HUGGETT, Frank E., Victorian England as seen by PUNCH,
Sidgwick & Johnson 1978

HUC, Evariste Régis, Christianity in China, Tartary and   2208.bb.8
Thibet 1857,
    Life and Travel in Tartary, Thibet and China 1867   10057.aa.39

INGLIS, Brian, The Opium War, Hodder & Stoughton   09059.pp.30
1976

LATOURETTE, Kenneth Scott, A History of Christian   4763.g.4
Missions in China, SPCK 1929
    A History of the Expansion of Christianity 1800–1914   4533.ff.22
Eyre and Spottiswoode
    These Sought a Country: Tipple Lectures, 1950 edn. Harper   4807.e.25
& Brothers

LEGGE, Helen E., James Legge (1815–97), Religious Tract   04429.1.37
Society 1905

LEGGE, James, The Famine in China, 1878 edn. The   11102.b.20
Nestorian Monument (Oxford University Lecture)
    1888 edn.   4532.ee.13/14

LINDSAY, H. H. Report to the Hon. East India Company
on a Voyage to the Northern Ports of China 1832 (voyage
of the Lord Amherst)

LINTON, E. Lynn, A Night in a Hospital (from magazine
Belgravia) 1879

LOCKHART, William, *The Medical Missionary in China*, 10058.d.16
1861 edn.
MacGILLIVRAY, Donald, *A Century of Protestant* 4764.ff.11
Missions in China (Centennial Conference Historical
Volume), Shanghai 1907
McGILVARY, Daniel, *A Half-Century among the Siamese and
the Lao*, Fleming, Revell & Co. 1912
McNEUR, George Hunter, *Liang A-fa*, Oxford University
Press China Agency 1934
MARTIN, W. A. P., *A Cycle of Cathay*, 1896 010056.g.7
MEDHURST, W. H. Sr., *China: Its State and Prospects*, 571.g.10
John Snow 1838
    A Glance at the Interior of China in 1845, Shanghai 10055.c.25
Mission Press 1849
MEDHURST, Sir Walter H., *Curiosities of Street Literature* 10057.aaa.16
in China, 1871
    The Foreigner in Far Cathay, Edward
Stanton 1872 010058.ee.35
MICHIE, Alexander, *Missionaries in China*, Edward 4767.ccc.10
Standford, Ldn. 1891
    An Englishman in China: as illustrated in the Career of Sir 09057.d.3
Rutherford Alcock, Wm. Blackwood & Sons, Edin.1900 2 vols.
MORRIS, E. W., *The London Hospital*, Edward Arnold 1910
MORRISON, Mrs. Robert, *Memoirs of . . . Robert Morrison*,
Longmans 2 vols 1839
MORSE, Hosea Ballou, *The International Relations of the* 2386.c.17
Chinese Empire, (9 vols) vols 1–3 1910
MOULE, Arthur E., *The Story of the Cheh-Kiang Mission*, CMS
1879
MÜLLER, George (ed. G. F. Bergin), *Autobiography:
Narrative*, J. Nisbet & Co. Ltd. 1905
NEATBY, Mrs. Thomas, *The Life and Ministry of Thomas Neatby*,
Pickering & Inglis
NEILL, Rt. Rev. Stephen C., *A. History of Christian Missions*,
(Pelican History of the Church) Penguin Books 1964
NEVIUS, Helen S. C., *The Life of John Livingston Nevius*, 4985.eee.5
Revell 1895
NORTH CHINA HERALD (newspaper) 1854 et seq British
Library, Colindale
ORR, J. Edwin, *The Second Evangelical Awakening in
Britain*, Marshall Morgan & Scott 1949
PADWICK, Constance E., *Henry Martyn: Confessor of the
Faith*, Inter-Varsity Fellowship 1922
PARLEY, Peter, *China and the Chinese*, Simpkin Marshall 10058.a.26
1843

PARLIAMENTARY PAPERS 1831–32 Vols VII, X, XI,
XXXVI, XLI (*see* Foreign Office 1840–60 opium
wars) 1857 XLIII relating to the opium trade with
China
PIERSON, A. T., *George Müller of Bristol*, Jas. Nisbet & Co.
Ltd. 1905
POLLOCK, John C., *Hudson Taylor & Maria*, Hodder &
Stoughton
POLO, Marco, *The Book of Ser Marco Polo, The Venetian, 1298*,
First printed edition 1477 (*see* YULE)
POTT, HAWKS, F. L., *A Short History of Shanghai*, Kelly 010056.aaa.46
& Walsh 1928
PUNCH, *PUNCH Panorama 1845–65* (*see* HUGGETT, F. E.)
ROWDON, H. H., *The Origins of the Brethren*, Pickering
& Inglis 1967
SELLMAN, R. R., *An Outline Atlas of Eastern History*,
Edward Arnold Ltd.
Sianfu: The Nestorian Tablet WP.4683.49
SMITH, Arthur H., *The Uplift of China*, The Young People's
Missionary Movement of America 1909
STOCK, Eugene, *A History of the Church Missionary* 4765.cc.28
Society, Vols I–III 1899–1916
TAYLOR, Dr. & Mrs. Howard, *Hudson Taylor in Early Years:
The Growth of a Soul*, CIM and RTS, 1911
 *Hudson Taylor and the China Inland Mission: The
Growth of a Work of God*, CIM and RTS, 1918
 Hudson Taylor's Spiritual Secret, CIM, 1932
TAYLOR, Mrs. Howard (M. Geraldine Guinness), *The Story of the
China Inland Mission*, 2 vols, 1892, Morgan & Scott
 Behind the Ranges: A Biography of J. O. Fraser, CIM
TAYLOR, J. Hudson, *China: Its Spiritual Need and Claims*,
1st–6th edns. 1865 et seq, CIM
 China's Spiritual Need and Claims, 7th edn. 1887, CIM
8th edn. 1890, CIM
 A Retrospect, 1875, CIM
 After Thirty Years, 1895, Morgan & Scott and CIM
THOMPSON, R. Wardlaw, *Griffith John: The Story of
Fifty Years in China*, The Religious Tract Society 1907
WALEY, Arthur David, *The Opium War through Chinese* 09059.pp.30
Eyes, London, 1958
WANG, Mary, *The Chinese Church that will not Die*, Hodder
& Stoughton
WOODCOCK, George, *The British in the Far East*,
Weidenfeld & Nicolson, 1969 (A Social History of the
British Overseas)

WURTZBURG, C. E., *Raffles of the Eastern Isles*, Hodder
  & Stoughton, 1954
YULE, Sir Henry, *The Book of Ser Marco Polo the Venetian*,
  1878, 2 vols.

INDEX

HUDSON TAYLOR & CHINA'S OPEN CENTURY
Book One: Barbarians at the Gates

Foreword by Donald Coggan

Hudson Taylor was one of the world's greatest missionaries of all time. He has been described as one of the five most influential foreigners who came to China in the nineteenth century.

Dr A J Broomhall, with full access to much previously unpublished material, has written the definitive history of this remarkable man.

'Barbarians at the Gates', the first of six books, provides the essential background: a clear understanding of the land and people of China, together with Chinese attitudes to the Western 'barbarians', knocking at their gates with ambitions of trade and empire, and to the Christian predecessors who paved the way for Hudson Taylor.

Joint publication with the Overseas Missionary Fellowship.